T0135803

THE PLE CONFERENCE 2013
Learning and Diversity in the Cities of the Future

Ilona Buchem, Graham Attwell, Gemma Tur (Eds.)

**4th International Conference
on Personal Learning Environments**

Beuth University of Applied Sciences
Berlin, Germany

Monash University
Melbourne, Australia

July 2013, Proceedings

Research Report 2013
Beuth University of Applied Sciences

Forschungsbericht 2013
Beuth Hochschue für Technik Berlin

Editors

Prof. Dr. Ilona Buchem
Professor for Digital Media and Diversity
Beuth University of Applied Science Berlin
Department I Economics and Social Sciences
E-Mail: *buchem@beuth-hochschule.de*

Graham Attwell
Educational Researcher
Pontydysgu – Bridge to Learning
Associate Fellow at the Instutute for Employment Research
University of Warwick
E-Mail: *grahamattwell@googlemail.com*

Dr. Gemma Tur
University of the Balearic Islands
Department of Applied Pedagogy and Educational Psychology
E-Mail: *gemma.tur@uib.es*

Forschungsbericht 2013
Beuth Hochschule für Technik Berlin

Bibliografische Information der Deutschen Nationalbibliothek
Die Deutsche Nationalbibliothek verzeichnet diese Publikation in der Deutschen Nationalbibliografie; detaillierte bibliografische Daten sind im Internet über *http://dnb.d-nb.de* abrufbar.

ISBN 978-3-8325-3811-8

Logos Verlag Berlin GmbH
Comeniushof, Gubener Str. 47,
10243 Berlin
Tel.: +49 (0)30 42 85 10 90
Fax: +49 (0)30 42 85 10 92
INTERNET: *http://www.logos-verlag.de*

PREFACE

The Conference on Personal Learning Environments is now an established annual international, scientific event and a reference point for the current state of the art in research and development in Personal Learning Environments (PLE). The PLE Conference creates a space for researchers and practitioners to share concepts, case studies and research related to the design, development and implementation of Personal Learning Environments in diverse educational contexts including formal and informal education. The PLE Conference takes place annually, each time in a different country and city. The first event was held in Barcelona, Spain in 2010, the second in Southampton, UK in 2011, and the third in Aveiro, Portugal in 2012 together with a parallel event in Melbourne, Australia.

Building on the previous conferences, the 4th PLE Conference took place at Beuth University of Applied Sciences in Berlin, Germany together with a parallel event at Monash University in Melbourne, Australia. As Chair and Organising Committee members of the PLE Conference 2013 we am very pleased to present a wide range of contributions that we received and welcomed in Berlin and Melbourne. The contributions included in these proceedings encompass empirical research studies, literature reviews, theoretical treaties and descriptions of workshops and alternative sessions held at both venues in July 2013.

Personal Learning Environments (PLE) is an approach in Technology-Enhanced Learning (TEL) based on the principles of learner autonomy, ownership and empowerment. PLEs are integrated, individual environments for learning which include specific technologies, methods, tools, contents, communities and services constituting complex learning infrastructures, enhancing new educational practices and at the same time emerging from these new practices. This represents a shift away from the traditional model of technology-enhanced learning based on *knowledge transfer* towards a model based on *knowledge construction and sharing*. In PLEs learning happens by drawing connections from a growing and diverse pool of online and offline resources to plan, organise, create, network, engage and reflect in permeable spaces. Although much research is presently focused on MOOCs, the very emergence of MOOC and the increasing uptake on online resources for learning in different contexts is opening the debate on pedagogic approaches to the use of different technologies for learning, including PLEs.

The 4th PLE Conference focused on the theme of "Learning and Diversity in the Cities of the Future", among others addressing the issue of smart cities, one of the key research priorities worldwide and the strategic direction of Beuth University of Applied Sciences Berlin. The conference addressed the following questions:

- How can Personal Learning Environments support diversity, cross-boundary learning and interdisciplinary transformation of urban spaces?
- How to design and implement Personal Learning Environments as part of interconnected social and technological infrastructures of smart cities?
- What PLE scenarios can be envisaged to enhance learning and diversity in cities of the future?

The conference programme tackled the main theme and the three questions within three days, including the pre-conference and the two main conference days, which encompassed a number of engaging formats such as un-keynote speakers, research sessions, interactive sessions, workshops, pecha kucha sessions, demonstrations and posters. In fact, the mix of conference and un-conference formats of the PLE Conference is one of its unique features – our aim has always been to involve conference participants in conversation and interaction, hence our participants can be called "The People Formerly Known as the Audience", following Jay Rosen's phrase.

The papers included in the Proceedings provide rich and valuable theoretical and empirical insights into Personal Learning Environments. The PLE Conference 2013 received 75 submissions and welcomed almost 100 delegates from Europe, Asia, Australasia, North and South America and Africa. In 2013 we did not only engage the participants in dialogue but also within the conference proposal process. To enhance the participatory character of the PLE Conference the review process was based on the shepherding idea. This means that the authors were offered support by experienced shepherds (mentors), who helped those submitting proposals by making suggestions for improvements in the process of writing the final versions of submissions. In this way we enhanced the quality of submissions and helped authors qualify for publication in one of the two Special Issues with selected best papers.

It was noticeable that the debate over PLEs has matured over the past four years. Rather than more abstract discussion on the definition and nature of PLEs, many of the contributions focused on studies of PLE implementation. At the same time the contexts in which PLEs are being developed and used are widening, encompassing informal learning and learning in the workplace and community as well as through educational institutions. The introduction of new technologies such as smart phones, tablets and cloud computing are also providing a powerful infrastructure for PLE development.

Two special edition of journals have already been published based on contributions to the PLE Conference 2013 conference. The first was a Special Issue of the EU eLearningPapers, Issue No. 35, entitled "Personal Learning Environments",[1] The second is the Special Issue of the Journal of Literacy and Technology, JLT, Volume 15, No. 2, titled "Personal Learning Environments: Current Research and Emerging Practice"[2].

1 *http://openeducationeuropa.eu/en/paper/personal-learning-environments*
2 *http://www.literacyandtechnology.org/current-issue.html*

We hope that papers in these proceedings inspire your research and practice, taking forward the field of Personal Leaning Environments to address the challenges of learning and diversity in smart cities.

July 2014

Ilona Buchem *Gemma Tur* *Graham Attwell*

EDITORS:

Prof. Dr. Ilona Buchem
Beuth University of Applied Science Berlin
Department I Economics and Social Sciences
E-Mail: *buchem@beuth-hochschule.de*

Dr. Gemma Tur
University of the Balearic Islands
Department of Applied Pedagogy and Educational Psychology
E-Mail: *gemma.tur@uib.es*

Graham Attwell
Educational Researcher
Pontydysgu – Bridge to Learning
E-Mail: *grahamattwell@googlemail.com*

CONFERENCE ORGANISATION

GENERAL CHAIR AND BERLIN CONFERENCE CHAIR:

Ilona Buchem, Beuth University of Applied Sciences Berlin

Programme Chairs:

Ilona Buchem, Beuth University Berlin
Arunangsu Chatterjee, University of Plymouth
Martin Wolpers, Frauenhofer FIT

Melbourne Conference Chairs:

Sarah Pasfield-Neofitou, Monash University
Sarah McDonald, Monash University

Review Process:

Mandy Rohs, University Duisburg-Essen
Ademar Aguiar, University of Porto
Arunangsu Chatterjee, University of Plymouth
Luis Pedro, University of Aveiro:
Cristina Costa, University of Salford
Agnieszka Chrzaszcz, AGH Kraków

Website and Media:

Ilona Buchem, Beuth University
Tobias Hölterhof, University Duisburg-Essen

Chair of the Organising Committee (and liaisons with Australia):

Graham Attwell, Pontydysgu
Cristina Costa, University of Salford

Pre-Conference Chairs:

Kamakshi Rajagopal, Open University
Sabine Reisas, University of Kiel

MEMBERS OF THE ORGANIZATION COMMITTEE

Ademar Aguiar – University of Porto (Portugal)
Agnieszka Chrzaszcz, AGH Kraków (Poland)
Andreas Auwärter – Koblenz-Landau University (Germany)
Annette Pedersen – University of Copenhagen (Denmark)
Arunangsu Chatterjee – University of Leicester (UK)
Carlos Santos – University of Aveiro (Portugal)
Cristina Costa – Salford University (UK)
Firmino Alves – University of Aveiro (Portugal)
Frances Bell – University of Salford (UK)
Gemma Tur – University of the Balearic Islands (Spain)
Graham Attwell – Pontydysgu (UK)
Hugh Davis – University of Southampton (UK)
Ilona Buchem – Beuth University of Applied Sciences (Germany)
Joyce Seitzinger – Deakin University (Australia)
Linda Castañeda – University of Murcia (Spain)
Lisa Harris – University of Southampton (UK)

Luís Pedro – University of Aveiro (Portugal)
Kamakshi Rajagopal, Open University (NL)
Mandy Rohs, University Duisburg-Essen (Germany)
Mar Camacho – Universitat Rovira i Virgili (Spain)
Maria Perifanou – University of Athens (Greece)
Martin Wolpers – Fraunhofer Institute of Applied Information Technology (Germany)
Mónica Aresta – University of Aveiro (Portugal)
Ricardo Torres Kompen – Entrelaza – Asociación Tecnosocial (Spain)
Sabine Reisas, University of Kiel (Germany)
Sara Almeida – University of Aveiro (Portugal)
Sarah Pasfield-Neofitou, Monash University
Sarah McDonald, Monash University
Su White – University of Southampton (UK)
Tobias Hölterhof, University Duisburg-Essen (Germany)

MEMBERS OF THE SCIENTIFIC COMMITTEE

Ademar Aguiar
Fernando Albuquerque Costa
Sara Almeida
Firmino Alves
Mónica Aresta
Graham Attwell
Andreas Auwärter
Dr. Igor Balaban
Dr. Frances Bell
Prof. Dr. Ilona Buchem
Prof. Dr. Mar Camacho
Dr. Linda Castañeda
Dr. Arunangsu Chatterjee
Dr. Mohamed Amine Chatti
Prof. Dr. Gráinne Conole
Prof. Dr. John Cook
Prof. Dr. Alec Couros
Dr. Cristina Costa
Catherine Cronin
Agnieszka Chrzaszcz
Hugh Davis
Assoc. Prof. Dr. Martin Ebner
Dr. Palitha Edirisingha
Prof. Dr. Antonio Dias de Figueiredo
Dr. Denis Gillet
Assoc. Prof. Dr. Carlo Giovanella
Mark van Harmelen
Lisa Harris
Lehosław Hojnacki
Tobias Hölterhof
Prof. Dr. Malinka Ivanova
Prof. Dr. Isa Jahnke
Nick Kearney
Dr. Ralf Klamma
Prof. Dr. Thomas Köhler
Moshe Leiba
Prof. Dr. Tobias Ley
Prof. Dr. Johannes Magenheim
Dr. Stefania Manca
Prof. Kerstin Mayrberger
Sarah McDonald
Dr. Alexander Mikroyannidis
Felix Mödritscher
José Mota
Sarah Pasfield-Neofitou
Annette Pedersen
Luis Pedro
Dr. Mar Pérez-Sanagustín
Dr. Maria Perifanou
Jeff Piatek
Kamakshi Rajagopal
Dr. Maria Ranieri
Prof. Andrew Ravenscroft
Prof. Dr. Peter Reinmann
Dr. Wolfgang Reinhardt
Sabine Reisas
Dr. Mandy Rohs
Dr. Nancy Rubin
Carlos Santos
Maren Scheffel
Dr. Sandra Schoen
Joyce Seitzinger
Paulo Simões
Prof. Dr. Peter Sloep
Mark Smithers
Dr. Thomas Strasser
Dr. Gemma Tur
Ricardo Torres Kompen
Timo van Treeck
Dr. Riina Vuorikari
Prof. Dr. Steven Warburton
Prof. Dr. Steve Wheeler
Su White
Fridolin Wild
Prof. Dr. Martin Wolpers
Dr. Maria Zajac

CONTENTS

CONTENTS

CONTENTS

Learner Control in Personal Learning Environments: A Cross-Cultural Study

Ilona Buchem, Gemma Tur, Tobias Hoelterhof

ABSTRACT

Changing power relations and the shift in control have been some of the key issues driving the discussion in Technology-Enhanced Learning (TEL) in the last years. As opposed to deterministic approaches to designing learning, such as the system approach in instructional design, emancipatory approaches, such as Personal Learning Environments (PLE), emphasizes the ***shift of control and ownership*** *from the educator or the designer to the learner, bestowing decision making and choice upon the learner, not only in terms of choosing the content or the sequence of learning steps, but first and foremost the choice of the learning tools and the use of these tools to support one's own learning, including co-creation of learning content and fostering of Personal Learning Networks (PLN). In this paper we describe the results of an international, cross-cultural study exploring the role of ownership and control in Personal Learning Environments. Our study is rooted in the theory of psychological ownership and utilizes research instruments developed in the predecessor study by [Buc 12]. The study was conducted in winter and spring 2013 at three different universities in Germany and Spain including students from six different courses, i.e. three courses in media sociology in Germany, two online master programs in educational media and educational leadership in Germany and a teacher education program in Spain. An online survey was used to collect data in two languages – German and Catalan. Following the concept of ownership proposed by [Buc 12], the study is based on the assumption that a learning environment becomes a Personal Learning Environment when the learner (subjectively) feels the owner this environment and perceives herself/himself to able to exercise control over this environment. The study presented in this paper aims at advancing our understanding of the role of psychological ownership in contect of PLE, especially in relation to* ***learner control****. This paper specifically explores ownership and control in context of ePortfolio practice. Finally, this article provides a contribution to methods of measuring the impact of PLEs.*

Note: *This article has been published in the Special Edition of the Journal of Literacy and Technology: "Personal Learning Environments: Current Research and Emerging Practice". The link to the JLT Special Issue is: http://www.literacyandtechnology.org/uploads/1/3/6/8/136889/jlt_special.pdf*

Introduction

Personal Learning Environments (PLE) is an approach to using technology for learning, focusing on self-directed and self-regulated uses of tools and resources by the learner [Buc 11]. It is capturing the *personal activity*, or how the learner uses technology to support own learning, rather than developing *personalised platforms*, that lies at the heart of the PLE research. The first survey about the role of ownership and control in context of Personal Learning Environments was conducted in 2012 at two universities in Germany [Buc 12]. This study was rooted in the theory of psychological ownership by [Pie 01], [Pie 03] and reported on empirical findings from an online survey and analysis of educational practice, exploring multiple relationships between ownership, control and learning in context of technology-enhanced learning environments created in the process of creating ePortfolios. The results of the study indicated that control of *intangible elements* of a learning environment, such as control of content or personal data, is more strongly related to the feeling of ownership of this learning environment than is the control of *tangible elements*, such as technical tools (e.g. Web 2.0 services). The underlying assumption was that not every learning environment – not matter how personalized – automatically becomes a PLE, but that it is the perception of the individual learner that makes a learning environment to a PLE. Further, the hypothesis is that this perception depends on whether the learner develops a feeling of ownership and control of the learning environment. More specifically, it was argued that the perception of a learning environment as a PLE is related to the feeling of ownership of intangible elements rather than tangible ones [Buc 12]. The results of the study indicated that learners perceive a learning environment as a PLE even if they do not have the full control of all elements of this environment and do not in fact own them. For example, Web 2.0 services do not belong to the learner in terms of legal or intellectual proprietorship, and yet learners may feel in control when using them. The follow-up research presented in this paper further explores the role of psychological ownership and learner control in PLEs from a cross-cultural perspective.

Theoretical Background

Learner control has been one of the key research interests in the field of technology-enhanced learning. In the early years, learner control was analyzed mainly within technology-enhanced instructional delivery systems, such as computer-assisted learning programs including intelligent tutoring systems. Recently, the socio-constructivist paradigm in technology-enhanced learning and the emergence of Personal Learning Environments have introduced new lines of research in the area of learner control.

Research on learner control in 1980s and 1990s was to a wide extend embedded in the instructional design paradigm. This prescriptive approach to learner control

focused on control as a choice of a pre-defined set of elements, including learning paths (e.g. lesson branching) and learning materials (e.g. examples and exercises) in computer-supported settings. Later, in web-based settings, new types of learner control have been explored, including informational control enabled by hypertext and hypermedia systems [Wil 89]; [Lin 01]. Within the instructional design framework learner control has been pre-programmed by the designer and conceptualized as choices provided within computer-delivered instruction, for example in form of *control of sequence* (i.e. control of sequencing of topics or exercises), *control of level*, (i.e. control of the difficulty level or degree of difficulty within a learning sequence), *control of pacing* (i.e. control of speed of presentation of learning content), *control of display* (i.e. control of viewing materials from a selection including examples, exercises or quizzes), *control of support* (i.e. control of using system advice such as recommendation on learning materials) [Mer 83], [Lau 87], [Mil 91], [Chu 92]. A number of authors including [Buc 11] have argued that this type of conceptualization of learner control allows for system adaptivity and individual customization but not for a genuine co-/design of a learning environment by the learner.

More recently research on learner control in context of PLE has moved beyond computer assisted programs, intelligent tutoring systems and learning management systems towards authentic learning contexts mediated by technology in which the learner may have a greater control of both tangible or intangible elements of a learning environment [Buc 12]. [Buc 11] carried out an extensive literature review on Personal Learning Environments and showed that learner control in context of PLEs has been conceptualised broader in relation to different dimensions of learner activity. Based on the activity theory framework (extended triangle) these authors analysed learner control in PLEs in five dimensions: objectives, tools, rules, community and tasks.

The results of the grounded theory analysis pointed towards a multi-dimensional notion of learner control in PLEs, which goes beyond the previous conceptualizations of learner control in terms of scope (Table 1).

Table 1: Dimensions of learner control in PLEs [Buc 11: 10–11]

DIMENSIONS OF LEARNER CONTROL	EXAMPLES OF LEARNER ACTIVITIES
A. Control of objectives	The learner (subject) can: • Determine learning goals and outcomes • Manage data, services, resources, content • Use scaffolding and guidance
B. Control of tools	The learner (subject) can: • Select and use tools according to own needs • Reuse and remix content • Aggregate and configure tools based on own preferences

DIMENSIONS OF LEARNER CONTROL	EXAMPLES OF LEARNER ACTIVITIES
C. Control of rules	The subject can: • Configure the environment according to own preferences • Negotiate rules of communication and collaboration with teachers, peers, communities • Negotiate intellectual property rights
D. Control of social base	The learner (subject) can: • Choose with whom to communicate • Choose who can communicate with him/her • Initiate discussions and collaborations
E. Control of tasks	The learner (subject) can: • Specify own needs (e.g. user profile) • Self-monitor own progress • Adjust performance based on (peer) feedback

The examples of learner control in Table 1 indicate that the concept of learner control in PLEs envisages learner control far beyond skipping forwards and backwards as part of a pre-programmed sequencing strategy or choosing between viewing examples or consulting a glossary as part of a display strategy. The notion of learner control in the PLE approach goes as far as allowing learners to determine their own learning goals, selecting and aggregating a wide range of available (not necessarily pre-selected) tools, negotiating rules, initiating (and not only engaging in) discussions and collaborations and adjusting learning based on self-monitoring the learning progress (versus automated recommendations). In comparison to earlier instructional principles of learner control, the PLE approach resembles more of an activity of "building a house" rather than "furnishing a house". Thus, while instructional design approaches have focused on *micro-level strategies of learner control* within a pre-determined system (manipulation of small instructional elements), the PLE approach has focused on *meta-level strategies of learner control* within an open system (management of the entire learning process) with learner control being inherent to the construction of PLEs.

Learner control is related to the concept of ownership, and both concepts are related to the notion of "agency" in terms of the human capacity to make choices and to impose those choices on the world [Buc 11]. Ownership has been considered as a critical issue for learning. Allowing learners to own their learning process means to allow learners to engage with the process itself, which is a crucial factor for the effectiveness of the learning process [Big 11]. In context of technology-enhanced learning, a number of approaches consider ownership as a crucial concept for learning. For example, the "folio thinking" approach to ePortfolio practice has emphasised the role of ownership of ePortfolio for ensuring the use of ePortfolio as a basic learning strategy, integrated into all educational activities and sustainable in the lifetime [Cou 06], [Joy 09], [Che 09], [Che10], [She 11]. In this research context, the relationship between control,

motivation and ownership have been considered to be mutually supportive. For example, the study by [Shr 13] rooted in the [Mil 01] framework of ownership, showed that students and teachers considered the feeling of control as vital for the ownership of ePortfolio. As [Bar 04] argue, the greater the control of students over their ePortfolio, the more intrinsic motivation towards learning they develop.

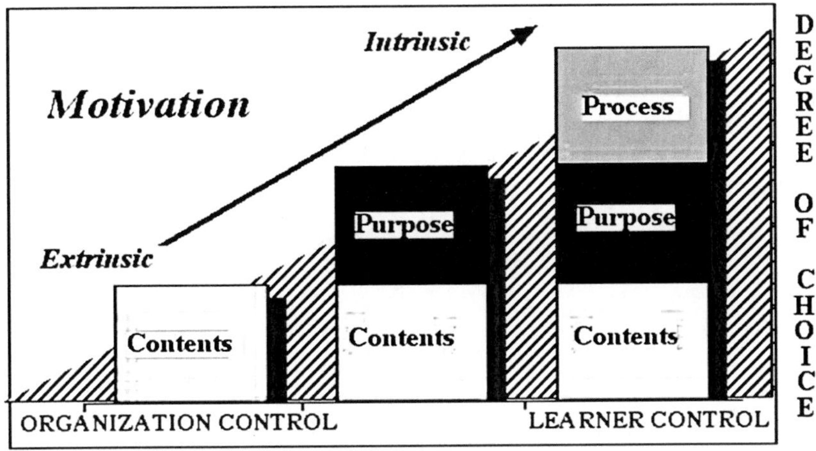

Figure 1: Learner ownership and control of ePortfolio [Bar 04]

However, the varying forms and degrees ownership have been seldom differentiated both in literature related to PLEs and ePortfolios as well as in publications addressing the ownership of learning in general. Also there has been little clarity about what type of ownership and control (e.g. technical, legal, psychological, social) and over what elements (e.g. goals, information, services) may be effective for learning. As [Buc 11] point out, it is possible to conceive of ownership of learning from various perspectives, e.g. in a *technical* sense (e.g. the learner is technically responsible for aggregating and configuring services), *legal* sense (e.g. the data and content legally belongs to the learner) or *psychological* sense (e.g. the learner feels an owner of the learning environment). As the study by [Buc 12] indicated, it is also possible that the learner can "control" the environment (e.g. select sources of information, reuse and remix content) without actually "owning" all its constituting parts. In context of ePortfolios, [Att 05] and [Att 07] highlighted some important issues related to ownership by distinguishing different agents owing different ePortfolio processes [Att 12]. Attwell focused on the ownership of different processes related to learning and pointed out that in educational settings different ePortfolio processes are owned by different agents. For example, reflecting is "owned" by the learner (the learner controls this process), assessment is "owned" both by the learner and external agents whilst accreditation is "owned" only by external agents, such as educational institutions.

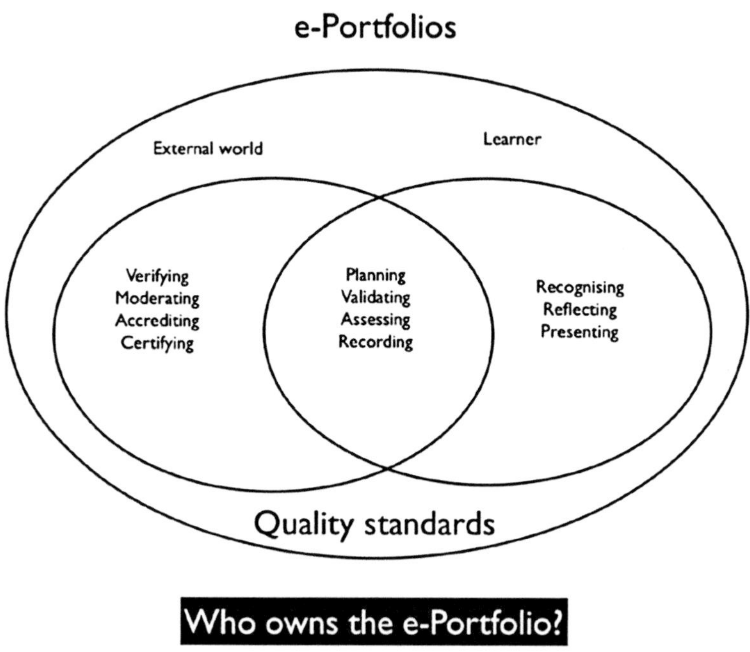

Figure 2: ePortfolio processes ownership [Att 05], [Att 07], [Att 12]

However, ownership in context of PLE comprises both processes and elements of learning, such as digital tools used to construct a PLE. Nowadays, the nature of the relationships brought about by social networks, as well as the shift of the external world's learning agents, has highlighted the importance of the control of intangible elements of learning including personal data in order to improve the sense of ownership [Att 12] This is the central point of interest explored by [Buc 12] and in this paper.

To explore the relation between ownership and control one can refer to philosophical investigations about ownership in general and self-ownership in particular, e.g. [Dan 92], [Bro 93]. For example, the concept of self-ownership, which is related to the individual autonomy [Pat 02], can be defined as a psychological condition of a person (disposition), which is expressed in actions and in the general attitude towards oneself and the world [Dwo 88]. Personal "autonomy" in the sense of self-governance or self-rule ("autos" meaning self and "nomos" meaning rule), involves choosing, defining,

being able to make preferences and take decisions [Dwo 88]. As such the notions of personal ownership and personal autonomy are closely linked to the notion of control. Learner autonomy regarded as learner's psychological relation to the process of learning [Lit 91], is also closely linked to taking responsibility for one's learning. Autonomous learners are capable of independently setting learning goals, choosing learning materials and methods, making choices in organizing learning and defining criteria for evaluation [Kno 75], [Kno 80]. Owning a learning environment is to some extent similar to owning physical objects such as books or digital devices. In context of PLEs, ownership is rooted in a learner-controlled use of technology, especially the ability to create, design, and operate an environment according to personal preferences [Buc 11], [Buc 12]. According to moral and philosophical investigations about ownership, the dependency between the learner and the environment can be characterized as "control ownership", whereas "control" may be used to refer to the ability of a person to be the final arbiter of what is to be done with an object [Chr 94: 128]. In this sense to own a learning environment means to be able to use, control, modify or even destroy it in an independent way without the consent of others. Ownership in terms of control means a private use of an object. In addition the common meaning of ownership also implies the ability to sell or gain income from ones property. Thus ownership and control are part of individual autonomy [Chr 94: 167). This is yet to emphasize that the concept of learner control pertinent to the concept of PLEs radically differs from previous conceptualizations of learner control in technology-based learning. In the PLE sense of learner control, the learner can build, use, change, adjust, abandon, lend, cede or even destroy a learning environment or its parts without the consent of a teacher or another external agent.

Research design

The study presented in this paper is guided by the following research questions: *How are control and ownership of learning environments perceived by learners from different national and academic cultures and how do these perceptions impact learning?*

The conceptual model applied in the present research study used the Antecedents-Consequences Model (ACM) proposed by [Buc 12]. Based on theoretical underpinning of psychological ownership, the underlying assumption of the ACM is that psychological ownership is influenced by a number of factors (antecedents, such as students' perceived control of different elements of a learning environment) and leads to certain outcomes (consequences, such as level of engagement, creativity and productive uses of media). Based on the results of the first study, it was expected that a learning environment is perceived as a PLE if learners develop a feeling of ownership towards the elements of this environment. The present study encompassed three main groups of variables, i.e. (a) perceived control as a factor influencing psychological

ownership (Antecedents), (b) the measure of psychological ownership itself, and (c) learning effects (Consequences) resulting from ownership (Figure 3).

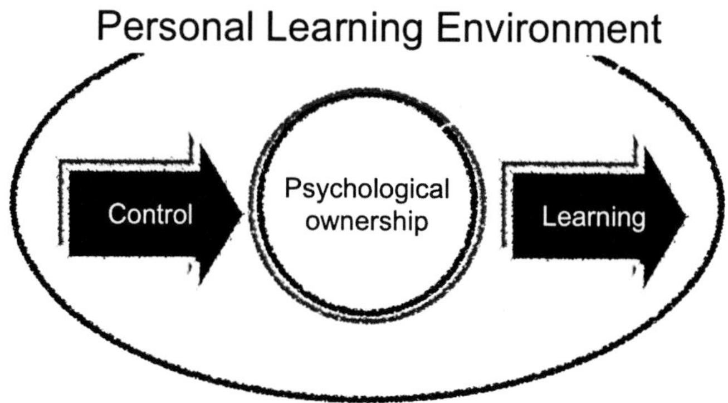

Figure 3: The Antecedents-Consequences-Model (ACM) of the study

The study incorporated the concept of psychological ownership by Pierce et al. (2001) applied in the study by [Buc 12]. According to this model, ownership comprises *five dimensions,* i.e. (1) sense of responsibility, (2) sense of self-identity, (3) sense of accountability, (4) sense of self-efficacy, and (5) sense of belongingness. *Sense of responsibility* is related to protecting and enhancing the object of possession, which may include improvement, control and limiting access to others. *Sense of identity* is viewed as part of the self-concept and is established, maintained, reproduced and transformed through interactions with tangible and intangible objects of possession. *Sense of accountability* can be defined as an expectation to hold others accountable and to be held accountable for what happens to and with objects of possession. *Sense of self-efficacy* is based on the concept developed by [Ban 97] and describes the belief in one's ability to reach goals, master difficult situations and succeed in relation to both tangible and intangible objects of possession. *Sense of belongingness* relates the feeling of attachment to places, objects and people [Pie 01], [Ave 09].

Research method

The present study is an extension of an earlier study by [Buc 12], which was conducted at two universities in Germany with 50 students from three different university courses and disciplines. An online survey including three scales, i.e. psychological ownership scale, control scale and learning effects scale, was applied to collect data. The present study revised and adjusted the three scales from the study by [Buc 12] based on reliability measures from the first study and on feedback from experts in the PLE

community. The current study was conducted with a wider and more diverse group of learners in terms of age, language, cultural background and the area of study. Given the international study sample, the survey was created in two language versions (English and Catalan) and conducted using online tools LimeSurvey and Google Forms. The research applied quantitative and qualitative methods to triangulate conclusions. Quantitative data was analysed with SPSS and R software. Qualitative data obtained by means of open questions in the survey was analysed and discussed with students in respective courses.

Despite different educational contexts of learners participating in the study, all students in the sample used Web 2.0 tools to construct their PLEs as part of ePortfolio practice in university course. Students from all courses used different Web 2.0 tools to support and document their learning during one semester. Following the idea formulated by [Con 10] about the need for systematical integration of the social web in higher education, Web 2.0 tools were introduced as instruments for learning, knowledge construction and collaboration. The study sample included 76 students from the following courses:

1. *General Studies Program at Beuth University of Applied Sciences Berlin (Germany)*: The general studies program (Studium Generale) at Beuth University is an open, university-wide program aiming at academic and career development of students from all accredited programs. Students who participated in the study were enrolled in two courses in media sociology, i.e. "Web 2.0 and the Society" and "Mobile Web and the Society". The sample for this research study included 45 bachelor and master students from various programs including economics, computer sciences, engineering and media design. Both courses integrate the concept of PLEs and ePortfolios into their coursework. ePortfolios are primarily used to support research-based learning as students work in small groups on own research projects throughout the semester. The aim is to foster the use of digital media to create own PLE beyond the requirements of the course. Students in the course "Web 2.0 and the Society" created their ePortfolios combining different Web 2.0 tools, such as Wordpress, Tumblr, Twitter, Flickr, Storify, Prezi, ScoopIt and SlideShare. Students in the course "Mobile Web and the Society" used Mahara as a main hub in which different artefacts and media (e.g. YouTube videos, RSS feeds) were mashed and aggregated to create ePortfolios.

2. *Teacher Education Programme at the University of the Balearic Islands (Spain):* This program integrates the concept of PLEs and ePortfolios into coursework. ePortfolios are created by students using Web 2.0 tools, in this way extending their PLEs. The aim is to develop a positive attitude towards using technology in education. The study sample comprised of 24 student teachers consisting of first and second-year students who study to become Infant Education Teachers. Student teachers at the local branch in Ibiza of the Balearic Islands University create

and maintain their ePortfolios throughout their stay at the university. In this way students document their learning and identity development as Infant Education teachers as well as use ICT for learning during their education as teachers so that the experience is consistent enough to use ICT as future teachers. The project has run since 2009/2010 and its evolution has been positive [Tur 11], [Tur 12a], [Tur 12b], [Tur 13]. The ePortfolio project is based on three approaches by [Bar 09], [Bar 10], [Bar 11], [Cam 09], [Cam 10], and [Zub 09]. First, based on Barrett's work, students build their ePortfolio in three main steps: students create artefacts, document learning in a chronological order and finally present their ePortfolios. Second, based on Cambridge's work, ePortfolios are used to foster the development of students' *networked selves* and *symphonic selves* which are closely related to Barrett's three steps. Third, based on Zubizarreta, students collaborate and reflect while documenting their learning.

3. *Online Master Programs at the University Duisburg-Essen (Germany):* The master programs "Educational Media" and "Educational Leadership" are designed as part time study and blended learning with one or two on-campus events per semester. The programs count around 100 participants per semester and are held in German language. Participants mainly come from Germany and German speaking countries. The sample from these courses comprised of 7 students from different courses. These courses integrate the concept of PLEs into their coursework. New students are introduced to the learning systems and become acquainted with a personal weblog. According to the concept of a "social hub", the social learning management system of the study program focuses on connecting students' PLEs [Höl 12]. A basic set of tools is offered by the system for learners including a collaborative synchronous text editing tool, an internal personal weblog, a poll tool, a messaging system. In discovering the potential of Web 2.0 for collaboration and synchronous communication, students can choose an internal weblog managed by the learning system or an external weblog hosted on the web. Weblogs are used as tools to express the learning process which corresponds with the ePortfolio approach. As part of ePortfolio students form groups and cooperate to work on assignments. Students are given assignments for blogging, reflecting and discussions in their weblogs. Using weblogs is required in order to be permitted to the examination at the end of the course.

Research results

The study comprised a cross-cultural sample of 76 students from three different universities and courses as described in the previous section (i.e. "Berlin sample", "Ibiza sample" and "Duisburg sample"). Descriptive statistics related to these samples are summarized in Table 2.

Table 2: Descriptive statistics of the study sample, n = 76

	BERLIN (GERMANY)	IBIZA (SPAIN)	DUISBURG (GERMANY)
Language	German	Catalan	German
Study area	General Studies	Teacher Education	Online Master
Sample size	45 students	24 students	7 students

Below the results of several statistical tests are summarized following the key research question: *How are control and ownership of learning environments perceived by learners from different national and academic cultures and how do these perceptions impact learning?*

(A) **Psychological ownership:** These five dimensions of psychological ownership, i.e. sense of responsibility, sense of self-identity, sense of accountability, sense of self-efficacy, and sense of belongingness, were measured across the three samples based on the scale with five items rated on the Likert scale from 1 (fully agree) to 5 (fully disagree). Thus the lower the values, the more positive the result. Table 3 summarizes statistical results for ownership scale.

Table 3: Statistics of psychological ownership (m = mean, sd = standard deviation), n = 76. Likert scale 1–5: 1 = fully agree, 5 = fully disagree

		BERLIN n = 45	IBIZA n = 24	DUISBURG n = 7	TOTAL n = 76
1.1	Sense of responsibility	m = 1.78 sd = .95	m = 2.29 sd = .91	m = 2.14 sd = .90	m = 1.97 sd = .95
1.2	Sense of self-identity	m = 2.41 sd = .99	m = 1.83 sd = .96	m = 2.71 sd = .96	m = 2.29 sd = 1.02
1.3	Sense of accountability	m = 2.36 sd = .80	m = 1.92 sd = 1.02	m = 2.86 sd = .69	m = 2.26 sd = .90

	BERLIN n=45	IBIZA n=24	DUISBURG n=7	TOTAL n=76
1.4 Sense of self-efficacy	m=2.23 sd=1.03	m=1.75 sd=.79	m=3.29 sd=1.5	m=2.28 sd=1.09
1.5 Sense of belongingness	m=2.07 sd=.86	m=2.38 sd=.77	m=3.86 sd=1.07	m=2.33 sd=.95
Total of 5 items	m=2.21 sd=.96	m=2.03 sd=.92	m=2.97 sd=1.15	m=2.23 sd=.99

As Table 3 shows, the lowest (most positive) values across all five items measuring the five dimensions of psychological ownership were reached by the Ibiza sample with m=2.03 and the lowest standard deviation of sd=.92. This means that Ibizan students developed the strongest feeling of ownership of their learning environments. In general, students in all three samples developed a sound sense of ownership towards their learning environment with the m=2.23 and sd=0.99. These results may indicate that students perceived their ePortfolio based learning environment as their PLE, for example students felt responsible for it, could identify with it, felt accountable for and attached to the learning environment they created. Yet, the cut-off point for a learning environment becoming a PLE to the individual learner is not straightforward. Further studies should investigate the relationship between the ownership values and PLE in more detail. As far as results for single dimensions are concerned, the lowest (most positive) values across all three samples were reached for dimension "sense of responsibility" with the m=1.97 and sd=.95. In this respect, most positive values were reached for Berlin students with m=1.78 and sd=.95, meaning that students in Berlin felt more responsible for their learning environment than students in other two samples. Since the sense of responsibility (item 1.1) towards the learning environment was the most salient dimension of psychological ownership in all three samples, especially in Berlin sample, a possible interpretation is that ePortfolio practice promotes the responsibility of own learning, independent from the national or academic culture. It is also interesting to highlight the fact that the lowest values related to accountability (item 1.3) are achieved by Ibiza students, who are assessed to 50% based on their ePortfolio performance. Further research should further investigate the question raised by this result: Is there a relationship between type of assessment (e.g. ePortfolio) and ownership, especially the sense of accountability?

(B) **Learner control:** The theory of psychological ownership by [Pie 01], [Pie 03] defines control as one of the three key mechanisms (besides engagement and identity) through which psychological ownership develops. The overall aim of ePortfolio work in the courses participating in the study was to enhance learner control in the sense of the PLE concept of learner control. However, the intended design may be

realised otherwise in situ or perceived differently by students. Therefore, it was not the "designed control" but "perceived control" that was measured to explore students' perceptions. The concept of perceived control was defined to encompass seven dimensions of control with items derived from the research by [Buc 11] and applied in the first study by [Buc 12]. These seven dimensions were: (1) control of technology, (2) control of objectives, (3) control of content, (4) control of planning, (5) control of design, (6) control of access rights, and (7) control of personal data. Altogether 7 items were applied to measure perceived control. Table 4 summarises the values for perceived learner control across the three samples.

Table 4: Statistics of perceived learner control (m = Mean, sd = Standard Deviation), n = 76; Likert scale 1–5: 1 = fully agree, 5 = fully disagree

		BERLIN n = 45	IBIZA n = 24	DUISBURG n = 7	TOTAL n = 76
2.1	Control of technology	m = 2.2 sd = 1.1	m = 2.63 sd = .77	m = 3.57 sd = 1.4	m = 2.46 sd = 1.1
2.2	Control of objectives	m = 2.47 sd = 1.06	m = 2.5 sd = .88	m = 2.86 sd = 1.46	m = 2.51 sd = 1.04
2.3	Control of content	m = 2.36 sd = 1.13	m = 2.42 sd = .78	m = 1.71 sd = 1.89	m = 2.41 sd = 1.11
2.4	Control of planning	m = 1.78 sd = .93	m = 2.67 sd = 1.13	m = 2.14 sd = 1.95	m = 2.09 sd = 1.17
2.5	Control of design	m = 2.33 sd = 1.13	m = 1.88 sd = 1.33	m = 3.86 sd = 1.21	m = 2.33 sd = 1.3
2.6	Control of access right	m = 2.16 sd = 1.21	m = 2.88 sd = 1.3	m = 2.71 sd = 1.6	m = 2.53 sd = 1.35
2.7	Control of personal data	m = 2.49 sd = 1.22	m = 2.42 sd = 1.34	m = 3.43 sd = 1.62	m = 2.55 sd = 1.3
Total 7 items		m = 2.25 sd = 1.13	m = 2.48 sd = 1.12	m = 3.13 sd = 1.64	m = 2.43 sd = 1.22

As Table 4 shows, the lowest (most positive) values across the seven dimensions of perceived learner control were reached by the Berlin sample with the average value of m = 2.25. This results raises the question why Berlin students felt more in control of their learning environments than students in other samples? It seems that differences in instructional design are a more plausible explanation than cultural differences. Differences in perception of control can be further explored in specific dimensions. For example, students in Berlin felt strongly in control of planning (item 2.4), while students in Ibiza felt strongly in control of design (item 2.5) and students in Duisburg felt strongly in control of content (item 2.3). These differences may be related to different instructional designs in respective courses. For example, it may be that students in Berlin were given more freedom to plan while students in Ibiza were given more freedom to design. These also could be cultural differences related to educational principles of course instructors. At the same time the values of perceived control in terms of visual and structural design (item 2.5) are in general negative for the Duisburg sample. The reason may be that students used tools embedded in the learning management system that allowed for only little customisation of the look and feel. Furthermore, the blog functionality used by students in Duisburg was for technical reasons readable by all other students in the study program, which may explain negative values of perceived control of access rights and data privacy (items 2.6 and 2.7) in the Duisburg sample. These results compared to positive values of ownership may indicate that although students in Duisburg felt the owners of their learning environments, there were technological limitations which negatively effected the perception of control. However, the ex ante examination of the relationship between different instructional designs and different perceptions of control has certain limits as freedom to make choices which educators grant to students is to a large extent determined in context. Granting control is a negotiation process and takes place in interaction between instructors and students. Further studies could therefore apply other methodologies, such as interactional analysis, to determine the degrees of freedom granted to students in practice and compare these with measures of perceived control. Nevertheless, the differences in perceived control could be attributed to cultural differences, especially related to discipline cultures. A possible explanation is that students of technical disciplines in Berlin attached more value to control of planing (item 2.4), while students of pedagogy in Ibiza attached more value to control of design (item 2.5). These hypotheses should be tested in further studies, as the implications of cross-cultural differences are relevant for culture-sensitive designs of learning environments. Since perceived control related to planning was the most salient dimension of learner control among all students in the all three samples, control of planning seems to be an important design feature independent of national or discipline culture. The negative values, however, were reached for control of objectives, control of access rights and control of personal data. In general, these results can be understood both in terms of instructional designs and cultural differences, such as learner control versus institutional control. As learning objectives may have been imposed and perceived as compulsory by students, further research on PLE designs in formal education should attempt to explore new ways of establishing learning objectives with students. It should be explored further, if institutional control related to learning objectives is meaningful in context of PLEs at all and how a balance between educational objectives and learner autonomy could be reached.

Further, negative results were reached for perceived control of personal data. This again may be the result of institutional applications of technology which from students

perspective lack flexibility and transparency. However, it could also be a cultural issue, especially in terms of data privacy concerns in the academic culture. Further research on PLE designs should try to improve perceived learner control in relation to personal data.

The comparison of results in Tables 3 and 4 reveals some interesting findings of possible relationships between perceived control and ownership. First, students in Duisburg achieved most positive results in control of content (item 2.3) and at the same time most negative results in the feeling of responsibility (item 1.1). This may mean that being able to control the content has no significant effect on the feeling of responsibility. The correlation analysis seems to support this interpretation. At the same time, there is a strong relation between the sense of self-efficacy (item 1.4) and the control of personal data (item 2.7) in the Duisburg sample (r=.835). However, these observations would need to be further tested, e.g. by means of regression analysis. Also students in Duisburg did not achieve any significant values in any item related to psychological ownership despite – or perhaps because of – the fact that ePortfolio assignments were compulsory. Further research should try to understand how compulsory tasks in context of PLEs affect learner control and ownership. Second, findings reveal that students in Berlin obtained most positive values in control of planning (item 2.4) and at the same time most positive values in the sense of responsibility (item 1.1). Further research should investigate how perceived control of planning affects the sense of responsibility. Third, students from Ibiza achieved the most positive values in control of design (item 2.5) of their ePortfolio and at the same time the most positive values in the sense of self-identity (item 1.2). The correlation analysis confirms this relationship, r=.425. This may mean that Ibiza students focused on designing the representations of their identity in their ePortfolio practice. Further research should explore the role of perceived control of design on the sense of self-identity and the PLE becoming a part of the self-concept.

(C) **Cross-cultural differences:** Beyond descriptive statistics and correlation analysis, t test for independent means were computed to compare parameter values of the three key variable sets, i.e. learner control, psychological ownership and learning effects, across the three samples representing different cultures in terms of fields of study and nationality. Altogether nine t tests were calculated for pairs of independent samples and the significance assessed at the .05 level. The results of the t tests are summarized in Table 5.

Table 5: T test results (m = mean, df = degree of freedom, p = probability), n = 76

	STATISTICS
Learner control	Berlin (m = 2.25) & Duisburg (m = 3.18): *t = -3.2174*, df = 50, p ‹ .05** Berlin (m = 2.25) & Ibiza (m = 2.48): *t = -1.4716*, df = 67, p › .05* Duisburg (m = 3.18) & Ibiza: (m = 2.48): *t = 1.9635*, df = 29, p ‹ .05**
Psychological ownership	Berlin (m = 2.21) & Duisburg (m = 2.97): *t = -2.9571*, df = 50, p ‹ .05** Berlin (m = 2.21) & Ibiza (m = 2.03): *t = 1.1396*, df = 67, p › .05* Duisburg (m = 2.97) & Ibiza (m = 2.03): *t = 3.3174*, df = 29, p ‹ .05**
Learning effects	Berlin (m = 2.99) and Duisburg (m = 3.30): *t = -0.9281*, df = 50, p › .05* Berlin (m = 2.99) & Ibiza (m = 2.26): *t = 4.0059*, df = 67, p ‹ .05** Duisburg (m = 3.30) & Ibiza (m = 2.26): *t = 4.0787*, df = 29, p ‹ .05**
	* p › .05 = non significant ** p ‹ .05 = significant

Results in table 5 indicate that there was no significant difference in how students in Berlin and Ibiza perceived learner control and psychological ownership. This may indicate that instructional designs in Berlin and Ibiza did not differ in a significant way. However, due to significant differences in perceived control and ownership in the Duisburg sample, instructional design in Duisburg was explored in more detail. In fact, instructional design in Duisburg was different as most students could not freely choose a tool to create their ePortfolios but had to use a blogging tool embedded in the learning management system. The t-tests also reveal significant differences in learning effects of students in Berlin and Duisburg compared to students in Ibiza. Possible predictors are explored in the section below.

(D) **Learning effects:** The Antecedents-Consequences-Model of the study considers learning effect as a consequence of ownership and control. This is based on the assumption that the sense of ownership and perceived learner control influence how students engage and develop their learning environments. Learning effects in the study were explored using a measure with six dimensions: (1) time invested (students willingly invested time in learning), (2) student engagement (students did more than was required by the teacher), (3) student creativity (students tried something new), (4) interest orientation (students followed their interests), (5) self-direction (students felt they were learning for themselves), (6) intrinsic motivation (learnig was more important than grades), (7) social learning (students collaborated to learn), (8) future use (students expect to create a similar learning environment in the future), (9) continued use (students expect to continue to use their learning environment after the course), (10) transfer (students expect to transfer the PLE idea to other areas), and (11) transformation (PLE practice changed the way students learn). Since psychological ownership and control have been viewed

as positive resources for impacting attitudes, e.g. higher commitment, responsibility [Ave 09], [Pie 01], [Pie 03]; [Van 04], it was expected that both ownership and control had a positive impact on the learning effects. Learning effect statistics are summarised in Table 8.

Table 8: Statistics of learning effects (m = mean, sd = standard deviation), n = 76; Likert scale 1–5: 1 = fully agree, 5 = fully disagree

LEARNING EFFECTS	BERLIN n = 45	IBIZA n = 24	DUISBURG n = 7	TOTAL n = 76
3.1 Time invested	m = 2.6 sd = 1.07	m = 2.58 sd = .72	m = 2.86 sd = 1.35	m = 2.62, sd = .99
3.2 Student engagement	m = 2.78 sd = 1.33	m = 2.54 sd = 1.02	m = 3.71 sd = 1.38	m = 2.79, sd = 1.27
3.3 Creativity	m = 2.71 sd = 1.12	m = 2.08 sd = .78	m = 3.14 sd = 1.21	m = 2.55, sd = 1.08
3.4 Interest orientation	m = 2.42 sd = .99	m = 2.13 sd = .9	m = 2.71 sd = 1.38	m = 2.36, sd = 1.0
3.5 Self-direction	m = 2.71 sd = 1.2	m = 2.38 sd = .71	m = 3.86 sd = 1.21	m = 2.71, sd = 1.13
3.6 Intrinsic motivation	m = 3.29 sd = 1.2	m = 2.54 sd = .78	m = 4.29 sd = .76	m = 3.14, sd = 1.15
3.7 Social learning	m = 3.06 sd = 1.05	m = 2.46 sd = .78	m = 2.86 sd = 1.21	m = 2.86, sd = 1.02
3.8 Future application	m = 2.96 sd = 1.20	m = 1.91 sd = .93	m = 2.86 sd = 1.57	m = 2.62, sd = 1.24
3.9 Continued use	m = 3.6 sd = 1.21	m = 2.33 sd = .96	m = 3.43 sd = 1.13	m = 3.18, sd = 1.26
3.10 Learning transfer	m = 3.4 sd = 1.29	m = 2.33 sd = .87	m = 3.14 sd = 1.57	m = 3.04, sd = 1.28
3.11 Learning transformed	m = 3.33 sd = 1.07	m = 1.58 sd = .83	m = 3.43 sd = .97	m = 2.79, sd = 1.28
Total of 7 items	m = 2.99 sd = 1.21	m = 2.26 sd = 0.88	m = 3.3 sd = 1.28	m = 2.79, sd = 1.18

As Table 8 shows the self-assessment of learning effects in general among students from all three samples reached on average slightly higher (more negative) values (m = 2.79) than ownership (m = 2.23) and control (m = 2.43). Students in Berlin and Ibiza (compared to students in Duisburg) invested more time in the development of their learning environments, were more engaged and more creative, followed their interests more strongly and felt more strongly that they were learning for themselves. These are interesting results which may indicate that the instructional design in Duisburg, which was more compulsory and allowed for less freedom of choice, contributed to less positive learning effects. However, intrinsic motivation, social learning, future applications, continued use, learning transfer and transformation of learning as dimensions of learning effects reached positive values only in the Ibiza sample. There is a striking difference especially in the perception that ePortfolio practice transformed own learning (item 3.11). This indicates that the ePortfolio practice in the Ibiza sample had the deepest impact on learning as it transformed the way students learn.

In general, highest (most negative) values were reached for dimensions "continued use" (m = 3.18) and "intrinsic motivation" (m = 3.14). This means that on average students in all three samples felt it was rather unlikely they will continue to use their learning environments created during the course and that grades (extrinsic value) were no less important than learning (intrinsic value). Lowest (most positive) values were reached for dimensions "interest orientation" (m = 2.36) and "students creativity" (m = 2.55). This means that students in all three samples followed their interests and engaged in creative practice.

In order to explore the impact of perceived learner control and psychological ownership on learning effects, several statistical tests were conducted, i.e. bivariate correlations and regression analysis. The correlation analysis shows that there is an overall significant correlation between control and ownership ($r = .41$, $p < .01$) and a significant relationship between learning effects and ownership variables across all samples ($r = .68$, $p < .01$). These results can be interpreted as of validation of the Antecedents-Concequences Model applied in this study. Table 9 summarizes correlation coefficients.

Table 9: Correlation results of the Antecedents-Consequences Model

	PERCEIVED CONTROL AND OWNERSHIP (MEANS)	OWNERSHIP AND LEARNING EFFECTS (MEANS)
All samples	$r = .41$, $p < .001$***	$r = .68$, $p < .001$***
	*** $p < .001$ = highly significant	

Also the results of the linear regression analysis with learning effects as dependent variable and ownership as independent variable for all samples indicate that psychological ownership is a good predictor of learning effects (R Square = .46), explaining almost 50 % of variance. Perceived control, on the other hand, explained under 20 % of variance (R Square = .17). The proposed model should however be tested in further studies with larger samples.

Discussion

This paper presented the concept of learner control and ownership in context of Personal Learning Environments and the results of a cross-cultural study aiming at exploring possible differences in perception of control and ownership of learning environments by learners from different national and academic cultures. The study presented in this paper also proposed a measure of "learning effects" which can be used to explore the impact of perceived control and ownership on learning. The results of the study indicate that there may be certain cultural differences in perception of control and ownership of learning environments, such as attaching more value to planning in technical academic cultures rather than to control of design as compared to other discipline cultures, including pedagogy. These differences should be, however, explored in more detail in further studies, as the implications may be important for promoting PLE design and practice by students from different academic backgrounds. However, it seems that a number of differences in perceptions of control and ownership may be best explained by differences in instructional designs, especially in relation to how much freedom of choice and thus control is granted to students in their PLE practice in formal settings, e.g. higher education.

As the results of the study indicate, compulsory tasks and choice of media, little possibilities to adjust the look and feel of PLE tools as well as application of institutional tools such as learning management systems which from students' perspective provide little control and transparency of personal data, may have a negative impact on learning. The responses in the survey express a disjunction between the instructional design aimed at activating students for ePortfolio work by formal (compulsory) assignments and the student perception of their ePortfolio as a PLE. On the other hand, as survey responses indicate, especially control of planning and control of design have a positive impact on learning. This is reflected, among others, in willingly investing time in learning, following their interests and being creative in ePortfolio practice or even the perception that ePortfolio practice altogether transform the way they learn. Thus perceived learner control, especially control of planning and control of design (both intangible elements of Personal Learning Environments) should be considered an important element of PLE practice and PLE design.

Conclusions

This paper provides a contribution to the discussion on learner control in context of Personal Learning Environments. In line with the study by [Buc 12], the results presented in this paper point out to the fact that perceived control of intangible elements, such as planning and design, may have more positive effects on learning than control of tangible elements, such as technical tools. This study also reveals the impact of different PLE designs on learning.

It seems that more freedom of choice (e.g. objectives, tools) as well as flexibility (e.g. planning) and transparency (e.g. personal data) may be beneficial to learning effects. The future implication may be that learner control as postulated by the PLE approach can be advanced to the next level, at which learners are able not only to choose but also to create, for example developing the components of their PLE. This would require learners to develop new skills, such as coding, as well as technical tools to become low-threshold and user-friendly. Finally, this paper uncovers the topic of control and ownership from a cross-cultural perspective and indicates that specific elements of control may be more valued by learners from different national and academic cultures. As a recommendation for further research, future studies should also explore the possibilities of mobile technologies for enhancing perceived learner control and psychological ownership in relation to Personal Learning Environments and its impact on learning.

REFERENCES

[Ade 10] *Adell, Jordi; Castañeda, Linda (2010):* Los entornos personales de aprendizaje (ples): Una nueva manera de entender el aprendizaje. In: R. Roig Vila & M. Fiorucci (Eds.) Claves para la investigación en innovación y calidad educativas. Alcoy: Marfil – Roma TRE Universita degli studi.

[Att 05] *Attwell, Graham (2005):* Recognising learning: Educational and pedagogic issues in e- portfolios. Retrieved 1 March 2014 from *http://es.scribd.com/doc/24852254/Recognising-Learning-Educational-and-pedagogic-issues-in-e-Portfolios-Graham-Attwell*

[Att 07] *Attwell, Graham (2007):* E-Portfolios – the DNA of the personal learning environment? Journal of Elearning and Knowledge Society, 3(2), 39–61. Retrieved 1 March 2014 from *www.pontydysgu.org/wp.../eportolioDNAofPLEjournal.pdf*

[Att 12] *Attwell, Graham. (2012):* Who owns the e-portfolio? Pontydysgu. Bridge to learning. Retrieved 1 March 2014 from a *http://www.pontydysgu.org/2012/09/who-owns-the-e-portfolio*

[Bar 04] *Barrett, Helen; Wilkerson, Judy (2004):* Competing paradigms in portfolio approaches. Electronic portfolios. Retrieved 1 March 2014 from *http://electronicportfolios.org/systems/paradigms.html*

[Bar 09] *Barrett, Helen (2009):* Balancing 2 faces of eportfolios. Retrieved1 March 2014 from *http://electronicportfolios.com/balance/index.html*

[Bar 10] *Barrett, Helen (2010):* Balancing the two faces of eportfolios. Educação, Formação & Tecnologias, 3 (1), 6–14. Retrieved 1 March 2014 from *http://www.eft.educom.pt/index.php/eft/article/viewFile/161/102*

[Bar 11] *Barrett, Helen (2011):* Balancing the two faces of eportfolios. In S. Hirtz, K. Kelly (2011) (Eds.). Education for a digital world. Innovations in education, 2, British Columbia Ministry

of Education, 291–310. Retrieved 1 March 2014 from *http://www.openschool.bc.ca/info/edu/7540006133_2.pdf*

[Big 11] *Biggs, John; Tang, Catherine (2011):* Teaching for quality learning at university. Maidenhead, UK: McGraw-Hill and Open University Press.

[Bro 93] *Brown, L. Susan (1993):* The Politics of Individualism: Liberalism, Liberal Feminism, and Anarchism. Montréal/New York/London: Black Rose Books.

[Buc 11] *Buchem, Ilona; Attwell, Graham; and Torres, Ricardo (2011):* Understanding personal learning environments: Literature review and synthesis through the activity theory lens. Proceedings of the The PLE Conference 2011, 10th – 12th July 2011, Southampton, UK. Retrieved 1 March 2014 from: *http://journal.webscience.org/658*

[Buc 12] *Buchem, Ilona (2012):* Psychological Ownership and Personal Learning Environments. Do possession and control really matter? Proceedings of the PLE Conference 2012, Aveiro, Portugal. Retrieved 1 March 2014 from *http://revistas.ua.pt/index.php/ple/article/viewFile/1437/1323*

[Buc 13] *Buchem, Ilona; Pérez-Sanagustín, Mar (2013):* Personal Learning Environments in Smart Cities: Current Approaches and Future Scenarios. eLearning Papers, 35, November 2013. Retrieved from *http://openeducationeuropa.eu/sites/default/files/asset/In-depth_35_1.pdf*

[Cas 13] *Castañeda, Linda; Adell, Jordi (2013):* La anatomía de los PLEs. In L. Castañeda y J. Adell (eds) Entornos personales de aprendizaje: claves para el ecosistema educativo en red, Alcoy: Marfil, 11–28.

[Che 09] *Chen, Helen L. (2009):* Using E-Portfolios to Support Lifelong and Lifewide Learning, In D. Cambridge, B. L. Cambridge, K. B. Yancey, eds., Electronic Portfolios 2.0: Emergent Research on Implementation and Impact. Sterling, VA: Stylus, 29–39.

[Che 10] *Chen, Helen L.; Light, T. Penny (2010):* Electronic Portfolios and Student Success: Effectiveness, Efficiency, and Learning. Washington, D.C.: Association of American Colleges & Universities.

[Chr 94] *Christman, John (1994):* The myth of property: toward an egalitarian theory of ownership. New York: Oxford Univ. Press.

[Con 10] *Conole, Gráinne; Alevizou, Panagiota (2010):* A literature review of the use of Web 2.0 tools in Higher Education. HEA Academy, York, UK. Retrieved1 March 2014 from *http://oro.open.ac.uk/23154/*

[Cou 06] *Cousin, Glynis (2006):* An introduction to threshold concepts. Planet Special Issue on Threshold Concepts and Troublesome Knowledge, 17, 4–5. Retrieved from *www.gees.ac.uk/planet/p17/gc.pdf*

[Chu 92] *Chung, Jaesam and Reigeluth, Charles M. (1992). Instructional prescriptions for learner control. Educational Technology 32(10), 14–20.*

[Dan 92] *Dan-Cohen, Meir (1992):* Responsibility and the Boundaries of the Self. *Harvard Law Review* 105, (5), 959–1003.

[Dwo 88] *Dworkin, Gerald (1988):* The Theory and Practice of Autonomy. Cambridge: Cambridge University Press.

[Hoe 12] *Hölterhof, Tobias; Nattland, Axel; Kerres, Michael (2012):* Drupal as a Social Hub for Personal Learning. Proceedings of the PLE Conference 2012, Aveiro, Portugal. Retrieved 1 March 2014 from: *http://revistas.ua.pt/index.php/ple/article/view/1453*

[Joy 09] *Joyes, Gordon; Gray, Lisa; Hartnell-Young, Elisabeth (2009):* Effective practice with e-portfolios: How can the UK experience inform practice. Same Places, Different Spaces. Proceedings Ascilite Auckland 2009, 486–495. Retrieved 1 March 2014 from *www.ascilite.org.au/conferences/auckland09/procs/joyes.pdf*

[Kea 13] *Kearney, Matthew; Shuck, Sandra; Burden, Kevin; Aubusson, Peter (2013):*Viewing mobile learning from a pedagogial perspective. Research in Learning Technology, 20, 1–17. Retrieved from *http://www.researchinlearningtechnology.net/index.php/rlt/article/view/14406*

[Kno 75] *Knowles, Malcom S. (1975):* Self-directed Learning. New York. Association Press.

[Kno 80] *Knowles, Malcom S. (1980):* The Modern Practice of Adult Education. From Pedagogy to Andragogy. Chicago: Follett.

[Lau 87] *Laurillard, Diana M. (1987):* Computers and the emancipation of students: giving control to the learner. Instructional Science 16(1), 3–18.

[Lit 91] *Little, David (1991):* Learner Autonomy: Definitions, Issues and Problems. Dublin: Authentik.

[Mer 83] *Merrill, M.David (1983):* Component display theory. In C.M. Reigeluth, ed. Instructional-design theories and models, 279–334. Hillsdale, NJ: Erlbaum.

[Mey 03] *Meyer, Jan; Land, Ray (2003):* Threshold concepts and troublesome knowledge: Linkages to ways of thinking and practising within the disciplines. Enhancing Teaching-Learning Environments in Undergraduate Courses. Occasional Report 4. Retrieved 30 June 2013 from *http://www.etl.tla.ed.ac.uk/docs/ETLreport4.pdf*

[Mil 91] *Milheim, William D.; Martin, Barabara L. (1991):* Theoretical bases for the use of learner control: three different perspectives. Journal of Computer-Based Instruction 18(3), 99–105.

[Pat 02] *Pateman, Carole (2002):* Self-Ownership and Property in the Person: Democratization and a Tale of Two Concepts. The Journal of Political Philosophy, 10, (1), 20–53. Retrieved 1 March 2014 from: *http://www.sscnet.ucla.edu/polisci/faculty/pateman/Self-Ownership.pdf*

[Pie 01] *Pierce, John L.; Kostova, Tatiana; Dirks, Kurt T. (2001):* Toward a theory of psychological ownership in organizations. Academy of Management Review, 26, 298–310.

[Pie 03] *Pierce, John L., Kostova, Tatiana; Dirks, Kurt. T. (2003):* The state of psychological ownership: integrating and extending a century of research. Review of General Psychology, 7, 84–107.

[Ro 09] *Roder, John; Brown, Mark (2009):* What leading educators say about Web 2.0, PLEs and e-portfolios in the future. In Same places, different spaces. Proceedings ascilite Auckland 2009, 870–882. Retrieved 1 March 2014 from *http://www.ascilite.org.au/conferences/auckland09/procs/roder.pdf*

[She 11] *Shepherd, Craig. E. and Skrabut, Stan. (2011):* Rethinking electronic portfolios to promote sustainability among teachers. TechTrends, 55, (5), 31–38. Retrieved from *www.springerlink.com/index/611H10281598516J.pdf*

[Shr 13] *Shroff, Ronnie H.; Trent, John; Ng, Eugenia. M. W. (2013):* Using e-portfolios in a field experience placement: Examining student-teachers' attitudes towards learning in relationship to personal value, control and responsibility. Australasian Journal of Educational Technology. 29, (2), 143–160.

[Tur 11] *Tur, Gemma (2011):* Eportfolios and PLEs in Teacher Education. First results. Proceedings of the The PLE Conference 2011, 1–10, Southampton, UK. Retrieved 1 March 2014 from: *http://journal.webscience.org/578/*

[Tur 13] *Tur, Gemma (2013):* Projecte de portafoli electrònic amb eines de la Web 2.0 als estudis de Grau d'Educació Infantil de la UIB a la Seu d'Eivissa.Estudi de cas. Thesis. University of the Balearic Islands. TDX database. Retrieved from *http://www.tdx.cat/handle/10803/111339*

[Tur 12a] *Tur, G.emma; Urbina, Santos (2012a):* PLE-based ePortfolios: Towards Empowering Student Teachers' PLEs through ePortfolio Processes. Proceedings of the PLE Conference, University of Aveiro, Portugal. Retrieved 1 March 2014 from *http://revistas.ua.pt/index.php/ple/article/view/1438*

[Tur 12b] *Tur, Gemma; Urbina, Santos (2012b). Documentando el aprendizaje en portafolios electrónicos:* una experiencia con herramientas de la Web 2.0. Congreso Internacional Edutec 2012, 656–669. Retrieved 1 March 2014 from *http://gte.uib.es/pape/gte/sites/gte.uib.es.pape.gte/files/aprendizajeeportfolios.pdf*

[Wi 89] *Wilson, Brent.G.; Jonassen, David H. (1989):* Hypertext and instructional design: some preliminary guidelines. Performance Improvement Quarterly 2(3), 34–49.

[Zub 09] *Zubizarreta, John (2009):* The Learning Portfolio. Reflective Practice for Improving Student Learning. San Francisco: Jossey Bass.

CONTACT DETAILS

Prof. Dr. Ilona Buchem
Beuth Universty of Applied Sciences
Department I – Economics and Social Sciences
Luxemburger Street 10
13353 Berlin
Phone: +49 (0)30 450 452 43
E-Mail: *buchem@beuth-hochschule.de*

Dr. Gemma Tur
University of the Balearic Islands
Department of Applied Pedagogy and Educational Psychology
Calvari Street 1
07800 Ibiza (Balearic Islands)
Phone: +34 (0)971 398 020
E-Mail: *gemma.tur@uib.es*

Dr. Tobias Hölterhof
University of Duisburg-Essen
Learning Lab
Forsthausweg 2
47057 Duisburg
Phone: +49 203 3799 1557
E-Mail: *tobias.hoelterhof@uni-duisburg-essen.de*

A pedagogy-driven framework for integrating Web 2.0 tools into educational practices and building personal learning environments

Ebrahim Rahimi, Jan van den Berg, Wim Veen

ABSTRACT

While the concept of Web 2.0 based Personal Learning Environments (PLEs) has generated significant interest in educational settings, there is little consensus regarding what this concept means and how teachers and students can develop and deploy Web 2.0 based PLEs to support their teaching and learning activities. In this paper a conceptual framework for building Web 2.0 based PLEs is proposed. The framework consists of four main elements, including (i) student's control model, (ii) learning potential of Web 2.0 tools and services, (iii) project-based teaching approach, and (iv) technology-enhanced learning activities. The main purpose of the framework is to assist teachers to design appropriate Web 2.0 based learning activities. Students then can accomplish these learning activities to develop their PLEs and complete their learning projects.

Note: *This article has been published in the Special Edition of the Journal of Literacy and Technology: "Personal Learning Environments: Current Research and Emerging Practice". The link to the JLT Special Issue is: http://www.literacyandtechnology.org/uploads/1/3/6/8/136889/jlt_special.pdf*

Introduction

In recent years innovations in web technologies along with the new learning requirements laid down by the knowledge society have led to the emergence of three fundamental shifts in technology enhanced learning (TEL) including: (i) a shift from a focus on content to communication, (ii) a shift from a passive to a more interactive engagement of students in the educational process, and (iii) a shift from a focus on individual learners to more socially situated learning [Con 07]. There is overwhelming evidence corroborating the notion that Virtual Learning Environments (VLEs), as the mainstream in TEL initiatives, despite some successes, have failed to address these shifts [Cha 10], [Att 10], [Dow 06]. These systems mainly follow and support the learning from technology approach [Jon 95] manifested in technology-push, course-centered, content-based, and teacher-driven educational processes [Cha 10], [Att 10]. As a result, the underlying assumption of these systems presumes a passive and controlled role for students in their educational practices [Dro 07].

Personal Learning Environments (PLEs) have been suggested as a solution for the challenges mentioned above [Att 07], [Dow 06], [Val 12], [Dab 12]. An overwhelming number of authors contended that PLEs, as rooted in socio-cultural and constructivist theories of learning and knowledge building as well as facilitated by the popularity of Web 2.0 tools and social software, have potential to support collaborative learning, communities of practice, personal development, self-directed and lifelong learning [Lee 10], [Wil 09], [Joh 08], [Dre 10]. According to [Att 07], PLEs are activity spaces in which students interact and communicate with each other and experts the ultimate result of which is the development of collective learning. As argued by [Lee 10], the conceived goal of PLEs is to enable students, not only to consume content, but to remix, produce, and express their personal presentation of knowledge. Furthermore, it has been argued that PLEs presume and support an active role for students by placing them in the center of their learning processes, corroborating their sense of ownership of learning, and enhancing their control in educational process [Dow 06], [Buc 12].

Knowing the potential of PLEs, the question how to develop Web2.0-based PLEs in educational settings to address these challenges is posed. Indeed, while there is an increasing number of suitable Web 2.0 tools, robust theoretical-based technological and pedagogical roadmaps to build PLEs are unavailable. As a result, educators at different educational levels are forced to adapt and rethink their teaching approaches in conjunction with the advent of new web technologies and the learning requirements of the knowledge society "without a clear roadmap for attending to students' various needs" [Kop 08]. Furthermore, while supporting student's control appears to be an essential aim of PLEs [Att 07], there is little consensus regarding what this concept means and how it is to be attained by developing Web 2.0 based PLEs [Väl 10], [Buc 12].

Inspired by these observations, in this paper we develop a framework to support teachers in facilitating the main dimensions of student control by designing appropriate learning activities using the learning potential of Web 2.0 tools and services.

Framework for developing Web 2.0 based PLEs

Supporting the personal development of students and enhancing their control in educational process by using web technologies are the main objectives of building and deploying PLEs [Joh 08], [Dre 10]. [Sca 06] argue that in order to help students to acquire the required skills for learning and working in the knowledge-based society, they should participate in designing and developing their learning environments. Along similar lines some authors remarked that the participation of students in designing and developing their learning environment can strengthen their control in educational process [Val 10], [Dre 10]. Applying this approach to developing and deploying PLEs requires adopting a constructivist-based learning with technology concept [Jon 95]. From the perspective of this concept, instead of leaving technology to the hands of instructional designers to "predefine and constrain learning process" of students, it should be given to students to use as constructing tool to support their personal development and learning by building their learning environments and expressing what they know.

In an attempt to formulate a solution to support student's control in educational process by developing and deploying Web 2.0 PLEs, we proposed a conceptual framework (Figure 1). The framework illustrates how Web 2.0 technologies, the student's control model and the teaching process should interact with each other in order to define appropriate technology-enhanced learning activities to be accomplished by students to build and apply their PLEs. According to this framework, by facilitating the student's control through student-centric instructional approaches (i.e. project-based learning), it is likely that students will start to engage in several learning activities by means of Web 2.0 tools. As a result, it can reveal the ways that they employ technology to manage their learning process providing the teacher with opportunities to acquire a deep understanding and knowledge about students' learning process as a means to improve their teaching process. Moreover, the engagement of students and teachers with Web 2.0 technologies can help them to explore the affordances and learning potential of these technologies and operationalize these affordances to enrich their educational practices.

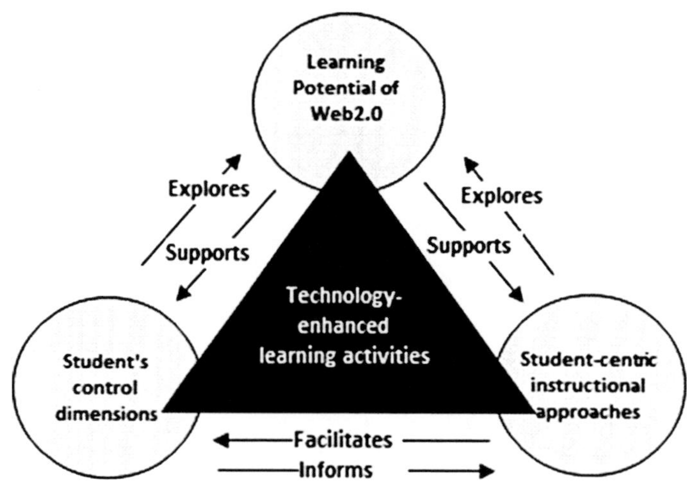

Figure 1: A conceptual framework for developing Web 2.0 PLEs

Student control model

Supporting students to achieve more control over their learning process and become autonomous learners is pivotal to the learner-centric learning theories such as self-reg-

ulated and self-directed learning theories [Dab 12]. Student's control over the learning process is concerned with the degree to which the student can influence and direct her learning experiences and it relates to several aspects of the educational process, including the selection of what is learned, the pace and strategies of learning, the choices of methods and timing of assessments, and choosing learning resources such as online communities and networks, web tools, and content [Kir 02], [Dro 07], [Val 10], [Buc 12]. As stated by [Kir 02], strengthening of student's control over the educational process will place the student in a "position of importance" and by giving them the feeling of more control over their learning experience, it will be more rewarding for the student. Along similar lines, [Buc 12] demonstrated that there is a significant relationships between perceived control, sense of ownership and uses of a learning environment. Accordingly, [Buc 12] argued that supporting student's control opens an opportunity to make choices during the learning activity to effect certain learning outcomes and perceive the learning activity with more personal meaning.

Figure 2 presents the suggested model to support student control in PLEs. We developed this model by adopting and appropriating the learner's control dimensions model proposed by [Gar 87]. According to [Gar 87], learner control is not achieved simply by supporting their independency. Rather than it can be attained only by establishing a dynamic balance between independence (i.e. learner's freedom to choose what, how, when, and where to learn), power (i.e. cognitive abilities and competencies) and support (i.e. learning resources the learner needs in order to carry out the learning process and keep control over learning process) through the process of communication between teachers and students.

To support the active and constructing roles of students in PLEs, we translated power, support and independence dimensions into the active roles a student should undertake in PLE-based learning, namely knowledge producer, socializer, and decision maker, respectively. The student's control model is based on the assumption that students in order to be in control of their learning process should act as (i) knowledge producers to achieve control by acquiring relevant cognitive capabilities, (ii) socializers to keep control by learning skills needed to seek support, and (iii) decision makers to practice control through the personal endeavors to manage web technologies for enriching their learning experiences. The model also explains how to make a balance between these roles by supporting and encouraging activities for co-producing knowledge, developing personal knowledge management strategies, and developing personal learning network. Furthermore, by considering the PLE as output, not input, of the learning process, the model underscores the constructivist-based nature of the PLE-based learning.

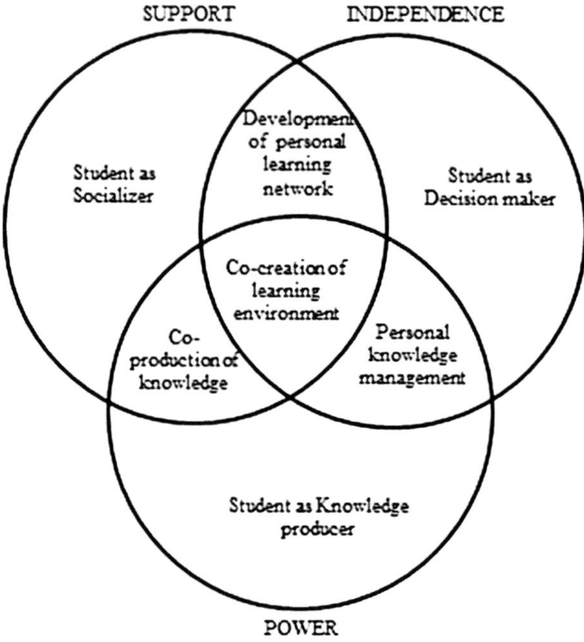

Figure 2: The proposed model for supporting student control in Web 2.0 PLEs

Student-centric instructional approaches

To support and corroborate student control, teachers should adopt a more activity-oriented and student-centric rather than lecture-based teaching approach. Project-based learning (PBL) is an appropriate approach to support student control model.

Firstly, PBL can support the knowledge producer role of students through involving them in knowledge building and higher-level cognitive activities such as engagement with more complex problems and pursuing solutions to them, asking and refining questions, collecting and analyzing data, knowledge and idea presentation, drawing conclusions, and creating artifacts [Blu 91], [Che 07].

Secondly, through participating in designing and doing learning projects, students can acquire personal and metacognitive skills needed to improve their decision making skills such as designing plans or experiments, time and project management, making predictions, selecting appropriate content and, choosing relevant web tools [Che 07].

Thirdly, PBL can develop the social skills of students through collaborating with peers and experts, communicating their ideas and findings to others, improving their willingness to accept peer critiques and revise their projects, and promoting them to work collaboratively in groups to achieve the projects objectives [Blu 91], [Che 07].

Finally, the involvement of the students in defining and completing the project "can create a sense of accomplishment and control for students which is absent in traditional classroom instruction" [Kea 98].

Learning potential of Web 2.0 tools and services

Web 2.0 tools and services are receiving intense and growing interest across all sectors of the educational industry as means for facilitating the transformation of learning [Ale 06], [Cou 10], [Lee 10]. These tools and services can support creative and collective contribution, knowledge producing and the development of new ideas by students [Nel 09]. Furthermore, they can provide students with "just-in-time" and "at-your-fingertips" learning opportunities in a way that typical learning management systems cannot [Dun 11].

In order to investigate the ways that Web 2.0 technologies can support student control model, we need to elicit their learning potential. Due to the steadily increasing heterogeneity of Web 2.0 technologies and ambiguousness of Web 2.0 concept, it is difficult to reach consensus about the meaning, notion, and borders of Web 2.0 technologies. Hence, we need to consider the gravitational core and underlying concepts of Web 2.0 to depict a picture of their learning potential and map them to the elements of the student's control model. [Ale 06] enumerated the gravitational core and underlying concepts of Web 2.0 as below:

- Social software: a software application which provides an architecture of participation for end users to support collaboration and harnessing of collective intelligence by extending or deriving "added value" from human social behavior and interactions [O'Reilly 05].
- Micro-content: a metaphor for the nature of user-generated content in Web 2.0 including blog posts, wiki conversations, RSS feeds, podcasts, vodcasts, and tweets, compared to the page metaphor of Web 1.0. Openness: refers to the free availability of web tools and user-generated content.
- Folksonomy: user-generated taxonomies which are dynamic and socially or collaboratively constructed, in contrast to established, hierarchical taxonomies that are typically created by experts in a discipline or domain of study [Dab 11].
- Sophisticated interfaces: refer to the drag and drop, semantic, widget-based websites created by using AJAX, XML, RSS, CSS, and mashup services [Bow 10].

The potential of Web 2.0 to support students as knowledge producers

Web 2.0 is drawing several new perspectives to knowledge development within educational settings, which were not possible before.

Firstly, as asserted by [Mej 05], the openness nature of Web 2.0 makes it possible for social software applications to impact knowledge building process within classroom by connecting the classroom activities "to the world as a whole, not just the social part that exists online". Indeed, by considering the knowledge building as a "civilization-wide" process, these technologies afford students to "connect with civilization-wide knowledge building and to make their classroom work a part of it" [Sca 06].

Secondly, in recent years, affected by increasing attentions towards social approaches of learning and knowledge building, a fundamental shift in technology enhanced learning from a focus on content to a focus on co-constructing knowledge and communication around the content has been emerged [Con 07]. [Gun 97] illustrated five developmental stages for co-constructing knowledge in collaborative learning environments including (i) sharing and comparing of information, (ii) discovering of inconsistency among the information, (iii) negotiating the meaning and co-construction of knowledge through social negotiation, (iv) testing and modification of co-constructed knowledge, and (v) agreement and application of newly constructed knowledge and meaning. Arguably, the architecture of participation and openness aspects of Web2.0 can facilitate the communicational process and information needed to support the co-construction of knowledge by students.

Thirdly, Web 2.0 can support the appropriation of content by students. Appropriation as the "ability to meaningfully sample and remix media content" [Jen 06] makes student simultaneously as the producer and consumer of content and can be understood as a learning process in which students learn through picking several content (sampling) and putting them back together (remixing) to produce new content and knowledge objects such as ideas, discussions, conversations, comments, replies, concept maps, webpages, podcasts, wikis, and blog posts [Jen 06]. Appropriation as a student-driven knowledge producing strategy is in line with the new knowledge development approaches which underscore the importance of increasing the students' capacity to know more rather than what currently they know, through equipping them with competencies required to engage with social and technological changes. Combining the participatory, micro-content, and openness aspects of Web 2.0 facilitates a unique sort of participatory appropriation process known as "collaborative remixability" that recombines the information and micro-content generated by students to create new content, concepts, and ideas [Lee 10], [Che 07], [Ale 06].

Taken together, different aspects of Web 2.0 can enrich the learning experiences of students and nurture their cognitive skills by providing them opportunities to practice "learning by doing" [Bro 89], to experience "learning with technology" [Jon 95], and construct a personal presentation of knowledge and share it with others. In addition, by involving students in active construction of knowledge, teachers can achieve a comprehensive understanding of the ways that students learn, the sorts of content and technology they use, and the patterns of interactions they establish as a means to improve their teaching practices.

The potential of Web 2.0 to support students as socializers

The value and real power of Web 2.0 technologies is in their sociability aspect. This sociability aspect has changed the way that "participations" spread and people behave by making it feasible to build connections and networks between them [Boy 07]. From a learning perspective, the sociability aspect of Web2.0 offers students learning opportunity that is in line with their normal ways of learning and can enable them to integrate the explicit and tacit dimensions of knowledge [O'Re 05]. On this basis, as stated by [Dab 11], the inextricable link between "learning as a social process" and sociability aspect of Web 2.0 is transforming learning spaces, perspectives and interactions.

Web 2.0 can support the socializer role of students in three levels. Firstly, it can facilitate student-centered instruction. Indeed, Web 2.0 can trigger deep and active interactions between teacher and students through supporting conversational interactions; social feedback; and social networks. As a result, it can improve the negotiated control between teacher and students and raise levels of students' engagement and motivation [Lee 10], [Att 07]. Secondly, Web 2.0 can foster interaction and social learning between students. By getting help of social software, students can participate collaboratively with each other to the "authorship of content", obtain support and guidance from others, work together as a learning community, and share their resources, knowledge, experiences and responsibilities [Bow 10]. Social bookmarking and RSS services can provide a great way to support students to bookmark, tag, and disseminate information, people, and learning experiences. These tags then can be arranged to develop tag clouds to visualize the ways that students are working and learning [Ale 06]. Being able to have access to other students' tags cloud provide the opportunity for students to see each other experiences and competencies resulting in being aware of the new streams of information, supporting vicarious and social learning and triggering students' reflection [Dab 11]. Additionally, as pointed out by [Dab 11], folksonomy as a context-based mechanism for supporting social tagging and sharing the personal experiences of people can be seen as the "language of a community to form connections" between the members of the community. In classroom settings students can use this language to communicate and support "socio-semantic networking" and create learning environment through tagging, annotating and sharing web resources and learning experiences. Thirdly, the social and openness aspects of Web 2.0 make it possible to connect students to "More Knowledgeable Others" outside of the classroom boundaries [Att 10]. As claimed by [Peñ 12], this possibility can broaden the horizon of students' personal development by making a close link between PLEs and Zone of Proximal Development, or ZPD, [Vyg 78] concepts. According to [Peñ 12], PLEs could be understood both as the ZPD and the full set of More Knowledgeable Others in terms of "people of flesh and blood", open educational resources, and all sorts of digital content. Accordingly, he contends that PLEs can extend the borders of students' ZPD by providing them with more developmental opportunities and support.

The potential of Web 2.0 to support students as decision makers

As the locus of control is shifting from institutions and teachers to students, the decision making abilities of students as the core part of self-directed and self-organizing learning behaviors are gaining more attention. Web 2.0 can support the decision making role of students in three dimensions.

Firstly, the abundance of Web 2.0 tools along with the intensive contact of today's students with technology provide an unprecedented opportunity for supporting self-organizing and self-directing students to explore the web to satisfy their heterogeneous learning needs [Vee 06], [Bro 00]. According to [Bro 00], the permanent contact of today's students with web technologies and the open nature of web, provide them with opportunity to be the discoverers and thinkers of relevant technologies and learning resources and then to be the conveyors of them to their educational settings. As a result, students are intensively showing a new behavior called bricolage, i.e. "the ability to find something – an object, tool, document, a piece of code – and to use it to build something you deem important", which is compatible with their natural spirit of exploration [Bro 00]. This technology-induced behavior can provide an exploratory-based learning situation which educators can use to corroborate the role of students as decision makers by prompting them to manage their learning process through designing and developing personal knowledge and technology management strategies [Rah 13a], [Rah 13b].

Secondly, selecting the most appropriate technologies to support teaching and learning activities is becoming more and more complicated due to the growing heterogeneity of available web tools and resources [Cou 10]. This growing heterogeneity can trigger several learning processes and corroborate the role of students as decision makers in educational process. As illustrated by [Cou 10], the heterogeneity of Web 2.0 tools and services is enforcing teachers and students to acquire new skills in order to discover learning affordances of these tools and integrate them in their educational processes. As a result, choosing what to learn, what tools to use, how to find the right tool or content, and what community to join are becoming prevalent processes in today's learning and position decision making as an important learning skill for educators and students [Sie 04]. Moreover, according to [O'Re 05], the features and functionalities of Web 2.0 tools are considered to be in a "perpetual beta" state. On this basis, the permanent and extensive contact of students with Web 2.0 tools beside "unceasing development" of these tools can posit students as pioneer explorers of new functionalities of Web 2.0. As a result, it can change the expectations from the students and open a great opportunity for them to act as decision makers, co-designers, and partners in educational processes.

Thirdly, the sophisticated interfaces of Web 2.0 support easy development of the drag and drop, semantic, widget-based websites by using AJAX, XML, RSS, CSS, and mash-up services. As a result, students can use these technologies to manage their

learning activities not only by remixing of content but also by mashing up of tools and services. This feature of Web2.0 along with the provision of opportunity for students to make decision regarding their learning trajectory, can provide possibility for them to develop their PLEs by adding their personal choices including learning content, tools, and peers into them. Figure 3 summarizes the learning potential of Web 2.0 and depicts a map between these potential and the elements of the student's control model.

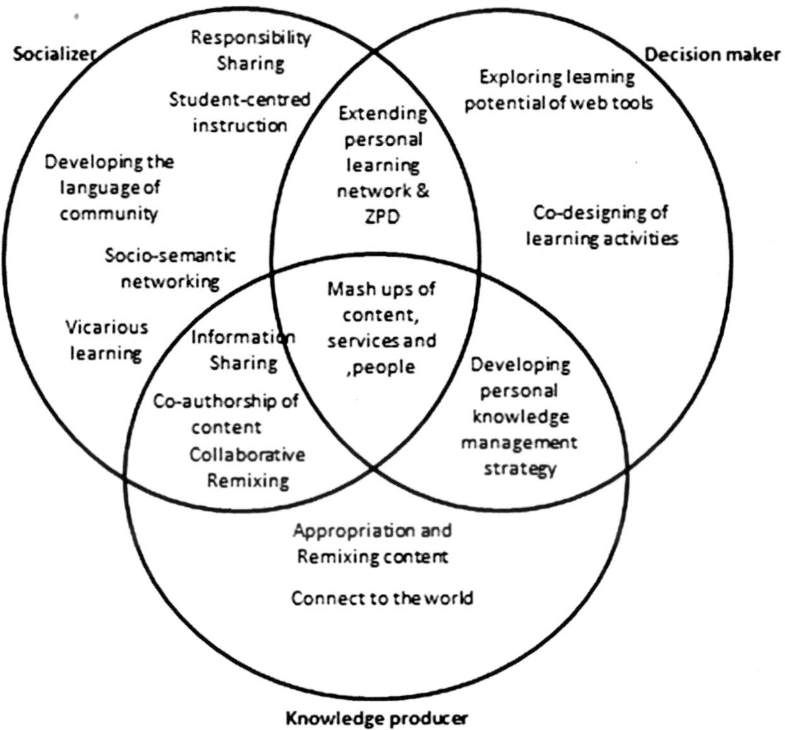

Figure 3: Mapping the learning potential of Web 2.0 into student control model

Technology-enhanced learning activities

To design technology-enhanced learning activities, we adopted and appropriated the Bloom's digital taxonomy map proposed by [Chu 08]. Bloom's taxonomy [Blo 56] represents the cognitive process dimensions as a continuum from lower order thinking skills to higher thinking skills being: knowledge, comprehension, application, analysis, synthesis, and evaluation. [And 01] revised Bloom's taxonomy by assigning a number of sup-process to each dimension and defining creating as a new higher order thinking skill. Thus, the revised Bloom's taxonomy has proposed a new continuum of thinking process consisting of remembering, understanding, applying, analyzing, evaluating and creating sub-processes. [Chu 08] extended the revised Bloom's taxonomy and proposed Bloom's digital taxonomy map by assigning digital learning activities to these cognitive processes as below:

- Remembering: recognizing, listing, describing, identifying, retrieving, naming, locating, finding, bullet pointing, highlighting, bookmarking, social networking, social bookmarking, favorite-ing/local bookmarking, searching, googling.
- Understanding: interpreting, summarizing, inferring, paraphrasing, classifying, comparing, explaining, exemplifying, advanced searching, Boolean searching, blog journaling, twittering, categorizing and tagging, commenting, annotating, subscribing.
- Applying: implementing, carrying out, using, executing, running, loading, playing, operating, hacking, uploading, sharing, editing.
- Analyzing: comparing, organizing, deconstructing, attributing, outlining, finding, structuring, integrating, mashing, linking, reverse-engineering, cracking, mind-mapping, validating, tagging.
- Evaluating: checking, hypothesizing, critiquing, experimenting, judging, testing, detecting, monitoring, blog/vlog commenting, reviewing, posting, moderating, collaborating, networking, reflecting, (alpha & beta) testing.
- Creating: designing, constructing, planning, producing, inventing, devising, making, programming, filming, animating, blogging, video blogging, mixing, remixing, wiki-ing, publishing, vodcasting, podcasting, directing/producing, creating or building mash ups.

Figure 4 shows an example of mapping Bloom's digital taxonomy into the defined roles for students in the student's control model. Teachers can use this map to design appropriate technology-enhanced learning activities to assist and scaffold students to develop and deploy Web 2.0 based PLEs and accomplish their learning projects. According to this map, the PLE development process includes two sub-processes consisting of lower-order technology-enhanced learning activities, and higher-order technology-enhanced learning activities. To develop their PLEs students can start with accomplishing the lower-order technology-enhanced learning activities and then continue by running the higher-order technology-enhanced learning activities.

The map can support the key elements of the student's control model. Indeed, accomplishing learning activities such as advanced searching, tagging, blogging, twitting, mind mapping, and evaluating, remixing and appropriating of content can arguably provide students with the opportunity to acquire appropriate domain-specific knowledge, cognitive skills and competencies.

During this process which can be characterized as learning by doing and content building process, it is likely that students acquire technical skills about the web tools and their learning potential which, as argued by [Dre 10], can improve their autonomy during their learning processes. It should be noted that, to support the inherent personal development approach embedded in the PLE concept, appropriation of content should promote and facilitate a personal developmental trajectory for students. Indeed, without careful consideration of this developmental trajectory, according to [Sca 06], any activity-based learning experiences can easily decline to a form of "shallow constructivism" or "doing for the sake of doing." Accordingly, to avoid this drawback and to emphasize the importance of the process of content building, appropriate learning activities such as reflecting, self-evaluating, creating personal meaning from learning experiences, and evaluating the quality of online content are required. This type of learning activities can foster internal learning abilities such as self-reflecting and develop critical thinking regarding the options and range of possibilities to select and evaluate content.

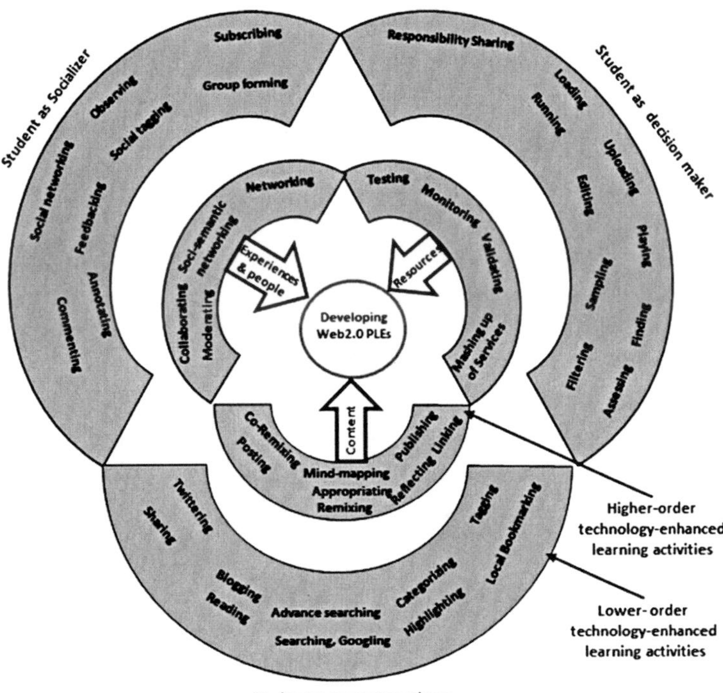

Figure 4: Mapping Bloom's digital taxonomy into student control model

The social context of learning environment can assist students to keep control by providing them learning resources and relevant support they need to overcome the difficulties faced during the learning process and assisting them to make appropriate decisions [Gar 87]. In technology-based learning environments such as PLEs, there are five sorts of interaction between the student and their social context, namely teacher-student, student-students, student-people outside of classroom, student-content, and student-interface [Moo 89], [Hil 94]. The first three interactions outline the socializer role, while the last two interactions are related to the knowledge producer and decision maker roles of student, respectively. By defining the social learning activities such as social tagging, annotating, and group forming the map can assist students to learn and practice the principles of being a socializer to seek and achieve needed support to keep their control.

The map can augment the decision making role of students by allowing them to find, use, assess, and introduce relevant web tools and services. It also can corroborate the role of students in planning and designing educational practices by allowing them to explore and introduce the learning potential of web tools. It also encourages them to develop personal knowledge management strategy through tagging, categorizing, filtering and mashing up of content and services.

Requirements for implementing the model

There is a set of prerequisite conditions needed to be considered in order to implement this approach in a classroom setting. These requirements include:

- Defining a learning project: The learning project gives a meaning and direction to the students' learning activities. It also defines the tangible and measureable learning objectives and expected outcomes needed by the assessment and evaluation rubric.
- Meeting technological requirements: i.e. providing reasonable access to Internet and required web tools, providing an initial technical platform to keep students' PLEs together and allow them to observe each other learning experiences.
- Providing initial support: i.e. appropriate learning content, a list of relevant experts outside of the classroom setting to contact, guidelines to evaluate the quality and validity of online content, training students the basic functionalities of the selected web tools, defining an appropriate group working mechanism, and defining appropriate assessment and evaluation rubric.

Summary

This paper proposes a pedagogy-driven framework for developing Web 2.0 based PLEs in educational settings. Supporting students' control through defining and adopting active roles in order to equip them with necessary competencies and skills needed to deal with the challenges of current knowledge intensive era is the main objective of this framework. Teachers can use this framework as a guideline to design appropriate enhanced

technology-based learning activities to scaffold and assist students to develop and deploy Web 2.0 based PLEs to accomplish their learning projects. Further research is supposed to be needed to test, evaluate and improve the roadmap introduced.

REFERENCES

[Ale 06] *Alexander, Bryan (2006):* Web 2.0: A new wave of innovation for teaching and learning? Educause review 41(2), 32.

[And 01] *Anderson, Lorin W.; Krathwohl, David R.; Bloom, Benjamin Samuel B (2001):* A taxonomy for learning, teaching, and assessing: A revision of Bloom's taxonomy of educational objectives. Allyn & Bacon.

[Att 07] *Attwell, Graham (2007):* Personal Learning Environments-the future of eLearning? eLearning Papers, 2(1), 1–8.

[Att 10] *Attwell, Graham (2010):* Personal learning environments and Vygotsky. Retrieved June 2013 from: *http://www.pontydysgu.org/2010/04/personal-learning-environments-and-vygotsky/*

[Blo 56] *Bloom, Benjamin S.; Engelhart, M. D.; Furst, Edward J.; Hill, William H.; Krathwohl, David (1956):* Taxonomy of educational objectives: Handbook I: Cognitive domain. New York: David McKay, 19(56).

[Blu 91] *Blumenfeld, Phyllis C.; Soloway, Elliot; Marx, Ronald W.; Krajcik, Joseph S.; Guzdial, Mark; Palincsar, Annemarie (1991):* Motivating project-based learning: Sustaining the doing, supporting the learning. Educational psychologist, 26(3-4), 369–398.

[Bow 10] *Bower, Matt; Hedberg, John G.; Kuswara, Andreas (2010):* A framework for Web 2.0 learning design. Educational Media International, 47(3), 177–198.

[Boy 07] *Boyd, Danah. (2007):* The significance of social software. BlogTalks reloaded: Social software research & cases, 15–30.

[Bro 89] *Brown, John Seely; Collins, Allan; Duguid, Paul (1989):* Situated cognition and the culture of learning. Educational researcher,18(1), 32–42.

[Bro 00] *Brown, John Seely (2000):* Growing up Digital: How the web changes work, education, and the ways people learn. Change: The Magazine of Higher Learning, 32(2), 11–20.

[Buc 11] *Buchem, Ilona Attwell, Graham; Torres, Ricardo (2011):* Understanding Personal Learning Environments: Literature review and synthesis through the Activity Theory lens. Proceedings of the second PLE Conference,(pp. 1–33). Southampton, UK.

[Buc 12] *Buchem, Ilona. (2012):* Psychological Ownership and Personal Learning Environments: Do sense of ownership and control really matter? Proceedings of the 3th PLE Conference, Aveiro, Portugal. Retrieved from: *http://revistas.ua.pt/index.php/ple/article/view/1437/1323*.

[Cha 10] *Chatti, Mohamed Amine; Ridwan Agustiawan, Mohammad; Jarke, Matthias; Specht, Marcus (2010):* Toward a personal Learning Environment Framework. International Journal of Virtual and Personal Learning Environments, 1(4), 66–85.

[Che 07] *Chen, Pearl; Chen, Huei-Lien (2007):* Knowledge building and technology dynamics in an online project-based learning community. International Journal of Technology in Teaching and Learning, 3(2), 1–16.

[Chu 08] *Churches, Andrew (2008):* Bloom's taxonomy blooms digitally. Tech & Learning, 1.

[Con 07] *Conole, Grainne (2007):* Describing learning activities. Rethinking pedagogy for a digital age: Designing and delivering e-learning, 81–91.

[Cou 10] *Couros, Alec (2010):* Developing Personal Learning Networks for Open and Social Learning. Emerging Technologies in Distance Education, 109–128.

[Dab 11] *Dabbagh, Nada; Reo, Rick (2011):* Tracing the Roots and Learning Affordances of Social Software. Web 2.0-Based E-Learning: Applying Social Informatics for, 1.

[Dab 12] *Dabbagh, Nada; Kitsantas, Anastasia (2012):* Personal Learning Environments, social media, and self-regulated learning: A natural formula for connecting formal and informal learning. The Internet and Higher Education, 15(1), 3–8.

[Dow 06] *Downes, Stephen (2006):* Learning Networks and Collective Knowledge. Instructional Technology Forum, available: Retrieved from: *http://it.coe.uga.edu/itforum/paper92/DownesPaper92.pdf.*

[Dow 07] *Downes, Stephen (2007):* Learning networks in practice. Emerging Technologies for Learning, 2, 19–27. Retrieved from: *http://www.downes.ca/files/Learning_Networks_In_Practice.pdf.*

[Dre 10] *Drexler, Wendy (2010):* The networked student model for construction of personal learning environments: Balancing teacher control and student autonomy. Australasian Journal of Educational Technology. 26(3), 369–385.

[Dro 07] *Dron, Jon. (2007):* Control and constraint in E-Learning: Choosing when to choose. Idea Group Publishing.

[Dun 11] *Dunlap, Joanna C.; Lowenthal, Patrick R. (2011):* Learning, unlearning, and relearning: Using Web 2.0 technologies to support the development of lifelong learning skills. E-Infrastructures and Technologies for Lifelong Learning: Next Generation Environments, George D. Magoulas, ed.(Hershey, PA: IGI Global, 2010), 46–52.

[Gar 87] *Garrison, D. Randy; Baynton, Myra (1987):* Beyond Independence in distance education: The concept of control. The American journal of distance education, 1(3).

[Gun 97] *Gunawardena, Charlotte N.; Lowe, Constance A.; Anderson, Terry (1997):* Analysis of a global online debate and the development of an interaction analysis model for examining social building of knowledge in computer conferencing. Journal of Educational Computing Research, 17(4), 397–431.

[Hil 94] *Hillman, Daniel CA; Willis, Deborah J.; Gunawardena, Charlotte N. (1994):* Learner–interface interaction in distance education: An extension of contemporary models and strategies for practitioners. The American Journal of Distance Education, 8(2), 30–42.

[Jen 06] *Jenkins, Henry (2006):* Confronting the challenges of participatory culture: Media education for the 21st century (Part two).Chicago: MacArthur Foundation.

[Joh 08] *Johnson, Mark; Liber, Oleg (2008):* The personal learning environment and the human condition: From theory to teaching practice. Interactive Learning Environments, 16, 3–15.

[Jon 95] *Jonassen, David H; Reeves, Thomas C. (1995):* Computers as cognitive tools: Learning with technology, not from technology. Journal of Computing in Higher Education 6.2: 40–73.

[Kea 98] *Kearsley, Greg; Shneiderman, Ben (1998):* Engagement Theory: A Framework for Technology-Based Teaching and Learning. Educational technology, 38(5), 20–23.

[Kop 08] *Kop, Rita; Hill, Adrian (2008):* Connectivism: Learning theory of the future or vestige of the past? International Review of research in open and distance learning, 9(3).

[Kir 02] *Kirschner, Paul A (2002):* Can we support CSCL? Educational, social and technological affordances for learning. In P. A. Kirschner (Ed.), Three worlds of CSCL: Can we support CSCL? (pp. 7–47). Heerlen, The Netherlands: Open University of the Netherlands.

[Lee 10] *Lee, Mark JW; McLoughlin, Catherine (2010):* Web 2.0-based E-learning: applying social informatics for tertiary teaching. Information Science Reference, 43–69.

[Mej 06] *Mejias, Ulises (2006):* Teaching social software with social software. Innovate: Journal of Online Education, 2(5).

[Moo 89] *Moore, Michael G. (1989):* Editorial: Three types of interaction. The American Journal of Distance Education, 3(2), 1–6.

[Nel 09] *Nelson, Jennifer; Christopher, Angela; Mims, Clif (2009):* Transformation of Teaching and Learning. TechTrends 53(5), 81.

[O'R 05] *O'Reilly, Tim (2005):* What Is Web 2.0. Design patterns and business models for the next generation of software. Retrieved from: *http://oreilly.com/web2/archive/what-is-web-20.html.*

[Pen 12] *Pena-Lopez, Ismael (2012):* Personal Learning Environments and the revolution of Vygotsky's Zone of Proximal Development. In ICTlogy, #107, Barcelona: ICTlogy.

[Rah 13a] *Rahimi, Ebrahim; Van den Berg, Jan; Veen, Wim (2013a):* A framework for designing enhanced learning activities in web2.0-based Personal Learning Environments. In Proceedings of World Conference on Educational Multimedia, Hypermedia and Telecommunications 2013, p. 2222–2231. Chesapeake, VA: AACE.

[Rah 13b] *Rahimi, Ebrahim; Van den Berg, Jan; Veen, Wim (2013b):* Investigating teachers' perception about the educational benefits of Web 2.0 personal learning environments. eLearning Papers, 35.

[Sca 06] *Scardamalia, Marlene; Bereiter, Carl (2006):* Knowledge building: Theory, pedagogy, and technology. The Cambridge handbook of the learning sciences, 97–115.

[Sie 04] *Siemens, George. (2004):* Connectivism: A learning theory for the digital age. Retrieved from: *www.elearnspace.org/Articles/connectivism.htm*

[Val 12] *Valtonen, Teemu; Hacklin, Stina; Dillon, Patrick; Vesisenaho, Mikko; Kukkonen, Jari; Hietanen, Aija (2012):* Perspectives on personal learning environments held by vocational students. Computers & Education, 58(2), 732–739.

[Väl 10] *Väljataga, Terje; Laanpere, Mart (2010):* Learner control and personal learning environment: a challenge for instructional design. Interactive Learning Environments, 18(3), 277–291.

[Vee 06] *Veen, Wim; Vrakking, Ben (2006):* Homo Zappiens: growing up in a digital age. Continuum International Publishing Group.

[Vyg 78] *Vygotsky, Lev (1978):* Mind and society: The development of higher mental processes. Cambridge, MA: Harvard University Press.

[Wil 09] *Wilson, Scott, Liber, Oleg; Johnson, Mark; Beauvoir, Phil; Sharples, Paul; Milligan, Colin (2009):* Personal Learning Environments: Challenging the dominant design of educational systems. Journal of e-Learning and Knowledge Society-English Version, 3(2).

FIGURES

CONTACT DETAILS

Ir. Ebrahim Rahimi, M.Sc.
E-Mail: *e.rahimi@tudelft.nl*

Prof. Dr. Jan van den Berg
E-Mail: *j.vandenberg@tudelft.nl*

Prof. Dr. Wim Veen
E-Mail: *w.veen@tudelft.nl*
Delft University of Technology
The Faculty of Technology, Policy and Management,
The Netherlands

Bridging Personal Learning Environments: Interfacing personal environments and Learning Management Systems: The example of a bookmarking tool

Tobias Hölterhof, Richard Heinen

ABSTRACT

This conceptual study investigates the ability to connect learners Personal Learning Environments (PLE) by a central, permeable and social Learning Management System (LMS). Within the exemplary scope of bookmarking tools as an element of learners PLE in Higher Education (HE), the relevance of this conceptual idea is shown with reference to the social bookmarking tool "Edutags" as well as by a survey about the heterogeneity and use cases of bookmarking tools in distance learners PLE. As the analysis shows the issue of connecting PLEs – a metaphor with can be adopted from "bridges" in graph theory and social network analyses – refers to a non dominant and inconsistent design of a LMS. Theoretical questions concerning the relation between personal and social, institutional and private, consistency and heterogeneity are addressed. As a framework for implementing the interface, the Content Management System "Drupal" is considered as well as the social Learning Management System "OnlineCampus Next Generation".

Note: *This article has been published in the Special Edition of the Journal of Literacy and Technology: "Personal Learning Environments: Current Research and Emerging Practice". The link to the JLT Special Issue is: http://www.literacyandtechnology.org/uploads/1/3/6/8/136889/jlt_special.pdf*

Personal Learning Environments in Institutions of higher education

Offering formal online learning opportunities at universities often depends on institutional learning environments, frequently referred as Learning Management System (LMS). In recent years, an increased interest has emerged in the personalization of online leaning processes. Most Higher Education (HE) institutions offer online learning opportunities through LMS. However, these systems do not seem to facilitate the level of personalisation and individualisation of learning required. In this context, the main question addressed in this article is how formal learning scenarios can be designed while fostering the concept of a Personal Learning Environment (PLE).

Regarding the scientific discussion about Personal Learning Environments it appears necessary to define PLE in more definite terms, since the spectrum of possible

understandings ranges from technological platforms to pedagogical ideas, from learning opportunities offered by institutions to informal opportunities opposing the integration in educational institution. Our central thesis is that PLE denotes as least a theoretical concept fostering the learning environment as belonging to an individual. The relation between the individual and the environment can be characterised in terms of ownership and control [Buc 11]. In doing so the person can own the environment in different manners. She or he can own and control the data and functions of the environment in a technological sense by deleting or expanding them. The data can also be owned by someone else while the learner is the legal owner of the functions and the data of the environment. At least the individual can feel the ownership and the control as a psychological aspect. Even though granting ownership and control to the learner may be realised by a central environment from a HE institution [Tar 09], the scientific discussion of PLE focuses on heterogeneous and decentralised systems, claiming the benefit from the wide range of generic tools on the web as quality, flexibility and pedagogical suitability [Wel 10]. The focus on personalisation and the learner as a pedagogical approach leads to a technological implementation of learning environments as a framework of less dominant, open and permeable systems with an inconsistent set of tools [Wil 09]. The inconsistency of tools means, the system is not restricted to one single tool per task, instead it is open to include multiple tools for the same purpose. This diversity of tools is considered to meet the demands of human individuality.

The personalisation of learning environments has to accompany learning as a social process. The learner is integrated in a social context that is essential for the learning process. So if one considers the heterogeneity of tools on the web as basis of a PLE, these tools usually include social aspects. A PLE is not an isolated environment. A PLE is social at least in its different components: messaging and communication tools, collaborative editing tools, weblogs and sharing tools [Att 07]. As the social and the personal aspects may represent two opposing poles of single dimension delimiting the concretion of PLE systems, the institutional inclusion of a platform is a second dimension that specify different kinds of PLE designs: a PLE can be a platform of an educational institution [Are 12], [Tar 09] and it can be a non-institutional personal arrangement of independent tools [Wil 09].

From the perspective of a higher education institution these two dimensions are essential for designing a system for technology-enhanced learning environment. A PLE as a personal arrangement of generic social media tools depends on the capacity of these tools to manage and determine the relationships between users. For example, Google+ and the collaborative text editing tools Google Docs own a dedicated user management as well as the note taking app Evernote, the social media platform Facebook and the synchronous communication tool Skype. The learners have to connect each other on every chosen tool. Building a group and especially building a formal learning context is a challenge and depends on further arrangements of frameworks. One approach of enabling social relations in PLE is to avoid generic social media tools. Mash-up, gadget or widgets are developed as components of PLE sharing the same background structure and can be arranged in special portal sites. According to this approach these arrangement portals are considered as a PLE. A widget based PLE serves the need of personalisation by offering functional learning objects that can be reused, individually arranged, shared and created. An example for this approach is the ROLE widget store combine with GRAASP as portal [Dah 12]. Another approach is the PLE design language LISL, that offers the possibility to use generic social media tools as well but doesn't face the mentioned problem with dedicated user management [Wil 08]. The portal can be hosted by an educational institution, serve as a central platform and build a unified formal learning context. While the widget based approach dissolves problems caused by the heterogeneity of tools, widgets are simple applications like todo-lists that hardly satisfy the needs of higher educational institutions.

Another approach is to combining generic tools through interfaces and APIs [Wil 09]. While this approach normally lacks a unified platform or portal, it benefits from the quality and richness of generic social media tools. Some standards for interoperation between generic tools already exist: rss-feeds and atom-feeds. Others need to be developed. An example for this kind of PLE is gRSShopper [Dow 10].

Technology enhanced learning in the context of higher educational institutions somehow depends on central platforms, especially for the needs of online study programs [Höl 12]. Instead of building a Learning Management System as a dominant system and consistent set of tools [Wil 09], the discussion about PLE and LMS should consider the design of open and permeable systems including a wide (and maybe inconsistent) range of generic tools. A strategy for integrating the demands of formal and institutional study programs in learners own Personal Learning Environment is through the implementation of "social hubs": a social hub connects the PLEs of different learners, including heterogeneous collaboration and learning tools as well as different devices, with the members of formal groups representing modules and courses of study programs [Höl 12]. The strategy is based on the Social Learning Management System (SLMS) instead of a common Learning Management System [Ker 11].

The "Online Campus Next Generation" is a Social Learning Management System used for technology enhanced learning in the online master programmes "Educational Media" and "Educational Leadership". The system realizes an approach of connecting generic web 2.0 tools instead of a widget based technology. Taking this system as an example as well as the masters programme, the following investigation develops a concept on how to connect different generic tools used in learners PLE. The mentioned aspects of heterogeneity are the first assumption for designing the concept. Accordingly, learners PLEs can contain an inconsistent set of tools, including redundancy. The second assumption concerns the understanding of PLE itself. Thus a Learning Management System for formal learning opportunities in higher education should focus on connecting the personal environments of the learners instead of offering a dominant

and central TEL system. With these assumptions the interaction between PLE and LMS can complement each other. The belief, sometimes suggested in the scientific discussion, that PLEs displaces LMSs, is unsustainable from the perspective of a formal master programme in higher education, because an LMS fulfils at least the function network and links the participants in a central und unified place.

Bookmarking tools in PLE

Bookmarking tools are created to help users to collect and structure web resources. Many of these tools use social tagging as a way to structure resources and contents. The idea of social tagging has become popular in many different web tools and is a standard tool in many social software applications [Mar 06].

Tagging means that users annotate digital objects with free chosen keywords [Gol 06]. Together with other tools, tags are used to describe single objects in the platform. For example in flickr tags are used to describe photos that are uploaded to the platforms. In social bookmarking platform the objects are links that refer to other websites or documents. A single learner describes an object by free chosen tags. In contrast to a hierarchically taxonomy, learners do not have to classify the object in a given set of terms. They are free to create their own system of classification. Describing an object by using tags can be seen as part of a learning process: Learners have to think about the tags that are most appropriate to describe an object. Therefore tagging is an active part of learning. The result of this learning activity is "tag cloud". In this cloud all tags are assembled and tags that are use more frequently are represented in a bigger scale. A tag cloud, therefore, can be regarded as a representation of a learner's concept of the subject.

So far we have described a personal tagging tool. The social aspect occurs when different learners start to share their tags and objects – in case of a bookmarking tool their bookmarks. In common social bookmarking tools the community of people share their tags and links and, therefore, their knowledge as an informal open community. In these communities, people can also build open or closed groups and networks by building friendships or following each other. But it is important to keep in mind, that in this place learning happens in an informal setting and manner. When using a social bookmarking tool, at the beginning learners can browse through the collection of resources by using the tags created by other users. While exploring the tag clouds they may pick up new tags they consider helpful for their own resources. Again the idea of the tag cloud and relevance of the tag indicated by the relative size of a word in the cloud become important support of the learning activities taking place in these bookmarking communities. For example, a learner can use tag cloud to explore the resources of a given area and may reflect and expand his or her own concept of this area and adopt certain tags to use with their own objects. A social bookmarking tool therefore is not only a tool that gives learners access to even more information, documents and resources. It also can help to build and extend knowledge by using tags. As we can see tags can be used by learners in two ways: learners can describe objects to elaborate their concept of the topic or they use tags of others to broaden their knowledge [Cre 12].

From the perspective of higher education learning communities in formal learning settings often share knowledge that is represented in texts which can be found on websites. They can use different tools of a LMS to do so. They can collect links in a forum or wiki – in both cases losing the benefit of tags and tag clouds. Therefore, a social bookmarking tool can be useful for learning in a formal setting using an LMS. Learners can collect resources from the web together and tag them to create a common knowledge base structured by a folksonomy build from the tags they used. However, here a problem occurs: What is the appropriate tool or web service to use? Is it part of the LMS offered by the institution or do they use a generic tool specialized on the task of bookmarking? And if the decision is to use a generic tool, how can they decide what tool they are going to use? If the tool is part of the LMS, the knowledge created remains in the LMS even when the students finish the course. Even if there is an export feature: during the course students would have to decide whether to use the usual tool or the course tool. Using generic tools is even worse. Students using different tools would hardly be able to know about the findings of their fellows.

Learners learn during their entire lifetime, that means learning is a lifelong learning process that now can be supported by social software of different types [Kla 07]. Therefore, learners who use the internet as a learning resource will most likely make a decision for one tool the like best regardless of the context. Learning in formal settings takes place only for a period of time. Learners come together to take a course or a seminar and then spread out again. It is not necessary that they build a community that lasts longer than the duration of the learning activity they share. For this purpose it seems to be useful to describe possibilities to bridge PLEs and LMS. In this way learners can use their usual bookmarking tools and amount of links, knowledge and groups they collected and formed within the tool when following a formal learning course. The idea of bridging PLE and LMS considers the use of different external bookmarking tools and the linking of them together in a formal learning scenario. As a result, learners may use their PLE to organize their own learning process, to create a knowledge base and to share resources.

In a formal learning scenario learners may use their knowledge and structures to obtain new information. New items shouldn't be stored in a new and course related bookmarking system or a bookmarking system of an isolated LMS. Learners might also want to transfer new items into their own PLE. So the Bridge has to serve two purposes: It has to offer an easy to use way to aggregate knowledge from a variety of bookmarking tools used in the learners PLEs (direction PLE to LMS) and a smart option for the user to integrate selected items into a PLE (direction LMS to PLE). As explained later the PLE in this case can be regarded as a bridge. Also to understand how different

tools can be bridged by the use of tags we have to take a closer look on tagging as the way individual and shared knowledge is represented. When it comes to social tagging another advantage is important. Social tagging means different learners objects can be described in different dimensions. The challenge is to correctly assign the resources of different origins to the corresponding courses and formal learning groups.

Edutags: exemplify a social bookmarking tool

As a result of a joined project between the University of Duisburg-Essen and the DIPF, the German Institute for International Educational Research as a member of the Leibniz Association, the social bookmarking system "Edutags" has been developed (see figure 1). Beside others the DIPF offers and operates the German "Eduserver", a server dedicated to educational resources. Edutags extends this server by a community oriented bookmarking system. With the focus on primary and secondary education, Edutags is a bookmarking tool for educators, teachers, pupil and also students to collect and classify a knowledge base of educational resources on the web. The system offers both a personal bookmarking tool combined with community and collaboration functions. The concept of Edutags is to offer teachers an easy to use system to collect, tag and share resources for daily teaching [Hei 11]. The service features:

- an integration into all common web browsers allowing to mark and classify any web resource within the web browser,
- suggestion of classification while bookmarking a resource, based on the community
- functions to explore and search web resources,
- management of groups and friendships, among the ability to share bookmarks
- interoperability with mobile devices and LMS.

The social bookmarking tool was established in 2011. Until now the tool counts 1.800 active users. The database contains more than 18.000 resources collected by users and shared in around 250 groups. With this spreading this tool is used in the PLEs of several students, learners and teachers for managing and collecting their private bookmarks as well as in learning groups, distance learning courses and LMS of schools and HE institutes.

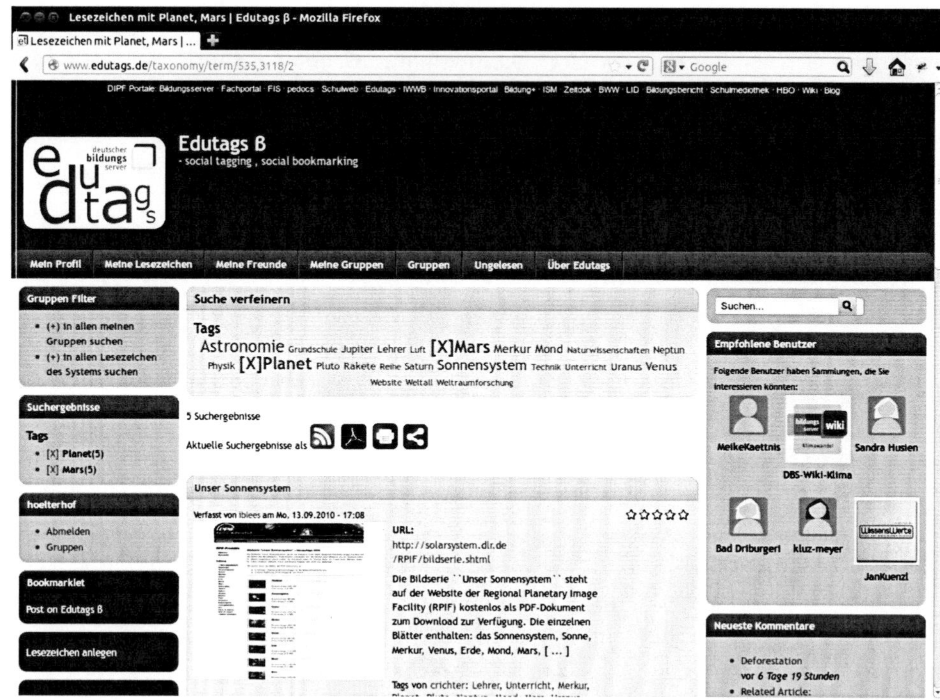

Figure 1: The social bookmarking tool "Edutags"

Investigating the use of bookmarking tools in distance learners PLE

For the scope of bookmarking tools as a central element of a PLE, the authors conducted a study to have a closer look at the heterogeneous use of bookmarking tools of participants of distance learning courses. The survey has been distributed in the Social Learning Management System of the master programmes "Educational Leadership" and "Educational Media" of the University of Duisburg-Essen as well as to the participants of a dedicated online course concerning Open Educational Resources "COER 13". In the online master programmes nearly 100 participants of the two programmes are familiar with Technology Enhanced Learning and distance learning scenarios. Also the participants of COER 13 are familiar with distance learning. The amount of return of the survey (n=32) can hence serve as an exemplary basis to illustrate the concept and not to draw further conclusions. This survey focuses on the plausibility of conceptual ideas and does not predicate the use of the final implementation.

Table 1: Frequency mentioned bookmarking tools in distance learners PLE (n=32)

Edutags	14	Webbrowser	14	Diigo	11	delicious	9	Google Bookmarks	7
Mr Wong	4	Pocket	3	Zotero	2	Instapaper	1	Readability	1
Xmarks	1	Pinboard	1	Evernote	1	ScoopIT	1	Kippt	1

The questionnaire first suggested several bookmarking tools (e.g. Delicious, Edutags, Google Bookmarks etc. as well as the bookmarking tool of the web browser) including the possibility to freely add other tools and asked the user to choose the tools they usually employ. The question offered the possibility to choose multiple tools and 59% of the respondents chose two or more tools. The most chosen tools in the sample are Edutags (marked 14 times), the bookmarking tool of the web browser (also marked 14 times), Diigo (marked 11 times) and Delicious (marked 9 times). The second question explored the use of bookmarking tools. They may either be used in a private way to bookmark content for oneself but also in a social way. The social way includes searching in the collections of the community, assign search results to the private collection and collect bookmarks collaboratively in groups. Clearly the private usage is the most common use case as 75% of the respondent marked that item as "often" and 94% as at least "sometimes". The two use cases searching and assigning results to the private collection are very similar: around 40% never used a tool that way, around 60% at least sometimes whereas searching is a little bit more common (20% "often") compared to assigning search results to the private collection (15% "often"). Finally the collaborative usage is somewhat more popular than the other two social usages. Concluding the private usage can be considered as the default usage for bookmarking tools, although the social usages showed also some relevance.

Table 2: Usage of bookmarking tools in distance learners PLE (n=32)

USE CASE ⇢	**PRIVATE USAGE**		**SOCIAL USAGE**					
⇣ FREQUENCY	**bookmark for oneself**		**search bookmarks**		**assign results to private collection**		**collect bookmarks in groups**	
never	2	6%	11	37%	11	41%	11	35%
sometimes	1	19%	13	43%	15	56%	15	48%
often	24	75%	6	20%	4	15%	5	16%

Note: The survey offered the possibility to skip answers. The percentage value is calculated against the amount of answers within the use case.

As the survey showed bookmarking tools are used as an element of learners PLE. Also social bookmarking is established and used. Therefore a concept of linking different bookmarking tools used by the participants of a formal learning scenario like courses of a master programme seems to be plausible and useful. One not even has to consider that distance learners already use multiple bookmarking tools and thus own expertise in using this tools as well as an amount of bookmarks stored in different systems. But also learners are at least familiar with the social usage of bookmarking tools.

Conceptual reflections and Interface Design

This article describes the design of an interface between bookmarking tools as an element of the learners PLE and the institutions SLMS realised as a "social hub". The design focuses on an interface is to be used in higher education courses, in particular a formal online master programme. This approach is geared to the structure of a bridge in graph theory and social media analysis insofar as it takes this structure as a design model. To focus the concept the above mentioned tools and systems are used as example: "Edutags" as a social bookmarking tool as well as "Online Campus Next Generation" as Social Learning Management System. Although this study focuses on a connection of specific tools, the interface needs to be designed as an open and universal connector suitable for many bookmarking tools.

Typically a PLE is illustrated as a network graph but as a special form of network. Scott Leslie collected 78 diagrams of PLEs on his wikispace "edtechpost". The diagrams have been created by educators, advanced learners and specialists. They have been collected from Leslie's own personal network and illustrate a personal view to the subject of PLE. After four years of collecting them he posted some of his observations concerning the diagrams [Les 12]. He remarked that the main metaphor used to illustrate a PLE is a network diagram, especially a hub-and-spoke network characterized by a centred hub at which all lines leaves like spokes. Not all diagrams show persons as the centre hub but also tools (like a web browser or a reader tool). Even if this observation is exemplary as it is based on a particular collection, one can find similar diagrams on scientific publications of PLE [Wil 09]. Further it corresponds to the characterisation of the relation between the subject and its PLE in terms of ownership and control.

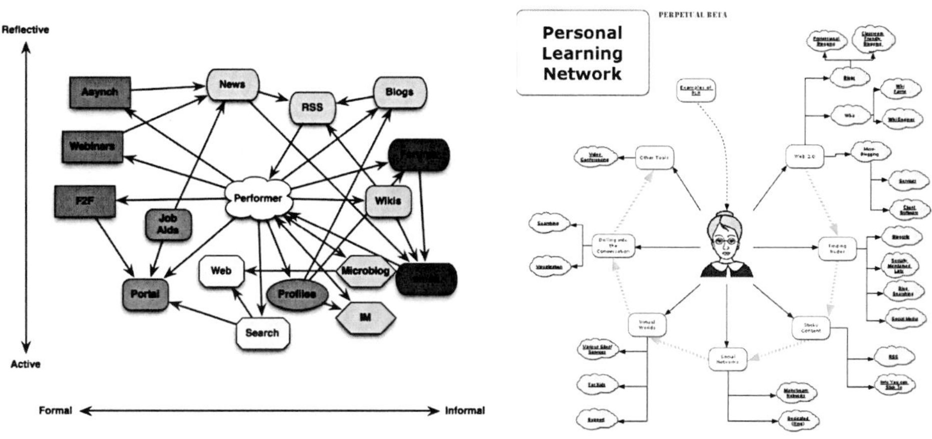

Figure 2: Diagrams illustrating PLE collected by Scott Leslie [Les 12]

Compared to the structure of the internet, these observations are interesting regarding the relation between personal and social in PLE: As Leslie explains: "While they [the PLE diagrams, TH] capture the individual user's perspective of being at the 'centre' of their network, these are not actually accurate representations of how internet networks as a whole look" [Les 12]. If one considers the internet as representing social relations between individuals, these ego-centred diagrams lack of social relations between the participants. These individual networks of tools and environments need to be connected to realise distance learning scenarios. Of course these connections can be done within the chosen tools by agreeing upon specific tools. But an agreement like this can serve as a limitation to the own environment. If we consider the personal learning environment as a basis to lifelong learning that stays persistent over multiple qualifications, participants of distance learning opportunities may need to change well established tools of their environment.

In social network analysis it is common to identify the vertices of a graph as actors and the edges as social relations between the actors. Several kinds of social relations have been analysed that way, e.g. E-Mail and forum messages sent between participants of distance learning course. From a perspective that considers a PLE not to be an institutional platform but the personal environment of a learner, one can suggest that an individual can only act on behalf of its environment. The diagrams collected by Leslie illustrate the network of tools a person uses to act, receive and react on the internet. Even E-Mail and forum messages are not send by the individual directly but on behalf of web browsers and E-Mail tools representing parts of the individuals environment. Thus with regard to PLE, vertices of social graphs can be environments of tools. These tools often realise relations to other individuals like E-Mails sent to others, friendships, posts to groups and bookmarks. In this way edges of a graph can be considered as one of the heterogeneous relations between the environments. This interpretation of vertices and edges of graph as personal environments and its relations to other personal environments can lead to the conceptual metaphor of bridging personal learning environments. Bridges in graph theory connect components of a graph, they are critical to the connectedness of a graph. If a bridge is removed from the graph, the resulting graph has more components than when the bridge is included [Was 94, 114]. Bridging PLEs with respect to the mentioned conceptual metaphor means to build connections between the tools of different environments; maybe by connecting multiple tools of the same kind in the context of a distance learning course.

Assigning items on behalf of tags

A challenge in bridging PLEs with regard to bookmarking tools is to identify the context of a bookmark resource. One has to consider that in higher education learners follow multiple courses. Thus a Social Learning Management System must be able to aggregate the bookmarks of participants of different courses. Lastly, because bookmarking tools are also used privately a learner must be able to decide if a resource is to be assigned to a formal learning context. An obvious way to solve that challenge is to use the tagging feature of bookmarking tools. As explained above, social bookmarking uses tags to identify resources. Because tags can be freely assigned by the learner, they can be used for different purposes. A requirement to automatically identify the formal learning context of a bookmark resource by its tags is a unique set of fixes tags used by all participants of a course to identify the context of the corresponding course. In other words, courses in social learning management systems need short acronyms (Figure 3). If the acronym of a course is used by a participant as tag for a bookmark resource the bookmark can be assigned to the course.

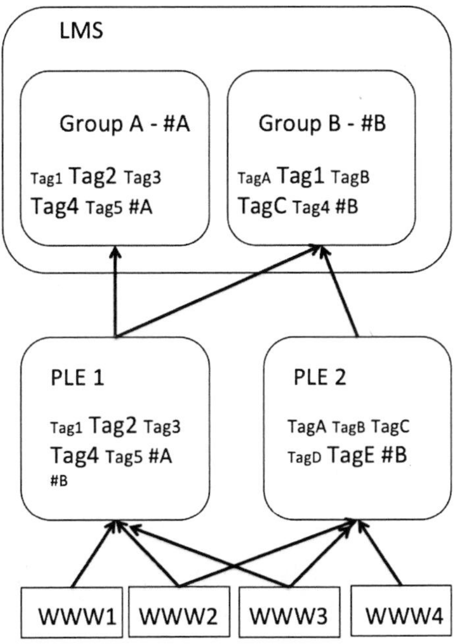

Figure 3: Concept of bridging PLEs: courses within the Learning Management Systems are marked with acronymes (here: "#a" and "#b") that matches tags used in learners PLE bookmarking tool

A closer look on adequate interfaces to export content from bookmarking tools shows that RSS feeds are widely-used for that purpose. Edutags as well as Diigo and Delicious, the three most frequently mentioned online bookmarking tools in the survey, support RSS feeds to export bookmarks of a user. Reading and handling RSS feeds is well established in most web developing environments. But with respect to the need to include users tags in the RSS feed. The situation looks different. It is not sufficient to somehow include the tags in the RSS feed, the tags need to be marked up so they can be identified automatically. The specifications of RSS 2.0 provide an element that can be used to mark tags: the "category" element, according to RSS 2.0 Specifications: *http://www.rssboard.org/rss-specification*. Edutags supports marking tags in that way. Diigo like Delicious do not support the category element, maybe because the feeds do not support RSS specification version 2.0. Instead the tags are included in the description element as links. Of course this way of marking tags can also be processed automatically, but the markup style misses an official standard. At least the fact that both tools, Diigo and Delicious, include the users tags in the description elements shows that a PLE bridge can use bookmark tags to assign bookmark resources to courses. The required data is exported by the RSS feed.

To transfer the knowledge of a single learners PLE to the group within the Social Leaning Management System RSS feeds are reasonable. The learner can register the feeds of the own PLEs bookmarking tools to the LMS and as soon as the new bookmarks appears in the feed it is imported into the LMS as well and assigned to the course group according to the tag acronym. To save the benefit of the social tagging the LMS has to preserve the tags of the bookmarks and take care that the imported bookmarks within the LMS are marked with the same tags then in the generic bookmarking tool. The LMS can than build a new tag-cloud representing the knowledge of the group. This import procedure may produce duplicate bookmarks within the LMS because learners can tag the same web resource on different bookmarking tools all imported to the same group in the LMS. This might be regarded as a problem, but the doublet bookmarks referring to the same web resource keep meaningful information within the LMS. They also retain the relation to the learners bookmarking system expressing that a specific resource has been bookmarked and tagged by several learners. By accepting doublets, the bridge offers the opportunities to explore more of the learners collected knowledge.

In case a learner will add a resources from the LMS to his or he own PLEs bookmarking tool, this can be done in the same way other resources are added to the specific bookmarking tool: the user can use a generic javascript "bookmarklet", an adapted toolbar for the web browser as well as other ways offered by the bookmarking system. Via RSS this adopted bookmark will be integrated in the tag cloud of the learners group if the learner specified the group acronym as a tag while assigning the resource to the own bookmark collection. In this case the interface collects the resource in the next iteration, identifies the acronym and assigns the bookmark to the corresponding learning group in the LMS. Possible new tags broaden the knowledge base of the learning community.

Implementation using the Content Management System "Drupal"

The implementation of the specified interface is planned to use the Content Management System "Drupal" as framework instead of generic Learning Management Systems like Moodle. The decision to choose Drupal rests upon the Social Learning Management System that is currently used in the online masters programmes at the University of Duisburg-Essen. The "Online Campus Next Generation" is developed with Drupal to take advantages of the numerously social media modules developed and maintained by the Drupal community. The organic group module builds social relations between website users by forming groups. This module can be used to form courses as well as learning groups. Arranging learning content can be done by the books module featuring a hierarchical structure of pages. Content can consist of videos, audios, pictures, texts, pdf files as well as SCORM elements. Learning assignments, student submissions and teacher feedback can be realised by the workflow module in combination with several workflow extension modules. The workflow modules allows to specify a succession

of submission states like creation, editing, submitted, reviewed, finalised with corresponding fields to be activated and locked for feedback text, attachments etc. A more detailed description on how the “Online Campus Next Generation” is created on basis of the Content Management System Drupal is given in Hölterhof and Kerres [Höl 11].

The interface to bridge bookmarking tools used in learners PLEs to a SLMS like the “Online Campus Next Generation” can use the Drupal feed module and its extension modules. These modules allows to parse RSS 2.0 feeds and import the feed items as website content by mapping item fields to internal web content. In this way the interface can be configured almost without the need of programming. However a little customisation is necessary first to extract the bookmark tags from RSS feeds that do not use the category element. In this case a parser needs to be written that matches the tags within the description section of the feed. Second assigning the imported bookmarks to the corresponding courses on behalf of the acronym is a customisation task of Drupals feed modules as well. Lastly, the issue of creating tag clouds is a standard feature and can be realised by corresponding modules without the need of programming. So the Drupal community offers valuable modules and plugins to implement the interface, but still there is a need of customisation by programming.

Conclusion

The concept to bridge learners PLE is based upon the metaphoric idea of bridges in social network analyses. According to this metaphor, a bridge connects components of a graph that elsewhere stays isolated. An analysis of PLE diagrams by Leslie [Les 12] indicates the structure of PLEs to be an ego-centred hub and stroke structure. It has been argued that the need to connect PLEs can be derived from this structure because it stays in contrary to the connected structure of the internet. Regarding the example of bookmarking tools used in learners PLE this need can be concretised. As an exemplary survey showed, distance learning participants uses multiple bookmarking tools in private and social use cases within their PLE. To make available the knowledge and resources learners collected in their bookmarking tools to formal learning scenarios as learning courses in higher education, the bookmarking tools needs to be connected to the institutions Learning Management System.

As an exemplary environment to discuss an interface for connecting bookmarking tools as PLE components the Social Learning Management System “Online Campus Next Generation” is used as well as the social bookmarking tool “Edutags”. The mentioned LMS and bookmarking tool uses Drupal as framework. A challenge in realising this interface is to assign the learners bookmarks to the corresponding course within the LMS. To solve this need the courses are marked with acronyms. Bookmarks are imported by the LMS with the corresponding tags from the generic learners bookmarking tools and assigned to the courses by matching the tags to course acronyms. With this procedure, tag clouds can be formed out of the bookmarked web resources of the course learners.

This article shows the need of rich metadata in feeds as the RSS 2.0 standard offers. Feeds are an easy way to connect web tools used in PLEs but to preserve meaningful information collected in the bookmarking tools, tags and marks assigned to a resource by the learner needs to be considered as well. As a way to face dominant design and to include personalisation, Learning Management Systems needs to be designed as permeable systems.

REFERENCES

[Are 12] *Aresta, Mónica; Pedro, Luís; Santos, Carlos; Moreira, António (2012):* Building Identity in an Institutionally Supported Personal Learning Environment – the case of SAPO Campus. Proceedings of The PLE Conference 2013. Retrieved June 2013 from *http://revistas.ua.pt/index.php/ple/article/view/1428*

[Att 07] *Attwell, Graham (2007):* Personal Learning Environments – the future of eLearning? Lifelong Learning, 2, 1–8.

[Buc 11] *Buchem, Ilona; Attwell, Graham; Torres, Ricardo (2011):* Understanding personal learning environments: Literature review and synthesis through the activity theory lens. Proceedings of The PLE Conference 2011.

[Cre 12] *Cress, Ulrike; Held, Christoph; Kimmerle, Joachim (2012):* The collective knowledge of social tags: Direct and indirect influences on navigation, learning, and information processing. Computers & Education, 60 (1), 59–73. Retrieved May 2014 from *http://www.sciencedirect.com/science/article/pii/S036013151200200X*

[Dah 12] *Dahrendorf, Daniel; Dikke, Diana; Faltin, Nils (2012):* Sharing Personal Learning Environments for Widget Based Systems using a Widget Marketplace. Proceedings of The PLE Conference 2012. Retrieved May 2014 from *http://revistas.ua.pt/index.php/ple/article/view/1445*

[Dow 10] *Downes, Stephen (2010):* New Technology Supporting Informal Learning. Journal of Emerging Technologies in Web Intelligence, 2 (1), 27–33. Retrieved May 2014 from *http://ojs.academypublisher.com/index.php/jetwi/article/view/2461*

[Hei 11] *Heinen, Richard; Blees, Ingo (2011):* Social Bookmarking als Werkzeug für die Kooperation von Lehrkräften. In Griesbaum J.; Mandl Womser-Hacker (Eds.): 12. Internationales Symposium für Informationswissenschaften. Boizenburg. Verlag Werner Hülsbuch, 111–122.

[Höl 12] *Hölterhof, Tobias; Nattland, Axel; Kerres, Michael (2012):* Drupal as a Social Hub for Personal Learning. Proceedings of The PLE Conference 2012. Retrieved May 2014 from *http://revistas.ua.pt/index.php/ple/article/view/1453*

[Höl 11] *Hölterhof, Tobias; Kerres, Michael (2011):* Modellierung sozialer Kommunikation als Communities in Social Software und Lernplattformen. In Heiß, H. U.; Pepper, P.; Schlinghoff, H.; Schneider, J. (Eds.): Informatik 2011: Informatik schafft Communities. Bonn. Gesellschaft für Informatik, 433.

[Ker 11] *Kerres, Michael; Hölterhof, Tobias; Nattland, Axel (2011):* Zur didaktischen Konzeption von «Sozialen Lernplattformen» für das Lernen in Gemeinschaften. MedienPädagogik 2011, 09.12.2011. Retrieved May 2014 from h*ttp://www.medienpaed.com/Documents/medienpaed/2011/kerres1112.pdf*

[Kla 07] *Klamma, Ralf; Chatti, Mohammed Amine; Duval, Erik; Hummel, Hans; Hvannberg, Ebba Thora; Kravcik, Milos; Law, Effie; Naeve, Ambjörn; Scott, Peter (2007):* Social Software for Life-long Learning. Educational Technology & Society, 10 (3), 72–83. Retrieved May 2014 from *http://dspace.learningnetworks.org/bitstream/1820/910/4/ET%26S_socialsoftware.pdf*

[Les 12] *Leslie, Scott (2012):* Some Observations on PLE Diagrams. Blogpost. Retrieved May 2014 from *http://www.edtechpost.ca/wordpress/2012/12/19/ple-diagrams-observations/*

[Ref 02] *Reffay, Christophe; Chanier, Thierry (2002):* Social Network Analysis used for modelling collaboration in distance learning groups. In: Intelligent Tutoring Systems, 31–40. Retrieved May 2014 from *http://www.springerlink.com/index/b4197184w8667748.pdf*

[Tar 09] *Taraghi, Behnam; Ebner, Martin; Till, Gerald; Mühlburger, Herbert (2009):* Personal Learning Environment – a Conceptual Study. Proceedings of International Conference on Interactive Computer Aided Learning.

[Was 94] *Wasserman, Stanley; Faust, Katherine (1994):* Social network analysis: methods and applications, Cambridge. New York. Cambridge University Press.

[Wel 10] *Weller, Martin (2010):* The Centralisation Dilemma in Educational IT. International Journal of Virtual and Personal Learning Environments, 1(1).

[Wil 08] *Wild, Fridolin; Moedritscher, Felix; Sigurdarson, Steinn (2008):* Designing for change: mash-up personal learning environments. eLearning Papers, 9.

[Wil 09] *Wilson, Scott; Liber, Oleg; Johnson, Mark; Beauvoir, Phil; Sharples, Paul; Milligan, Colin (2009):* Personal Learning Environments: Challenging the dominant design of educational systems. Journal of e-Learning and Knowledge Society, 3(2).

CONTACT DETAILS

Dr. Tobias Hölterhof
University of Duisburg-Essen
Learning Lab
Forsthausweg 2
47057 Duisburg
Phone: +49 (0)203 3799 1557
E-Mail: *tobias.hoelterhof@uni-duisburg-essen.de*

Richard Heinen, M.A.
University of Duisburg-Essen
Learning Lab
Forsthausweg 2
47057 Duisburg
Phone: +49 (0)203 3799 2443
E-Mail: *richard.heinen@uni-duisburg-essen.de*

Gamifying Quantified Self Approaches for Learning: An Experiment with the Live Interest Meter

Benedikt S. Morschheuser, Verónica Rivera-Pelayo, Athanasios Mazarakis, Valentin Zacharias

ABSTRACT

We investigate the impact of gamification to increase students' motivation to use PLEs. An experiment was conducted with the Live-Interest-Meter (LIM), a Quantified Self (QS) application to improve learning during and after lectures. Results show that perceived fun has a positive effect on usage motivation and the motivation to use the LIM is with gamification significantly higher than without. Hence, gamification seems to be an appropriate enabler to engage people in using QS approaches as PLEs.

Note: *This article has been published in the Special Edition of the Journal of Literacy and Technology: "Personal Learning Environments: Current Research and Emerging Practice". The link to the JLT Special Issue is: http://www.literacyandtechnology.org/uploads/1/3/6/8/136889/jlt_special.pdf*

Introduction

Recently there has been a growing interest in the impact of gamification – "the use of game design elements in non-game contexts" [Det 11] – on motivation in several contexts, including business and education [Tho 12], [Lee 11]. In the context of learning, gamification may contribute to increase the motivation of students to use PLEs (Personal Learning Environments) and other learning tools in the future. In the case of informal learning, several tools have been developed and tested within the EU-Project MIRROR – "Reflective Learning at Work": *http://www.mirror-project.eu*, to support reflective learning at the workplace. Concretely, a set of these tools are self-tracking applications, also known as Quantified Self (QS) tools, i.e. tools that collect personally relevant information for self-knowledge, e.g. *http://www.quantifiedself.com*. One of them is the Live-Interest-Meter (LIM) [Riv 13], a QS application and PLE, which allows capturing, aggregating and visualizing feedback given to the lecturer with the aim of supporting reflective learning for both speaker and audience.

Studies with the LIM and other MIRROR apps have shown that the use of such QS reflective learning applications in educational and working contexts face a lack of motivation. The results of several studies conducted with the LIM showed concerns regarding the students' voluntary participation to give feedback and actively be involved

in the lectures [Riv 13]. With the goal to enhance the user's engagement, we examined whether gamification can increase motivation to use QS tools like the Live-Interest-Meter. We conducted an extended literature review on gamification, the QS community and learning through reflection in order to create a theoretical framework. We also analysed successes and failures of existing gamification approaches. Following, we conducted an experiment to analyse the users' intention to use an adapted version of the Live-Interest-Meter with and without gamification.

In the following, we present the background of our work, including gamification, its role in Technology Enhanced Learning (TEL) and related approaches. Next, the presented case study and the conducted experiment will be described in detail. Finally, we will outline our findings before concluding the paper.

Background

The use of game design elements in non-game contexts [Det 11], also known as gamification, represents a huge trend in Human-Computer-Interaction (HCI), marketing [Zic 11], enterprise [Sch 12] and education [Lee 11]. Already in the 1980s, [Mal 82] researched the positive impact of game elements in interfaces and suggested to use video game elements to enhance the interest, joy and satisfaction of computer systems. Following the predictions of analysts like [Gar 11] and gamification visionaries [Sch 10], [McG 11], it is likely that gamification will play an important role in future urban spaces, including new forms of gamified education [Cha 11]. Since the rise of gamification, education is a popular application field of this new motivation method. [Cha 11] examined that gamification in education and TEL can increase the learners' engagement, strengthen the social relations, raise satisfaction, help to identify personal strengths and weaknesses and give a more detailed personal feedback.

The use of gamification to support learning through self-reflection with QS tools has not been previously studied in detail. However, this combination has been successfully applied in many popular applications like Nike+, HealthMonth or Mint. All these examples motivate people with gamification to collect personal information about their behaviour. The target of our research is to transfer this approach to the education context and to examine, if gamification can improve the motivation to collect data and reflect on it with technology enhanced PLEs in order to improve personal learning.

Case study

The object of our research is an adapted version of the Live-Interest-Meter, a Quantified Self application and PLE that supports the reflective learning process for presenters and listeners. This version of the LIM, which was developed based on [Riv 13], consists of two main components: 1) the "Meter", a mobile app that allows capturing and visualizing live feedback in lectures and 2) the "LIM-Community", a web platform to review past presentations, analyse the personal learning behaviour and interact with other users. The Meter was designed to quantify and track the performance of the presenter as well as the context of the students during a lecture in order to improve the individual learning process. The tool allows listeners to evaluate a lecture in real time on a uni-dimensional meter, whose scale can be chosen from a preconfigured set (speed of speech, interest, difficulty and comprehension). The gathered data is aggregated and visualized to the users. If a certain threshold value is exceeded, the presenter will see a discreet hint and can react on it. This live feedback loop is illustrated in Figure 1.

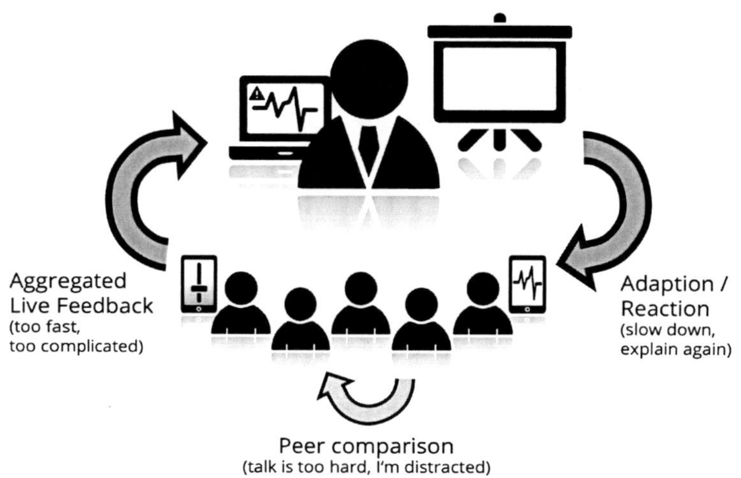

Figure 1: Schematic illustration of the LIM scenario

Participants can also compare their individual learning situation with peers. Therefore the Meter supports learners who can reflect on their own performance and improve their behaviour in comparison to peers but also the presenter, who gets real-time feedback about the lecture. Later, participants can reflect on a past lecture, by logging in into the LIM-Community. This web platform allows reviewing captured lectures, visualized and aggregated in graphs and enriched with collected metadata like date, time, topic and participants, and also context information (notes added by the audience). The students can discuss about lectures in forums and can evaluate their collected data. Thus, the LIM-Community can be used to recall information from past lectures combined with the associated events in the audience.

The combination of the Meter and the LIM-Community provides a PLE that helps regular attendees of lectures to visualize, understand and improve their personal learning process and behaviour.

Experiment: The gamified LIM

We conducted an online experiment with a 2x2 Latin Square design [Hic 73] to analyse the impact of gamification on the motivation to use the LIM, by examining the users' intention to use a gamified and a not gamified version of the app.

Gamification of the LIM

In order to keep the distraction of the students to a minimum during the lectures, gamification was only applied to the LIM-Community to foster the motivation to collect quantitative and qualitative data during lectures. In a software design process, based on Radoff's [Rad 11] player-centred design model, we selected multiple game mechanics and interface elements for the gamified version of the LIM, based on analysed needs of our target audience. We developed personas, derived from the surveyed participants of [Riv 13] and matched them with the player types of Bartle [Bar 96] and interviews of [May 09].

Central element of the gamified version is the personal "Knowledge Tree". This narrative element stands for the personal learning progress and grows with each lecture in which the user collects data with the LIM. Engagement in using the LIM or the accomplishment of tasks are rewarded with badges and points. The animated badges, e.g. little birds or squirrels (Figure 2), can be decorated in a tree branch, which represents a lecture. The overall personal progress is indicated in points and can be compared with other players in global leaderboards.

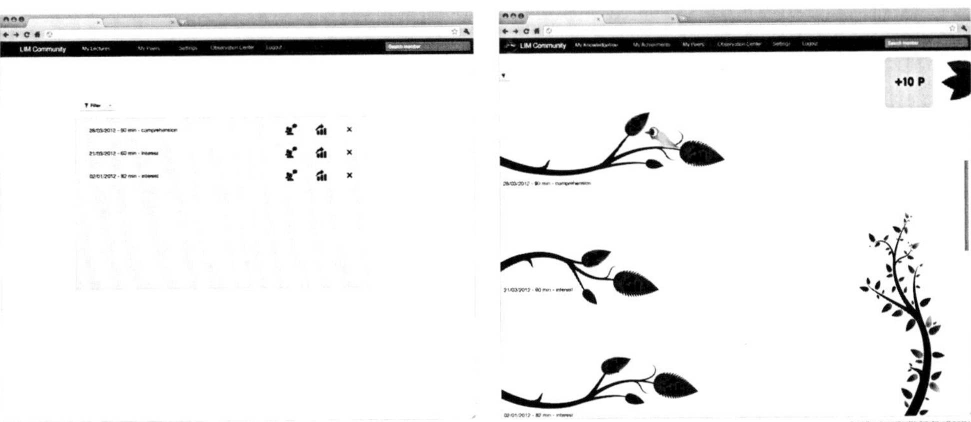

Figure 2: Prototypes of the LIM-Community. Left without gamification, right with gamification

Experiment

Considering successful gamified QS applications like Nike+ or HealthMonth, it seems that QS approaches can benefit from gamification. Therefore, gamification may be also an appropriate enabler to engage people in using QS approaches as PLEs for improving their personal learning experiences. Concerning our experiment, our first hypothesis was: H1: The intention to use the LIM with gamification (game elements, game mechanics, storytelling and playful design) is higher than without gamification.

Consequently, we also believe that gamification can support the motivation to keep tracking, according to QS, over a long-term period. Li et al. [Li 10] point out that a lack in motivation is one important barrier for its long-term success. We believe that suitable gamification elements are able to counteract that problem in a systematic and methodical manner. Therefore: H2: The intention to use the QS application LIM long-term and to visit the Community regularly is higher with gamification than without.

In general, it is assumed that gamification can enhance intrinsic motivation. Igbaria et al. [Igb 94] showed that "system usage is affected by both extrinsic motivation (usefulness) and intrinsic motivation (fun). Both are important in affecting the individual decision whether to accept or reject a new technology". Based on this, we believe this is also true for gamified QS-applications: H3: The perceived fun during the usage has a positive correlation on the usage intention of QS applications like the LIM.

We conducted an online experiment which was 20 days active and allowed us to achieve the appropriate target group. Each participant was randomly assigned to one of two groups. Group 1 (G1) evaluated first the non-gamified version of the LIM and then the gamified version, whereas group 2 (G2) evaluated the versions the other way around. After a short video introduction and checking the role of the participant in lectures, the gamified (G) or non-gamified version (O), depending on the group, was presented to the subjects (Figure 3). Subsequently, we asked the participants a set of questions. Afterwards, we presented them the other version of the LIM-Community and asked them the same questions. Finally, we asked demographical data and supplementary questions, like the interest to learn from personal QS data. The experimental design allowed us to perform two different analyses between the gamified and non-gamified version: the independent differences between the randomized and independent groups (between-subject) as well as the responses at the individual level (within-subject).

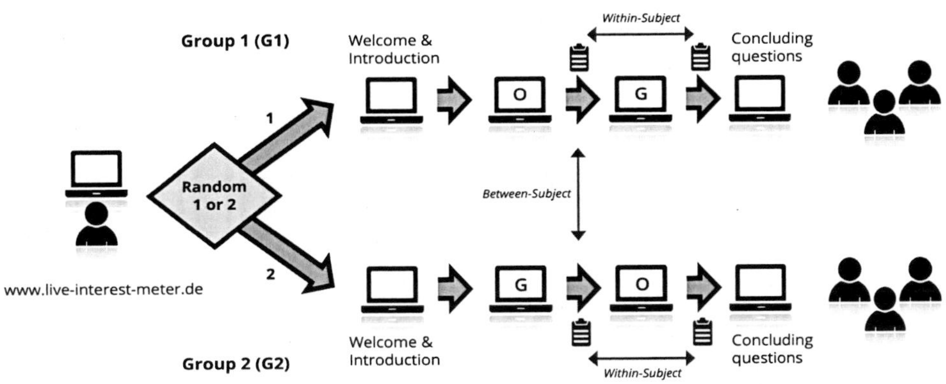

Figure 3: Structure of the experiment

The questions asked after each presentation were divided in four sections (Table 1). The intention to use the software – behavioural intention (BI1), which based on [Fis 75] is an indicator for the real usage – was derived from successful TAM studies of [Ven 00] and [Dav 89]. The questions about the long-term usage (BI2) were inspired by [Igb 94]. Perceived usefulness (PU) was operationalized with five items oriented at [Ven 00] and [Dav 89]. The questions were adapted to the LIM needs. To measure FUN, we used the proven construct from [Igb 94] consisted of a 7-point semantic differential with six pairs.

Table 1: Research factors, questions and reliability assessment

RESEARCH CONSTRUCT	QUESTIONS	CRONBACH'S ALPHA				SCALE
		GROUP 1		GROUP 2		
		G	O	G	O	
PU	General usefulness (i), usefulness to improve effectiveness (ii) and performance (iv), usefulness for self reflection (iii) and self improvement (vi)	0.898	0.897	0.917	0.945	7-point Likert-scale
FUN	rewarding /unrewarding (i), pleasant/unpleasant (ii), fun/ frustrating (iii), enjoyable/unenjoyable (iv), positive/negative (v), interesting/ uninteresting (vi)	0.925	0.868	0.910	0.929	7-point semantic differential

RESEARCH CONSTRUCT	QUESTIONS	CRONBACH'S ALPHA				SCALE
		GROUP 1		GROUP 2		
		G	O	G	O	
BI1	General intention to test (i) and use the meter(ii), the community (iii), the collected data (iv)	0.912	0.902	0.872	0.908	7-point Likert-scale
BI2	Intention to use the meter (i), the community (ii) and the collected data (iii) regularly	0.876	0.837	0.792	0.775	7-point Likert-scale

Data analysis and findings

During the online experiment, the website was visited by 607 unique visitors. Around 14 % of them participated in it. 70 complete valid data sets (according to control variables and having specified that the participant takes part in lectures regularly) were used for the analysis.

The automatic randomization resulted in 35 valid data records in G1 and 35 in G2. The distribution was homogeneous (Female G1: 13, G2: 13; male G1: 22, G2: 22; median age G1: 26, G2: 24; attend lectures regularly as student G1: 29, G2: 28; attend lectures regularly at work G1: 10, G2: 10; QS interest G1: 22, G2: 19). Therefore, the application of Pearson Chi-Square tests did not show significant differences in the groups, concerning demographic data and QS interest. We assessed the internal consistency of the measurement model by computing Cronbach's alpha coefficients for each of the four constructs PU, FUN, BI1 and BI2 in both groups and both versions (gamified (G) and not gamified (O)). All 16 were between 0,775 and 0,945 and showed a high reliability (Table 1).

Within-subject analysis

Figure 4 visualizes a descriptive analysis of the individual answers to the two LIM versions (G and O). Comparing the BI1 and BI2 item sums of each participant showed that both kinds of usage intention were in both groups with gamification higher than without.

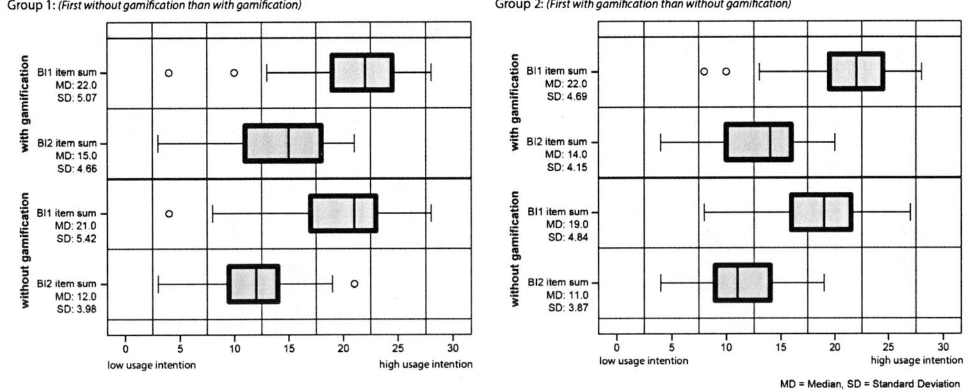

Figure 4: Boxplot of all BI item sums to compare within-subject differences in each group

We used non-parametric tests because the application of Kolmogorov-Smirnov-Tests showed that it is possible that BI1(G) (p=0.045) and PU(O) (p=0.046) are not normal distributed. For this reason, we verified our hypotheses 1 and 2 by using Wilcoxon signed-rank tests. The analysis reveals that the intention to use the LIM (BI1) and the long-term and regularly use of the LIM and the LIM-Community (BI2) is with gamification significantly higher than without. These results support our hypotheses 1 and 2. Furthermore it was shown that also perceived fun is with gamification significantly higher (Table 2).

Table 2: Results of the within-subject analysis, Wilcoxon signed-rank test

COMPARISON			N	SUM OF RANKS	P (ONE-TAILED)
PU	G – O	Negative ranks	17	478.00	0.025*
		Positive ranks	35	900.00	
		Ties	18		
		Total	70		
FUN	G – O	Negative ranks	12	298.50	0.00**
		Positive ranks	46	1412.50	
		Ties	12		
		Total	70		

COMPARISON			N	SUM OF RANKS	P (ONE-TAILED)
BI1	G – O	Negative ranks	10	280.00	0.00**
		Positive ranks	46	1316.00	
		Ties	14		
		Total	70		
BI2	G – O	Negative ranks	12	239.00	0.00**
		Positive ranks	43	1301.00	
		Ties	15		
		Total	70		

* is one-tailed significant at 0.05 level.
** is one-tailed significant at 0.01 level.

Between-subject analysis

The within-subject analysis is based on the individual comparison of both versions of the LIM. With the between-subject analysis we tried to determine whether the results are comparable, even if the participants only know one alternative. A tendency for the gamified version was also recognized in this analysis, in which we examined only the independent first answers in each group i.e. the answers to the not gamified version (O) in G1 and the answers to the gamified one (G) in G2. The intention to use the LIM (BI1 & BI2) was with gamification higher than without gamification (Figure 5). However, our hypotheses could not be verified with tests due to the small sample in the between-subject observation.

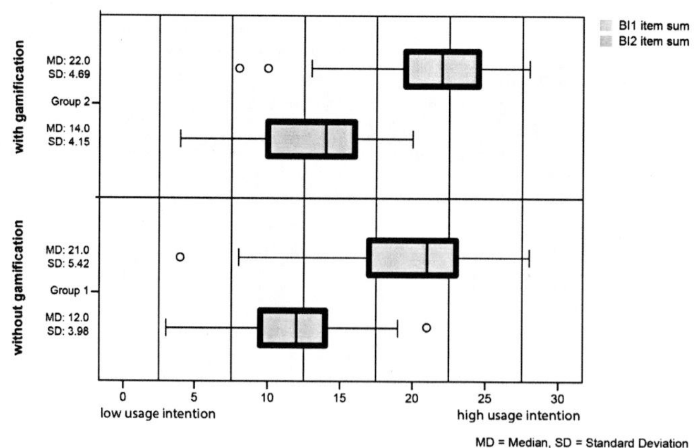

Figure 5: Boxplot with the BI item sums of the first answers in each group to compare between-subject differences

Correlation analysis

To test H3, Spearman's rank correlation coefficients for FUN, BI1, BI2 and PU were calculated (Table 3). All group-spanning correlation coefficients were one-tailed positive significant at $\alpha=0.001$ (with Bonferroni correction). The results show a positive correlation between FUN and BI1 & BI2 in both cases. It can be concluded that perceived fun during the usage (FUN) has a positive impact on the usage intention (BI) of QS applications like the LIM – in general (BI1) higher than in long term (BI2). This finding supports our third hypothesis and compared with the results from the within-subject analysis, it can be said that gamification can increase perceived fun (Table 2), which have a direct influence on the intention to use an application like the LIM. Furthermore, the correlations show that PU has a positive significant impact on BI with higher correlation coefficients than between FUN and BI (Table 3). These findings follow the results of [Igb 94], which measured a stronger influence of PU on BI compared to FUN on BI.

Table 3: Group-spanning Spearman-Rho correlations between FUN, PU, BI1 and BI2

WITH GAMIFICATION		GROUP-SPANNING	
SUMS OF		BI1	BI2
FUN	correlation coefficient	.691***	.561***
PU	correlation coefficient	.743***	.679***
WITHOUT GAMIFICATION		GROUP-SPANNING	
SUMS OF		BI1	BI2
FUN	correlation coefficient	.732***	.572***
PU	correlation coefficient	.773***	.569***
*** p < 0.001 (with Bonferroni correction).		N=70	

Additionally, a group-spanning comparison of the individual responses yielded that 62 out of 70 participants (88.57 %) are willing to test the LIM (independent from gamification) and 64.14 % (47 out of 70) recognized clear benefits in using the LIM at study or work. Additionally, 45 out of 70 (64.28 %) replied to the question "If you would use the Meter in a lecture once a week, how often would you login into the LIM-Community" (B3) that they would login once a week or more frequently.

Conclusions

In this study we showed that gamification can increase the motivation to use QS applications, like the Live Interest Meter, to collect personal data about the own learning and improve the learning process. The hypotheses H1-H3 were supported by the statistical analysis of the experimental results. The general as well as the long-term intention to use the LIM were with gamification higher than without. According to [Fis 75] and [Dav 89] it can be argued that these intentions have a direct impact on the actual usage. Further, we could show that perceived fun has a positive effect on the motivation to use the examined PLE. Together with the finding that perceived fun is with gamification higher than without, we can conclude that gamification can increase the motivation for using the examined application. Considering the gamification findings and the result that nearly 2/3 of the respondents see clear benefits in using the LIM to improve their personal learning process, gamification seems to be an appropriate enabler to engage people in using QS approaches as PLEs for improving their learning experiences.

The present research has several limitations. First, the sample size was insufficient to validate the hypothesis between the groups with a between-subject test. However, meaningful tendency for gamification was indicated between-subject and the performed within-subject analysis showed high significant results. Furthermore, the measurement was hypothetical and self-reported. Larger experiments in real settings are planned to validate our results. However, this study provides a first important contribution to the successful use of gamification approaches for supporting individual reflective learning with QS tools as PLEs.

Acknowledgement

The project "MIRROR – Reflective learning at work" is funded under the FP7 of the European Commission (project number 257617).

REFERENCES

[Bar 96] *Bartle, Richard (1996):* Hearts, Clubs, Diamonds, Spades: Players who suit MUDs. In: Journal of MUD research, 1(1), 19.

[Cha 11] *Charles, Therese; Bustard, David; Black, Michaela (2011):* Experiences of Promoting Student Engagement Through Game-Enhanced Learning. In: Ma, M., Oikonomou, A., Jain, L. (Eds.). Serious Games and Edutainment Applications. London. Springer. 425–445.

[Dav 89] *Davis, Fred D. (1989):* Perceived usefulness, perceived ease of use and user acceptance of information technology. In: MIS Quarterly, 13(3), 319–340.

[Det 11] *Deterding, Sebastian; Dixon, Dan; Khaled, Rilla; & Nacke, Lennart (2011):* From game design elements to gamefulness: defining "gamification". In: Mindtrek 2011 Proceedings. New York. ACM. 9–15.

[Fis 75] *Fishbein, Martin; Ajzen, Icek (1975):* Belief, attitude, intention and behavior: An introduction to theory and research. Reading, Massachusetts: Addison-Wesley.

[Gar 11] *Gartner (2011):* Gartner Predicts Over 70 Percent of Global 2000 Organisations Will Have at Least One Gamified Application by 2014. Retrieved May 2014 from *http://www.gartner.com/it/page.jsp?id=1844115*

[Hic 73] *Hicks, Charles R. (1973):* Fundamental concepts in the design of experiments. New York: Holt, Rinehart and Winston.

[Igb 94] *Igbaria, Magid; Schiffman, Stephen J.; Wieckowski, Thomas J. (1994):* The respective roles of perceived usefulness and perceived fun in the acceptance of microcomputer technology. Behaviour & Information Technology, 13(6), 349–361.

[Lee 11] *Lee, Joey J.; Hammer, Jessica (2011):* Gamification in Education: What, How, Why Bother? Academic Exchange Quarterly, 15 (2), 1–5.

[Li 10] *Li, Ian; Dey, Anind Dey; Forlizzi, Jodi (2010):* A Stage-Based Model of Personal Informatics Systems. . In Proceedings of the SIGCHI Conference on Human Factors in Computing Systems, Atlanta, USA: ACM, 557–566.

[Mal 82] *Malone, Thomas W. (1982):* Heuristics for designing enjoyable user interfaces. In Proceedings of the 1982 conference on Human factors in computing systems, ACM Press, 63–68.

[May 09] *Mayer, Monica (2009):* Warum Leben, Wenn Man Stattdessen Spielen Kann? – Kognition, Motivation Und Emotion Am Beispiel Digitaler Spiele. Boizenburg: Werner Hülsbusch.

[McG 11] *McGonigal, Jane (2011):* Reality is broken. New York: The Penguin Press.

[Rad 11] *Radoff, Jon (2011):* Game On: Energize Your Business with Social Media Games. Indianapolis. Wiley Publishing, Inc.

[Riv 13] *Rivera-Pelayo, Verónica; Munk, Johannes; Zacharias, Valentin; Braun, Simone (2013):* Live interest meter – Learning from quantified feedback in mass lectures. In Proceedings of the Third International Conference on Learning Analytics and Knowledge (LAK '13), New York: ACM.

[Sch 12] *Schacht, Maik; Schacht, Silvia (2012):* Start the Game: Increasing User Experience of Enterprise Systems Following a Gamification Mechanism. In Maedche, A., Botzenhardt, A. & Neer, L. (Eds.) Software for People, Heidelberg: Springer, 181–199.

[Sch 10] *Schell, Jesse (2010):* When games invade real life. Retrieved May 2014 from *http://www.ted.com/talks/jesse_schell_when_games_invade_real_life.html*

[Tho 12] *Thom, Jennifer; Millen, David; DiMicco, Joan (2012):* Removing Gamification from an Enterprise SNS. In Proceedings of the ACM 2012 conference on Computer Supported Cooperative Work, New York: ACM.

[Ven 00] *Venkatesh, Viswanath; Davis, Fred D. (2000):* A theoretical extension of the Technology Acceptance Model: Four longitudinal field studies. Management Science, 46(2), 186–204.

[Zic 11] *Zichermann, Gabe; Cunningham, Christopher (2011):* Gamification by Design: Implementing Game Mechanics in Web and Mobile Apps. New York: O'Reilly Media.

FIGURES

CONTACT DETAILS

Dipl. Wirt.-Ing. Benedikt Morschheuser
University of Leipzig
Information Systems Institute
Grimmaische Straße 12
04109 Leipzig, Germany
Phone: +49 (0)341 9733 611
E-Mail: *Benedikt.Morschheuser@uni-leipzig.de*

Dipl. Inf. Verónica Rivera-Pelayo
FZI Research Center for Information Technology
Haid-und-Neu-Straße 10–14
76131 Karlsruhe, Germany
Phone: +49 (0)721 9654 818
E-Mail: *rivera@fzi.de*

Dr. Athanasios Mazarakis
Kiel University
ZBW – D3
Düsternbrooker Weg 120
24105 Kiel, Germany
Phone: +49 (0)431 8814 214
E-Mail: *ama@informatik.uni-kiel.de*

Dr. Valentin Zacharias
codecentric AG
Zeppelinstraße 2
76185 Karlsruhe, Germany
Phone: +49 (0) 174 2055 415
E-Mail: *valentin.zacharias@codecentric.de*

The mobile as an ad hoc PLE- Learning serendipitously in urban contexts

Ruthi Aladjem, Rafi Nachmias

ABSTRACT

In this paper we describe results from a pilot study of informal serendipitous learning interactions mediated by mobile technologies, during first visits to cities. The analysis of learning interactions revealed three themes that are discussed in this paper- the availability theme, the social theme and the awareness theme. Learning interactions were explored with the underlying premise of unveiling potential paths for consolidating discrete learning events into coherent learning experiences. We suggest that the mobile device serves as an "ad hoc PLE (Personal Learning Environment)" that offers on-demand support for learners, thus encouraging them to explore the city and to utilize opportunities for learning and interaction, while accommodating their individual needs and preferences.

Note: *This article has been published in the Special Edition of the Journal of Literacy and Technology: "Personal Learning Environments: Current Research and Emerging Practice". The link to the JLT Special Issue is: http://www.literacyandtechnology.org/uploads/1/3/6/8/136889/jlt_special.pdf*

Background and Introduction

Travel situations have long been recognized as holding substantial learning potential [Mit 98], [Fal 12]. In this context, a city may be regarded as an exploration ground; all is new and invites explanation, clarification, and further information. A visit to a new city carries endless learning opportunities, from the local language, the history of the city, its architecture, art, culture and so on. Travellers are often in a state of mind that makes them eager to learn and explore [Mit 98], [Fal 12] and learning takes an informal, serendipitous nature. By informal learning, we are referring to learning incidents that are not planned nor organized [Kle 73]; the term serendipitous learning accentuates the incidental and unplanned aspect of informal learning processes, though it does not suggest that learning is random, as it is in fact determined by the learner's goals, interests, and prior knowledge [Buc 11].

Before the age of smart mobile devices, tour books, tour guides, and paper maps served as the common support tools, for visitors looking to explore and learn more about their travel destinations. Information was thus limited to the scope of the book, preselected by an editor or an expert guide. A chance encounter with a point of interest that was not deemed as significant enough to appear in a tour book might have ended with no further investigation. As a result of the lack of immediate information, the learning interest that was evoked by the point of interest, might not have been fulfilled or further explored. This situation has changed dramatically since the oncoming of the social web and the advent of mobile devices, no longer is there a single source of information or lack of immediate support. The mobile's perpetual connectivity allows access as well as to information at anytime, anywhere, and on any topic of interest, as well as active contribution [Jen 06], [Kre 07], [Sca 06]. Furthermore, the mobile device has become one with the learner, carried everywhere at all times, holding vast potential for supporting learning in authentic settings and contexts. Learners are free to follow their personal interests, to define their own learning goals and to engage in active, collaborative, learning processes among learners with shared interests [Die 07], [Lau 07], [Sha 07]. The notion of a Personal Learning Environment (PLE) has been described from multiple perspectives with varying definitions and design directions [Hen 10], [Zho 13]. Adhering to a view of a PLE as an approach to the use of technologies, that is "comprised of all the different tools we use in our everyday life for learning" [Att 07], we suggest a view of mobile devices as potential ad hoc PLEs for travel situations; comprised of tools selected by learners according to their context dependent learning needs, as they arise in real time. Mobile services and technologies such as navigation tools, social networks and location-based applications, although not created specifically for learning purposes, may allow learners to engage in knowledge interactions through activities such as sharing, searching and reflection. By selecting applications that support their personal, context dependent needs as they emerge in real time, learners may potentially turn a city visit into a personal, active, and collaborative learning experience.

Following, we will describe the research approach of our pilot study, aiming at identifying and analysing informal serendipitous learning processes during urban explorations, supported by mobile devices. We will than present the main findings and discuss possible implications.

Research Approach

The pilot study was conducted as part of a PhD research, aimed at identifying and analysing key factors that play a significant role in incidental, serendipitous learning processes, supported by mobile technologies. The pilot takes a qualitative, learner-centred, approach that includes in-depth interviews with 10 early adopters of technology, who own a smart mobile device. Early adopters are often characterized with such personality traits as personal innovativeness, active information seeking, and intrinsic motivation for exploration [Aga 98], [Str 09]. These characteristics seem congruent with

desirable qualities of 21st century learners and with the socio-constructivist ideal of an active learner involved in constructing knowledge while interacting with a community in authentic settings [Sha 07], [Weg 98]. For the purpose of this study, any knowledge interaction that occurs outside of a formal learning environment is considered an informal learning incident [Kle 73], [Liv 99]. The research questions focused on the ways in which mobile tools and applications are being used in order to construct knowledge in authentic settings (the city). The analysis of learning interactions also considered the learning needs that emerged during the visit, the tools and applications that were used in order to support those needs, the types of learning activities (for example, "push" contributions or "pull" requests) and the contexts in which the activities took place.

Results

All subjects owned a smart mobile device (six subjects owned an iOS device and four owned an Android device). Subjects gave a detailed description of up to three recent visits that they had made to new cities (i.e., cities that they had not visited before), bringing the number of cities visited to a total of 21. All subjects reported that they had chosen to use their mobile device as the sole tool for support and communication during their visit; no additional artefacts (such as a paper map, a tour book, or a tour guide) were used. During their visit, subjects were continually engaged with their personal mobile environment, using versatile mobile applications; different applications were selected alternately to support different needs. It is beyond the scope of this paper to discuss all applications in detail, but they included: location-based navigation and information services (such as Google Maps, Yelp, TripAdvisor, Foursquare, Browser Search), social interaction tools (such as Facebook, Twitter, Google Talk), tools for real time documentation (such as Instagram, flickr, Evernote), real time scheduling services (such as bus and subway schedules), and translation tools (such as Google Translate, iTranslate). It was found that the tool selection was not necessarily based on the technical features that the applications offered but was context dependent; different applications often carried similar features (for example, both Facebook and Foursquare have location-based features and support "check-ins") but were used in different contexts and situations for different purposes. The determining factor seemed to be the way in which subjects interpreted the main purpose of the application and what they had felt would best suit their needs (for example, checking in on Facebook was described as an effective means for sharing with friends back home while checking in on Foursquare was often done for pertinent purposes such as seeing if there were other users at the current location and initiating new encounters).

Three major themes emerged from the analysis of learning interactions: the availability theme, the social theme, and the awareness theme. A description of each theme follows.

The availability theme

Walking around the city carrying a mobile device means that one is perpetually connected. Subjects had mentioned that the fact that information and communication are readily available and only a click away, affected their behaviours and decision-making processes. This seems, first and foremost, to have affected their personal sense of control over their environment. For example, one subject mentioned that "just knowing that I could not really get lost, allowed me to get lost in the streets, wandering aimlessly without a worry and just looking around."

Availability also affected the perception of the need to plan ahead; most subjects reported that they preplanned almost nothing for their trip because they knew that they would have their mobile with them. Only one subject stated that he regularly prepares a list of locations to visit; based on prior research and recommendations, he places the list on a mobile map that he uses to navigate in the city. However, he also noted, "If the applications worked perfectly, all the items on my list would appear on them anyway and this might have been redundant."

Availability also allowed subjects to make decisions in real time; in several cases, subjects received recommendations for nearby locations from friends who realized that they were nearby (as they saw their check-ins). In one instance, a subject checked in while in the north of Paris and a friend commented that he must visit the famous Père Lachaise cemetery; this visit later led to a college project on Oscar Wilde (who is buried at the cemetery) that was based on the information collected and shared during this unplanned encounter.

Finally, availability allowed for benefiting from location-based services and for the ability to learn in context. In fact, context was often the trigger for learning interaction, as one subject mentioned, "If I come across anything that seems interesting, I immediately look for more information by searching, posting a question on Twitter or simply by photographing, tagging and sharing."

Lack of an available connection and the high cost of mobile internet were mentioned as a major issue. Having an internet (Wi-Fi) connection was mentioned in the interviews as a basic and critical need; as one subject mentioned, "I am lost without my mobile and it must be connected all the time- I can't imagine my world without it".

The social theme

The ability to stay in touch with one's close social group (friends and family) as well as to be able to receive information from and contribute to a larger community, were mentioned throughout the interviews. Subjects had reported versatile ways and contexts in which they chose to use the social features available in different mobile applications.

Subjects, especially if traveling alone, kept a continuous communication with their close social circle; sharing and receiving feedback. This contributed to a feeling of a shared learning experience; as one subject noted, she felt as if "my friends were taking part in my expedition, even if they were not technically there."

The ability to benefit from social support formed on the basis of context or need was also mentioned; subjects regularly used location-based applications that are based on community contribution such as Yelp or Foursquare, to receive information on discoveries that they had reached.

Sharing, sometimes led to unexpected discoveries; for example, "I posted a picture of a café and a friend told me that an art gallery next door was just opening an exhibition."

Finally, though sharing was usually done in real time, social activity allowed subjects to return, virtually, to discoveries that they have shared; subjects also reported that they sometimes accessed previously shared items in order to add titles or insert tags.

The awareness theme

As a result of their intensive use of mobile social tools while exploring the city, subjects become more aware of the reciprocal nature of their activities. Subjects mentioned that they came to realize that their actions had more than a personal meaning and that their activities, such as sharing, contributing information, and answering questions, could affect others. One subject, for example, summed up by saying that "just as I have been depending on the courtesy of strangers so can my actions have meaning to others and not just to my personal group of friends." Realizing that their activities resonate, affected subjects' long-term tendency to be actively involved in knowledge contribution after the visit ended. Another subject said, "I had used foursquare years ago, when it was launched but after a while didn't really see the point anymore and stopped, after my trip I make a point of using it again as I realize that others will read and benefit from my reviews."

In summary, it was found that the use of the mobile as an ad hoc personal learning environment has contributed to a shift in the relationship between learners and the object of learning, while exploring the city. The mobile has contributed to an increased sense of control over the surroundings and allowed for true immersion with the dynamic city and all that it has to offer. The mobile device also allowed learners to interact with their community, as part of the learning process and had increased their awareness of the fact that their contributions can resonate and can benefit others, thus encouraging them to engage in knowledge building processes even once their visit was over.

Discussion and Conclusions

The pilot study illuminates the transformation that mobile technology has brought to the learning experience during visits to a new city. The study also highlights ways in which the mobile device can serve as a dynamic learning environment that is activated and controlled by learners, for exploration and learning. The wide array of tools and applications available to learners, all under the "umbrella" of the mobile device and the choice of this technology as the sole learning environment for exploring the city, suggest that the mobile serves as an on-demand personal learning environment, an ad hoc PLE for the visit. Effectively, learners are taking an active part in designing their PLEs [Hen 10] by selecting and utilizing dynamic components based upon their contextual needs and preferences, as they emerge in real time.

The mobile, serving as an ad hoc PLE, supports a serendipitous learning process. Learners do not need to, and often chooses not to preplan their visit, because of their reliance on the perpetual connection to contextual sources of information and to their own communities. This ad hoc PLE supports dynamic learning processes with extensive opportunities for immediacy that is needed both for the learners' changing needs as well as due to the city's static and always changing nature. With no predetermined plan and no expert to lead the way, learners are in control of the learning process; live concerts, parades, traffic jams and essentially everything that happens in the city, is injected, in real time, into the exploration process. Though a single interaction may seem trivial, this ad hoc PLE essentially connects discrete learning interactions onto a comprehensive personal learning experience [Ala 11], each interaction may lead to several potential trajectories and a final learning path can only be sketched aftermath.

With a feeling of control over their environment, largely due to the availability of resources and the social support received through the mobile PLE, learners are free to fully experience the city without worrying about getting lost. Learners undergo a truly serendipitous and immersive learning experience by engaging in authentic, contextual learning interactions. Personal points of interest that were not likely to appear in an expert tour book, now become meaningful learning activities as they are shared and interacted upon, thus changing the level of granularity of learning and increasing the array of potential learning triggers.

Learners are continually engaged in social collaborative learning activities such as responding to comments, tagging previously shared items or adding titles, these activities lead them to virtually revisit previously shared discoveries and view them through the diversified eyes of the community. Revisiting past learning experiences allow learners to engage in reflective and ultimately more profound learning experiences [Die 07], [Sha 07].

Due to their reliance on communal contributions, learners become increasingly aware of the notion that their own activities can hold more than just a personal value, realizing that their contributions resonate and can be of benefit to other learners in a virtual community. It can be said that through their own activities learners come to realize that they are a part of a dynamic collaborative knowledge construction process and that they are not just consumers of knowledge, but are also assigning meaning, sharing with the virtual community and changing the balance between contribution and receipt of information [Kre 07], [Sca 06].

In conclusion, a visit to a new city is a highly intensive and condensed exploratory experience that may serve as a microcosms and a reference point for demonstrating the potential of the mobile as an informal learning tool. The mobile device has trans-

formed the experience of serendipitous urban exploration and the ways in which learners interact with their surroundings and construct knowledge by serving as a powerful ad hoc PLE. Serendipitous learning processes could potentially be directed, with the support of the mobile PLE, to revolve around disciplines and areas that are relevant not only to informal, but also to formal learning objectives (such a History or Language Studies).

Finally, when considering the city of the future we envision a city visit as a truly personalized learning experience, we believe that urban planners and stakeholders should consider the need to cater for "mobile tourism" not only by making sure that an internet connection (WiFi) is freely available everywhere but mostly by planning mobile services that take into account and accommodate the personal needs of visitors interested in exploring and learning about the city.

REFERENCES

[Aga 98] *Agarwal, Ritu; Prasad, Jayesh (1998):* A conceptual and operational definition of personal innovativeness in the domain of information technology. Information Systems Research, 9(2), 204–215.

[Ala 11] *Aladjem, Ruthi; Nachmias, Rafi (2011):* Constructing knowledge via mobile devices–one interaction at a time. International Journal of Technology Enhanced Learning, 3(6), 599–607.

[Att 07] *Attwell, Graham (2007):* Personal Learning Environments--The future of eLearning? eLearning Papers, 2(1), 1–7.

[Buc 11] *Buchem, Ilona (2011):* Serendipitous learning: Recognizing and fostering the potential of microblogging. Form@ re-Open Journal per la formazione in rete, 11(74), 7–16.

[Die 07] *Dieterle, Edward; Dede, Chris; Schrier, Karen (2007):* "Neomillennial" learning styles propagated by wireless handheld devices, In Lytras, M. and Naeve, A. (Eds.) Ubiquitous and pervasive knowledge and learning management: semantics, social networking and new media to their full potential, Pennsylvania: Idea Group, Inc., 35–66.

[Fal 12] *Falk, John; Ballantyne, Roy; Packer, Jan; Benckendorff, Pierre (2012):* Travel and learning: A neglected tourism research area. Annals of Tourism Research,39(2), 908–927.

[Hen 10] *Henri, France; Charlier, Bernadette (2010):* Personal learning environment: A concept, an application, or a self-designed instrument? In: Information Technology Based Higher Education and Training (ITHET), 2010 9th International Conference on IEEE, 44–51.

[Jen 06] *Jenkins, Henry; Clinton, Katie; Purushotma, Ravi; Robinson, Alice J; Weigel, Margaret (2006):* Confronting the challenges of participatory culture: media education for the 21st century, MacArthur Foundation. Available at: *mitpress.mit.edu/books/full_pdfs/Confronting_the_Challenges.pdf*

[Kle 73] *Kleis, Russell J; Lang, Charles L; Mietus John R; Tiapula, Fia T. S (1973):* Toward a contextual definition of nonformal education. Nonformal Education Discussion Paper. Michigan: Michigan State University, 3–6.

[Kre 07] *Kress, Gunther; Pachler, Norbert (2007):* Thinking about the 'M-' in mobile learning. In Norman, A. & Pearce, J. (Eds.) Conference proceedings: long and short papers. 6th Annual Conference on Mobile Learning, 199–209.

[Lau 07] *Laurillard, Diana (2007):* Pedagogical forms for mobile learning. In Pachler, N. (Ed.) Mobile learning: towards a research agenda, London: WLE Centre, IOE, 153–175.

[Liv 99] *Livingstone, D. W. (1999):* Exploring the icebergs of adult learning: Findings of the first Canadian survey of informal learning practices. Canadian Journal for the Study of Adult Education, 13(2), 49–72.

[Mit 98] *Mitchell, Richard D. (1998):* Learning through play and pleasure travel: Using play literature to enhance research into touristic learning. Current Issues in Tourism, 1:2, 176–188

[Sca 06] *Scardamalia, Marlene; Bereiter, Carl (2006):* Knowledge building: theory, pedagogy, and technology. In Sawyer, K. (Ed.) Cambridge handbook of the learning sciences, New York: Cambridge University Press, 97–118.

[Sha 07] *Sharples, Mike; Taylor, Josie; Vavoula, Giasemi (2007); A theory of learning for the mobile age. In Andrews, R. & Haythornthwaite, C. (Eds.) The Sage handbook of eLearning research, London:* Sage, 221–247.

[Str 09] *Straub, Evan T (2009):* Understanding technology adoption: Theory and future directions for informal learning. Review of Educational Research, 79(2), 625–649.

[Weg 98] *Wenger, Etienne (1998):* Communities of practice: learning, meaning, and identity, Cambridge: Cambridge University Press.

[Zho 13] *Zhou, Hong (2013):* Understanding Personal Learning Environment: a literature review on elements of the concept. In Society for Information Technology & Teacher Education International Conference, Vol .1, 1161–1164.

CONTACT DETAILS

Ruthi Aladjem
Tel Aviv University
School of Education
Knowledge Technology Lab
E-Mail: *ruthalad@post.tau.ac.il*

Prof. Rafi Nachmias
Tel Aviv University
School of Education
E-Mail: *nachmias@post.tau.ac.il*

An exploratory study of the personal learning environments of security and investigation professionals

Antony E. Ratcliffe

ABSTRACT

This paper describes and discusses how security management and investigation professionals use Personal Learning Environments (PLE) for work-related learning and continuing professional development. It is based on an exploratory study, using a qualitative description approach. An online questionnaire was completed by 67 study participants in 17 countries, followed by Voice over Internet Protocol (VOIP) or telephone interviews with 11 of them. The study found that these professionals participate in online discussion groups and access networks and resources. Their collaborative activities in online spaces are limited for reasons that include security, privacy, authenticity of information, and employer restriction concerns. Many therefore may limit opportunities to learn from their local, national, and international peers within PLEs. This also limits discussions of digital literacy skills that might otherwise be expected. Study participants were limited to those who responded to a request for participation posted in online discussion groups. Further research may identify those who are more actively involved in online collaboration and identify reasons for different levels of participation. Presenting case studies of successful collaborative efforts may encourage others in the occupation, enhance continuing professional development, and contribute to the research literature connecting PLEs with careers. This study contributes to the literature on PLEs and digital literacy relating to adults and work-related learning.

Note: *This article has been published in the Special Edition of the Journal of Literacy and Technology: "Personal Learning Environments: Current Research and Emerging Practice". The link to the JLT Special Issue is: http://www.literacyandtechnology.org/current-issue.html*

Introduction

Many occupations require qualifications or certifications prior to employment. Voluntary, or non-compulsory, certification occurs during the developing career. Employees' educational studies may be formal, but they develop knowledge through informal learning for certification or overall work-related learning. Away from classrooms, their study may be independent – often in solitude – or it may include collaborative learning with others. Modern technologies make collaboration much easier, but employees may be missing opportunities to enhance their collaborative informal learning through using online technologies in occupational settings.

This paper describes and discusses how security management and investigation professionals (security professionals) use Personal Learning Environments (PLEs) for work-related learning and continuing professional development. Security professionals are in management, advisory, consultant, and investigative roles with broad responsibilities for the security and risk management of organisations. They meet face-to-face for collaboration and learning activities, and they earn professional designations, often by self-study or with face-to-face study groups. Some security professionals continue university education, often part-time and at a distance. They also participate in work-related online discussion groups (forums). The aim of this exploratory study was to gain an overview of how and the extent to which security professionals use PLEs and what digital literacy skills they need to do so, in advance of a broader study. The study was global because of the international nature of business and security threats: security professionals from around the world join online groups for informal learning.

Related literature

Personal Learning Environments and Personal Learning Networks

Online or blended (classroom and online) programs, both formal and non-formal, may offer online platforms for resource access and discussions, known as Virtual Learning Environments (VLEs) or Learning Management Systems (LMSs) [Wil 06]. An alternative approach for open and informal learning is the PLE. The PLE may include a structured VLE or LMS, but the PLE extends much further. The PLE may be described as a concept [Att 06], [Att 07], considering “a PLE is comprised of all the different tools we use in our everyday life for learning” [Att 07: 4). [Con 06] studied what higher education learners are using and how. Referencing this study, [Scl 08] stated, “there is strong evidence that students now see the personal computer as their primary learning tool, and this can be regarded as a de facto PLE” (p. 5). In addition to the personal use, institutions may offer PLEs they develop to support formal learning [Sal 11], [Scl 10] and commercialisation occurs with the development for educational institutions and business organisations.

At the end of the 2006 Association of Learning Technologies conference, at Edinburgh, United Kingdom, there was no definitive position on what the PLE was [Att 07]. A review of the literature by Fiedler and Väljataga [Fie 10] revealed that even those espousing the PLE as a concept or approach were still treating it as a technology. More recently, Buchem, Attwell, and Torres analysed in excess of 100 publications through an activity theory lens, identifying that there are “different conceptualisations of PLEs” [Buc 11: 3] and that “the majority of publications come from Higher Education” [Buc 11: 15]. It may be difficult to separate the thinking of the PLE as an approach to learning from the visualisation of how a PLE might look. Either way, a PLE “offers a

portal to the world" [Dow 06] with access to people and resources. Whether the PLE is a theory or concept, or a set of technological tools, there are places where the learners meet. According to Gee [Gee 04], "an affinity space is a place or set of places where people can affiliate with others based primarily on shared activities, interests, and goals, not shared race, class, culture, ethnicity, or gender" (p. 73). Jones and Hafner extended the term to "globalized online affinity spaces, where people can meet, interact, and build relationships and communities" [Jon 12: 115].

When learners come together, in person or online, they may be building a community of practice [Wen 98]. A community of practice forms with three essential elements: domain, community, and practice [Van 08], [Wen 06]. This acknowledges that members are actively practicing in relation to a domain while working together as a community. In contrast, an online discussion group (or meeting in person) may include those who join but do not actively participate. Those on the periphery might not be recognised as active members of a community, but they could be in the early stage of legitimate peripheral participation [Lav 91]. According to Lave and Wenger, legitimate peripheral participation is the process by which a new learner will join a community of practice and develop knowledge toward "full participation in the sociocultural practices of a community" [Lav 91: 29]. However, the mere presence of a discussion group may not meet the criteria to be a community of practice.

The research literature covers the PLE, but there is much less written about an associated term, Personal Learning Network (PLN) [Cou 10]. Couros's research relating to "the networked teacher" as a PLE [Cou 10: 124] led him to state, "My PLN definition is simple: personal learning networks are the sum of all social capital and connections that result in the development and facilitation of a personal learning environment" [Cou 10: 125]. Although the literature is not definitive about the relationship of the PLE to the PLN, the view in this study is that the PLN and personal web tools are components of the PLE, as illustrated by Wheeler [Whe 10]. Further, the current study adopts the view of the PLE as a concept, as previously attributed to [Att 07] above.

PLE and work-based learning

The study developed from an interest in how online communities, networks, and other resources are used to support work-related learning and continuing professional development. It sought to find evidence of PLEs and to identify the digital literacy skills presented in these environments. The learning investigated was informal, considered by Hager and Halliday [Hag 06] as that which is not formal, taking place beyond a formal structure, unintentionally or planned. The learning could also be to supplement that of a formal learning situation offering, "specified curriculum, taught by a designated teacher, with the extent of the learning attained by individual learners being assessed and certified" [Hag 06: 29]. Further, and likely related to workplace training sessions, informal learning could support non-formal learning that is defined as "non-credentialised but still institutionally-based and structured" [Sel 06: 7].

Younger workers are not necessarily more technologically inclined and higher users of a PLE. In one study, [Att 07] found that older workers made greater use of technologies. He speculated that it might be attributed to their responsibility level, access, and flexibility in their work. Attwell identified the potential uses of PLEs for continuing professional development, for sharing knowledge in organisations, and for training and development. He saw an opportunity for the PLE concept to be introduced in schools and used in relation to work and lifelong learning. Recently, researchers considered the competences of university students in two European countries and concluded that "students do not possess all needed technical, functional and social competences for self-organization, self-learning and self-cognition" [Iva 11]. This suggests that current workers and new entrants to the workforce may lack the necessary skills to establish and maintain a PLE. A discussion of digital literacy skills follows.

Adult learners participated in this research study. In andragogical theory, adults are responsible for their own learning [Kno 11]. Researchers such as [Bro 84], [Bro 86] and [Can 91] addressed self-directed learning and the PLE may be suited to support this kind of learning, whether it be informal or formal.

Digital Literacy and PLEs

An extensive review of the research literature on PLEs revealed that "only a few publications discuss what skills, abilities or competencies are necessary for developing and using a PLE [Wil 09], [Buc 11: 14]. Digital literacy skills, or digital literacies, are the skills that may be required by security professionals in an online environment. The research literature contains numerous related terms, sometimes used interchangeably, including digital literacies, digital literacy, and new media literacies [Coi 08]. Digital literacy skills may be considered under several frameworks. Gilster provided an early definition of digital literacy:

> *"the ability to access networked computer resources and use them....the ability to understand and use information in multiple formats from a wide range of sources when it is presented via computers." [Gil 97: 1]*

According to [Gil 97], literacy means much more than just reading, and he identified key competencies for digital literacy: "the ability to make informed judgments about what you find on-line....critical thinking"; the ability to read and move around using hypertext and hyperlinks; and "developing search skills" [Gil 97: 2–3]. Gilster pointed out that the Internet provides new ways of dealing with media [Gil 97: 34].

One digital literacy framework (referred to as media literacy) is that of [Jen 06] with 11 literacies: play, performance, stimulation, appropriation, multitasking, distributed cognition, collective intelligence, judgment, transmedia navigation, networking, and negotiation. These were found to be too detailed for the level of activity identified in this study. Rather, more adaptable to the study, Jones and Hafner discussed practices that can be expected in the digital world: "online gaming, social

networking, peer production and collaboration, and practices involving digital media in the workplace" [Jon 12: 14] . They described literacies as

> *"the ability to creatively engage in particular social practices, to assume appropriate social identities, and to form or maintain various social relationships"[Jon 12: 12]*

[Jon 12] identified that learning occurs within gaming and the associated online affinity spaces. They referred to 3-D virtual worlds, with Second Life as an example. While not a game in the same way as video games, virtual worlds provide opportunities for in occupational learning. Business case studies presented by [Kna 10] included one that may have appeal for security professionals. "Virtual Border Service Officer Training" used Second Life in an educational setting to role-play border crossing interviews with travelers entering Canada [Jon 12: 158–173]. The term 'digital' pertains to the tools being used. Social networking "has given internet users the ability to create the connections between the content based on social relationships" [Jon 12: 144]. [Jon 12] explained that "ordinary users of the internet" are able to make connections between people and the content that has been created online.

Digital Literacy and Security Professionals

As security professionals find or create information of interest, it can easily be shared with others. By its nature, social networking is often open and not anonymous, allowing the participant to be identified and establish credibility. Jones and Hafner [Jon 12] addressed privacy and not maintaining the anonymity that the Internet can otherwise provide. However, as discussed later in this paper, the study reveals that there are individuals who would prefer not to share their views openly. Not sharing may impact the attitude toward, and development of, digital literacy practices.

The skills of collaboration and peer production extend the ability of individuals to co-produce globally with colleagues. Through social networking technologies, the feeling of remoteness can be reduced [Jon 12]. As in more traditional groups, not all will want to participate equally, due to a lack of interest and/or skills. [Jon 12] described benefits and challenges of collaboration and peer production. They defined peer production, or commons-based peer production in full, as "massive numbers of people, who are distributed across the globe and connected to each other by digital networks, work together voluntarily to promote projects that they are interested in" [Jon 12: 158]. An example is Wikipedia.

Digital literacies at work pertain to the digital work environment. The framework by [Jon 12] recognised the information age, the global distribution of work, remote workers, team work models, and the workers who work on contract or encounter frequent job changes. Employers and employees are impacted by the needs and opportunities to adapt that are created.

Research Questions

Security professionals could not be expected to know the term, PLE, found in the research literature. It was anticipated that they could describe how they use online communities, tools, resources, and networks for their work-related learning and continuing professional development. It was also anticipated that digital literacy skills and practices would be identified. Considering the PLE as a concept, the research questions were to determine how PLEs are being established by security professionals who use online technologies in ways that support their learning. This included the tools they use, their networks, how they have developed skills, and whether they are actually taking advantage of opportunities to learn within a PLE.

Personal observations and knowledge of professional development in a few different occupations revealed that professional development programs, particularly through self-study, do not actively support or encourage what would be seen within a PLE. It was also known that security professionals network in person and online, but the extent of the application of online activity to learning was open to exploration. The main research question asked was: How are security management and investigation professionals using personal learning environments (PLEs) and digital literacies for work-related learning and, in particular, for continuing professional development? The sub questions were: (1) What web-based tools and resources are used as part of the PLE of participants? (2) What are the digital literacy skills required to function within a PLE? (3) How have participants developed digital literacy skills? (4) Are participants contributing within a participatory culture and online affinity spaces? (5) How is continuing professional development within work-related learning settings being supported through the use of a PLE?

Methodological Approach

The exploratory study occurred from August 19, 2012, until October 19, 2012, in two phases using an online questionnaire and online interviews. The results were to inform the research methodology, design, and data collection methods for a subsequent larger study.

The design aimed to explore the security management and investigation community, as widely as possible, to identify how security professionals use PLEs and to inform the design of the subsequent study. As a qualitative study, text responses in the questionnaire and semi-structured interview questions sought rich data. It was exploratory, so the qualitative description methodology provided "straight descriptions of phenomena" [San 00: 339].

Requests for participation were posted to 13 online forums (or groups) frequented by security management or investigation professionals globally, 12 on LinkedIn and one on the website of a professional association. LinkedIn is a professional networking, social media site. Members of LinkedIn maintain public profiles and may participate in a wide range of discussion groups. Four of the 13 LinkedIn groups were small and later determined to be inactive.

An online questionnaire invited participants to participate in an interview during either the exploratory study reported here or the later study. Thirty-five participants agreed to be interviewed. Purposive sampling selected questionnaire respondents who indicated they had something to share. Small batches of interview requests followed until 10 had been completed. An eleventh participant with limited access to telephone and online communication responded to questions by E-Mail. A Canadian service hosted the online questionnaire, and a summary of the research project was posted in online discussion groups to solicit participation in this study. An information sheet and an informed consent form preceded the questions. Questions asked, mapped to the research questions, were as follows:

1. What web-based tools and resources are used as part of the Personal Learning Environment of participants?
   - Which devices do you use to access the internet?
   - Are there restrictions on any of the software programs or applications you use for learning purposes that makes them inaccessible in your workplace? Please explain.
   - Beyond software and applications, are there other restrictions on any of the computers or hardware devices you use that prevent you from using them in your workplace for learning purposes? Please explain.
   - How often do you participate in each of these online activities, for personal, professional, or learning related purposes?
   - Please describe any other online activities you do for personal, professional, or learning related purposes and/or provide any comments on the above responses.
   - Which social media profiles do you maintain for personal and/or professional reasons, and what is your frequency of use?
   - Please identify any 'other' from the previous question along with frequency of use.
   - How do you use social media in relation to your continuing professional development?
   - Do you have a network of contacts not at your office with whom you communicate for work-related learning questions or relating to your continuing professional development?
   - Other than face-to-face, how do you connect with your network of contacts when you have questions relating to learning?

2. What are the digital literacy skills required to function within a Personal Learning Environment? and

3. How have participants developed digital literacy skills?
   - How comfortable are you with the following activities? (12 items identified)
   - Please comment on activities that you do not do or with which you have low comfort. It would be helpful to know your reasons.
   - How have you developed your computer skills to their present level?
   - When I encounter a challenge with online technologies, I tend to be one who will...
   - If being introduced to new online technologies or skills to assist my continuing professional development, I would prefer to experience them...

4. Are participants contributing within a participatory culture and online affinity spaces?
   - Are you involved in an online mentoring relationship?
   - What are the online tools and technologies that you use for the mentoring activity?
   - Do you participate in collaborative problem-solving other than working face-to-face?
   - How do you use technology to participate in collaborative problem solving?
   - Can you think of something you have created in an online environment for sharing with others?
   - If you answered 'yes' to the previous question, what did you create?

5. How is continuing professional development within work-related learning settings being supported through the use of a Personal Learning Environment?
   - Can you give an example(s) of how your learning has been assisted through online technology that would not have otherwise been possible or as effective? Please describe.

Online interviews

Personal interviews were conducted using Skype, a Voice Over Internet Protocol (VOIP). Participants chose videoconference, audio, or to receive a call to their telephone. With the participant's consent, each call was recorded by using a Skype add-on tool. A basic thematic analysis aided by a qualitative analysis program followed interview transcription. The following six guiding questions were asked to further investigate the research questions: (1) How would you describe your work-based learning over the past two years? How has it changed from the past? (2) I'm interested in the tools and technologies you use in relation to work-based learning, informal in particular. How have they changed, and how do you see them changing in the future years? (3) How

about your social networks? Can you describe your networks and how they are used for work-based learning? How have they evolved with new technologies? (4) In our digital world, it is easy to create learning resources and share them with others. What stands out that you have seen, whether you used it or not? (5) Again, think of digital resource opportunities, what have you created that has been shared and reused by others? (6) From your perspective, what is really being done well digitally in relation to learning? What remains to be done?

The term 'work-based learning' was used during the interviews. However, 'work-related' has appeared more appropriate. The explanation given to participants at the time of the interview clarified the focus on learning related to work, whether at a work-site or at another location including traveling.

Ethical Considerations

This study was in keeping with the University of Leicester Research Ethics Code of Practice, and the Association of Internet Researchers provides guidance for using online research methods through an E-Mail discussion list and an ethics guide [Ass 12], [Hoo 12]. Study participants gave informed consent after reading an information sheet as the start of the online questionnaire. The survey software, to support anonymity, did not collect the Internet address of the country of questionnaire access. Participants identified themselves at the end of the questionnaire only if they agreed to a personal interview. They could also E-Mail the researcher separately to avoid linking a name to the questionnaire.

Results

The exploratory study confirmed the ability to access participants, there is an interest in the research, and there is more to learn that will inform the security management community and academia. This section presents the data obtained during the questionnaire and interview phases.

Survey results

The questionnaire asked 22 questions to answer the research questions. Access to the online questionnaire occurred 137 times from August 19, 2012, until September 7, 2012 (20 calendar days). As the first step, 103 individuals acknowledged the informed consent, of which 67 (65 %) completed the questionnaire for inclusion in the results. Thirty-five (52 %) of those who completed indicated their willingness to participate in an individual interview during the exploratory study or main study. Questionnaire participants represented 17 countries (Table 1).

Table 1: Country of Residence of Questionnaire Participants

COUNTRY	NUMBER	PERCENTAGE
Canada	24	36
United Kingdom	15	22
United States of America	7	10
Australia	5	7
Bahrain, New Zealand, South Africa (2 from each country)	6	9
Burma, Cambodia, China, France, Hong Kong, India, Lithuania, Mexico, Romania, Russia (1 from each country)	10	15
Note. Rounding error of 1%.	67	99

All but one completing the questionnaire identified their ages (Table 2). Only one indicated being below the age of 35 years. The participants were predominantly male (Table 3).

Table 2: Age Range of Questionnaire Participants

AGE RANGE	NUMBER	PERCENTAGE
25 to 34	1	1
35 to 44	15	22
45 to 54	29	43
55 to 64	18	27
65+	3	4
Not answered	1	1
Note. Rounding error of 2%.	67	98

Table 3: Gender of Questionnaire Participants

GENDER	NUMBER	PERCENTAGE
Male	60	90
Female	6	9
Not answered	1	1

Interview results

Ten individual interviews were conducted from October 1 to 19, 2012, and an eleventh participant answered questions by E-Mail due to limited availability for telephone or online conferencing. Interview participants had identified themselves in the online questionnaire. Communications choices involved connecting on Skype with videoconferencing, connecting with just audio, or receiving a telephone call. Four chose to use videoconferencing, but for one a poor connection resulted in a Skype to telephone call instead. Six others received Skype to telephone calls. All 10 participants provided permission to record the interviews. The 10 interviews ranged in length from 21 to 78 minutes, with participants from Canada (60 %, n=6), the UK (20 %, n=2), South Africa (10 %, n=1), and Lithuania (10 %, n=1). The E-Mail interview involved a USA professional.

Data analysis

In this exploratory study, two major themes emerged: online activities and online challenges. The activities are what security professionals do and how they do it. The challenges encompass what they do not do and why they do not do it. Some coding was required to sort the data, so this was accomplished using NVivo for qualitative data analysis. The coding was kept broad to avoid "premature coding and sorting [which] are serious threats to analysis when researchers abdicate their full responsibility" [Tho 08: 144].

Online activities

Most participants responded to researcher requests in LinkedIn discussion group messages. While 67 % read discussion messages regularly, only 13 % responded to messages regularly. The other choices were 'infrequently,' 'tried it but stopped,' or 'never.' Questionnaire participants responded about their involvement with specific online activities. The percentage represents those who do the activity regularly: starting discussion topics by linking to an article, story, etc. (15 %), writing blog posts (7 %), posting updates on Twitter, Facebook, or other social media (29 %), gaming such as World of Warcraft (3 %), activities in a virtual world, such as Second Life (1 %). Participants completing the questionnaire identified other online activities with which they are involved: E-Mail, work related research, course work including research, online study portals, podcasts, course discussion boards, online training programs for software and products, Skype for overseas contacts, webinars, webcasts, and podcasts, virtual conferences, YouTube for research including conferences and speakers, educational programming from Khan Academy and iTunesU, news from local, national, and international sources, reading, restricted professional discussion groups or sites, Internet communities, including Reddit.com, language learning, completing professional certifications, mentoring, solving client problems beyond own experience, sharing organisation knowledge with the public, maintaining currency in relation to industry trends, relationships with learners when teaching within online course platform, finding hard copy text books to order, preferring over e-books.

Interview participants added the following online activities: presentations from BrightTALK and TED Talks, global communication, making learning continuous, even after the course ends, accessing the opinions of many people, from different sides of an issue, course learning from anywhere, E-Mail distribution lists, as frequent as several times daily, using videos from YouTube when teaching a subject area in which instructor does not have expertise, text alerts of major happenings before the news. The questionnaire and interviews explored what participants had created and shared. Responses included preparing materials for courses and workshops and sharing them online. Participants mentioned developing websites (for internal use by their organisation and for public consumption), databases, and a Wiki (an online document that can be edited by others). Some wrote papers, articles, and blog posts.

Participation on LinkedIn was the most prominent online activity to consume information and connect with industry colleagues. E-Mail (97 %) and telephone (81 %) are the most prominent methods of contact with colleagues and others. The preference for E-Mail allows messages to be selectively and easily sent to a large number. Privacy of the communication was a concern. Sending by E-Mail avoids others knowing about the nature of the enquiry when not appropriate, rather than asking within discussions groups. One security manager commented on networks for learning:

> *"Professional network sites like LinkedIn provide great opportunities for learning whether through posting links to articles, requesting assistance with research, or generating discussions. It makes it much easier to get a variety of perspectives and find out the differences and similarities in performing security work in different industries as well as different countries. Technology has evolved to the point where we can carry on real-time conversations with professionals in other time zones and can get immediate assistance as situations unfold instead of having to wait for "normal business hours" and adjust for time differences. Security never operates solely on normal business hours." Security manager, USA*

Online challenges

The second theme was the challenges of online activities. This section covers security professionals' decisions to avoid or minimise activities. It also includes restrictions placed upon security professionals in the workplace. A small number saw no need for online activities. Their comments included satisfaction with current methods, no need for online activities to develop a network, and no need for immediate information feeds. Online activities were a waste of time for some due to being of limited value and

because of the amount of 'noise' created. One participant made the following comment and highlighted the fear of employer criticism:

> *"I find that the forums are generally limited to people who are out of work and consultants who only speak for themselves, and people from large organizations don't necessarily participate because they don't feel that they are only speaking for themself, they don't want to be accountable for the things they are saying in those forums. But other than that, I really enjoy them, and for that reason I don't participate. I don't need my human resource department calling me about something I put online." Security manager, Canada*

Having limited time was a reason for reduced online activities. One participant stated that it was important for something to catch his attention and motivate immediate action. Another was attracted to activities that involved connecting with someone in a "leadership role." One participant expressed a lack of knowledge of what is available online, being only aware of webinars. Other comments included: "'entertainment' social media...a waste of time"; "I don't tweet, I think it's idiotic frankly"; "I dislike social media", "I think blogs are a waste of time: reading about some idiot and what he had for breakfast: nobody cares"; "I don't care about somebody's personal opinion on something. Like to me it ranks up there with blogging as a complete waste of time"; "Pre-recorded content webinars, I think are disastrous."

One participant observed: "Formal society groupings (corporations, governments, universities) have not fully grasped the big change in distributive, collaborative learning and how that will affect people in everyday real world." Another participant mentioned that social media are banned at work for productivity-related reasons. Another participant said that excessive personal use would result in a discussion with the employee about the use. Employer or other workplace restrictions were numerous. They included the following: rules against non-business use, prohibitions against downloads or the use of external and devices, emergency only use of the internet on mobile devices, restrictions to some websites and applications, special permissions required, personal devices not allowed, firewalls, outdated technologies, and compatibility issues not allowing access, equipment such as a webcam not provided.

Some participant and employer concerns related to security and sensitive activities. Concern about computer hacking and espionage encouraged the use of internal resources and prohibited USB devices in one company. Another participant spoke of vulnerability if able to access computers and turn on the camera remotely. There is concern about data remaining in existence and who might have unintended access to it. Identity theft is feared. Authenticity is also a concern. Before relying on information found on the Internet, participants wanted to validate the source. This was not always easy to do. A concern related to someone publishing online using the identity of another. One participant suggested that a reputable organisation should verify the credibility of what might be course offerings. Another participant was confident with his personal ability to identify suspicious material but added he could not be certain. These challenges appear to be beyond those strictly related to learning, but they may impact opportunities to access online communities, resources, and networks.

Discussion

The main research question asked, “How are security management and investigation professionals using PLEs and digital literacies for work-related learning and, in particular, for continuing professional development?” This question presumed that research study participants used PLEs and would demonstrate digital literacy skills, particularly since they were primarily recruited online. The research study questionnaire and individual interviews revealed a limited range of online learning activities, but the data provided a start at understanding why such activities might be limited or focused in online discussion groups.

Sub question 1 asked, “What web-based tools and resources are used as part of the PLE of participants?” There were no surprises; they use computers and mobile devices for Internet access, E-Mail, and telephone calls. Sub question 2 was, “What are the digital literacy skills required to function within a PLE?” The research literature answers this and provides skill frameworks. The study yielded limited finding of such skills, as participant activities were often limited to reading rather than identifying examples of activities such as peer production, collaboration, and gaming.

Sub question 3 enquired, “How have participants developed digital literacy skills?” They identified that they developed their skills attending courses, getting help from friends, family, and work colleagues, searching the World Wide Web, reading, exploring, and experimenting. There appears to be no lack of ability with the presence of willingness and support. Confidence was present: participants felt able to learn whatever was required in the ability to learn whatever is required for operating proprietary systems and following protocols. There was very little interest in gaming and virtual worlds, though one participant raised them as essential for teaching certain skills.

Sub question 4 was, “Are participants contributing within a participatory culture and online affinity spaces?” They appear to be online, but for many the level of activity is low. While SMIPs read and respond to discussion messages, and they might start discussions, many contribute infrequently. They are more likely to be consumers of information rather than producers or co-producers. Two participants expressed a preference for seeing the work of organisations and ‘thought leaders’ with noted expertise.

Sub question 5 asked, “How is continuing professional development within work-related learning settings being supported through the use of a PLE?” Discussion groups and various online resources were sought when information needs arose. Some SMIPs did contribute resources for others, but a primary activity was consuming the available

information. This suggests a different approach may be needed in the main study to identify possible examples of those creating and sharing content.

Prominent themes were security, privacy, and authenticity concerns in addition to not seeing a need for online activities, having a lack of interest, and having no time. These concerns are personal for many, but employers often have equipment, software, and access restrictions. Security threats are an ongoing concern. [Dal 13] explained that the very act of sharing socially is what can expose an individual to threat, such as providing personal information that could be used to create a security breach. These threats can indirectly result in a minimised use of online resources if the general use of computers and other devices is curtailed.

Despite the factors described that limited the activities, 67 participants provided data relating to their online activities. Online communities, tools, networks, and other resources are used for purposes of work-related learning and continuing professional development. A high use of the telephone and E-Mail may represent collaboration occurring in non-public spaces with 2 or more participants; however, the reported use of discussion groups demonstrates a lot of reading of the news and information posted by others.

Conclusion

This was an exploratory study of how security professionals are using their PLEs and digital literacy skills for work-related learning and continuing professional development. It was global and involved a total of 67 study participants from 17 countries. All completed an online questionnaire, and 10 participated in individual interviews, online or by telephone. An eleventh study participant provided input by E-Mail. In the questionnaire, study participants provided information that included devices they use, their technological skills, online activities, networks, collaboration, and learning. Those interviewed were asked more about their learning, tools and technologies, social networks, learning resources, and digital literacy practices. The participants, as security professionals, clearly accessed discussion groups and other resources for information to keep up in the industry or to answer questions that arise. Some create information for others, including linking to news stories and the blog post of themselves and others. Collaboration also takes place in private settings with the more traditional technologies of telephone and E-Mail. Some participants expressed their reluctance and caution when sharing in online spaces. More study participants could be seen to be consumers and users of information rather than creators. The data did not provide a lot of examples of security professionals contributing within the participatory environment. This might be attributed to many security professionals being in the early stage of legitimate peripheral participation, which may lead to greater participation as knowledge and comfort increases. At that time, examples of digital literacy practices may be more evident. This may provide examples to encourage other professionals to participate in the sharing of their knowledge while learning from others.

Future research

A subsequent and larger study (in progress) commenced with observations in online communities, followed by interviews with security professionals to more closely examine how online communities are used for work-related learning and professional development. Security professionals often work within environments with practices influenced by global events. The need to share and collaborate for work-related learning and continuing professional development is not expected to lessen. Observations, discussion, and interpretation may lead to a better understanding of their online communities and uses of networks and resources in the security management and investigation fields. There is much to be understood in this area of research, particularly beyond higher education settings and related to the workplace.

Acknowledgement

The assistance of Professor David Hawkridge, visiting Professor at the Institute of Learning Innovation, is appreciated for his editorial review and valued guidance.

REFERENCES

[Ass 12] *Association of Internet Researchers (2012):* Ethics guide. Retrieved January 7, 2013, from *http://aoir.org/documents/ethics-guide/*

[Att 06] *Attwell, Graham (2006, June 1):* Personal learning environments [Weblog]. Retrieved from *http://web.archive.org/web/20090114031041/http://www.knownet.com/writing/weblogs/Graham_Attwell/entries/6521819364*

[Att 07] *Attwell, Graham (2007):* Personal learning environments: The future of eLearning? learningpapers. Retrieved from *http://www.elearningeuropa.info/*

[Bro 84] *Brookfield, Stephen (1984):* Self-directed adult learning: A critical paradigm. Adult Education Quarterly, 35(2), 59–71.

[Bro 86] *Brookfield, Stephen (1986):* Understanding and facilitating adult learning. San Francisco. Jossey-Bass.

[Buc 11] *Buchem, Ilona; Attwell, Graham; Torres, Ricardo (2011):* Understanding personal learning environments: Literature review and synthesis through the activity theory lens. Paper presented at the PLE Conference 2011, Southampton. Retrieved from *http://journal.webscience.org/658/*

[Can 91] *Candy, Phillip (1991):* Self-direction for lifelong learning: A comprehensive guide to theory and practice. San Francisco. Jossey-Bass.

[Coi 08] *Coiro, Julie; Knobel, Michelle; Lankshear, Colin; Leu, Donald (2008):* Central issues in new literacies and new literacies research. In: Julie Coiro; Michelle Knobel; Colin Lankshear; Donald Leu (Eds.), Handbook of research on new literacies (pp. 1–21). New York. Routledge.

[Con 06] *Conole, Gráinne; de Laat, Maarten; Dillon, Teresa; Darby, Jonathan (2006):* Student experiences of technologies: Final report, JISC. 1–104. Retrieved from *http://www.jisc.ac.uk/publications/*

[Cou 10] *Couros, Alec. (2010):* Developing personal learning networks for open and social learning. In: George Veletsianos (Ed.), Emerging technologies in distance education. In: Terry Anderson (Series Ed.) Issues in Distance Education (pp. 109–128). Edmonton. AU Press. Retrieved from *http://www.aupress.ca/*

[Dal 13] *Daly, Jimmy (2013, June 14):* Mobile, cloud and social media are highly susceptible to hackers, edtechmagazine.com. Retrieved from *http://www.edtechmagazine.com/higher/article/2013/06/why-higher-education-target-hackers-phishers-and-spammers*

[Dow 06] *Downes, Stephen (2006):* Learning networks and connective knowledge. Retrieved October 22, 2011, from *http://www.downes.ca/post/36031*

[Fie 10] *Fiedler, Sebastian; Väljataga, Terje. (2010):* Personal learning environments: Concept or technology? Paper presented at the PLE Conference 2010, Barcelona. Retrieved from *http://pleconference.citilab.eu/*

[Gee 04] *Gee, James Paul (2004):* Situated language and learning: A critique of traditional schooling. New York. Routledge.

[Gil 97] *Gilster, Paul (1997):* Digital literacy. New York. Wiley Computers.

[Hag 06] *Hager, Paul; Halliday, John (2006):* Recovering informal learning: Wisdom, judgement and comunity. Dordrecht. Springer.

[Hoo 12] *Hooley, Tristam; Marriott, John; Wellens, Jane (2012):* What is online research? London. Bloomsbury.

[Iva 11] *Ivanova, Malinka; Chatti, Mohamed Amine (2011):* Competences mapping for personal learning environment management. Paper presented at the The PLE Conference 2011, Southampton. Retrieved from *http://journal.webscience.org/569/*

[Jon 12] *Jones, Rodney; Hafner, Christoph (2012):* Understanding digital literacies: A practical introduction. London. Routledge.

[Jen 06] *Jenkins, Henry; Clinton, Katie; Purushotma, Ravi; Robison, Alice; Weigel, Margaret (2006):* Confronting the challenges of participatory culture: Media education for the 21st century. Retrieved from *http://www.macfound.org/press/publications/white-paper-confronting-the-challenges-of-participatory-culture-media-education-for-the-21st-century-by-henry-jenkins/*

[Kna 10] *Knapp, Karl; O'Driscoll, Tony; (2010):* Learning in 3D. San Francisco. Pfeiffer.

[Kno 11] *Knowles, Malcolm; Holton III, Elwood; Swanson, Richard (2011):* The adult learner: The definitive classic in adult education and human resource development (7th ed.). Oxford. Butterworth-Heinemann.

[Lav 91] *Lave, Jean; Wenger, Etienne (1991):* Situated learning: Legitimate peripheral participation. New York. Cambridge University Press.

[Liv 08] *Livingstone, Sonia; Van Couvering, Elizabeth; Thumin, Nancy (2008):* Converging traditions of research on media and information literacies: Disciplinary, critical, and methodological issues. In: Julie Coiro; Michelle Knobel; Colin Lankshear; Donald Leu (Eds.), Handbook of research on new literacies (pp. 103–132). New York. Routledge.

[Sal 11] *Salinas, Jesús; Marín, Victoria; Escandell, Catalina (2011):* A case of an institutional PLE: Integrating VLEs and e-portfolios for students. Paper presented at the The PLE Conference 2011, Southampton. Retrieved from *http://journal.webscience.org/585/*

[San 00] *Sandelowski, Margarete (2000):* Whatever happened to qualitative description? In: Research in Nursing and Health, 23(4), 334–340. Retrieved from *http://www.wou.edu/~mcgladm/Quantitative%20Methods/optional%20stuff/qualitative%20description.pdf*

[Scl 08] *Sclater, Niall (2008):* Web 2.0, personal learning environments, and the future of learning management systems. Research Bulletin. Retrieved from *http://pages.uoregon.edu/not/LMS/future of LMSs.pdf*

[Scl 09] *Sclater, Niall (2010):* eLearning in the Cloud. International Journal of Virtual and Personal Learning Environments, 1(1), 10–19. doi: 10.4018/jvple.2010091702

[Sel 06] *Selwyn, Neil; Gorard, Stephen; Furlong, John (2006):* Adult learning in the digital age: Information technology and the learning society. London. Routledge.

[Tho 08] *Thorne, Sally (2008):* Interpretive description. Walnut Creek. Left Coast Press.

[Van 08] *van Harmelen, Mark (2008):* Design trajectories: Four experiments in PLE implementation. Interactive Learning Environments. Retrieved from *http://elgg.jiscemerge.org.uk*

[Wen 98] *Wenger, Etienne (1998):* Communities of practice: Learning, meaning, and identity. New York. Cambridge University Press.

[Wen 06] *Wenger, Etienne (2006):* Communities of practice: A brief introduction. Retrieved from *http://wenger-trayner.com/Intro-to-CoPs/*

[Whe 10] *Wheeler, Steve (2010, July 11):* Anatomy of a PLE [Web log message]. Retrieved from *http://steve-wheeler.blogspot.ca/2010/07/anatomy-of-ple.html*

[Wil 06] *Wilson, Scott; Liber, Oleg; Johnson, Mark; Beauvoir, Phil; Sharples, Paul; Milligan, Colin (2006):* Personal learning environments: Challenging the dominant design of educational systems. Retrieved from *http://hdl.handle.net/1820/727*

CONTACT DETAILS

Antony E. (Tony) Ratcliffe, M.Ed.
Institute of Learning Innovation
University of Leicester 106, New Walk
Leicester LE1 7EA, United Kingdom
Phone: +1 780 910 4354 Canada
E-Mail: *tony@ratcliffe.ca*

Connected older adults: conceptualising their digital participation

Linda De George-Walker, Mark A. Tyler

ABSTRACT

Older adults' experience of the digital divide is apparent and under explored. This paper presents a model for conceptualising older adults' digital participation by positioning self-efficacy theory, digital competence and personal learning environments together. We illuminate a pathway toward developing affordances in digital self-efficacy and digital participation for older adults.

Note: This article has been published in the Special Edition of the Journal of Literacy and Technology: „Personal Learning Environments: Current Research and Emerging Practice". The link to the JLT Special Issue is: http://www.literacyandtechnology.org/uploads/1/3/6/8/136889/jlt_special.pdf

Introduction

As folk move toward their latter years, they may experience acute complications in the process of ageing well: existing with a reduced income, health issues, and social dislocation due to no longer holding economic and socially valued roles. There has been some evidence to suggest that digital technologies have the potential to improve opportunities for older adults to socialise, access services and learning, and in turn improve their quality of life and enhance social capital; moreover some of the fastest growth in uptake of technology is occurring in older adult cohorts [Cot 12], [War 13]. Yet, these benefits may be accruing for relatively few older adults as the digital divide fails to narrow to any significant degree with older adults continuing to experience lower levels of digital technology use compared to younger people, and with apparent group differences in technology use within older adulthood [War 13], [Whi 12]. If, however, we wish to capitalise on the potential for older adults in an ageing population to "contribute to the re-forming of society" [Mar 09: 3] and for digital technologies to improve the health and wellbeing of individuals and communities, it is imperative that we seek to more fully understand what influences older adults' digital participation, including issues associated with the heterogeneity of older adulthood and technology access, but also choice and motivation.

With this in mind, our challenge in this paper is to map a model that signposts a path towards examination of ageing adults as they navigate the digital era (Figure 1).

Our conceptualisation has its basis in Bandura's (1997) self-efficacy theory, a motivational construct in the social cognitive tradition. Over the past decade, self-efficacy has appeared as a variable of interest alongside others for explaining older adults' digital technology use, but to the best of the authors' knowledge no self-efficacy framework integrating Personal Learning Environments (PLEs) and digital competence has been adopted to explain older adults' digital participation. In the paper, we first present an overview of self-efficacy theory and its association with older adults' digital participation. We then chart a path towards exploring how digital competences and PLEs might afford digital self-efficacy and digital participation and promote social connectedness, identity enhancement and the wellbeing of older adults.

Figure 1: Conceptualising older adults' digital participation

Self-efficacy theory and older adults digital participation

Self-efficacy can be defined as "beliefs in one's capabilities to organize and execute the courses of action required to produce given attainments" [Ban 97: 3]. Self-efficacy is a belief about capability rather than actual skills, and while both are required for effective functioning, Bandura asserts that self-beliefs are the critical factor for personal

agency, the exercise of self-control, and achievement [Ban 97]. Certainly, confidence that one can achieve beyond their capability is not likely to make it so, but if individuals do not believe they have personal capability, they will not attempt to do so irrespective of whether they have the skills. This may well be the case with some older adults as they confront the digital world with studies showing that those older adults with higher technology self-efficacy are more likely to be internet users, engage with Facebook, and adopt computer technology compared to those who feel less confident [Bel 13], [Cza 06], [Eas 00]. The implication is that seeking to develop older adults' technology-related confidence may prove valuable for cultivating older adults' digital participation.

Self-efficacy theory also specifies four antecedents or sources that influence self-efficacy judgments: enactive mastery experiences (previous accomplishments); vicarious experiences (observed or modelled experiences); verbal persuasion (verbal or social feedback associated with experience); and physiological and emotional states associated with experience. The self-efficacy judgments arising from these four sources affect goals, persistence, and motivation, which in turn affect behaviour and performance. Self-efficacy is cyclical, incorporating a feedback loop whereby performance and its consequences become new sources of efficacy information. That is, self- efficacy is both a product and a constructor of experiences. According to self-efficacy theory then, older adults' digital participation may be enhanced by seeking to improve their self-efficacy through the mechanisms associated with the sources of efficacy information. Practically this might be achieved by conceptualising digital technology training and support according to the sources of efficacy information, and although there are studies that have explored the impacts of training and support on older adult's digital participation [Rus 11] the authors know of no studies to date that have used the sources of efficacy information to guide the design, implementation or evaluation of technology-related learning and support experiences for older adults.

Additional to the sources of efficacy, comparison of one's personal competence in relation to the task and the nature of the setting also contribute to self-efficacy judgments. Personal competence can be considered as current functioning, which along with analysis of the current context, contributes to self-efficacy judgments that are a prediction of future capability. In the next section we argue that in our integrated self-efficacy model of older adults' digital participation the concept of personal competence is appropriately conceptualised as digital competences, and that PLEs offer a comprehensive approach to the analysis of contextual aspects that might influence older adults' digital self-efficacy judgments.

Integrating digital competences, personal learning environments, and self-efficacy theory

Older adults are reported as having the lowest levels of digital competence of all consumers, this being cited as a key factor for older adults' low digital participation [War 13]. What is digital competence? A simple search on the Internet and within the academic literature reveals an array of definitions and variations in the use of the term digital competences such as: technological literacy, e-literacy, internet literacy, and digital literacy; and it is often associated with other concepts such as information literacy, media literacy, visual literacy and communication literacy, all of which offer a particular nuanced perspective. Current major projects and models reported in the literature nevertheless tend to be framed in terms of either digital competences or digital literacies. Reviews of current definitions of these terms, two of which are offered below, indicate the concepts of digital competences and digital literacies may be similar in their intention and application:

> *[Digital competence] consists in being able to explore and face new technological situations in a flexible way, to analyze, select and critically evaluate data and information, to exploit technological potentials in order to represent and solve problems and build shared and collaborative knowledge, while fostering awareness of one's own personal responsibilities and the respect of reciprocal rights/obligations [Cal 08: 186].*

> *[Digital literacy is] the awareness, attitude and ability of individuals to appropriately use digital tools and facilities to identify, access, manage, integrate, evaluate, analyse and synthesize digital resources, construct new knowledge, create media expressions, and communicate with others, in the context of specific life situations, in order to enable constructive social action; and to reflect upon this process [Mar 05: 135].*

A review of various frameworks and models of digital competences and digital literacy also initially suggest they are interchangeable terms. For example, some models of digital literacy emphasise the notion of multiple digital literacies and refer to a range of technical, cognitive, motor, and socioemotional skill sets required for navigating the digital world. The model of [Esh 12], for example, refers to six digital literacies: photo-visual (understanding and communicating graphically), reproduction (manipulating digital material to create new and meaningful materials), branching literacy (constructing knowledge from non-linear navigation of hypermedia environments), information literacy (critical consumption of digital information), social-emotional literacy (communicating effectively in online contexts), and real-time thinking (processing and evaluating large volumes of digital information simultaneously). Similarly, several models of digital competence also reflect the multi-faceted skills needed to engage with the digital world. For example, the European Digital Competence (DIGCOMP) project has identified knowledge, skills and attitude (KAS) competences as necessary to engage with the digital world: information management (identify, locate, access, retrieve, store and organise information), collaboration (link with others, participate in online

networks and communities, interact constructively), communication and sharing (communicate through online tools, taking into account privacy, safety and netiquette), creation of content and knowledge (integrate and re-elaborate previous knowledge and content, construct new knowledge), ethics and responsibility (behave in an ethical and responsible way, aware of legal frames), evaluating and problem solving (identify digital needs, solve problems through digital means, assess the information retrieved, and technical operations (use technology and media, perform tasks and through digital tools) [Fer 12]. This model notes that these KAS competences may develop according to levels depending on age, depth of application, or cognitive complexity.

[Mar 09], however, offers a different take on conceptualising digital literacy, modelling it as three levels of engagement with the digital. The first level, digital competence, is according to Martin a precursor of digital literacy, and is the skill and differentiation of skill levels necessary for digital engagement. Similar to the notion of multiple digital competences presented above, Martin suggests that digital competence presents as levels of expertise to be mastered, from the basic to the complex, and includes such activities as finding and retrieving information on the web, using task specific software, generating content for web presentation and the like. At level two, digital usage emphasises the connect between a user (individual, group, or community) and the life situation to which the digital competence is being deployed. Successful doing can result when the user's digital expertise shapes a unique response to a task or problem [Mar 09]. In Martin's model, digital transformation is the third and final level of digital literacy. This stage is reached when innovation and creativity are used to stimulate change in personal and social circumstances and contexts. Digital usages offer the catalyst and conduit for these changes. When applied to older adults this may mean enabling and maintaining social networks by remaining connected through email, chat room and various instant-messaging opportunities; or challenging the societal perceptions about older adult consumers as they launch themselves into the convenience of online purchasing, participate in online social commentary through social networking sites, or engage in digitally mediated forms of learning. We argue that these transformational consequences of digital usages that shape identities and facilitate social inclusion are the critical aspects that may promote the observed improvements in older adults' health and wellbeing as a result of digital participation.

What is clear from this review of various definitions, models and frameworks is that digital literacy is more than being technologically savvy; the digitally literate have necessary knowledge, skills and attitudes in information management and communication, as well as being good technical operators. Further, these knowledges, skills and attitudes, although described as digital literacy in some models, may be more appropriately considered as digital competences, themselves only one component of what it means to be digitally literate. We argue that digital competence as a set of knowledge, skills and attitudes, and a sub-component of digital literacy, aligns best with the concept of personal competence in self-efficacy theory and is therefore an antecedent of digital self-efficacy. An increase in digital competence to varying degrees and with consideration of individual capability, circumstance and purpose will feed the self-efficacious position that feeds back into widening and deepening digital participation, a process that offers a cycle of contribution and development particularly into and through [Mar 09] usage and transformation levels of digital literacy. As degrees of self-efficacy increase, an increased motivation is experienced that prompts wider and deeper digital participation; and this in turn leads to the creative, innovative, and transformative activities that may promote older adults health and wellbeing.

As indicated in the definitions of digital literacy and competence provided above, and as detailed in Martin's model, digital participation is contextualised by the nature of the task to be achieved and the characteristics of the environment. Contextual influences are also crucial for self-efficacy judgments. It is here that we argue PLEs offer an opportunity to more fully conceptualise these individual and social aspects of context as they apply to digital self-efficacy and digital participation for older adults. PLEs are fluid and relational learning contexts in which individuals are both autonomous and interconnected; they appropriate available external (digital and non-digital) and internal tools, methods and resources within communities to problem solve, learn and develop [Buc 11]. While we could not locate studies looking specifically at PLEs and older adults' digital competence, digital participation, or digital self-efficacy, the literature demonstrates the importance of the personal and social context for older adults' digital participation. For example, there is evidence that approaches that are agentic and capitalise on the existing interests and needs of older adults can motivate digital technology use; and that staying connected with family and friends, the accessibility of aged based interest groups or intentional communities, the availability of support for technology assistance, less formal instructional settings, can influence older adults technology use [Bel 13], [Ree 11], [Kea 02], [Sel 03].

[Iva 11: 2] state that "a PLE can be viewed as a supporting tool for the enhancement of the learner's performance in his or her activities management as well as for the acquisition of knowledge, skills and expertise. Similarly, we model PLEs as personal and social affordances (including, but limited to the notion of "tools") that along with the sources of efficacy and digital competences can facilitate digital participation through building self-efficacy (Figure 1). Future research will be needed to clarify the key features of older adults PLEs related to their digital participation, and the specific relationships among older adults' PLEs and the other variables in our model.

Conclusion

Achieving positive experiences of the digital by older adults appears as a reasonable goal that accords well with the mentioned notions of social contribution and wellbeing. Digital engagement by older adults needs to be purposive and agentic, and we argue

that a means of achieving this is by the building of efficacious responses to particular experiences and contexts that afford learning. Further researching what these actually are, that is, which are most influential and which might best be leveraged to increase older adults' technology self-efficacy, appear as our next step toward deepening an understanding of older adults' digital terrain.

REFERENCES

[Ban 97] *Bandura, Albert (1997):* Self-efficacy: The exercise of control. New York. Freeman.

[Bel 13] *Bell, Caroline; Fausset, Cara; Farmer, Sarah, Nguyen, Julie; Harley, Linda; Fain, W. Bradley (2013):* Examining social media use among older adults. Paper presented at the ACM Conference on Hypertext and Social Media, Paris, France. Retrieved April 2013 from *http://dl.acm.org/citation.cfm?id=2481509*

[Buc 11] *Buchem, Ilona; Attwell, Graham; Torres, Ricardo (2011):* Understanding Personal Learning Environments: Literature review and synthesis through the Activity Theory lens, 1–33. In: Proceedings of PLE Conference, 10-12 July 2011, Southampton, UK. Retrieved March 2013 from *http://journal.webscience.org/658/*

[Cal 08] *Calvani, Antonio; Cartelli, Antonio; Fini, Antonio; Ranieri, Maria (2008):* Models and instruments for assessing digital competence at school. In: Journal of e-Learning and Knowledge Society, 4(3), 183–193.

[Cot 12] *Cotten, S. R., Ford, G., Ford, S., & Hale, T. M. (2012):* Internet use and depression among older adults. In: Computers in Human Behavior, 28(2), 496–499.

[Cza 06] *Czaja, Sara J.; Charness, Neil; Fisk, Arthur D.; Hertzog, Chistopher; Nair, Sankaran N., Rogers, Wendy A.; Sharit, Joseph (2006):* Factors predicting the use of technology: Findings from the Centre for Research and Education on Aging and Technology Enhancement (CREATE). In: Psychological Aging, 21(3), 333–352.

[Eas 00] *Eastin, Matthiew; LaRose, Robert (2000):* Internet self-efficacy and the psychology of the digital divide. In: Journal of Computer Mediated Communication, 6(1). doi:10.1111/j.1083-6101.2000.tb00110.x.

[Esh 12] *Eshet, Yoram (2012):* Thinking in the digital era: A revised model for digital literacy. In: Issues in Informing Science and Information Technology, 9, 267–276.

[Fer 12] *Ferrari, Anusca (2012):* Digital competence in practice: An analysis of frameworks. In: European Commission Joint Research Centre Technical Report. Luxembourg: Publications Office of the European Union. Retrieved April 2013 from *http://ftp.jrc.es/EURdoc/JRC68116.pdf*

[Gap 07] *Gapski, Harald (2007):* Some reflections on digital literacy. In: Vana Kamtsiou; Lampros Stergioulas; Frans Van Assche (Eds.), Proceedings of the 3rd International Workshop on Digital Literacy, Greece, September 17, 2007 (p.p. 49-55). The Netherlands, CEUR-WS. Retrieved April 2013 from *http://ftp.informatik.rwth-aachen.de/Publications/CEUR-WS/Vol-310/paper05.pdf*

[Iva 11] *Ivanova. Malinka; Chatti, Mohamed Ali (2011):* Competences mapping for Personal Learning Environment management. 1–13. In: Proceedings of PLE Conference, 10–12 July 2011, Southampton, UK. Retrieved March 2013 from *http://journal.webscience.org/569/*

[Kea 02] *Kearns, I., Tyrrell, J., & Bend, J. (2002):* Access, training and content: How to engage older people with ICTs. In: A report for Help the Aged. London. IPPR Trading.

[Mar 05] *Martin, Allan (2005):* DigEuLit–A European framework for digital literacy: A progress report. In: Journal of eLiteracy, 2(2), 130–136.

[Mar 09] *Martin, Allan (2009):* Digital literacy for the Third Age: Sustaining identity in an uncertain world. In: eLearning Papers, 12, 1–15. Retrieved April 2013 from *http://www.elearningeuropa.info/files/media/media18500.pdf.*

[Ree 11] *Rees Jones, Ian; Gilleard, Chris; Higgs, Paul; Day, Graham (2011):* Connectivity, place and elective belonging: Community and later life. Retrieved April 2013 from *http://www.ahrc.ac.uk/Funding-Opportunities/Research-funding/Connected-Communities/Scoping-studies-and-reviews/Pages/Scoping-studies-and-reviews.aspx*

[Rus 11] *Russell, Helen (2011):* Later life ICT learners ageing well. In: International Journal of Ageing and Later Life, 6(2), 103–127.

[Sel 03] *Selwyn, Neil; Gorard, Stephen; Furlong, John; Madden, Louise (2003):* Older adults' use of information and communications technology in everyday life. In: Ageing and Society, 23, 561–582.

[War 13] *Warburton, Jeni; Cowan, Sue; Bathgate, T. (2013):* Building social capital among rural, older Australians through information and communication technologies: A review article. In: Australasian Journal on Ageing, 32(1), 8–14.

[Whi 12] *White, Patrick; Selwyn, Neil (2012):* Learning online? Educational internet use and participation in adult learning, 2002 to 2010. In: Educational Review, 64(4). 451–469.

FIGURES

CONTACT DETAILS

Dr Linda De George-Walker
School of Human, Health and Social Sciences
CQUniversity, Bundaberg
Building 8, University Drive,
Branyan Qld 4670, Australia
Phone: +61 (07) 41507054
E-Mail: *l.degeorge-walker@cqu.edu.au*

Dr Mark Tyler
Adult and Vocational Education
School of Education and Professional Studies
Griffith University
Mt Gravatt Campus 176 Messines Ridge Rd
Mt Gravatt Qld 4122, Australia
Phone: +61 (07) 37356830
E-Mail: *m.tyler@griffith.edu.au*

Innovation, knowledge and sustainability with PLEs: an empirical analysis from SAPO Campus Schools pilots

Fátima Pais, Carlos Santos, Luís Pedro

ABSTRACT

Based on an empirical study of use cases of the SAPO Campus Schools (SCS) platform, this paper analyses preliminary data gathered from a group of pilot schools that have institutionally adopted SCS. Building on the concept of BA [Non 95] and in the assumption that SCS can become a school's BA, our main goal is to understand if and how these dimensions intersect in the use cases studied.

Note: *This article has been published in the Special Edition of the Journal of Literacy and Technology: "Personal Learning Environments: Current Research and Emerging Practice". The link to the JLT Special Issue is: http://www.literacyandtechnology.org/uploads/1/3/6/8/136889/jlt_special.pdf*

Introduction

Sapo Campus Schools (SCS), a project developed by the University of Aveiro (UA), SAPO and TMN within the SAPO Lab at the UA Research and Development facility, is a Web 2.0 platform specifically designed for schools (K1 through K12) that results from the reinvention of another, similar platform designed for Higher Education [San 09].

In September 2012, a group of pilot schools was chosen to sign a protocol making a commitment to promote the formal and institutional adoption and use of SCS. The signing of this protocol assured the participation of the different schools in this research project, making it easier to get feedback from users in a real setting. This feedback also allows the developer team to uncover flaws in the system and to get real and almost live input on how to improve the services provided.

On the other hand, these schools were also faced with the challenge of opening themselves, by promoting and encouraging openness, collaboration, production and content sharing. Because SCS makes it possible to create and manage personal learning spaces, from an individual perspective (teacher/student/other users), it was also important to discuss the concept of Personal Learning Environments (PLE) within each institution.

This process can become a catalyst for disruptive innovation [Chr 08] and the creation of spaces where new knowledge can emerge – BA [Non 95]. In the following section we will revisit these concepts, making way for the analysis of specific use cases that are currently under way in SCS. After that, we will discuss the methodological strategies behind this empirical analysis, followed by the cases themselves and some final remarks will be presented.

Background

Schools can become advocates for knowledge management through the creation of institutional learning spaces, where everyone can share, create and display knowledge. [Dru 02] refers to the creation of knowledge as an innovation source that has undergone change. [Pai 12] summarise the different types of innovation presented by [Chr 12] by stating that "(...) sustainable innovation is about making something better and disruptive innovation is about making something new". Hargreaves cited in [Fer 09] points out that the idea behind disruptive innovation is the opposite of that of sustainable innovation. [Fig 09] does not share this vision as he states that despite the high level of failure associated with sustainable innovation in education, this path can be explored. However, "the promising path to innovation in education systems is through disruptive innovation that quietly grows in the margins of the system, unobtrusively until starts changing it, irreversibly". We argue that SCS could be a vehicle for this innovation combined with institutionalization. [Mil 98] presents institutionalization as a change to be taken as normal, as something that is part of organizational life; and that has unquestionable resources of time, personnel and money available. The apparent paradox in the SCS conception – the institutional versus personal dichotomy – may actually be another catalyst for change. Considering knowledge creation and the role it plays in promoting innovation, SCS can actually support this space: BA. As stated by [Pai 12]: "BA is characterized by the involvement of people interacting in a given space, what sets it apart from ordinary human interaction, the main difference relying on the goal of these meetings: BA aims at creating knowledge" [Non 00].

SCS can, therefore, be an optimal space for schools that create and share knowledge, the kind of schools that [Che 08] consider to be" the cradles of innovative knowledge, [that] have a rich collection of intangible assets".

SCS Anatomy

SCS's design was based on a set of principles that had a direct impact on usage and user interaction. Openness, one of those fundamental features, involves two different kinds of issues. Because we are dealing with minors (students) that interact within a digital environment, the platform must be safe and in compliance with legal and regulatory requirements. Hence, all content published by users of a given school can only be accessed by other members of the same school, which includes not only other students, but also teachers, parents, guardians and other stakeholders, all previously

validated by the platform's institutional administrators. Inside SCS, all published content is visible to all members of the community, thereby achieving the digital metaphor of the school space. Another consequence of this openness is having a horizontal rather than a hierarchical outlook and structure. Within SCS all users have the same permissions, even though they can play different roles while performing different activities. This choice means that the community must have self-regulation mechanisms, with schools playing a key role in promoting digital citizenship and education. Another fundamental principle underlying the design of SCS is sharing, with a wide range of services being made available to users, making it possible for them to store, organize and share resources in different formats. The creation of blogs is not controlled or subject to institutional permission: any logged-in user can create all the blogs they wish and invite other to manage them. The same applies for photos, videos and the recently integrated file sharing service. Users can also create groups (open or closed; public or private) and make them available to the community.

The principle of personalisation is attained by the creation of a Personal Learning Environment (PLE). This personal and non-transferable dimension suggested by Westenbrugge cited in [Kom 09], makes it possible for users to construct their own PLE. Another key feature of SCE is institutionalization, in the way schools must make a commitment to promote the formal and institutional adoption and use of SCS. The combination of these two principles (institutionalization and personalization) was carefully thought out in order to "ensure to the educational agents the possibility of building and customizing their own PLE based on commonly-used Web 2.0 services, while simultaneously not restricting the range of potential learning activities that can be carried out in a diverse environment as the educational context" [Pai 12].

Methodology

The processes of adopting a new technology can be very complex and challenging, especially when they involve significant procedural changes. Even though the introduction of SCS by itself does not imply change, the way it is used by different agents in different school settings can be disruptive. Therefore, despite all the institutional support and commitment, and as seen from previous experiences and projects, full implementation and adoption can be very difficult. The use cases of SCS presented in this paper result from a pilot study group that benefitted from certified training workshops supervised by the University of Aveiro. These workshops were strategically designed not only to promote the institutional adoption and appropriation of SCS, but also to facilitate and promote the creation of PLEs at an early stage of their development.

These workshops took place between November 2012 and April 2013 and consisted of a total 30 hours work (15 face to face and 15 at a distance). After introducing some basic concepts and discussing the philosophy behind Web 2.0 and how it relates to teaching and learning dynamics, the participants had the opportunity to explore SCS and were challenged to develop and execute an educational project that involved the platform. These workshops became very important in promoting and supporting the appropriation of SCS, not only from a more technical perspective, but also and foremost because they allowed people to share and discuss their on-going progress, questions and problems in a constructive way. Based on this sharing and on the opinion of the users, participants often realigned their initial projects, gradually feeling more confortable using SCS and understanding its underlying principles.

From the group of pilot schools, three were chosen for this analysis. Even though these schools (hereafter referred to as school A, school B and school C) are geographically close (within a 50 km radius), they are very different from each other. School A is located in a fishing village and has 378 students (ages 3 to 15) and around 40 teachers. School B is located in a rural setting. It is attended by 2606 students (ages 3 to 18) and has 241 teachers. It is a cluster school made up of 10 different establishments, 8 of which are geographically dispersed. School C is located in an urban and industrialized area and is a junior/high school attended by students from the 7th to the 12th grade. It is a former industrial school known for its use of technology with 971 students and 134 teachers.

As previously described, all schools had to sign a protocol and were institutionally and formally bound to the project, also having access to specific training and support. Nevertheless, because of the different settings and features, the adoption and use of SCS was very diverse. The perceptions and feedback gathered both online and throughout the onsite training sessions, made it clear that even though schools officials have initially been very welcoming and receptive of the project, they adopted different strategies that influenced and constrained the way SCS was used by teachers and/or students. These perceptions are supported by the statistical data gathered from the platform.

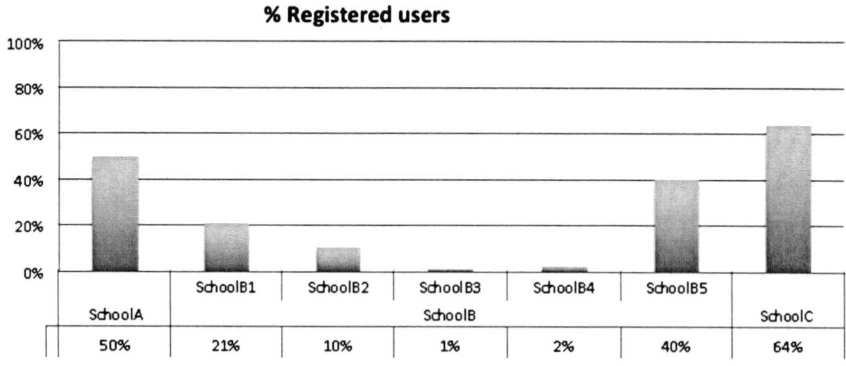

Figure 1: Percentage of registered users

In order to analyse the chart you have to keep in mind the specific features of each school. Students attending school A are between 3 and 15 years old. The 50 % registered users refer to the total number of students, including those who are too young to use the platform by themselves. School B is a very particular case. As mentioned before, this is a cluster school made up of 10 different establishments, and only 5 of those schools have registered users. While school B1 is attended by 13 to 18 year students, students in B2 are between 10 and 12. B3 and B4 are nursery/preschools (ages 3 to 5) and B5 is a primary school (ages 6 to 9). With older students (ages 13 to 18) in school C, all students are autonomous and could register themselves. Drawing from this analysis, schools A, B5 and C are arguably those that stand out.

Even though the number of users can be considered an objective source of data, it is important to complement this analysis with the activity reports of each school. In order to get a more complete and comprehensive analysis, a user activity rate was defined. This rate was based on the ratio between the number of registered users and the activity in each school (number of comments, states, photos, videos, links and posts). The results can be seen in the chart below:

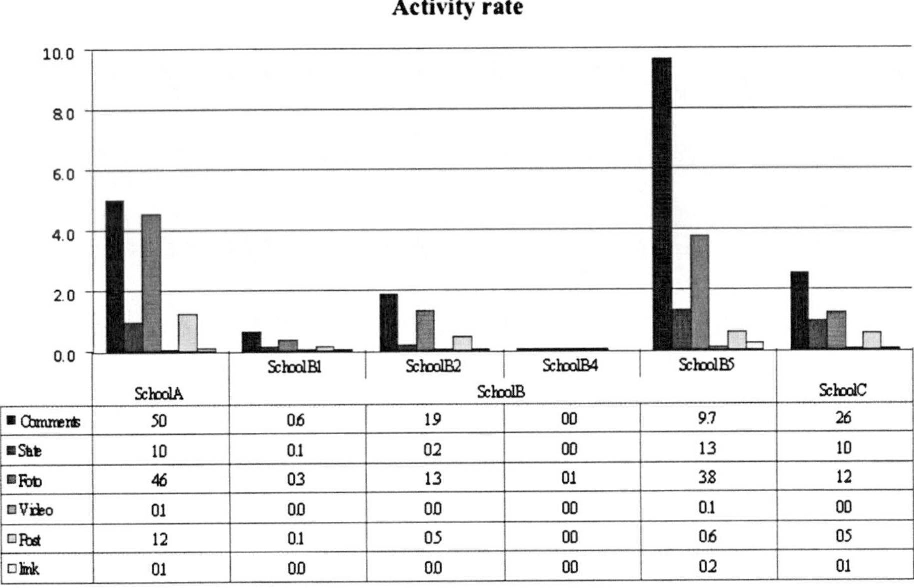

	SchoolA	SchoolB1	SchoolB2	SchoolB4	SchoolB5	SchoolC
		SchoolB				
Comments	50	0.6	1.9	00	9.7	26
State	10	0.1	0.2	00	1.3	10
Foto	46	0.3	1.3	01	3.8	12
Video	01	0.0	0.0	00	0.1	00
Post	12	0.1	0.5	00	0.6	05
link	01	0.0	0.0	00	0.2	01

Figure 2: Activity Rate

In the following analysis, School B4 will be left out because there was no activity other than the registration. The chart confirms the idea that schools A, B5 and C are those with more registered users and that are globally more active. However, as we can see from the results in school B5, there is no direct correlation between the number of registered users and each school's activity. Even though it has the lowest number of registered users of the 3, school B5 is the one with the highest activity rate.

After defining and validating the choice of schools to be analysed, it was important to select specific use cases within these schools. These cases were selected based on different criteria that included creativity in using the platform, the impact on student engagement and content creation. Because these projects were publically presented and discussed as part of the training workshops, in addition to the data from the platform itself, this analysis also included interviews with school administrators and the input of the teachers involved.

In school A, the project selected – "AEC (Curriculum Enrichment Activities) for all" – clearly illustrates the potential and the impact that SCS can have in younger audiences. Working with 6 to 9 year old students, the teachers involved in the project created a blog and different groups in which all students could post information, photos or videos regarding not only classroom or school activities, but also other content they found relevant. The different spaces were also used for collaborative projects and to promote contests that involved the school community. Besides being very engaging and involving a great number of students, this project also prompted other teachers to develop their own ventures within SCS. The fact that it played a significant role supporting other initiatives is widely recognized and was pointed out by the school's administrator in an interview.

The "GeoSapo" project from school B, was also selected because of its impact. A more personal endeavour, it involved a group of motivated teachers that created an engaging project that appealed to other teachers and even other schools. At a first stage, the project aimed at publicising a wide range of activities that promoted the local geopark, but it quickly evolved into something more dynamic, taking full advantage of Web 2.0 features. This project was at the core of a process that can lead to disruptive innovation.

In school C we have selected two cases to analyse: "Weekend Discussions" and "The 3R Club". The first example was selected because of its diversity and levels of participation. Unlike the previous cases, it has a very different background and goals, with SCS being used to support discussions on topics that are not usually discussed in the classroom. After a process of negotiation, the teacher and the students agreed that every Friday, a student would have to suggest a topic to be discussed synchronically the following Sunday, from 7:00 to 8:00 p.m. The second project – "the 3R club" – did not have a predefined audience, but supported an already existing recycling group that was open to all students. Because it was the first time the teacher responsible for the project worked with social networking services there were some initial reservations. But, despite the initial scepticism, SCS became a cohesive agent, with a high level of engagement, with more and more challenges being posted every week. Nevertheless, it is also important to mention that not all projects developed within the platform succeeded in promoting participation and engagement. In some cases, like in school C, at least one project had virtually no interaction. One thing that emerges consistently in all schools involved is the personal dimension that embodies the concept of PLE and can easily be found in the examples described. Using SCS, teachers and/or students

create and regularly update blogs about their own personal interests and share photos, videos and links, also commenting and interacting in different ways.

In the following sections of this paper, we will examine these cases more comprehensively, systematically revisiting their unique and differentiating features, as well as common and constant elements that make up the processes and may be drivers for disruptive innovation. Setting out to describe some examples of how a Web 2.0 platform is being used in different schools and relating that with innovation and knowledge creation processes, this study does not intend to thoroughly analyse each particular case, but rather draw a broader picture, exploring possibilities that have already been noticed.

Use Cases

Use Case 1: Project "AEC for all" (school A)

The Portuguese government has recently created the Curriculum Enrichment Activities (AEC), in an attempt to meet families' needs by adjusting schools schedules. This is a funded programme that aims at broadening the primary school curriculum and ensuring a full day education. Arguing that schools should offer more than just curricular activities and that they should promote physical education, sports, arts, technology, scientific inquiry and foreign language education, the Ministry of Education developed a regulatory framework to ensure that after regular classes, children can stay at school and engage in pedagogically enriched activities.

At school A students can take part in Study Room, English as a Foreign Language, Sports, Arts and Story Time. Even though they are not compulsory, most students are enrolled in these activities. Considering only those attending English and Arts classes and whose teachers took part in the training workshop, this particular use case involved a total of 112 students.

When asked to come up with a project that combined features of Web 2.0 and SCS and that was within the scope of the AEC, the teachers involved tried to create an articulated and interactive space, where all participants could share authorship and publish content. To be accessed outside the classroom, this space would be used to showcase the work being done in the different activities. Using a blog, participants should regularly post texts, pictures and videos displaying their work, so that other members of the community could comment on it. This blog was created and then shown to the students. In order to showcase the features of the platform and make it easier for students to register, a demo-user for each class was created. The first interactions within the SCE took place using these demo-users in the classroom, as students started to register themselves.

After this approach and due to difficulties in the registration process, the teachers involved asked for parents' permission to register the students in the platform. At the time of this analysis, 58 students were registered in SCS and listed as blog authors. Of those 58, 51 took active part in the blog either by publishing post or comments.

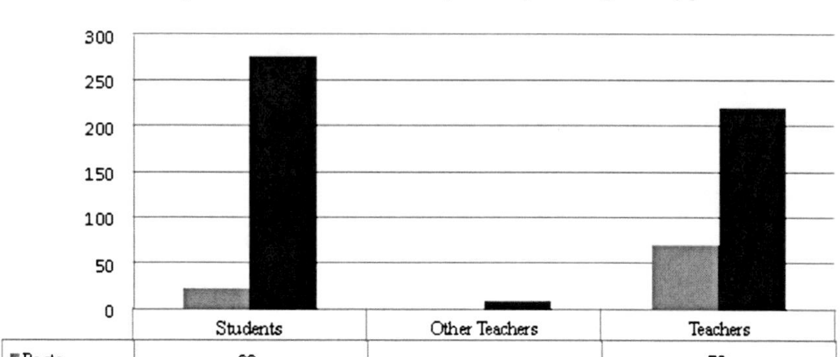

	Students	Other Teachers	Teachers
Posts	22		70
Comentários	276	9	220

Figure 3: Use case 1 – Activity distributed by participant/user type/role

As can be seen in figure 3, in the time frame analysed, 92 posts and 505 comments were published. Because it is a blog open to the community, of the 505 comments some are made by other teachers and students who are not directly involved in the AEC project.

Overall, and even though most content was published by the teachers, students were very active in commenting. In fact, as can be seen in figure 2, there was a steady increase in student participation. This may indicate a growing familiarity with the platform, with students feeling more confident to interact as they become more autonomous. In addition to this, student activity tends to mirror teacher activity, repeating the pattern.

Monthly distribution of activity (nr. of post and comments

120
100
80
60
40
20
0

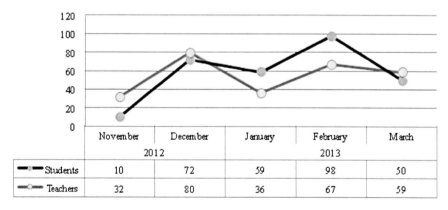

	November	December	January	February	March
	2012		2013		
Students	10	72	59	98	50
Teachers	32	80	36	67	59

Figure 4: Use case 1 – Activity – monthly distribution

If you analyse the blog activity more closely, you can also observe that activity peaks in the blog are concurrent with specific school events, such as the school's Christmas party or the celebration of Valentine's day. In that way the activity timeline in the platform seems to replicate the school calendar and activities, with user participation decreasing significantly in school holidays. Figure 5 shows an example of students' activity. Following a collaborative writing task in the classroom, students went online and published a Valentine's Day poem. This post was commented on by other students and also by teachers. Soon after this post, students from other classes also posted their own poems on SCE.

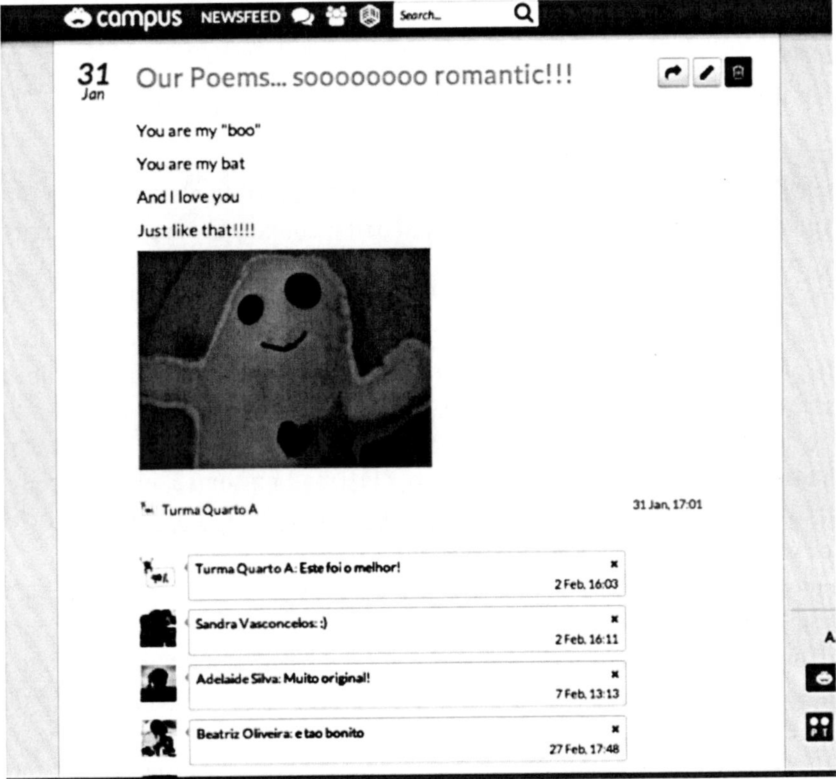

Figure 5: Use case 1 – Student activity

Even though some of the activities were carried out during classes, most students interactions took place outside the classroom, after school hours or during study breaks (between 10:00 and 10:30 am and 3:00 and 3:30 p.m).

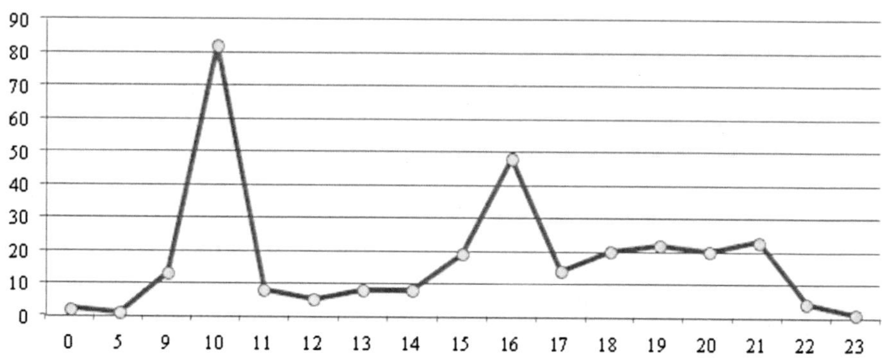

Figure 6: Use case 1 – Student participation: daily distribution

An empirical analysis of the number of posts and comments also suggests that this blog evolved from being a display of the work being done by the students to become a sharing, collaborative and socialization space, combining formal and informal learning and interaction. In addition to publishing information related to content presented in class, such as a song or the life and work of a given artist, it was possible to identify some of the students' interest areas and problems, which were later addressed in other settings. When a link to a game was made available, for example, students were asked to post their scores in English, making it possible for one of the teachers to pinpoint common mistakes. At another time, after reading some confusing comments about an Albert Einstein cartoon, another teacher took the opportunity to carry out a research assignment about prominent scientific personalities.

The blog was also used to answer questions about the platform and troubleshooting. Many of these comments dealt with personalisation of the space, with students asking how they could change their profile photo, and with publishing content ("How do I publish a video?", "Can you help me post a photo?", "I forgot how to publish a video."). Even though some of these problems were initially recurrent, they become less noticeable as students became more independent in accessing the platform. The role played by older and more autonomous students in answering less-experienced users questions and helping them register and take part in the community should also be noted.

The data gathered suggests that users were very enthusiastic in participating and interacting with each other and with the published content. However, mostly due to the age of the users, participation was disorganised and at times chaotic, making it impossible to categorise the type of comments and find content patterns. Many students published content and asked questions outside the blog and tried to address specific people rather than focus on space.

Students' comments also suggest that they were interested in synchronous communication with other users, often using comments and posts to chat. Another indication of the users' lack of experience was that, when trying to comment on something, they would report the content as inappropriate. This could signal that it would be important to have other ways of interacting with content than writing comments.

Use Case 2: GeoSAPO (School B5)
School B5 is a recently remodelled school with a strong connection to the surrounding environment and located in a rural setting and near a geological park. Each classroom, for example, is named after a geological element that can be found in the geological park (for example, the "trilobite room"). In addition to these more symbolic features, and because nature and ecology are a very important part of the curriculum, the school has also developed many projects in this area, the most recent being the "Earth Experiences" programme.

Aiming at extending the scope of this programme and "developing multidisciplinary activities that promote the Geopark", five teachers from this school decided to use SCS to support and publicise their work. Even though it was the first time they worked with web 2.0 platforms, working closely together as a team, the teachers involved managed to overcome the different obstacles they faced. The first problem involved the registration process. Due to the age and lack of experience of their students, they had to create E-Mail addresses and register them. This required getting parental consent and working with the families, making them aware of this opportunity of working together with their children and allowing them to actively engage in their learning. In addition to registration, teachers also had to be creative in order to keep the younger children from forgetting their logins and passwords. They designed a personal and non-transferable card with each user's information and monitored their activity closely.

With many registered users, the project became a big hit. In order to address curricular questions, different spaces where created within SCS, with the different classes taking part and participating keenly. The participation is demonstrated in the chart below:

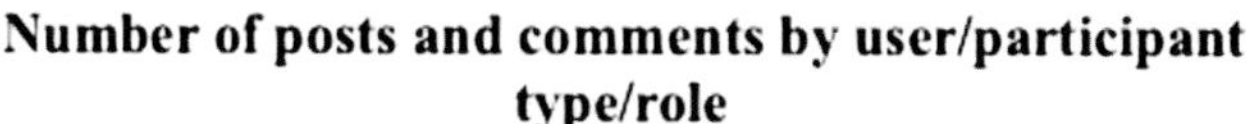

Number of posts and comments by user/participant type/role

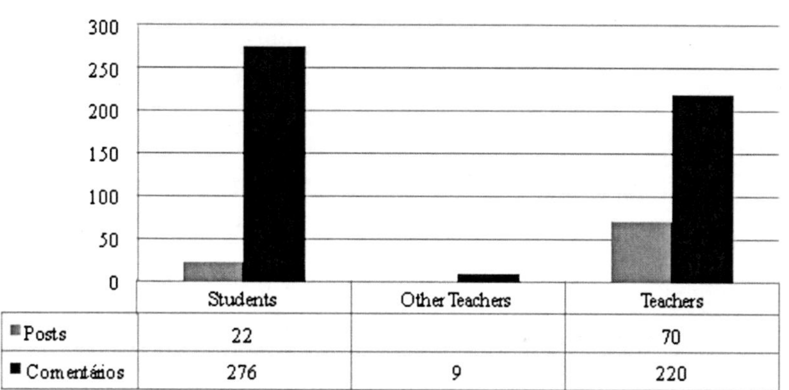

	Students	Other Teachers	Teachers
Posts	22		70
Comentários	276	9	220

Figure 7: Use case 2 – Activity distributed by participant/user type/role

This chart confirms what was said previously in the methodology section: school B5 has the highest activity rate of all the schools considered in this study, with students not only reacting (number of comments) but also producing content (number of student posts). Moving beyond the initial project, many students also spontaneously created blogs and posted their own content, as can be seen in the following examples:

- Fun PEB09 – a place where all the PEB09 (the author's classmates) can laugh. A 4th grade student created a blog where he could post jokes. This is an interesting example because the author asked his classmates to join him, so they would not only react to what was being written, but also post their own jokes and funny stories.
- Infinite Music: A third grade student who was passionate about music and the transverse flute, created a blog where she would post videos, photos and texts on this topic.

The chart above also provides important data regarding teacher participation. There is a significant number of comments from teachers who are not involved in the project. As we mentioned before, school B is a cluster school made up of 10 different establishments, and all of them can access content published by the different schools. Many of the comments from other teachers are also from different schools. This dynamic led to collaboration between schools, with school B5 positively influencing and driving other teachers and students to develop their own projects. This was a two-way influence and collaboration, as users from other schools would often interact with users from school B5.

In order to support the GeoSAPO project, teachers at school B5 created a "GeoSAPO time". Every Wednesday morning, students taking part in the project would meet in the school library to share what they had learnt throughout the week, ask questions about SCS and prepare competitions and challenges. Because it was difficult for some younger students to keep up with all the activities, older students would often monitor and help them. These meetings went viral, with other students becoming curious and eager to take part in the project.

Another distinctive feature of this project is that it involved people outside the school. Parents were key players in adopting and using the platform, as it supported their involvement in their children's school activities. This evidence is also supported by the following chart:

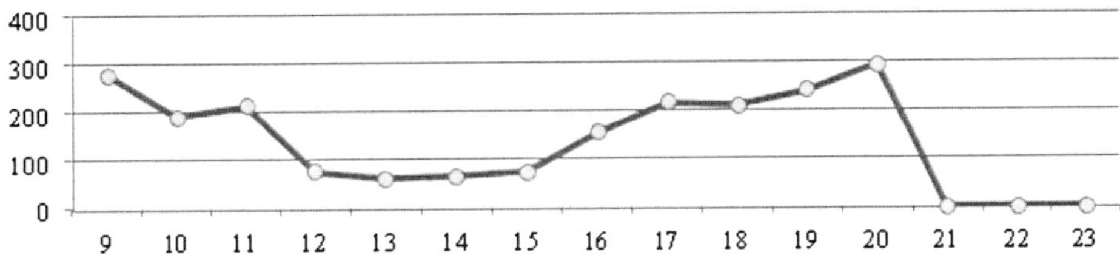

Figure 8: Use case 2 – Student participation: daily distribution

Most activity in SCS took place after 5 p.m., outside school hours. Even though the time alone is not enough to determine parental participation, there are other indicators that support this assumption:

(A) Most students that log-in after 5 p.m. are 3 to 5 years old and do not know how to read and write;

(B) Some posts are co-signed by parents, showing their support in using the platform;

Throughout the whole process it is also important to mention the interaction strategies adopted by the teachers involved, who would readily answer all their students' questions and provide stimulation. They also developed an informal user policy and promoted online safety. According to them, this was SCS' most significant benefit: that it made it possible for them to showcase their work in a safe environment within the school community.

Use Case 3: The 3R Club (School C)

In Portugal there is a national programme that encourages the collection and recycling of plastic bottle caps, with several companies exchanging them for orthopaedic

material. Carrying on the work of previous years, the 3R (Reduce, Reuse, Recycle) club from school C is involved in this campaign and aims at raising people's awareness for this movement. Working closely with local authorities and CERCI (a centre for the rehabilitation and integration of people with disabilities) the club is always reaching out to the community and trying to find new active members. When asked to come up with a project involving her students, Web 2.0 services and SCS, one of the teachers responsible for the club, together with a group of 9th grade students, outlined a plan of action that included:

1. The creation of the "3R Club Blog" where different events could be publicized.
2. Researching and posting creative projects that used recyclable and reusable materials;
3. Advertising collection points throughout the school;
4. The creation of a group in SCS where participants could work together in order to design two bottle caps collection containers. All caps collected should then be recycled, with the funds raised proceeding to the local CERCI.

In the following chart we can see the number of posts and comments on the blog, according to the type of user.

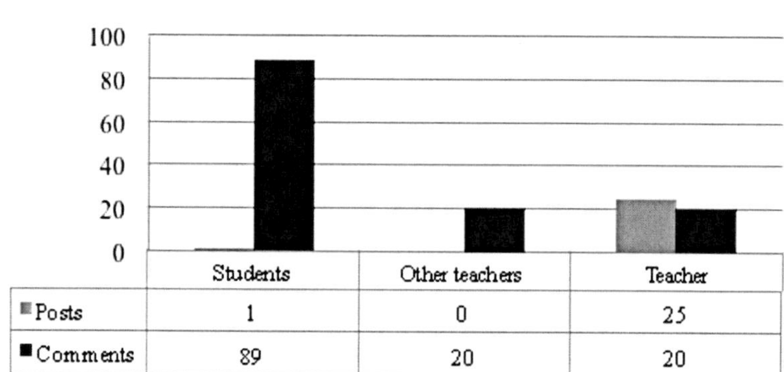

	Students	Other teachers	Teacher
Posts	1	0	25
Comments	89	20	20

Figure 9: Use case 3 – Activity distributed by participant/user type/role

Even though, when compared to others, this blog did not have a significant number of contributions, there are some distinctive features that should be taken into account and are relevant for this analysis. On the one hand, it was a new experience for all those involved, as the teacher responsible for the blog had never worked with Web 2.0 services before. Nevertheless, she prompted student participation, asking them for comments, posting

challenges and even giving out rewards. In one of these challenges, the teacher posted a picture of a container somewhere in the school, asking students to guess where it was:

> *Is it a giant candy, a vase? No! It's a hidden plastic container used to collect plastic caps from those who drink water or yogurt at school. Have you seen it? Where is it? Have you ever used it? I don't think so. I keep seeing caps in the regular bin. Why don't we use the recycling bins and put the caps on a separate container? There will be a sweet award for the first to guess where this cap collector is!!*

Student feedback was immediate and the winner was given a chocolate bar. But the most interesting aspect of the project was the fact that, as the different challenges were issued, many of the discussions extended beyond SCE, taking place in and outside the classroom. According to the teacher in charge, many students that were not involved in the project would question her about the challenges and the results.

Because it is a non-curricular project, most interactions took place after classes. In the following chart we can see the daily distribution of student activities (number of posts and comments).

Daily and hourly distribution of students participation (number of post and comments

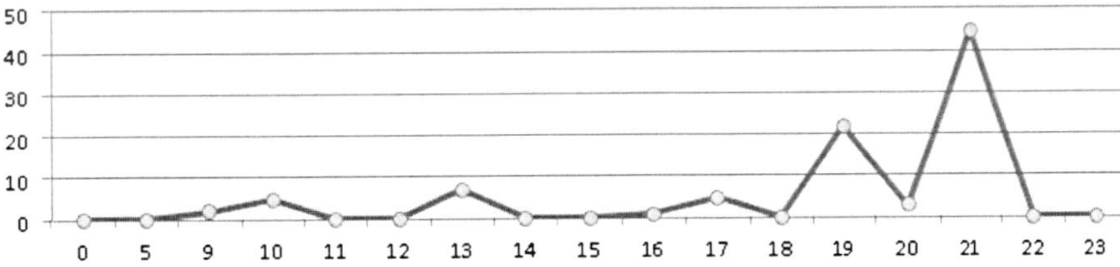

Figure 10: Use case 3 – Student participation: daily distribution

In order to publicize the project and the different club activities posted in the blog, the teacher also used the school's mural, regularly reaching out to all members of the community and inviting other students to take part in the project. This was considered to be an effective strategy. Another interesting feature of the project was the fact that many other teachers also engaged in the discussions. This interaction played an important part in keeping students motivated and making the project known.

As mentioned previously, one of the challenges issued involved the creation of two cap collection containers. Open to the school community, in order to enter the competition participants had to publish rough drafts that would then go through a selection process. With the help of teachers and students, two drafts were chosen. Because there were many constraints associated with the construction process, in one of the training sessions the teacher supervising the project asked for the cooperation of arts teachers and students. Another teacher attending the workshop offered to help and working collaboratively (both teachers and students) they built the container below (Figure 11) that won a municipal award.

Figure 11: Container

Use Case 4: You speak, I speak, we speak (school B)

Involving an 11th grade class (students ages 16–17), this project was open to the community and, according to the teacher in charge, aimed at "promoting the use of Web 2.0 as a way of bringing participants closer and developing their critical sense". Reaching outside the classroom and moving away from formal content, it consists of using SCE to promote a weekly debate with students. Having started in January, every week a different student would post a topic, some context and a few questions on a blog in order to kickoff the discussion. This discussion took place synchronously, using comments on the post. Because it required participants to be online simultaneously, a meeting time was negotiated and agreed upon. Participants agreed to meet every Sunday from 7:00 to 8:00 p.m. Participation was optional and there was no kind of reward or compensation other than taking part in the discussion and sharing personal thoughts and opinions. The topics discussed were diverse and can be seen in Table 1.

Table 1: Use case 4 – Discussion themes

MONTH	DISCUSSION THEME
January	Young writers
	Teenage pregnancy
	First Sexual Intercourse
	STD (Sexually transmitted diseases)
February	Media
	Drugs
	Doping and performance enhancing drugs
	Can a teacher be a friend?
March	Domestic Violence
	Homosexuality
April	Sports in Adolescence
	Music festivals
	Precocious Youth
	Young people and social networks

In the period covered in this analysis, 18 students (from a total of 24) took part in the discussions. The following figure illustrates the distribution of activities within of the group:

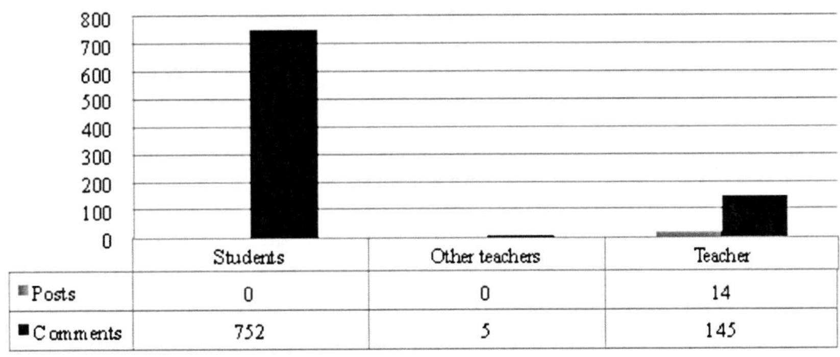

Figure 12: Use case 4 – Activity distributed by participant/user type/role

As can be seen in the chart, from January to April there were 14 posts, each for a different topic, generating 752 student comments. An empirical analysis of the comments indicates that the teacher took on the role of mediator, moderating the discussion: the students played the most active role. The following chart details the distribution of the blog activity throughout the time considered in this analysis:

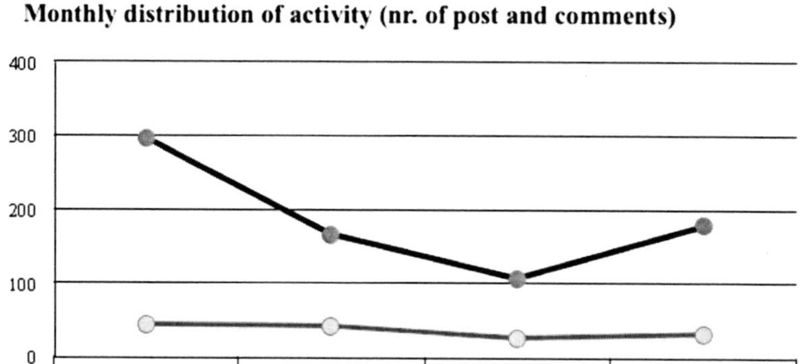

Monthly distribution of activity (nr. of post and comments)

	January	February	March	April
Students	298	167	107	180
Teacher	44	42	26	33

Figure 13: Use case 4 – Activity: monthly distribution

The graph shows that after a very promising beginning, the blog activity decreased and became more stable. Much like in other cases described before, in March, in the weeks corresponding to the Easter holidays, there is a further decline in the number of interventions. If we overlap the data from the graph with the topics covered in the discussions, in January all but one dealt with sexuality. These topics appeal to the target audience and seem to arouse their curiosity. If you go through the comments, you can see there are still many myths and misconceptions surrounding these matters. In addition to the sensitivity and the intimate nature of these particular subjects, the fact that the debate was public had an impact in the discussions. When discussing and commenting on this project, other teachers said that they followed the blog and the interactions but did not feel confortable enough to engage in the discussions, given their personal nature.

Even though the students taking part in the debates belonged to the same class and had known each other for at least two years, after the first discussion many revealed other sides of their personalities. In the first discussion, for example, one of the students shared a passage of a poem he wrote. His classmates, who were not aware of his interest in poetry, reacted immediately, expressing their surprise. Students' engagement in the discussions was not limited to text. They shared many links related to the topics being discussed, adding to the debate.

Final considerations

The current activity of SCS is not limited to the practices briefly described above. SCS is already a platform where information, knowledge and experiences can be shared and can be considered a quality step forward towards the elimination of hierarchical institutional barriers.

To some extent, the use cases described evidence that SCS can help institutions overcome these barriers: teachers and students are at the same level, the only difference between them lying on the setting and the role they play at a given moment. In the schools described it is usual for students to ask questions regarding curricular content. These questions are answered not only by other students, but also by teachers. Moving beyond independent projects or individual blogs, the schools' murals are used to showcase different activities and to discuss all sorts of issues, prompting and adding value to the interactions taking place.

SCS is a Web 2.0 platform based on SAPO core technologies that promote communication, sharing and collaboration in schools (K1 through 12). It also reveals the built-in dimension of a Personal Learning Environments (PLE), making it possible to create and manage personal spaces with all the PLE features within the institutional whole that makes up a school. The focus on the platform should not, however, be viewed from a technical standpoint that instrumentalises the PLE, but rather from a humanist perspective that values the individual or groups of individuals and their control over their learning activities – both formal and non-formal [Fie 10]. SCS can, therefore, be considered an institutionally supported PLE in which the focus is on the schools' commitment as a whole, rather than on isolated initiatives from teachers or students.

As we have seen from the use cases, in SCS, each school establishes its own network, using elements of their community. This option can be seen as a limiting aperture, but is related to privacy issues mostly due to the age of the target audience. This fact was particularly relevant in schools A and B. [Chr 08] refers to disruptive innovation not only as something concerned with the improvement of a product (as sustaining innovation) but also with a radical change of paradigm and principles that underlie the product or process. Disruptive processes usually take place in smaller groups, slowly and gradually being adopted by larger groups. Of the cases described, this can be best seen in school B5, where SCS has been the catalyst for change. With an initial small group of active participants, its use has steadily spread to the rest of the school and is already promoting change in practices and procedures.

[Ang 09: 207) identify some characteristics that a platform that supports and sustains innovation process should incorporate:

"Collaboration, knowledge sharing and exchange, reciprocal trust, recognized ownership, reinforcing and enlarging innovation stake-holders' networks, clear network visualization, simple and reliable technology (...): all these factors need to be taken into account to develop effective IT tools aimed at supporting and boosting innovation processes."

Even though some of the characteristics mentioned by Angehrn, et al. do not depend on the technological platform itself but rather on use, SCS can be viewed through these lenses in order to verify if it meets the conditions thought necessary for innovation.

[Chr 10] argue that combining change and innovation, and using technology as a catalyst for a disruptive, student-centered process, can be the key to have a school fitting the values of today's knowledge society. The same authors also suggest that the personalization of teaching accommodates students' multiple intelligences, as postulated by [Gar 93] and can play a pivotal role in this process. BA can be translated as place and is defined as "a shared space that serves as foundation of knowledge creation" [Non 05: 1]. Even though there are pieces of evidence that suggest it can become BA, and thus promote disruptive innovation, it is still early to draw definite conclusions. If in fact SCS is becoming part of the school ecosystem, only time will tell if these changes will be sustainable on the long run.

Acknowledgements

A special thank you those who contributed to this paper especially to Sandra Vasconcelos and Jorge Braz. Research done in partnership with the PTDC/CPE-CED/114130/2009 project, funded by FEDER funds through the Operational Programme for Competitiveness Factors – COMPETE and National Funds through FCT – Foundation for Science and Technology (Portugal).

REFERENCES

[Chr 08] *Christensen, Clayton M.; Horn, Michael B.; Johnson, Curtis W. (2008):* Disrupting class: How disruptive innovation will change the way the world learns, Vol. 98, McGraw-Hill New York.

[Dru 02] *Drucker, Peter F. (2002):* The discipline of innovation. Harvard Business Review, 80, 95–104.

[Fer 09] *Ferrari, Anusca; Cachia, Romina; Punie, Yves (2009):* Innovation and Creativity in Education and Training in the EU Member States: Fostering Creative Learning and Supporting Innovative Teaching: Literature review on Innovation and Creativity in E&T in the EU Member States (ICEAC). JRC Technical Note, 52374.

[Fig 09] *Figueiredo, A. Dias (2009):* Innovating in Education, Educating for Innovation. 7th EDEN Open Classroom Conference – The European School 2.0. Oporto.

[Kom 09] *Kompen, Ricardo; Edirisingha, Palitha; Monguet, Josep (2009):* Using Web 2.0 applications as supporting tools for personal learning environments. Best Practices for the Knowledge Society.

Knowledge, Learning, Development and Technology for All, 33–40.

[Mil 98] *Miles, Matthew (1998):* Finding keys to school change: a 40-year odyssey. International handbook of educational change, 1, 37–69.

[Non 05] *Nonaka, Ikujiro; Konno, Noboru (2005):* The concept of "Ba": Building a foundation for knowledge creation. Knowledge management: critical perspectives on business and management, 2(3), 53.

[Non 00] *Nonaka, Ikujiro; Toyama, Ryoko; Nagata, Akiya (2000):* A firm as a knowledge-creating entity: a new perspective on the theory of the firm. Industrial and corporate change, 9(1), 1–20.

[Non 95] *Nonaka, Ikujiro; Takeuchi, Hirotaka (1995):* The knowledge-creating company: How Japanese companies create the dynamics of innovation: Oxford University Press, USA.

[Pai 12] *Pais, Fatima, Santos, Carlos:* Pedro, Luis (2012): Sapo Campus Schools as a Disruptive Innovation Tool: Could it be the Educational Ba? PLE'12 Conference Proceedings. Retrieved from: *http://revistas.ua.pt/index.php/ple/article/view/1434*

[San 09] *Santos, Carlos; Pedro, Luis (2009):* SAPO Campus: a social media platform for Higher Education. Research, Reflections and Innovations in Integrating ICT in Education, 2, 1104–1108.

FIGURES AND TABLES

CONTACT DETAILS

Fátima Pais
University of Aveiro
Departamento de Comunicação e Arte
Campus Universitário de Santiago 3810-193 Aveiro – Portugal
Phone: +351 (0) 234 370389
E-Mail: fpaiswww@gmail.com

Carlos Santos
University of Aveiro
Departamento de Comunicação e Arte
Campus Universitário de Santiago 3810-193 Aveiro – Portugal
Phone: +351 (0)234 370389
E-Mail: *carlossantos@ua.pt*

Luís Pedro
University of Aveiro
Departamento de Comunicação e Arte
Campus Universitário de Santiago 3810-193 Aveiro – Portugal
Phone: +351 (0)234 370389
E-Mail: *lpedro@ua.pt*

Personal Learning Environments in Smart Cities: Current Approaches and Future Scenarios

Ilona Buchem, Mar Pérez-Sanagustín

ABSTRACT

With the increasing number of the global population living in densely populated and technologically advanced urban spaces, the notion of smart cities is gaining importance, especially in view of citizen engagement, learning and participation. We propose to consider smart cities as learning spaces and call for innovative pedagogical approaches for using technologies embedded in physical environments to support connected and ubiquitous learning in smart cities. In this paper, we discuss smart cities as spaces for constructing Personal Learning Environments. Our special focus is on mobile and locative media, which open new possibilities of interaction with the surrounding environment. In technology-rich infrastructures such as smart cities, physical objects, including buildings, works of art or points of interests, can become part of the learning environment. When mediated through technologies, e.g. by means of mobile and locative media, the surrounding physical environment and the digital environment can be dynamically merged into augmented, ad-hoc Personal Learning Environments. In this paper we give a short introduction to smart cities, smart citizens and smart city learning, and go on to outline some innovative applications of mobile and locative media in urban spaces, including open badges, smart glasses and mobile tagging, and discuss their potential for learning. Followed by these examples, we discuss educaching as an approach to smart city learning and provide some practical examples based on the example of etiquetAR, a mobile, locative application that allows creating interactive tags to support augmented learning experiences. We then present the results of an international, explorative study on smart city learning, which we conducted with educators from Europe, North America, South America, Middle-East and Asia-Pacific. Based on the synopsis of current research and practice and the results of our study, we argue for an extended view of Personal Learning Environments which are not permanent, but created ad-hoc and adjusted dynamically by connecting virtual and physical spaces in smart cities.

Note: This article has been published in the Special Edition of the eLearning Papers, Issue No. 35 "Personal Learning Environments". The link to this Special Issue is: http://openeducationeuropa.eu/en/paper/personal-learning-environments

Defining Smart City Learning

The notion of "smart cities" has recently triggered a lot of technology-focused discussions and research, including the Horizon 2020 strategy of the European Commission, naming smart, inclusive and sustainable growth, security and citizenship and Global Europe, as well as stimulating interactions between the societal challenges and the development of generic enabling and industrial technologies as key concerns of the European Union [COM 11]. In view of the "smart cities" agenda, Horizon 2020 focuses on smart urban applications enabling innovative solutions targeting energy efficiency (e.g. alternative energy sources), smart transport (e.g. new mobility concepts), enabling technologies (e.g. nano-science, bio-science), but also understanding social, economic and cultural issues that are involved in the transformation of urban centers into smart cities [COM 11: 60-61]. Eurocities, the network of major European cities bringing together over 130 of Europe's largest cities and addressing several policy areas related to living in cities, emphasise the role of smart cities as living labs for market, public, social and cultural innovations [Eur 12]. Smart cities can be also viewed as smart learning environments, i.e. environments which exploit new technologies and approaches, such as ubiquitous and mobile learning, to support people in their daily lives in a proactive yet unobtrusive way [Mik 12]. In this sense smart cities as smart learning environments utilize the idea of ambient intelligence by integrating diverse computation, information and communication resources into a united framework of an ambient intelligent space [Coo 09], [Mik 12].

Although smart cities can be approached from several dimensions, such as technological, human or institutional (see a complete review about these different approaches in [Nam 11]), in this paper we adopt a human-centered perspective. Following the definition by [Woo 01], we understand the concept of smart cities as "the integration of technology into a strategic approach to sustainability, citizen well-being, and economic development". From this perspective smart cities can be viewed as complex ecosystems supported by technological infrastructures transforming citizen engagement, learning and participation. In our view, the notion of smart cities goes far beyond technologies and technological infrastructures. We argue that smart cities cannot be smart without smart citizens. In order to achieve sustainable societal changes we first and foremost need smart citizens, who are knowledgeable and empowered to actively use technologies to transform living environments to smart spaces. As Horizon 2020 points out, building resilient and inclusive societies entails enhancing societal awareness and participation of citizens in decision-making [COM 11]. We believe that is is necessary to refocus the strategy of smart cities from smart technologies and infrastructures to smart citizens. As [Hil 13] points out, the danger of the smart city vision predicated on feedback loops delivering information to influence citizen attitudes and behaviour is that citizens may become passive in response to technological infrastructure becoming active.

Refocusing the concept of smart cities from smart technologies to smart citizens is also closely linked to learning in smart cities. This issue has been just recently raised as a response to current smart city policies. The initiative on Smart City Learning and the related International Observatory on Smart City Learning are dedicated to the future of learning in smart cities and intend to foster a change in the current reflection on smart city learning [Gio 13a]. In this context, a number of articles propose new conceptualisations of smart cities: [Gio 13b] emphasize citizen involvement with the city and propose to consider cities as "open libraries" containing a huge number of resources, such as buildings or artworks, that can be used for learning; [Cal 13] suggest to think about smart city learning as a navigation of trajectories in terms of space, time, roles and resources, which can be supported by connecting episodes across past, present and future experiences; [Sin 13] propose the notion of "technology enhanced places", i.e. places with embedded technologies, supporting new kinds of learning, especially constructing contextual knowledge by moving and operating in an authentic environment; [McC 13[emphasises the importance of attention in context of ambient urban computing and proposes embodied cognition making use of environmental features as building blocks for thought as a framework for smart city learning.

Inspired by the concepts outlined above, we define smart city learning from a human-centered perspective as learning of locally and globally interconnected citizens, who use smart technologies to learn by using, sharing, remixing and co-constructing learning resources, and in this way actively contributing to solving societal, environmental, political and economic challenges. From this perspective, the "smartness" of the learning environment is determined primarily by the citizens and their uses of smart technologies rather than technologies themselves. Derived from the technological viewpoint of "smart" as expressed by [Pos 09], we define smart learners as active, networked, autonomous and in control of own resources. The proposed conceptualisation of smart city learning is thus akin to participatory urbanism, i.e. uses of "emerging ubiquitous urban and personal mobile technologies to enable citizen action by allowing open measuring, sharing, and remixing of elements of urban living marked by, requiring, or involving participation, especially affording the opportunity for individual citizen participation, sharing, and voice" [Pau 09]. While participatory urbanism focuses on engaging in grassroots efforts including citizen science, smart city learning is a broader term and encompasses formal, informal and mixed learning experiences in urban spaces.

Extending the view of Personal Learning Environments

Technological advancements, such as positioning systems, wireless technologies, ubiquitous computing and the increasing adoption of mobile technologies, allow citizens to connect anytime and anywhere, linking remote places, resources and people. This pertains not only to urban but also increasingly to rural and remote areas. In smart cities, however, technological infrastructures and digital ecosystems build far more complex and advanced interconnections, opening new opportunities for constructing Personal

Learning Environments. The rapid adoption of connected technologies, devices and networks across growing urban landscapes has been termed as urban computing [Pau 09]. With the ever increasing number of urban citizens (with approx. 75 % of the global population living in urban centers), the growth of digital infrastructures and the proliferation of interconnected personal digital tools such as smartphones and the recently emerging wearable computing, traditional physical constraints of time and space transcend and the notions of sociality, spatialization and temporalization have to be redefined [Gol 14], [Pau 09]. Taking as point of departure Meyrowitz's concept of "glocality" and Cereau's concept of "practiced places", we propose a conceptualization of Personal Learning Environments (PLE) as permeable physical and virtual spaces, which are dynamically constructed through the subject's practice of movements across physical and virtual spaces. While understanding "space as a practiced place" [Cer 88], new media and technologies expand our practice, or the "movements of everyday life" beyond the local. As our "practices" in physical and virtual spaces become interlaced, our spatial experience changes: "We live in glocalities, where the local and the global coexists" [Mey 05]. However, no matter how sophisticated technologies are, "the localness of experience is a constant" [Mey 05: 21]. As human beings we cannot detach ourselves from our local, physical experience, but as we use technologies, the localness and the virtuality of our experience become tightly fused. This happens for example when we move in a physical place (e.g. city), which is a relational environment with different elements distributed in a coexisting relationship [Cer 88], with a group of people (e.g. students) using mobile devices (e.g. smartphones, tablets) to interact with subjects (e.g. social media users) and objects (e.g. digital content) which are not within our immediate physical proximity. In this sense, PLE are constructed through the practice of "movement" across spaces. [Sha 09] differentiate between mobility in the physical space, mobility of technology, mobility in conceptual space, mobility in social space and mobility in time, as different types of movement in terms of "flows across locations, timed, topics and technologies". We believe these notions are applicable to constructing Personal Learning Environments, especially with mobile and locative media. By moving across spaces, contexts, concepts and time we are able to capture and share our personal learning experiences in new ways. For example, from the perspective of ubiquitous computing encompassing smart devices, smart environments and smart interactions (Smart DEI), learners in smart cities are provided with enhanced mobility, interaction and control possibilities [Pos 09], all enabling new forms of learning across multiple contexts. In this respect, [Pér 13a] propose three central attributes of technologies capable of supporting smart city learning. These include multi-channel, multi-objective and multi-context learning. First, technologies for smart city learning have to support multi-channel learning, which is an active and participatory process engaging diverse agents and supporting multi-directional conversations in multiple channels in the smart city ecosystem. Second, technologies for smart city learning have to support multiple-objective learning, which supports learners in following personal, idiosyncratic objectives and learning patterns.

Third, technologies for smart city learning have to support multi-context learning, which enables not only learning anywhere and anytime, but also combining physical and virtual spaces transforming urban elements into learning resources [Pér 13a].

Thus, we can think of constructing Personal Learning Environments in smart cities as blending spaces that together create opportunities for learning in networked and integrated urban infrastructured [Shar 13]. In smart cities, personal resources may be augmented with infrastructures and data embedded in the city by using personal devices such as smart phones, smart watches or smart glasses, all capable of enhancing our interactions with both physical and digital world. Based on the key principle of Personal Learning Environments, it is the learner that becomes the main actor in such augmented spaces. In smart city learning, learners may transform multiple spaces into a personal environment for learning by both interacting with the environment and connecting to other learners in order to receive, share, remix and co-create information. As the "Innovating Pedagogy 2013" report points out, the new emerging learning experiences take on diverse pedagogical forms [Shar 13]. Thereby, seamless learning, crowd learning, geo-learning or citizen inquiry seem to be especially relevant in context of smart city learning. Seamless learning describes an emerging pedagogical practice of connecting learning across settings, technologies and activities. As a pedagogical method, seamless learning aims at creating a seamless flow of learning experiences across such contexts as formal education and daily life. Seamless learning results from learners extending their personal technologies for learning across times and locations, blending learning with everyday life [Shar 13]. Crowd learning focuses on harnessing the knowledge of many people and utilizing "the power of the mass" to support learning experiences. By applying mobile technologies in crowd learning, the information flows between the crowd and the learner, and the expertise of the crowd can be accessed anytime and anywhere on learner's personal device. In this sense, crowd learning transfers ownership of the learning process to the learner but at the same time requires tools and mechanisms to guide learners, recognise their progress, and reward contributions [Shar 13]. Geo-learning refers to learning in and about locations. Geo-learning can take place in both indoors or outdoors, and utilizes context-aware and position-based technologies for mixing physical and digital elements. In geo-learning experiences, the technology is used to add interactive points and layers of digital information to physical spaces, which offers the possibility of interconnecting locations and social settings, as well as facilitating the exchange of information across contexts. Connecting contexts may be seen as a way of stimulating seamless learning, for example by moving themes explored in the classroom to outdoor settings and flowing back to the classroom to enrich lessons [Shar 13]. Finally, citizen enquiry as a pedagogical approach combines inquiry-based learning and citizen activism in order to support creative knowledge building, citizen investigations and scientific practices of social value [Shar 13].

These and other new pedagogical approaches may be applied to support smart city learning. Since any moment in the city can become a "learning moment", in which peo-

ple can relate their knowledge from different contexts, constructing Personal Learning Environments becomes ad-hoc and dynamically adapted by the learner to the current context rather than pre-designed to equip the learner with necessary tools to cope with upcoming situations. From this perspective, ubiquitous learning, i.e. detecting and identifying the surrounding context to provide guidance, resources and collaborators for learning [Yan 09], provides new reference points for conceptualising Personal Learning Environments in context of smart city learning. These include but are not limited to mobility, location awareness, interoperability, seamlessness, situation awareness, social awareness, adaptability and pervasiveness [Yan 09].

Smart City Learning Practices

Given the new technological opportunities and pedagogical practices, this section outlines some of the current applications of emerging media in urban spaces. Then, the results of an international, explorative study which aimed at eliciting educational scenarios in context of smart city learning are presented and discussed from the perspective of constructing Personal Learning Environments.

Digital Badges

Badges are symbolic representations of an accomplishment, skill, quality or interest [Kni 12]. Digital badges have become popular due to geolocation services such as Foursquare, which award users with badges for check-ins at different locations. More recently, Open Badges, an initiative of Mozilla and MacArthur Foundation, have explored badges as elements of learning and applied badges to set goals, stimulate motivation, recognise and represent achievements, and communicate learning success across contexts, supporting open credentialing and accreditation for formal and informal learning [Kni 12]. Open Badges are designed to build a badging ecosystem with badges being issued and displayed across different contexts and learning environments to form living transcripts of learners' skills and competencies [Kni 12]. As such Open Badges offer a flexible mechanism not only for motivating learners or recognising achievements but also for communicating personal accomplishments, skills and evidence of learning across diverse learning spaces. In this sense badges can be viewed as boundary objects, crossing boundaries between existing divisions such as formal and informal learning or academic and professional achievement [Buc 11]. With tools and infrastructures for badging constantly improving, there is yet much room for educators to explore new approaches to using badges for learning [Sha 13].

Among numerous examples to support motivation and recognise achievement in online learning environments [San 13], there have been yet few examples of using badges to merge the physical and virtual learning spaces in context of smart city learning. The first citywide implementation of a badge ecosystem was the Chicago Summer of Learning [CSO 13]. In 2013 the City of Chicago incorporated badges to support learning in the city building on partnerships with youth-serving organizations, museums and cultural institutions, philanthropists, businesses and citizens. Young people in Chicago could explore, play and learn with the different organisations and citizens by following exploratory challenges, making own projects, developing skills and earning badges throughout the smart city learning experience. The Summer of Learning in Chicago focused on Science, Technology, Engineering, Arts and Mathematics (STEAM) and enabled young people in Chicago to gain learning and work experiences using the city as a learning environment. By earning badges participating citizens could unlock citywide challenges which supported developing new skills by connecting to people, building real-world artifacts and communicating achievements across learning contexts by publicly displaying badges. Chicago Summer of Learning with its applications of mobile and locative media allowing for embedding learning in smart cities, supported learners in constructing Personal Learning Environments on-the-go. Students could construct their Personal Learning Environments ad-hoc, by combining online and in-person experiences as well as using technologies for collaboration and recognition of learning and achievement through Open Badges. Partnering with schools, enterprises, families and community organisations and allowing students to create and navigate multiple learning pathways, allowed to blur traditional divisions between formal and informal learning and to explore new learning opportunities by connecting physical and virtual learning spaces.

Smart Glasses

Google Glass is one of the most popular augmented reality eyewear. With augmented reality applications becoming commonly available to the general public, mainly due to technological advances in mobile computing and sensor integration, educators and learners can seize new opportunities for learning [Fit 12]. For example, AR browser applications, including Wikitude, Layar or junaio are used by smartphone users to explore the surrounding environment, such as finding new, interesting places, events and activities in close proximity. Other AR applications, such as Google Goggles application for smartphones, which enables search based on visual recognition, and Google Glass including an AR spectacle with overlaid contextual information, enable users to search, record and share what is seen in the surrounding environment. These and other AR applications rely on the context as a critical aspect of supplementing or augmenting the physical surroundings through additional, overlaid information, thus blending reality and virtuality into what is called mixed reality [Fit 12]. Mobile uses of AR allows to blend physical and virtual environments based on an ever changing geographical position of the user, serving as a mechanism for personal or individual experiences. As such mobile AR may enhance not only spatial but also temporal mobility, enabling learners to use resources on-the-fly, at a time and place convenient and relevant to them [Fit 12]. While AR applications have been used in such fields as medicine or mechanics, only recently educators have started to explore educational uses of wearable technologies based on

AR. Wearable AR, such as Google Glass, enable to take the learning experience to the outdoors, such as in smart city learning, allowing for situated learning including situative embodiment as proposed by the embodied cognition approach [Bar 07].

The Google Glass device as a wearable technology operated by voice commands enables the user to connect to internet services, contacts and social networks, record video and display information in a hands-free mode. Google Glass may provide educators and learners with new possibilities for hands-free perspective media capture and augmented networked learning experiences [Hay 12]. Some of the first explorations of Google Glass in education is STEMbite by [Heu 13], an educator selected as Glass Explorer by Google, teaching live physics lessons using Google Glass. As part of this teaching experience - STEMbite - a YouTube channel with a series of bite-size videos have been set up to show the math and science of everyday life from a unique first-person perspective [Heu 13]. It is the shift in perspective, from watching a lecturing teacher, to seeing as if through the eyes of a teacher, that allows for new teaching and learning experiences. One of the examples includes the transmission from the Large Hadron Collider at CERN in Switzerland to students in the USA. This type of educational transmission from at the eye-level perspective capture allows both educators and learners to capture the surrounding environments and participate in just-in-time activities. In this way learners can construct Personal Learning Environments by linking physical and virtual learning spaces and participating in glocal learning activities, including virtual field trips with embedded communication with both local and remote peers, educators and experts.

Mobile Tagging

Thanks to such technologies as Global Positioning Systems (GPS) or tag-based augmented reality technologies including Quick Response (QR) codes, physical spaces can be transformed into digitally augmented spaces where the digital and the physical merge. These technologies, in combination with the software on mobile devices detecting the position of the user and providing context-aware learning depending on the location, offer new opportunities for learning based on the principles of geocaching. Geocaching appeared as a treasure hunting game with a GPS-enabled device in a physical space in the late 1990s. Geocaching has been played throughout the world by adventure seekers equipped with GPS devices, called geocachers, who locate hidden containers, called geocaches, in physical outdoor settings and then share their experiences offline and online [Zec 12]. In the recent years, geocaching has developed as an approach to designing localised learning activities, which utilize the benefits of ubiquitous computing in outdoor settings. As such geocaching concept, methods and tools have been making their way in education under the name of educaching [Dob 07]. Educaching encompasses a range of applications and scenarios, such as providing learning content in caches which can be found with the help of location services, also in form of mobile learning games, linking physical surroundings to digital learning content.

etiquetAR is a web-mobile-based application for generating interactive tags to support the design and enactment of mobile learning experiences [Pér 13b]. etiquetAR is based on the idea that digital tags, e.g. QR codes, can work as digital layers of information that extend and transform physical spaces into digitally augmented learning spaces. The etiquetAR application includes a set of functionalities that are especially suitable to support smart city learning. First, etiquetAR allows users to create own tags with the image of a QR code linking physical objects to multiple digital resources. Users can create interactive tags linking with one or a list of resources, all associated with a particular profile that learners can select when creating tags. The profile functionality allows users to adapt their learning path according to own needs or interests. Second, tags generated with etiquetAR can be read with any QR code reader, allowing users with diverse devices with different operating systems to participate in learning. Third, etiquetAR tags can be commented on, which enables users to contribute new ideas and opinions about resources associated to a particular code. The comment functionality allows for micro-blogging and in this way supports conversations as part of smart city learning. Since anyone can generate tags attachable to any urban element, urban spaces can be transformed into blended spaces, which at the same time can be extended by anyone in the city. etiquetAR can be used as a service for generating indoor and outdoor learning experiences based on educaching and analysing the type of scenarios that emerge from its usage. In this context, etiquetAR tags act as geocaches that are distributed and attached to objects in the city. Tags can be generated, personalized and commented on by any user, allowing for building communities of knowledge associated to particular urban spaces. In this way, etiquetAR can support multi-directional conversations through multiple channels allowing learners to engage in multiple communication and follow multiple learning paths.

Most educaching scenarios, such as environmental education [Zec 12], involve the uses of GPS technology to situate the geocaches and guide the learners along the interactive adventure. However, the potential of tag position-based technologies such as QR codes or NFC for educaching experience in closed places such as museums, has not yet been fully explored. Moreover, compared with other position-based technologies such as GPS, that directly shows resources when the user is positioned in a particular location, tag position-based technologies are specially interesting in learning situations in which a voluntary user-information interaction is expected. In this context, tags can be seen as digital layers of information allowing for an ad-hoc construction of Personal Learning Environments. By enabling learners to discover different places and dynamically constructing learning spaces, educaching promotes ubiquitous, playful and exploratory learning in both outdoor and indoor settings. As such educaching can be seen as an approach to constructing Personal Learning Environments (PLE) by connecting local and global perspectives (glocality) and moving across different physical and virtual places (spaces). In educaching experiences, learners construct their knowledge

by solving game-like challenges and creating game-like challenges for other learners, using various tools to localise physical objects and relate digital information to these objects, as well as by interacting with other educaching participants, both within and outside of physical proximity. Based on the understanding of Personal Learning Environments (PLE) as self-directed uses of technology by the learner to support own learning [Buc 11], educaching involves appropriation of tools and resources by the learner, who constructs own spaces for learning by selecting, aggregating and creating resources from physical and virtual spaces.

Exploring Scenarios for Smart City Learning

In order to understand how educators envisage constructing Personal Learning Environments in context of smart city learning, we conducted an international, exploratory study with educators from around the world. Altogether 16 educators from different higher education institutions in countries in Europe, North America, South America Middle-East and Asia-Pacific participated in the study and contributed their ideas and visions on smart city learning. The study consisted of two parts both based on an online survey, in which educators were invited to reflect about possible smart city learning scenarios. In the first part of the survey, related to possible uses of etiquetAR for educaching in context of smart city learning, selected five educators were asked to describe (1) a use case scenario using etiquetAR, including its main objectives, who will participated and what activities would they perform, (2) how learners would create their PLE in their scenarios and (3) what will be the personal environment composed of. Three exemplary scenarios elicited in the first part of the survey are presented in Table 1.

Table 1: Examples of educaching scenarios elicited in the first part of the study

QUESTION	EDUCATORS' ANSWER
EDUCATOR 1 (1) The scenario	**Setting**: I would like to design and run a connectivist MOOC (cMOOC) on learning technologies. As part of the logo of this MOOC there will be a QR code generated with etiquetAR. Every week I would suggest a topic for discussion. Students may discuss online but also gather physically in groups at different locations in cities. One of those participating in the physical meetings will print the logo of the course and use it at a banner stuck on the wall at the meeting place (e.g. a cafeteria or pub). After the discussion one of the participants will scan the QR code, adding the main conclusions of that meeting as a comment to the question posed by me (the instructor). That will happen in all the cities where learners gather for face-to-face discussions.

	Objectives and theme: Discussing about given questions on learning technologies (e.g. the role of MOOCs nowadays, the potential of mobile devices in face-to-face classes). The theme would be Technology Enhanced Learning. **Participants and roles:** Me (instructor) in the role of facilitator for the discussions. Learners as the ones who actually discuss selected topics. **Activity plan:** Weekly face-to-face meetings and online discussions. **Organization**: I will pose a weekly question, analyze the conclusions of the discussion in every face-to-face group, analyze the contributions in further online discussion, and then I will set my own conclusions. **Complementary social media tools**: Foursquare and meetup for organizing the meetings; Facebook and Twitter for further online discussions.
(2) Learners PLE creation	There is no central platform like an LMS in this MOOC. The contributions to the course are distributed across a number of web 2.0 tools.
(3) PLE composition	The PLE will be constructed using Foursquare, Meetup, Facebook, Twitter and some other tools that students will want to add by their own initiative.

EDUCATOR 2	
(1) The scenario	**Setting**: The context of my informal learning scenario uses etiquetAR in a technological fair. The different exhibitors are tagged using etiquetAR so that a visitor can approach them and know more about the technology or service exhibited. There are several profiles of visitors: techies, businessmen, investors, etc. Each of them will have personalized information from the tags, as well as a communication channel by means of the comments. **Objectives and theme**: The concrete learning objective depends on the learner profile. It is different for a techie and a businessman. But a common objective is to be aware of new technologies and services in their field, find out what other participants think about them, and collect enough information about them to further explore/investigate the most relevant. **Participants and roles:** In this informal learning setting, there will be learners (the visitors) and a basic learning content (the info about the products and services) provided by the vendors, that is used by the organizers to tag the exhibitors in the fair. **Activity plan:** As previously described, the main activity would be for the visitors to walk around the fair, find out more about the products and services, and provide comments about them to share with their profile peers. Once the fair is finished, the information collected would help them to choose some products and services to investigate in depth. **Complementary social media tools:** Social media could be used jointly with etiquetAR to detect trendy products in the fair. An integration of one of them, for example twitter, with etiquetAR comments would be nice to open the conversation about the products and services to the world.

(2) Learners PLE creation	The visitors create their PLEs by deciding which exhibitor resources to visit and what media tools to use in order to be part of the conversation. With the personalized information collected (e.g. links, tutorials, interesting comments), visitors can continue learning after the event. Maybe some of them will report about what they learnt in the fair to their bosses using etiquetAR and social media.
(3) PLE composition	The learning resources would be the information associated with the exhibitors, as well as the interaction with the salesmen. It is an unstructured learning setting, in which the learners (visitors) decide about the next learning steps, creating their Personal Learning Environments as they move on.

EDUCATOR 4	
(1) The scenario	**Setting**: Adapting a physical environment to support language learning. **Objectives and theme**: The theme would be a location-based and multilingual learning experience focusing on vocabulary learning. The objectives would be to learn the vocabulary of more than one language. **Participants and roles**: Teachers would have the role of resource creators. Learners would have the role of participants in one or more languages. **Activity plan**: 1. Checking for information of an object in the physical space; 2. Providing more information about an object; 3. Performing an assessment about the information of an object. **Complementary social media tools**: Probably a learning management system.
(2) Learners PLE creation	By providing more information, either general or contextual, about each object in the physical space.
(3) PLE composition	The physical space, the objects that can be visited, commented and assessed about.

We analyzed all five educaching scenarios proposed by the educators as summarized in Table 1 in relation to three research question related to smart city learning addressed in the first part of the explorative study, i.e.: (1) What types of educaching scenarios can support smart city learning? (2) What types uses of tag-based technologies can support construction of PLEs? (3) How can etiquetAR provide guidance for PLE construction in educaching scenarios?

Regarding the first question about the type of educaching scenarios designed to support smart city learning, we could derive three main characteristics of smart city learning scenarios:

1. Smart city learning scenarios combine exploratory learning activities carried out in informal or non-formal outdoor and indoor settings, combining both open and closed physical locations with online environments. Such exploratory learning activities occur in several spatial locations in which learners can freely explore me-

diated interactions.

2. Smart city learning scenarios promote discussions and reflections about physical spaces with the learning objectives being to actively interact with other ideas and context of other learners, such as contributing comments to proposed tags. Discussions and reflections aims at making learners aware about physical objects in different locations by providing information adapted to individual profiles.
3. Smart city learning scenarios are learner-centered, where the learner plays an active role in each learning activity with teachers acting as facilitators in the activity. Learners play the role of contributors adding comments and ideas to complement information provided by peers.

Regarding the second question related to the uses of tags supporting the construction of Personal Learning Environments, we could see that teachers propose the construction of PLEs composed of social media tools in combination with the use of interactive tags, as created with etiquetAR. Especially, educators view tools such as Facebook and Twitter as part of educational scenarios, followed by uses of Learning Management Systems, wikis and other Web 2.0 tools.

Regarding the third question about the type of guidance provided by tools such as etiquetAR for supporting PLE construction we could identify three different generic strategies, i.e.:

1. Constructing PLEs by interacting with people, mediated by technologies, such as tags, as a communication channel to receive and leave information. An example of this type of strategy is the scenario proposed by Educator 2, in which visitors to a trade fair learn by connecting to other visitors and exhibitors, e.g. by leaving comments about different exhibits.
2. 2Constructing PLEs by interacting with objects, mediated by technologies, such as tags, adapted to user profile. An example of this type of strategy is the scenario proposed by Educator 4, in which students receive information in different languages about an object in the city.
3. Constructing PLEs by interacting with tools, mediated by technologies, such as tags, in combination with other web-based tools. An example of this type of strategy is the scenario proposed by Educator 1, in which students can use complementary tools integrated in a MOOC.

In the second part of the survey, we invited selected educators to describe their visions of future smart city learning scenarios with emerging technologies, including badges, augmented reality and wearable computing. Several exemplary scenarios elicited in the second part of the survey are presented in Table 2.

Table 2: Examples of smart city learning scenarios with emerging technologies.

TECHNOLOGICAL FOCUS	EDUCATORS' SCENARIO
(1) Pervasive technologies	Learning in smart cities will mostly be constructed out of short fragmented interaction with pervasive technology serving as a consolidating umbrella by documenting, aggregating and connecting discrete interactions into a larger whole, allowing for revisiting, self-reflection and ultimately, for a deeper learning experience. Learning will become highly personal and personalized, embedded sensors will become prevalent both in the learners' environment (i.e. the city) as well as physically embedded on the learners body and on wearable items, allowing for technology to serve as a true extension of the self, collecting explicit and implicit cues from the learner for the purpose of highlighting, mediating and supporting learning opportunities. Learning, with the mediation of pervasive technologies, will have a social context as learners will increasingly become a part of a connected group of learners, be it their real life peers or ad hoc groups of learners who share a common interest or simply a common location.
(2) Open Badges	Well, let me try to imagine a learning scenario in smart cities. I think (or I hope) that in the future each person will have his own device to learn (1:1). Nowadays we can see many students with notebooks and smartphones and a few students with tablets. Internet connection will be provided by cities for everyone and everywhere. In future cities learning will be supported by localization in context, e.g. the system will recognize learner's location and provide adequate information, helping to find people who have similar interests and indicating appropriate learning resources based on the context. Especially, technologies such as Open Badges will be used to communicate expertise (including non-formal expertise of non-scholars), and will be supported by game-based approaches such as gamification which together with social networks will be integrated into curricula and considered as part of the learning environment.
(3) Mobile Tagging	Learning in educational contexts will be different. For example learning about geography, such as climate change, population growth, demographic changes or urbanisation will be supported by using different geo-localisation apps on mobile devices. As far as learning about history, QR codes will be attached to different places and historical information will be displayed with the help of AR applications. In civic education, learning about neighbourhoods will be supported by e-badges displayed in bus stations, supermarkets etc., transforming open spaces into places for learning about the city. SNS will be used to support learning about policies, local governments, to post pictures and trace places of local interests, mapping events and public transportations with geo-localisation apps. QR codes will be used to open the appetite for learning. For example, chains of QR codes will be used to support storytelling and team-based adventures.

(4) Augmented Reality	In the future we will learn history in a different way. A historian will be able to analyze developments of a given battle way back in time. Historians will be able to visit a battlefield and not only reenact history by using augmented reality, but also change the conditions under which the battle took place, change the compositions of the armies, change the hour of the day, the weather ... and learn how it all affected one side or the other side's victory by actually seeing it, not just being told about it and having to believe it. In this train of thought, augmented reality used for simulation will automatically lead to experimentation. With a major difference - so far experimentation has been something mostly reserved for experimental sciences. Augmented reality can definitely contribute to bringing experimentation into social sciences.More than providing contextual information, we should be thinking on how augmented reality can bring knowledge into many fields of science and learning, by enabling simulation and, thus, experimentation in many fields and situations. The main limitation for 3D environments was that input still used to be 2D, e.g mouse movements over the screen. With augmented reality, input can match output and a 3D environment enables a full and comprehensive learning experience. And this will surely change the way we work, have fun and, of course, learn.
(5) Smart objects	I guess that in the future the locations/objects themselves will present people/groups different and challenging learning opportunities. I also believe that the technology involved will not be intrusive because natural interfaces will be used. And yes, that kind of challenge will be drawn by educators but also by learning peers as I believe that learning and assessment/validation will suffer major changes and that peer assessment will be increasingly important. I believe the future will bring new and totally different teaching and learning scenarios in which objects will be able to communicate with us and with other things in order to create exciting learning opportunities. I think that in a near future students will be able to directly interact with objects and that those objects will be, in a "real" sense, learning objects, posing challenges and providing exciting learning opportunities to them. One example of something that we are currently working on: the idea that in a chemistry lab you can learn through direct manipulation and interaction with lab objects, learning all the security procedures needed to use them. The idea is to use natural interfaces and invisible computing techniques.
(6) Google Glass	In the future we will use opportunities of wearable computers for improvement of educational processes (e.g. Google Glass videos for young teachers). We can collect video data about best practices from leading educators at universities (e.g. Youtube channel "Google Glass in professional practice"). For example, young surgeons (or students of medical faculty) will be able to watch through Google Glass video how experienced surgeon performs open heart surgery. Also young educators (e.g. faculty of education) will be able to watch how leading lecturer interacts with the students in the classroom. Young teachers can observe the behavior of the lecturer (voice volume, direction of gaze, movement in the classroom). It will be possible to see how students react on different methods

	of teaching. That means Google Glass give us opportunities to watch from teacher's side on professional situations. And every young teacher around the world by video channel "Google Glass in professional practice" will be able to improve his/her teaching skills.
(7) Mobile social media	Mobile social media is inherently collaborative, but requires a significant rethink of assessment design, utilizing collaborative user-content generation tools such as Vyclone for collaborative video. In the future lecturers will engage with and model the educational use of mobile social media within the curriculum. This requires reconceptualizing mobile social media from a purely social domain to an academic and professional domain of use. For example: Google Maps or Google Earth will be used as a collaborative platform to collate/curate student projects from around the world, where student teams link their geotagged content within a shared Google Map. This adds the dimension of authentic context to student projects, with the ability for students around the world to share in the experience of learning of others within the original context. Linking geotagged content from a variety of new and emerging mobile Apps makes this a relatively simple yet dynamic and collaborative experience. Example Apps include: Vyclone for collaborative video recording, the online YouTube video editor for collaborative video editing and annotation, Flickr, Instagram, and Picasa for collaborative photo sharing/curation, Junaio for embedding QR tags within augmented reality etc. Academic rigour can be achieved by requiring students to annotate their content using accepted referencing styles, yet turning this into a collaborative curation activity via creating shared Mendeley or Zotero libraries etc. Specific activities will depend upon each students' context, and should be student negotiable, however the collaborative element of such projects needs to be clearly defined, as student experience of being active members within an authentic professional global community of practice is one of the goals of such projects.

The analysis of the second part of the survey reveals some key technologies envisaged by educators to play a central role in supporting smart city learning. These include pervasive technologies, augmented reality, mobile tagging including QR codes and geotagging, digital badges, mobile social media, smart objects and wearable computing including Google Glass. To sum up, the first exploratory results about possible smart city learning scenarios together with the educaching designs proposed by educators, are the first evidence indicating that a wide range of emerging technologies, going far beyond web 2.0 or social media, may be used to support learners in constructing their Personal Learning Environments in context of smart city learning.

Discussion

Current technologies allow transforming smart cities into augmented spaces for learning in which constructing Personal Learning Environments is happens ad-hoc and is adjusted dynamically to individual learner's context. The challenge is to understand how

Personal Learning Environments may be constructed as part of smart city learning. In this paper, we have reviewed some of the current techno-pedagogical approaches and practices in the field and presented our understanding of smart city learning. Based on the preliminary results of our international, explorative study we could identify three key generic strategies for constructing Personal Learning Environments in context of smart city learning. These include constructing Personal Learning Environments by interacting with people, objects and tools. The review of current literature and the results of our explorative study suggest, that the conceptualisation of Personal Learning Environments in context of smart city learning has to be extended to the view of PLEs as merged physical and virtual learning spaces which are constructed ad-hoc as learners move across spatial, temporal and conceptual contexts. To support learners in constructing their Personal Learning Environments in context of smart city learning, we need to understand what pedagogical strategies and technological uses could be most effective to do so. In this paper we have introduced educaching with a mobile tagging service etiquetAR as an example of a combination of pedagogical approach and technological application supporting smart city learning. This paper is just a preliminary exploration of smart city learning. We intend to elicit further scenarios across various educational contexts to understand what emerging technologies and pedagogical approaches could be employed to support learning in smart cities.

Acknowledgements

This work has been partially funded by the Spanish Ministry of Economy and Competitiveness with the EEE project (TIN2011-28308-C03-01 and TIN2011-28308-C03-03), by the eMadrid project (S2009/TIC-1650) funded by the Regional Government of Madrid and by post-doctoral initiative Alianza 4 Universidades. We would like to thank all educators who participated in our explorative study aiming at eliciting educational scenarios for smart city learning. Our thanks go to Rutrut Aladjem, Patricia Scherer Bassani, Carlos Alario-Hoyos, Thomas Cochrane, Mike Cosgrave, Iria Estévez-Ayres, Gabriela Grosseck, Israel Gutiérrez, Moshe Leiba, Derick Leony, Juan Alberto Muñoz Cristóbal, Luis Pedro, Ismael Peña-López, Tony Ratcliffe, Verónica Rivera Pelayo, Daniyar Sapargaliyev.

REFERENCES

[Bar 07] *Barab, Sasha; Zuiker, Steve; Warren, Scott; Hickey, Dan; Ingram-Goble, Adam; Kwon, Eun-Ju; Kouper, Inna; Herring, Susan C. (2007). Situationally embodied curriculum:* relating formalisms and contexts. Science Education 91(5), 750-782.

[Buc 11] *Buchem, Ilona; Attwell, Graham; Torres, Ricardo (2011). Understanding Personal Learning Environments:* Literature review and synthesis through the Activity Theory lens. pp. 1-33. Proceedings of the The PLE Conference 2011, Southampton, UK.

[Cal 13] *Calori, Ilaria Canova; Rossitto, Chiara; Divitini, Monica (2013). Understanding Trajectories of Experience in Situated Learning Field Trips. Interaction Design and Architecture(s) Journal - IxD&A, 16, 2013, 17-26. Retrieved from http://www.mifav.uniroma2.it/inevent/events/idea2010/doc/16_3.pdf*

[Cer 88] *Certeau, Michel de (1988). The Practice of Everyday Life. Berkeley:* University of California Press.

[COM 11] *COM (2011). COUNCIL DECISION establishing the Specific Programme Implementing Horizon 2020 - The Framework Programme for Research and Innovation (2014-2020). Retrieved from http://eur-lex.europa.eu/LexUriServ/LexUriServ.do?uri=COM:2011:0811:FIN:en:PDF*

[Coo 09] *Cook, Diane J.; Augusto, Juan C.; Jakkula, Vikramaditya R. (2009). Ambient Intelligence:* Technologies, Applications, and Opportunities. Pervasive and Mobile Computing 5, 277–298.

[Dob 07] *Dobyns, Sally M.; Dobyns, Megan S.; Connell, Elisabeth E. (2007). EDUCACHING:* Capturing the spirit ofthe hunt for learning. Teaching for High Potential. Washington, D. C.: National Association for Gifted Children.

[Eur 12] *Eurocities (2012). EUROCITIES statement on Horizon 2020. Retrieved from http://nws.eurocities.eu/MediaShell/media/EUROCITIES%20statement%20Horizon%202020.pdf*

[Ghi 09] *Ghiani, Giuseppe;. Paternò, Fabio; Santoro Carmen; Spano, Lucio Davide (2009). UbiCicero:* A location-aware, mutli-device museum guide, Interacting with computers, 21(4), 288-303.

[Gio 13a] *Giovanella, Carlos (2013). International Observatory on Smart City Learning. Retrieved from http://www.mifav.uniroma2.it/inevent/events/sclo/index.php?s=166*

[Gio 13b] *Giovenella, Carlos; Iosue, Aandrea;. Tancredi, Aantinello; Cicola, Fabrizio; Camusi, Andrea; Moggio, Fabrizia; Baraniello, Vincenzo; Carcone, Simone; Coco, Silvio (2013) Scenarios for active learning in smart territories. Interaction Design and Architecture(s) Journal - IxD&A, N. 16, 2013, 7-16.*

[Gol 04] *Golloway, Anne (2004). Intimations of everyday life:* Ubiquitous computing and the city. Cultural Studies, 18 (2-3).

[Hay 12] *Hayes, Andrew (2012). Reflections:* Glass & Mobile Learning. Transactions On Mobile Learning 2012, anzMLearn. Retrieved from *http://bit.ly/19gyj6V*

[Heu 13] *Heuvel, Andrew (2013). STEMbite:* An Experiment in Teaching with Google Glass, edutopia blog. Retrieved from *http://bit.ly/18JdgAl*

[Hil 13] *Hill, Dan (2013). Essay:* On the smart city; Or, a 'manifesto' for smart citizens instead. City of Sound. Retrieved from *http://www.cityofsound.com/blog/2013/02/on-the-smart-city-a-call-for-smart-citizens-instead.html*

[Fit 12] *FitzGerald, Elisabeth; Adams, Anne; Ferguson, Rebecca; Gaved, Mark; Mor, Yishay; Rhodri, Thomas (2012). Augmented reality and mobile learning:* the state of the art. In: 11th World Conference on Mobile and Contextual Learning (mLearn 2012), 16-18 Oct 2012, Helsinki, Finland, 62–69. Retrieved from *http://oro.open.ac.uk/34281/1/ARpaper_FINAL.pdf*

[Kni 12] *Knight, Eric; Casilli, Carla (2012). Mozilla Open Badges. Game Changers:* Education and Information Technologies. EDUCAUSE 2012. Retrieved from *http://net.educause.edu/ir/library/pdf/pub7203cs6.pdf*

[Lic 08] *Licoppe, Christian; Diminescu, Dana; Smoreda, Zbigniew; Ziemlicki, Cezary (2008). Using mobile phone geolocalisation for 'socio-geographical' analysis of co-ordination, urban mobilities, and social integration patterns. Tijdschrift voor Economische en Sociale Geografie - 2008, 99 (5), 584-600.*

[McC 13] *McCullough, Malcolm (2013). Attention in Urban Foraging. Interaction Design and Architecture(s) Journal - IxD&A, 16, 2013, 27-36. Retrieved from http://www.mifav.uniroma2.it/inevent/events/idea2010/doc/16_3.pdf*

[Mey 05] *Meyrowitz, Joshua (2005). The Rise of Glocality:* New Senses of Place and Identity in the Global Village. Electronic Media, 21-3.

[Mik 12] *Mikulecký, P. (2012). Smart Environments for Smart Learning. DIVAI 2012 – 9th International Scientific Conference on Distance Learning in Applied Informatics.*

[CSO 13] *CSOL (2013). Chicago Summer of Learning. Retrieved from http://chicagosummeroflearning.org/about*

[Nam 11] *Nam, Taewoo; Pardo, Theresa A. (2011). Conceptualizing smart city with dimensions, people, and institutions. Proceedings of the 12th Annual International Digital Government Research conference:* Digital Government Innovation in Challenging Times, ACM, 292-291.

[Pau 09] *Paulos, Eric; Honicky, R., Hooker, Ben (2009). Citizen Science:* Enabling Participatory Urbanism. In M. Foth (Ed.), Handbook of Research on Urban Informatics: The Practice and Promise of the Real-Time City. Hershey, PA: Information Science Reference, 414-436.

[Pér 13a] *Pérez-Sanagustín, Mar; Buchem, Ilona; Kloos, C Delago (2013). Multi-channel, multi-objective, multi-context services:* The glue of the smart cities learning ecosystem. Alpine Rendez-Vous 2013, Workshop 3: Smart Cities Learning, 28-29 January 2013, Villard-de-Lans, Vercors, France.

[Pér 13b] *Pérez-Sanagustín, M., Martínez, A., Delgado Kloos, C. (2013) etiquetAR:* Tagging Learning Experiences. Scaling up Learning for Sustained Impact. Lecture Notes in Computer Science, 8095, 573-576.

[Pos 09] *Poslad Stefan (2009). Ubiquitous Computing:* Smart Devices, Environments and Interaction. Wiley.

[San 13] *Santos, Jose Luis; Charleer, Sven; Parra, Gonzalo; Klerkx, Joris; Duval, Eric; Verbet, Katrien (2013) Evaluating the use of Open Badges in an Open Learning Environment. Scaling up Learning for Sustained Impact. Lecture Notes in Computer Science, 8095, 314-327.*

[San 11] *Santos, Patricia; Pérez-Sanagustín, Mar; Hernández-Leo, Davinia; Blat, Josep (2011) QuesTInSitu:* From tests to routes for assessment in situ activities, Computers & Education, 57(4), 2517-2534.

[Sha 09] *Sharples, Mike; Arnedillo-Sánchez, Inmaculada; Milrad, Marcelo; Vavoula, Giasemi (2009). Mobile learning:* Small devices, big issues. In: Balacheff, N.; Ludvigsen, S.; Jong, T. de; Barners, S. (Eds.) Technology-Enhanced Learning, Springer: New York, 233-249.

[Sha 13] *Sharples, Mike; McAndrew, Patrick; Weller, Martin; Ferguson, Rebecca; FitzGerald, Elisabeth; Hirst, Tony; Gaved, Mark (2013). Innovating Pedagogy 2013:* Exploring new forms of teaching, learning and assessment, to guide educators and policy makers. Retrieved from *http://www.open.ac.uk/personalpages/mike.sharples/Reports/Innovating_Pedagogy_report_2013.pdf*

[Vit 12] *Vitale, John L.; McCabe, Michael; Tedesco, Stephen; Wideman-Johnston, Taunya (2012). Cache Me If You Can:* Reflections on Geocaching from Junior/Intermediate Teacher Candidates, International Journal of Technology and Inclusive Education (IJTIE), 1 (1).

[Woo 11] *Woods, Eric; Bloom, Eric (2011). Smart Cities:* Intelligent Information and communication infrastructure in the government, buildings, transport, and utility domains. Pike Research.

[Yan 08] *Yang, Stephen J.H., Okamoto, Toshio, Tseng, Shian-Shyong (2008). Context–Aware and Ubiquitous Learning. Educational Technology & Society, 11 (2), 1-2.*

[Zec 12] *Zecha, Stefani (2012). Geocaching, a tool to support environmental education!?– An explorative study. Educational Research eJournal, North America, 1, July. 2012. Retrieved from http://www.erej.ua.es/rdd/article/view/36/24*

CONTACT DETAILS

Prof. Dr. Ilona Buchem
Beuth Universty of Applied Sciences
Department I Economics and Social Sciences
Luxemburger Street 10
13353 Berlin
Tel: +49 30 4504 5243
E-Mail: *buchem@beuth-hochschule.de*

Assistant Prof. Dr. Mar Pérez-Sanagustín
Pontificia Universidad Católica de Chile
Department of Computer Science
Av. Vicuña Mackenna 4860, Edif. San Agustín, 4º Piso
7820436 Santiago de Chile
Tel: +56 2 2354 7407
E-Mail: *mdelmar.ps@gmail.com*

Decentralized badges in educational contexts: the integration of Open Badges in SAPO Campus

Carlos Santos, Luís Pedro, Sara Almeida, Mónica Aresta

ABSTRACT

Nowadays it is still difficult to achieve recognition for learning developed in informal contexts. To attenuate this situation, a badging system was integrated in SAPO Campus in order to support the interaction and assessment processes occurred inside and beyond the classroom. Opposed to the usual top-bottom approach, this paper presents the concepts of user-generated and peer-support badge attribution, discussing the potential of badges in the promotion of a participatory learning community.

Note: *This article has been published in the Special Edition of the eLearning Papers, Issue No. 35 "Personal Learning Environments". The link to this Special Issue is:* http://openeducationeuropa.eu/en/paper/personal-learning-environments

Introduction

An essential part of the European strategy to meet future challenges is to build higher skills through better education and training systems (CEC 08). This will only be possible if lifelong learning becomes a reality, allowing people to acquire key competences such as problem solving, self-management, learning to learn, creative thinking [EC, 2008], and updating skills throughout their lives.

In this context, lifelong learning plays an important role today, as jobs and the skills required for them are changing [Ala 10]. In a lifelong learning approach, learners themselves are the main motivational instance; in other words, there is a high level of "ownership of learning" [Kel 12]. In a context where the digital technologies support the construction of connective knowledge as a result of learners' active role in interacting with information and collaborating with other learners [Dic 06], it is, however, often difficult to achieve recognition for skills, competences and learning developed in informal contexts [Goli 12].

In this scenario, the use of games and game-like elements in non-game contexts, which is called gamification [Det 11], could raise the users' engagement by using personalized and immediate feedback and motivating self-regulated learning through reward systems and competitive social mechanisms [Dom 13]. With these principles in mind, the SAPO Campus (URL: *http://campus.sapo.pt*) team has developed and integrated a badging system, supported by Mozilla Open Badges Technology. In this paper we will present the approach that guided the development of SAPO Campus' badging system that aims to break up the traditional top-bottom perspective to create and attribute badges. Its potential in the promotion of new ways of assessment and the development of truly participatory learning communities is discussed.

The potential of badges in educational contexts

Game-based learning has existed for a long time but still faces a main challenge: humans always have had the ability to engage and learn through gaming, but the natural drive to learn through games has a dismissive meaning, especially from the viewpoint of the formal educational systems [Kel 12]. According to [McG 11] cited in [Lee 11], the formal educational systems (e.g. schools) already have several gaming practices and elements – students get grades for correctly complete their assignments – however, contrary to what happens in games, this fails to engage students. As pointed by [Kel 12] users are not equally affected by games but there are a few main drivers responsible for their engagement with games:

- Immediate feedback: Users are able to see obvious and continuous progress and realize the effects of their actions through any type of measurement (e.g. points or badges). Also, they are able to compare their performances with others and become more easily motivated to compete with them.
- Collaboration: In some games collaboration can provide mutual benefits for players to achieve mastery, however the collaboration has also a competitive side between teams and between the players of the same team.
- Control and ownership: Games have a high potential to stimulate the notion of players' control and ownership. As the consequences remain in the game, the players have more freedom to try out different strategies and develop their own ways to solve the problem.
- Game-content: The gaming experience is more attractive and motivating when certain innovativeness and aesthetic is guaranteed by the game.

The incorporation of game features in several non-game domains as marketing, health and education has become increasingly recognized [Lee 11]. This phenomenon called gamification [Det 11] can enhance learners' motivation and increase self-directed learning, helping learners getting comfortable and engaged upon the overall learning process [Gro 12]. According to [And 12] gamification is the "interactive online design that plays on people's competitive instincts and often incorporates the use of rewards to drive action – these include virtual rewards such as points, payments, badges, discounts and free gifts; and status indicators such as friends counts, leader boards, achievement data, progress bars and the ability to level up". Game-like elements are used in several contexts. Corporations such as Samsung assign badges to motivate

their employees and services such as Foursquare assign badges as users check-in at locations [Far 13]. Mozilla is a non-profit company that wants to contribute to a better way for credentialing experiences, knowledge, interests and skills [Bel 13]. In this context, they have built the Open Badges Infrastructure (OBI) that makes possible for badges issued by different companies to be shareable across the Web.

Badges have been used for hundreds of years in military context as symbols of authority and control. Nowadays badges are used in the virtual world, being sometimes representations of the real world [Hal 12]. To [Ant 11], badges are digital artefacts with some visual representation, symbols of achievement representing the experience and mastery of an individual or group [Kni 12]. According to [Bar 12] badges could bring some advantages for learning, such as:

- Democratize learning and promote lifelong learning skills: the process of earning a badge is itself a learning process and can lead others to learning [Hal 12]. In this context, badges enable achievements beyond themselves, allowing and extending learning [Gold 12]. Additionally, badges can be viewed as a tool for developing the metacognitive skills required today in order to achieve success in formal and informal spaces, giving value to what is being learned, supporting connections and developing strategies for negotiating and shaping the learning environment [Bar 12].
- Promote alternative ways of assessment: in a context where lifelong learning is becoming increasingly recognized, a broader range of assessment tools is needed to achieve important learning goals [She 00]. Badges can serve as an alternative way of assessment, a new way to receive formative and summative evidence-based feedback [Bar 12].
- Improve users' engagement and motivation: if badges are not used just as another quantitative assessment system, they can actually promote motivation, inspiring individuals to greater mastery through "goal settings, instruction, reputation, status/affirmation and group identification" [Ant 11, p.1]. In this context, badges can express the values of a particular community, allowing for a self-directed gratification among the group and encouraging participatory learning [Bar 12].

In the next section, we will describe the main principles and concepts that guided the development and integration of a badging system – supported by the Mozilla Open Badges Technology – in the SAPO Campus platform.

The integration of Open Badges in SAPO Campus: a decentralized approach

Towards a SAPO Campus definition

SAPO Campus (SC), developed by the University of Aveiro and PT Communications/ SAPO, is an institutionally supported platform, specifically designed for educational contexts offering some social media services and features such as photos, videos, blogs, links and status [Pedr 12], in order to support the natural interaction that occurs inside and beyond the classroom walls and allow for the development of collaborative-based communities of learning.

Although formal educational institutions are not always equipped and prepared to bring the outside world into the classroom in order to enhance and enrich the learning process, the authors believe that the institutional adoption of SC and other social media platforms may promote changes not only in the way people interact and relate with each other, but also in the overall learning processes and methods [Pai 12].

In SAPO Campus each school establishes its own community/network. Nevertheless, users also have the possibility to build their own personal network by following people from any school with public activity. Being an institutionally supported platform that aims to encourage openness and sharing values, SC needs to balance the institutional and individual dimension. In this context, each institution must define its own privacy rules and provide an acknowledged space for secure content publishing, while users are able to share contents that, along with the content shared by the community they follow, are automatically aggregated in the newsfeed area.

The social dimension of the platform has also an important role. Along with the institutional area where the user can get access to all content shared by the other members and interact with different users and interests, in SAPO Campus users are able to create groups and participate in other communities based on shared interests. In this context, with the possibility of creating different groups or communities based in different interests, each user is able to establish different kinds of connections, which leads to the emergence of different knowledge hubs with different purposes and potentialities.

In order to enhance the development of truly participatory learning communities and promote new ways of assessment, a mechanism for creating, assigning and supporting badges was developed and integrated in SAPO Campus.

Integrating decentralized badges in SAPO Campus

Supported by the Open Badges Infrastructure (OBI) and taking into account the main principles of Mozilla Open Badges, badges earned in SAPO Campus are digital images having metadata 'baked' into them (e.g. name, description, criteria, etc.). Hence, they are portable and can be added to users' [Mozilla] backpack along with other badges earned in other contexts and platforms, in order to promote the development of an open and decentralized system where the learner is sovereign [Bel 13].

The SC badging system comprises two main types of attribution: automatic and manual. While the automatic attribution is integrated in a challenge-based tutorial that allows users to earn badges as a result of completing specific and predetermined challenges (e.g. visit the different areas of the platform or follow at least one user), the manual system allows the participation of the community – school administrators,

teachers, learners and other members – to create, attribute and support the attribution of badges. However, OBI doesn't provide yet this type of interaction although they present something similar in the roadmap, designated by "Endorsement".

In our opinion, in order to be sustainable this system must be supported and nurtured by the whole community and not only by the school administrators. In this context, SAPO Campus approach tries to break up with the traditional top-bottom perspective for the creation and attribution of badges, through the promotion of two main concepts: user-generated badges and peer-support for badge attribution.

User-generated badges

One of the features of most badging systems in digital platforms is that users do not have the power to create their own badges. It's expected that users must only try to achieve the challenges created and promoted by space owners in order to get the final compensation, the badge. SAPO Campus approach recognizes two main level of users. Educational institutions are at the first level and it looks somehow obvious that they need to have the power to decide the badges that are most suitable to their own context(s).

Our first concern related to institutions was to create a set of predefined badges that the institution (through school administrators) is able to activate and use, for instance, badges representing school roles such as teacher, student or guest (Figure 1). These badges will only be visible to the community if the institution decides to activate them. One exception to this rule is the "Fã do SAPO Campus" ("SAPO Campus fan") badge that is activated by default. The first tests conducted by the team showed that it was critical to have at least one badge activated at the institution initial setup to allow users, and even administrators, to get curious and discover this functionality.

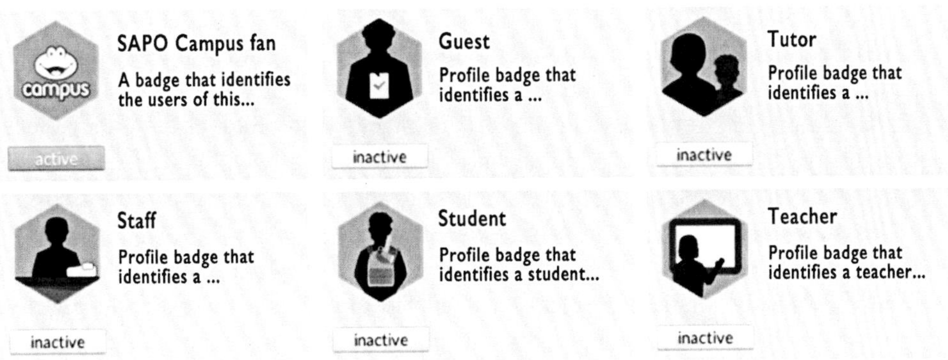

Figure 1: Predefined platform badges

Institutions are also able to create their own badges by using the Badge Constructor Tool integrated into the platform (Figure 2) that allows them to easily create new and unique badges by selecting and combining a set of different elements (frameworks, backgrounds, images, colours and an optional text label).

Figure 2: Create new badges on the platform using the Badge Constructor Tool

Institution badges are attributed by the administrator(s) to users and become automatically visible in their SC profile. Badges can be attributed to users in 3 different ways: (1) in the user's profile by clicking on the Mozilla Open Badges icon and selecting the desired badge; (2) in any public activity item, being possible to associate the badge to the specific content that has motivated the attribution; (3) in the badges' page, allowing to select multiple users at the same time.

At a second level we decided that it was critical to let any user to create and assign their own badges. For instance, it could be a teacher that aims to have badges for their classes or it could be a group of students that would like to create some badges related to a topic of their own interest. SAPO Campus allows this by making possible to create and attribute badges in the context of groups. As any user can create groups, all users are able to create new badges through the same set of elements mentioned above and attribute them to its members. In this particular context the badge recipient will be able to accept, reject or make the badge visible only inside the group (Figure 3).

This type of control mechanism is critical to assure that badges aren't used with bad intentions that could culminate in a new type of undesired bullying. An additional protection mechanism was also implemented to block the badge edition after being assigned for the first time. Hence, it is not possible to offer a badge with a positive meaning that, after accepted, could be converted to a negative one.

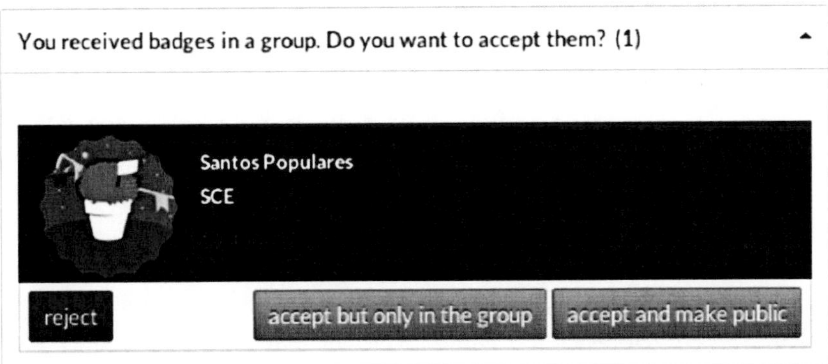

Figure 3: Accept or reject badges in the context of a group

We believe that this feature will allow a greater involvement of the whole community (teachers, school administrators, students or other members) in creating and attributing badges in different contexts with different purposes (e.g. having the best performance in a classroom activity or win an extracurricular contest). We also recognize that it's still possible to go further in this approach, for instance, allowing any user in any context to create a new badge and suggest it to be accepted by the institution or by the group owner. This type of functionality will be part of our future research. Another topic still under discussion is the possibility of extending the Badge Constructor Tool by allowing users to upload their own content to build the badge or even to upload a complete badge image directly to the platform.

Peer-support for badge attribution

One major difficulty related with manual badge attribution mechanisms is the required effort from users responsible for that task. A good decision process requires that administrators follow all the activity from their community and that they have the capability to remember all the badges and the respective decision process that, quite regularly, could be based on a subjective set of rules.

Our first implementation of badges in the platform occurred during the PLE Conference 2012 in Aveiro and we've learned by our own experience how difficult and time consuming that task could be. We believe that the best approach to this problem could be the distribution of this task across the community. Any user could contribute to the administrator task by showing their support for a specific badge to a specific user.

Administrators are notified of each endorsement and have access to a tool that helps them in the decision process of attribution of badges. The same set of principles is also applied for groups. In the platform interface, badge attribution and support are very similar actions. The interface is basically the same but the action available depends on the user role in that specific context. Support is available for any user of the community and for group members. Support and/or attribution are only available to administrators or group owners.
Badge attribution and support follow a set of rules:

- the attribution of badges by administrators is always done in the name of the institution. It is not a specific administrator that attributes the badge. It is the institution and users don't have the opportunity to know the person responsible for it;
- administrators are also able to support a badge as a normal user. In this case, it is the user that supports the badge, not the institution;
- supports previous to the badge attribution are only visible to administrators or group owners. This rule is important to avoid the discussion about the badge attribution decision process that could be questionable regarding only the quantitative part of the process;
- after the badge attribution all supports are made public.

Peer-support for badge attribution was built mainly to help the decision process. But as stated in the last two points, we decided also to make the process public. After receiving the badge, the user will be able to view the number of supports and who supported the attribution. On the page of the user badge, it is also possible to comment and see other users that also have received the same badge (Figure 4), which may reinforce the credibility, the competition and the sense of belonging to the community.

Figure 4: Page of the user badge

The table below summarizes the process of creating, attributing and supporting badges on SAPO Campus, stating where, how and who is able to do those actions.

Table 1: Create, attribute and support badges on SAPO Campus

	CREATE	ATTRIBUTE	SUPPORT
Where	Institutions and groups	Institutions and groups	Institutions and groups
Who	School by group administrators	School by group administrators	Any user
How	By using the integrated Badge Constructor Tool	By clicking on the Mozilla Open Badges icon on: • The user profile • The page of the badge • Any public activity item	By clicking on the Mozilla Open Badges icon on: • The user profile • The page of the badge • Any public activity item

Current research

In order to understand the relevance of the use of automatic badges as a strategy to promote users' engagement and motivation, a pilot test was conducted in October 2012 with beginner users of SAPO Campus. They were asked to complete an introductory tutorial of the platform, discovering the existence of badges and how they could be earned. We aimed to understand the impact of badges on their desire to complete the tutorial and their general attitude towards being rewarded with badges. The main results revealed that earning badges has contributed for users to feel more engaged with the tutorial challenges (automatic badging system) and that students would like to be able to earn more badges as a result for completing other activities occurring inside or outside the classroom context [San 13].

To systematically improve the system according to the user's needs, and with the manual system for badges attribution fully available, a second test is being conducted in order to characterize the use of manual badging system and to understand the users' opinion about the potential of this system in the promotion of news ways of assessment and interaction in order to enable the development of truly participatory learning communities.

In this context, some preliminary usage data (quantitative) was collected regarding the activity of the manual badging system. The graph below (Figure 5) represents the number of badges created, attributed and supported since the system was launched in May, 17th 2013.

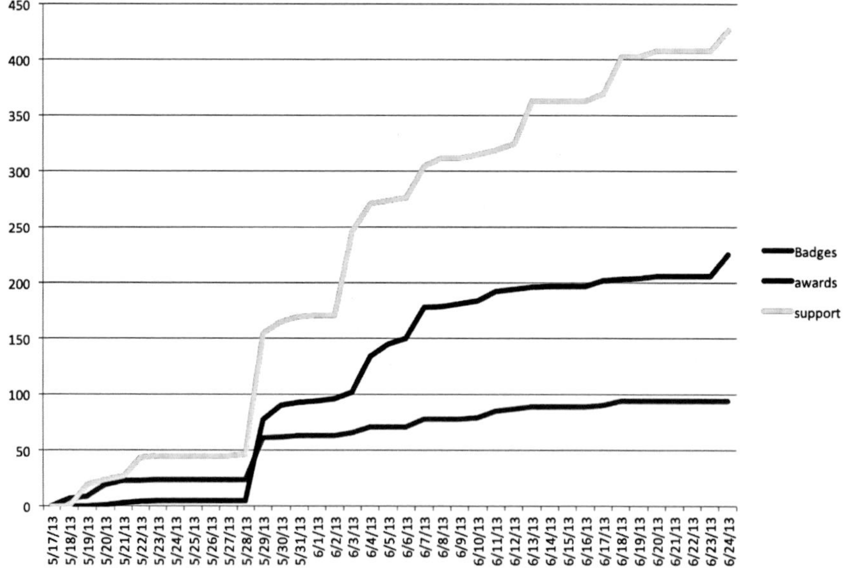

Figure 5: Progress of badges creation, attribution and support

The number of created badges has progressively increased, reaching 94 in June 24th 2013. The same happens with badge attribution and support reaching, in the same period, 225 attributions and 427 supports. It is important to note that there was no specific promotion and dissemination of the service apart from a post that was made in the SC blog team announcing the integration of the badging system. We believe that this blog post may have influenced the significant increase in badge creation, attribution and support verified in that day.

These preliminary results are very interesting because they are showing that, even without guidance and launched in a very late and very busy phase of the academic year, SC users are adopting the system and using its main features. However, they are insufficient to understand the users' opinion about the potential of the system in the promotion of new ways of assessment and interaction. In this context, a survey will be developed focusing in the aforementioned issues to be answered by a heterogeneous group of users: learners from all educational levels, teachers and school administrators. The collection of data at different groups and levels of education aims to understand the differences (if any) between users, regarding their experience and opinion about the decentralized approach for manual badging system and its potential to enhance the development of richer learning environments.

Taking users' feedback into account, new elements as images, backgrounds and frameworks can be added and the recommendation of new badges that the user can win (similar to what happens with the recommendation of people the user may know or content he or she might be interested in) can be introduced at the platform. In this context, the collected data will allow us to adjust the system in order to accomplish the needs of SAPO Campus users and to characterize the usage scenarios of the manual system for create and attribute badges.

Conclusions

This paper presented the approach that guided the SC R&D team in integrating a system, supported by Mozilla Open Badges technology, for creating and attributing badges in the platform. This approach, trying to break with the traditional way badges are used and attributed in the educational field, introduces two major concepts: user-generated badges and peer-support for badge attribution.

These concepts refer to the idea that creating and attributing badges should not be exclusive of a few users and that the whole community should be involved, participating in and supporting the attribution decision process. However, as SC is an institutionally supported platform designed mainly for educational contexts, it is also important to guarantee the validity of the whole process. This means that, in the institutional context, only the school administrators are able to create and attribute badges that are automatically attached to the user profile. Nevertheless, all users can support the attribution of badges before or after the attribution. Badges can also be freely created and attributed in groups. Any user can create a group and, in this context, he or she can create and attribute badges that must be accepted (being publicly visible or only visible inside the group) or rejected by its members.

With the manual system fully available, some preliminary data about the activity of create, attribute and support badges was collected. The first results show that SC' users are progressively adopting and using the system and its main features, specially the support. In this context, it would be interesting to further collect more data in order to characterize the usage scenarios and to understand the users' opinion about the system and its potential in the promotion of truly participatory learning communities.

Acknowledgments

The authors would like to acknowledge University of Aveiro, SAPO and TMN for the scientific, financial and technical support to the SAPO Campus project and the Labs SAPO/UA R&D activities. This work is part of the Shared Personal Learning Environments (ref: PTDC/CPE-CED/114130/2009) project funded by FEDER funds through the Operational Programme for Competitiveness Factors – COMPETE and National Funds through FCT – Foundation for Science and Technology (Portugal).

REFERENCES

[Ala 10] *Ala-Mutka, Kirsti (2010):* Learning in informal online networks and communities. JRC-IPTS. Luxembourg.

[Ant 11] *Antin, Judd; Churchill, Elizabeth (2011):* Badges in social media: A social psychological perspective. Human Factors, ACM, 1–4.

[And 12] *Anderson, Janna Quitney; Rainie, Lee (2012):* Gamification: Experts expect 'game layers' to expand in the future, with positive and negative results. Pew Research Center's Internet & American Life Project. Washington, D.C.

[Bar 12] *Barry, Joseph (2012):* Six ways to look at badging systems designed for learning. Global kids Online Leadership Program. Retrieved May 2013 from *http://www.olpglobalkids.org/content/six-ways-look-badging-systems-designed-learning*

[Bel 13] *Belshaw, Doug (2013):* Answering your questions about open badges. Retrieved May 2013 from *http://dougbelshaw.com/blog/2013/05/08/answering-your-questions-about-open-badges*

[CEC 08] *Commission of the European Communities (2008):* Communication from the Commission to the European Parliament, the Council, the European Economic and Social Committee and the Committee of the Regions. An updated strategic framework for European cooperation in education and training. Brussels.

[Det 11] *Deterding, Sebastian; Dixon, Dan; Khaled, Rilla; Nacke, Lennart (2011):* From game design elements to gamefulness: defining "Gamification". In Lugmayr, A., Franssila, H., Safran, C., & Hammouda, I. (Eds.) Proceedings of the 15th International Academic MindTrek Conference: Envisioning Future Media Environments, Finland: ACM, 9–15.

[Dic 07] *Dickey, Michelle D. (2007):* Game design and learning: a conjectural analysis of how massively multiple online role-playing games (MMORPGs) foster intrinsic motivation. Educational Technology Research and Development, 55 (3), 253–273.

[Dom 13] *Domínguez, Adrián; Saenz-de-Navarrete, Joseba; DeMarcos, Luis; Fernandéz-Sanz, Luis; Pagés, Carmen; Martinéz-Herráiz, José-Javier (2013):* Gamifying learning experiences: practical implications and outcomes. Computers & Education, 63, 380–392.

[EC 08] *EC (2008). Lifelong Learning for Creativity and Innovation:* A Background Paper. Retrieved May 2013 from *http://www.sac.smm.lt/images/12 %20Vertimas %20SAC %20Creativity %20 and %20innovation %20- %20SI %20Presidency %20paper %20anglu %20k.pdf*

[Far 13] *Farber, Matthew (2013):* Gamifying student engagement. Retrieved May 2013 from *http://www.edutopia.org/blog/gamifying-student-engagement-matthew-farber*

[Gold 12] *Goldberg, David Theo (2012):* Badges for learning: Threading the deedle between scepticism and evangelism. Retrieved May 2013 from: *http://dmlcentral.net/blog/david-theo-goldberg/badges-learning-threading-needle-between-skepticism-and-evangelism*

[Goli 12] *Goligoski, Emily (2012):* Motivating the Learner: Mozilla's Open Badges Program. Access to knowledge, 4 (1).

[Gro 12] *Groh, Fabian (2012):* Gamification: State of the art, definition and utilization. In Asaj, N. et al. (Eds.) Proceedings of the 4th Seminar on Research Trends in Media Informatics, Germany: Institute of Media Informatics, Ulm University, 39–46.

[Hal 12] *Halavais, Alexander. M. C. (2012):* A genealogy of badges: Inherited meaning and monstrous moral hybrids. Information, Communication and Society, 15 (3), 354–373.

[Kel 12] *Kelle, Sebastian (2012):* Game design patterns for learning. Centre for Learning Sciences and Technologies: Dutch Research School for Information and Knowledge Systems.

[Kni 12] *Knight, Erin; Casilli, Carla (2012):* Case Study 6: Mozzilla Open Badges. In Oblinguer, D. (Ed.). Game Changers: Education and Information Technology. Educause Publications, 279–284.

[Lee 11] *Lee, Joey J. & Hammer, Jessica (2011):* Gamification in education: what, how, why bother? Academic Exchange Quarterly, 15 (2).

[She 00] *Shepard, Lorrie A. (2000):* The role of assessment in a learning culture. Educational Researcher, 29 (7), 4–14.

[Pai 12] *Pais, Fátima; Santos, Carlos; Pedro, Luís (2012):* Sapo Campus Schools as a disruptive innovation tool: could it be the educational Ba? Retrieved May 2013 from *http://revistas.ua.pt/index.php/ple/article/view/1434*

[Ped 12] *Pedro, Luís; Santos, Carlos; Almeida, Sara; Koch-Grunberg, Tim (2012):* Building a shared personal learning environment with SAPO Campus. Retrieved May 2013 from *http://revistas.ua.pt/index.php/ple/article/viewFile/1426/1312*

[San 13] *Santos, Carlos; Almeida, Sara; Pedro, Luís; Aresta, Mónica; Koch-Grünberg, Tim (2013):* Students' perspectives on badges in educational social media platforms. 13th IEEE International Conference on Advanced Learning Technologies. Beijing, China (Paper ID: 89).

FIGURES

Figure 1	Predefined platform badges
Figure 2	Create new badges on the platform using the Badge Constructor Tool
Figure 3	Accept or reject badges in the context of a group
Figure 4	Page of the user badge
Figure 5	Progress of badges creation, attribution and support

CONTACT DETAILS

Carlos Santos
University of Aveiro
Departamento de Comunicação e Arte
Campus Universitário de Santiago 3810-193 Aveiro – Portugal
Phone: +351 (0) 234 370389
E-Mail: *carlossantos@ua.pt*

Luís Pedro
University of Aveiro
Departamento de Comunicação e Arte
Campus Universitário de Santiago 3810-193 Aveiro – Portugal
Phone: +351 (0) 234 370389
E-Mail: *lpedro@ua.pt*

Sara Almeida
University of Aveiro
Departamento de Comunicação e Arte
Campus Universitário de Santiago 3810-193 Aveiro – Portugal
Phone: +351 (0) 234 370389
E-Mail: *saraalmeida340@gmail.com*

Mónica Aresta
University of Aveiro
Departamento de Comunicação e Arte
Campus Universitário de Santiago 3810-193 Aveiro – Portugal
Phone: +351 (0) 234 370389
E-Mail: *m.aresta@ua.pt*

Using Gamification to Improve Participation in a Social Learning Environment

Jorge Simões, Rebeca Redondo, Ana Vilas, Ademar Aguiar

ABSTRACT

This paper presents a gamification framework applied in a K6 Social Learning Environment leading to a gamified system. The use of this system is expected to achieve a rise in motivation to use the platform with students becoming more loyal users. It is also expected that they will be more deeply involved and engaged in educational activities supported by the environment. The proposed gamification framework includes an architecture and a guide to help the development of gamified activities.

Introduction

This paper describes work in progress for a proposed framework implementing gamification in a Social Learning Environment (SLE). The framework is an architecture for the integration of game elements in an existing and fully functional K6 SLE – schoooools.com [Sim 11] – leading to a gamified environment. Along with the architecture, a step-by-step guide is provided to give teachers a tool to help them use game elements in school activities. It is intended that in this way the gamification experience will be meaningful and engaging for the students.

An SLE is a particular way to look at the concept of Personal Learning Environments (PLE). According to Attwell and Costa [Att 09], PLEs "are made-up of a collection of loosely coupled tools, including Web 2.0 technologies, used for working, learning, reflection and collaboration with others." They can be seen as "spaces in which people interact and communicate and whose ultimate result is learning and the development of collective know-how". The concept is fluid but it is clear that a PLE is not a technology but an approach or process [Jon 12]. They support self-directed and group-based learning and they are user centered. It is a way to use Information and Communication Technologies (ICT) in education where students are put in charge of the learning process. The approach has great capacity for flexibility and customization and therefore a PLE is different from person to person.

Rather than an approach or process, a SLE is a technological platform including or allowing access to different tools and applications, namely Web 2.0 applications. These tools help students to learn and socialize. The PLE approach implies a high level of autonomy necessary to manage all the available tools. However, such a level of autonomy may be difficult to achieve for younger students, who are less proficient independent learners [Sim 11]. They must be accompanied and guided in their use. In basic education, involving students from 6 up to 12 years old (K6), security and privacy play an important role. A SLE can address all these features, if implemented as an integrated platform closely connected to the real school. In such platforms, teachers and parents should also play an important role as active users. But, as with traditional Learning Management Systems (LMS), SLEs need motivated and engaged users to be effective. The proposed architecture and guide address this problem.

The research initially looked at several gamified applications, in educational and non-educational contexts, to find which game elements are used and how they are used. This preliminary work shows that, although some proposals for gamification frameworks have been made, there is not any commonly accepted framework or set of guidelines to develop gamified applications nor an architecture defining the components and building blocks of such applications. Mostly, these proposals are step-by-step guides, based on simple observations of existing applications.

The contribution of this research is to provide a framework including an architecture to develop gamified applications, applied to a social learning environment, and a guide to help teachers use the core concepts of the framework. This paper follows previous work about the main features that a gamification framework should include [Sim 12a].

This paper is organized as follows: Section 1 provides the purpose and the motivation of the ongoing research and the objectives of the paper; Section 2 provides the background for the proposal, defines some of the concepts and includes an overview of existing gamification frameworks; Section 3 presents a proposal for a gamification framework that includes an architecture and a guide to create meaningful gamified experiences within the framework; Section 4 shows how the framework will be applied in a K6 social learning environment and the last section concludes and provides future directions for this research work.

Background

The increasing use of ICT in educational contexts resulted in e-learning systems initially supported by a LMS. They give support to learning activities based on learning theories and models used before the rise of ICT in schools. Today, learners are not compatible with these models even if supported by these new tools [Sim 11]. The quality of e-learning systems often is negatively valued by users with a lack of motivation for its effective use. Web 2.0 brought new ways for people to collaborate in the creation and sharing of their own content. It is now possible to create collaborative spaces for teachers and students, social, informal and also personal. Concepts such as PLEs have contributed to this approach.

Along with the introduction of ICT in the classroom, the increasing popularity of video games has led to a trend known as Game-Based Learning (GBL). Games have attracted the attention of educators and have been used in schools for a long time. Video games are highly engaging and academics, like Marc Prensky or James Paul Gee [Sim 12a] advocate their potential to increase engagement in learning contexts. This increasing popularity of video games and their potential for use in schools to enhance and support learning, gave rise to a movement known as serious games. Serious games are video games that have a learning objective, rather than being played just for fun and pleasure [Uli 11].

To apply GBL, different approaches have been followed like using commercial video games for educational purposes, developing specific educational games (serious games) and allowing the students to build their own games. These approaches each have drawbacks: commercial video games' contents are limited and may not be complete and accurate, producing serious games with the quality of commercial games requires large budgets and allowing students to create games requires teachers with expertise in game design and game development [Sim 12a].

The gamification of education is another way to use game thinking and game elements in learning contexts and is an alternate approach to GBL. The term gamification began to be mentioned by the media in October 2010 [Sim 12a]. It can be defined as the use of game design elements in non-game contexts, to drive game like engagement in order to promote desired behaviours. This definition extends the known and widely quoted definition from Deterding, Dixon, Khaled and Nacke [Det 11]: "the use of design elements characteristic for games in non-game contexts".

In this section, we will first look at Social Learning Environments, the concept of gamification for education and existing gamification frameworks.

Social Learning Environments

[Har 09] defines a SLE as "a place where individuals can work and learn together collaboratively (both formally and informally) with others – in course groups, study groups or in project and team spaces". A SLE "equips learners with the tools necessary to collaborate and participate with teachers and peers both inside the classroom and beyond the walls of the school" [Sch 12]. It is a virtual space where students, individually or in groups can gather to co-create content, share knowledge and experiences, and learn. It includes a number of social elements that provide an open environment for students to work, co-create, communicate and learn collaboratively. As PLEs should not just be user-centered but they should also focus on the community and in the users' social interactions [Att 12], a SLE can be seen as an implementation of the PLE concept with a focus on the social interaction between users and also covering issues like security and privacy. These features are addressed by platforms like schoooools.com, a virtual space that gives response to the strong need for environments designed specifically for younger audiences [Sim 11]. Schooools.com is closely connected with schools and is simple, easy to use and, above all, safe. It also allows students to build their own personal learning environment in a controlled and teacher-oriented way. Teachers can moderate the interactions, manage misunderstandings and foster participation.

A SLE like schoooools.com takes advantage of the benefits of social learning without putting young students' safety at risk. As social networks create participatory environments, open social media sites have issues concerning online predators, cyber bulling, access to inappropriate content and other undesirable situations [Sch 12]. These issues can be addressed by the use of appropriate SLEs, specifically designed for these particular users.

Gamification of Education

The Horizon Report 2013 Higher Education Edition [Jon 13] identifies video games together with gamification as one of the emerging technologies to impact on higher education in a horizon of two to three years. Not only in higher education but also in general, education has been one of the areas identified with a high potential for the application of gamification [Lee 11]. In fact, the education system already incorporates game elements as students receive credits for completing assignments and when they move up a level to the next grade. Gamification and traditional education share the same objectives [Mar 13].

The gamification of education approach has the advantage of introducing what really matters from the world of video games without using any specific games, unlike the GBL approach. The purpose is to find the elements that make good games enjoyable and fun to play, adapt and use them in learning contexts. Thus, students learn, not by playing specific games but through the feeling that they are playing games.

Assuming that children and teens like to play video games [Uli 11] but are not sufficiently engaged in school activities [Sim 11], leading to demotivation, gamification of education is a process to induce motivation in those activities and to get students engaged by changing their behaviours.

An example of gamification of education is the Khan Academy, a project with a platform including several game elements such as achievement badges and points. Some classroom experiences are also known like the Ananth Pai's classes [Cho 13b] and Paul Andersen experiences [Ren 12] among others [Dun 13]. Several web applications for education are also available like ClassDojo, to improve students' behaviours and engagement or GoalBook to track students' progress.

These applications are gamified systems. For the purpose of this paper, a gamified system is any non-game context with the addition of game elements.

If the context is digital, then the gamified system comprises a software application incorporating those game elements. The system can be a website or a web application.

It can run on a server and be accessed by a computer with a web browser or it can be an app running on a smartphone storing data in the cloud. The system can be built as a gamified system from the start or elements of gamification software can be added to an existing application. Examples include gamification platforms like PunchTab or CaptainUp that provide tools to power websites, blogs and web applications. These tools can be simple add-ons or plug-ins to monitor and reward the players' activities. In this approach, users take a passive role since they cannot control what is monitored and must just let the system watch their actions. If the context is non-digital, a software system can be used to support the addition of the game elements and to monitor users' activities. The software system may rely on specific devices or other applications to access data from the non-digital context or it may need the intervention of a human user. In both cases, digital or non-digital contexts, the purpose of the gamified system is to engage users and influence their behaviour in order to achieve the system's objectives more efficiently.

In this paper, the target users of a gamified system, those whose behaviours are to be changed, will be called players. Players may have an active or a passive role in their relation to the system. The system might have other categories of non-player users that act as mediators between the system and the non-game context. If the context is non-digital, mediators are needed, either human users or a specific device. These mediators are the interface between the software system and the non-digital context.

Most current gamified systems rely on providing some form of rewards for activities carried out by the player. These systems use all the common game mechanisms such as badges, levels, leader boards, achievements and points. This is what Nicholson [Nic 12] calls BLAP (Badges, Levels and Leader boards, Achievements and Points) gamification and Werbach and Hunter [Wer 12] refer as the PBL (Points, Badges and Leader boards) triad. These elements act mainly on the players' extrinsic motivation.

To be effective on a long-term basis, gamification must be more than just adding these kind of elements to a non-game context. A good gamified system should also act on the intrinsic motivation of the players. If a person performs a task for the tasks' own sake, it means he or she is intrinsically motivated to perform that task. This is what happens when people play games. Gamification, in its quest to generate a game-like level engagement in non-gaming contexts, must create a meaningful experience and not only rely on commonplace extrinsic rewards. Nicholson [Nic 12] calls this approach "meaningful gamification".

According to [Csi 90], in order to be intrinsically motivated to perform a task, a person must be kept in a state between anxiety (if the challenge exceeds the person's abilities) and boredom (if the person feels that the task is too easy). This is a state known as flow. Clear goals, a sense of control, immediate feedback and, above all, a balance between skill and challenge are some of the factors that contribute to flow.

Fun is something commonly associated with video games. Fun is hard to define and means different things to different people. But, as [Kos 05] points out, fun in the context of video games arises out of mastery. For a videogame to be fun, it must develop an ability to master the next step in the game. Fun, resulting from mastery and from the sense of control that leads to flow, must also be part of a meaningful gamified application.

Relatedness [Wer 12], the desire to interact and connect with others, is one of the innate human needs leading to intrinsic motivation. It shows the importance for a player in a gamified application to be connected to other users and be part of a meaningful community. If the player earns a reward it has no meaning if the player cannot show it to other players. Game elements from social games must therefore be part of a gamified application. Hence, gamified systems must not only address the players' extrinsic motivation but also consider how to drive the players' intrinsic motivation. It should focus on how to create meaningful experiences, provide a sense of relatedness among players, improve their social recognition, give autonomy and purpose to their actions. It also must keep the players in a state of flow and provide a fun experience.

There are some other issues to consider when gamifying education [Mar 13]. Games foster competition and that could be a problem and potentially demotivating for some students. Students' profile, age and genre must be addressed regarding competition. On the other hand, it can help students compete with themselves. Fun and socially accepted competition can also reduce the gap between students that enjoy competition and the students that dislike it. The cost of gamifying learning activities must also be considered along with the training that will be required for teachers.

Gamification Frameworks and Platforms

Some gamification frameworks have already been proposed but their scientific validation is unknown. The most consistent appears to be the framework proposed by [Wer 12]. This framework is a six step guide to assist the design of a gamified system. A similar proposal from [Mar 12] also includes a sequence of steps (eight questions that the system designer must answer) to develop a gamified system. Marczewski's approach addresses the process in a more iterative way. [Kap 12] also proposes a methodology based on a sequence of steps to guide the design of gamified systems. It is, however, a more restrictive approach since the proposed gamified systems are essentially serious games, rather than the gamified systems as defined here.

Another framework is Octalysis [Cho 13a] that defines a set of eight fundamental motivators of behaviour (core drivers), which influence human activities. These motivators are presented in the form of an octagonal graph. Octalysis is more a tool to provide a deep analysis of gamification rather than a true framework. [Kum 13] proposed a player centered design methodology with five steps. This methodology is focused on the enterprise context and aims to apply gamification in business software. The steps are similar to approaches by [Kap 12] and [Mar 12]. The players are at the centre of the

design and development process. It also addresses legal and ethical considerations and points out that the gamified systems must be able to stimulate positive emotions in the players, like fun.

These frameworks are just step-by-step guides to support the design of gamified systems or to help the analysis of implementations. They do not deal with the structure and the architecture of the systems. To implement and deploy meaningful gamified applications, capable of providing long-term engagement and behaviour change, it is necessary to define a framework including both an architectural view and a design and implementation guide. The framework proposed in this paper focuses not only on how to apply game elements to develop a gamified application but also on what should be the architecture of such an application and the main components that should be included. In Simões, Redondo and Vilas [Sim 12a] the characteristics of a framework for gamification in education are outlined together with its objectives and purpose.

Some GBL frameworks can be found in [Sim 12a] but these are focused on the use and design of educational games. The MDA framework [Hun 04], a formal approach to understanding games. These frameworks are for games and as gamification is not the same as games, new and appropriate frameworks are needed for the design of gamified systems.

Gamification Framework

This paper proposes a framework for a family of software systems: gamified applications. Based on a definition by Stevens and Pooley [Ste 00], a gamification framework is a suitable architecture for gamified systems, together with common functionalities. The aim of this kind of framework is to support the implementation of gamified systems. It describes how a collection of elements (objects in the software engineering domain) work together. The architecture describes how the system will be built. [Ste 00]. The core concepts supporting the framework and an overview of game elements and how they are related with those concepts is discussed in this section.

The architecture states what should be the structure of a gamified system, which main building blocks should be considered and why and how they are related to each other. Besides this structure, which game elements to use and in which part of the architecture should they be considered and how they contribute to the purpose of each block is also addressed. A proper architecture should allow the system to produce meaningful gamification experiences. A guide to help designers achieve this goal complements this feature.

Core Concepts

Zichermann [Zic 11] identifies three recurrent concepts in gamified systems: feedback, friends and fun. Feedback is a way to communicate immediately with the players and tell them the results of their activities. This communication can contribute to maintaining a high level of involvement. Friends relates to the social context, where collaboration and the sharing features of social games play an important role, creating a meaningful community. Fun represents the inherent components of amusement and delight found in games. In the proposed framework, these three elements are included and completed with flow, the concept from [Csi 90]. Finally, a gamified system must provide a game experience to its users and so, gameplay is another core concept addressed by the framework. Fun and flow should be considered in a cross-sectional design of the system, transversal to the other components.

Game Elements

There is no consensus about how to name the set of components and features from video games that can be used in non-game contexts. It is common to find terms like "game mechanics", "game dynamics", "game techniques", "game attributes" or "game metaphors" [Sim 12b]. For the purpose of this paper the term "game elements" was chosen. It includes the common designation, widely used, of "game mechanics".

Among these game elements, some are used to inform players about their performance and progress in the game, other elements are to reward players; some elements have to do with the dynamics of the game and the progression of the players (gameplay mechanics). In our proposal, game elements are associated with the core concepts identified in the previous section (Table 1). Feedback can be materialized through rewards; hence the core concept of feedback and rewards uses game elements like points, badges or progress bars.

Table 1: Core Concepts vs. Game Elements

CORE CONCEPTS		GAME ELEMENTS
Flow & Fun	Feedback & Rewards	Points, progress bars, badges, trophies, leader boards
	Friends	Sharing, inviting friends, give/trade/ask for virtual goods, leader boards (social graph)
	Gameplay	Levels, intermediate goals, clear objectives, fun failure, rules, virtual economy, reward schedule

The concept of friends can be implemented by using features to engage with other players, make new friends or share and give virtual goods. A leader board, commonly associated with competition, can be used to foster the power of socialisation to change behaviour [Zic 11]. Like in many social games, leader boards can also be used to visualise the players' social graph.

The gameplay concept includes the game dynamics that represent the players' progress. Elements like clear objectives, intermediate goals, levels, a reward schedule

is included in this core concept. The reward schedule defines the frequency and the conditions for their assignment. The virtual economy sets the rules for the transaction of virtual goods in the systems' context. Fun failure is the possibility of repetition after failure without this being regarded as negative but rather making it fun, inducing in the player a sense of control.

The transversal components of flow and fun are achieved through the way that gamified activities are set in the system. [Zic 13] points out that mastery and progress are what makes gamified experiences fun. The sense of mastery and progress can be implemented through elements in the gameplay, friends and feedback and reward concepts. The same goes for flow. The player can be kept in a flow channel when or he or she is optimally challenged by tasks that are neither too easy nor too hard [Csi 00]. This could be achieved by providing immediate feedback, intermediate goals and different levels of progression. In this way the challenge is balanced with the players' skills.

Architecture

Some existing proposals address the issue of defining the structure of gamified applications. The SAP Gamification Platform [Her 13], expected to be released in the second half of 2013, is a platform for enterprise software that highlights building blocks for any gamified application. It includes modules like "Player Management", "Achievements", "Analytics", "Rules of Game" and "Rule Optimizer". The platform can be integrated with an application in a non-game context, adding game elements. Events in the non-game application are sent to the platform and through the "Analytics" and "Rules of Game" modules, the achievements are sent back to the application. [Kol n.d.], calls what is considered in this paper as a gamified system a "gamification platform" and describes the building blocks for this kind of application: "Connectors", "Tracking Engine", "Rewards Engine", "Gaming Engine", "Reputation Engine" and "Analytics Engine".

Both proposals highlight the components necessary for a gamified system, but a more formal description of an architecture, from a software engineering perspective, is needed. This paper proposes an architecture based on six main building blocks (Figure 1), represented as UML packages.

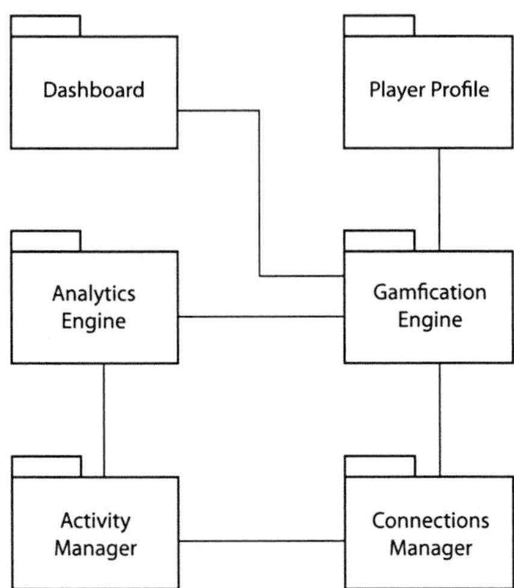

Figure 1: Architecture for a Gamified Application: Main Components

This architecture is a typical three-tier model for a software architecture (Figure 2) with a presentation tier (users' interface), a logic tier (system's logic) and a data tier (data interface). In the data tier, the block identified as "Activity Manager" gets data from a source outside of the system or from the players' activities while the "Connections Manager" manages the links with external applications, for example, by publishing the players' achievements in a social network.

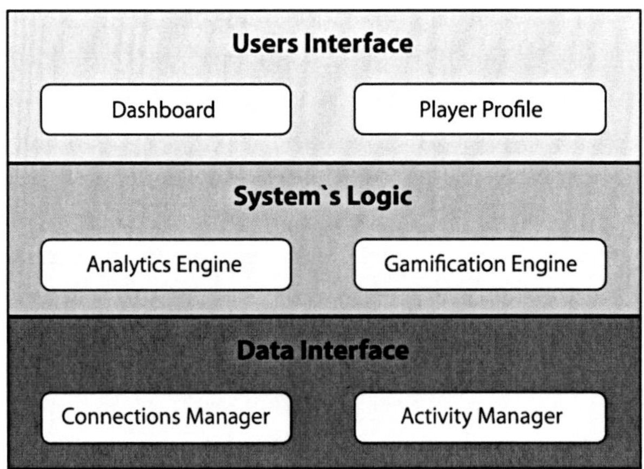

Figure 2: A Three-tier Architectural Model for a Gamified Application

The architecture's building blocks are explained below.

Analytics Engine

The way players get feedback for their action is crucial. By tracking certain variables related to players' actions, a gamified system can find patterns, trends and correlations and be able to provide immediate and accurate feedback in a fun and engaging way. Data analytics play an important part in gamified systems, therefore an analytics engine must be part of these systems. Analytics are the algorithms and data used to measure key performance indicators [Wer 12].

Activity Manager

To feed the analytics engine, the system must also include an activity manager, a component able to monitor and read the data generated by users' activities. The activity manager can obtain data from a mediator, a human user or an external device if the non-game context is in the real world or directly from the players' activities if the context is digital. To manage players' activities, the gamified system can use one or more of the following four approaches to monitor and collect the data for the activity manager:

- Automatically, by the system itself: the actions of the players on a website or web application are monitored by the system. The gamified system is the website or web application powered by generic gamification platforms. Examples include PunchTab or CaptainUp.
- Using an external device: a smartphone or another device or gadget is used to keep track of what the player is doing in a non-digital context. The device synchronizes with a website to upload the data. The players take an active part in the process since they can control whether to use the system or not, what to track, what to share or what to achieve. The best known example is Nike+. Zamzee is a similar application targeting children in lower socio economic environments.
- Relying on the players: In these systems, the players have full control over the data collected. Data can only be uploaded by the players using an app in a smartphone or logging into a website. The players are active players. Examples are EpicWin, an app for smartphones, and HabitRPG.
- Relying on a special user: a human user monitors the players' activities and is responsible for uploading the data. This user can also be a player with special privileges. Players are passive players because they cannot act upon what is being monitored. ClassDojo is an example of this approach where students are the players and teachers act as mediators. Other examples, targeting younger audiences are Chore Wars and HighScore House (motivating children and teens to do chores with parents as mediators).

Gamification Engine

A gamification engine should provide the game elements and the rules to establish the gameplay for the target activities. The gamification engine is closely related to the activity manager and to the analytics engine. This engine establish the "Rules of Game" as in Herger's proposal [Her 13] and is also related to the block called "Rule Optimizer". It should include a toolbox for game elements, a virtual economy manager and a reward scheduler.

Player Profile
The "Player Profile" is a component for players to define their profile within the gamified system. It is the place to store the player's achievements, using game elements (badges, points, trophies), to report feedback and where the player can set which outside applications or social networks can be used to publish their personal gamification data.

Dashboard
The "Dashboard" is designed to allow non-player users access the system. These users can be mediators between the software system and a non-digital context or can be some kind of system administrators. Other system stakeholders can also access the system through this interface. The dashboard is a component to evaluate the results and the behaviour change that the gamified activities are producing. It allows the gamification administrators to tune the system by changing and improving the rules and it displays the results according to Key Performance Indicators (KPI) defined for the activities.

Connections Manager
The "Connections Manager" is designed to establish links with the non-game context and to publish the players' achievements, e.g. badges or trophies, in a social network or other similar applications. Gamified systems relying on external devices to keep track of what the player is doing need a connection with those devices. These devices must be synchronized, through some kind of physical connection, with a website to upload the data. The data collection process may involve connections to external devices, and any gamified system outputting the players' social graphs must have connections to social networks and other social applications.

Guide
This guide is intended to help a designer of a gamification scenario in a digital or non-digital context. It assumes that the designer has a gamified system built on the proposed architecture. The designer can then use the system as a tool. The gamification framework is therefore completed with this guide.

The designer should first be aware of what is to be gamified and what are the benefits in motivating people, the players, to change their behaviours.

What behaviours need to be changed and what are the appropriate activities that can make these change happen should be the first concern of the designer. The designer

must also be aware of the context and the profile of the players. The decision to design a more competitive or more cooperative system must take into account who the players are (Table 2 – Non-game context characterization).

Table 2: Reference Guide to Apply Gamification

1.	Non-game context characterization	1.1.	Context's nature: digital or non-digital 1.2. Identify target activities 1.3. Identify target behaviours 1.4. Players' profiles characterization
2.	Set the system's objectives	2.1.	Define the goals in relation to the target behaviours 2.2. Quantify the goals (KPIs)
3.	Select game elements	3.1. 3.3.	Feedback and rewards 3.2. Social interaction (friends) Gameplay 3.4. Flow and fun
4.	Select meaningful data	4.1. 4.5.	Define the process to monitor and collect data 4.2. Define the actions to be monitored 4.3. Define the rules 4.4. Data analysis regarding systems' objectives (2.2) Select game elements for feedback
5.	Evaluate results	5.1.	Compare results with the objectives 5.2. Optimize rules if needed

The goals for the gamified system should then be set according to the target behaviour. These goals must be quantified with appropriate metrics (Table 2 – Set the system objectives). Game elements (Table 2 – Select game elements) should be chosen according to the core concepts of feedback and friends. How and when players should be rewarded is addressed at this stage. Players receive immediate feedback through rewards and other game elements. Then, they can adjust their actions in order to get closer to the goals. The gameplay set in the gamified context should implement these feedback loops. Feedback loops push users toward the target behaviours [Wer 12]. These loops have a central role in any gamified system: players perform actions and then they receive feedback. Feedback increases motivation and leads the players to further actions. The progression of the players through the activities should keep them in a flow channel (the activity should not be neither too easy nor too challenging), allow for repetition after failure and allow multiple courses of action. When players start their target activities, the system monitors their actions and collects relevant data according to the objectives that were set (Table 2 – Select meaningful data). Data is analysed and the actions of the players are evaluated against the goals (Table 2 – Evaluate results).

Applying a Gamification Framework on a Social learning Environment

The proposed framework has been applied to schoooools.com. The platform users, children from 6 to 12 years old, as with most LMS users, often need motivation to increase their participation and to be involved in the platform activities. From this starting point, the gamification of the schoooools.com will allow us to promote users' engagement and fidelity and to foster student motivation.

The guide to the social gamification framework will help teachers to gamify their teaching processes by helping them choose the appropriate game elements respecting learning objectives, student profile, nature of contents, desired behaviours, assessment, etc. The platform will provide the necessary tools to build the gamified learning process by, as an example, allowing the teacher to personalize and adapt badges, trophies or virtual goods or the kind of rewards that students can get.

Schoooools.com as a gamified system is, at the moment, a system where the non-game context is digital (the SLE itself). The activities that are monitored are the actions performed by the players (the students who are the application users) within the SLE. The players are passive players.

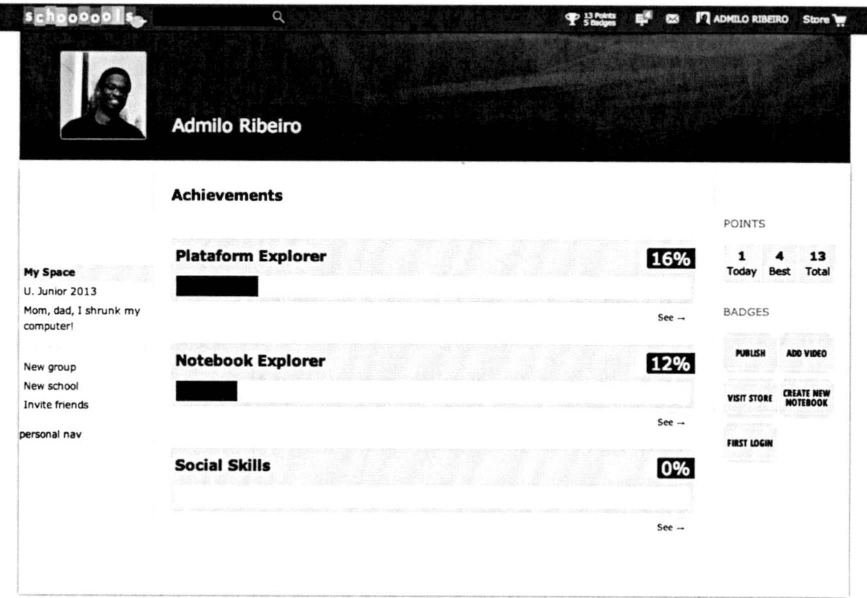

Figure 3: Schoooools.com: Categories of Achievements

All the players' actions in the system are monitored and recorded. A set of rules is established for some of those actions and for each of them the player can get points and badges. The first time a user executes some of those actions, he or she earns

a badge. Points are earned each time the action is executed. In the player's profile, points earned each day are displayed, along with the total amount of points and the best daily achievement. The actions that are considered as players' achievements are divided into three categories: "platform explorer", "notebook explorer" and "social skills" (Figure 3). A specific game element, a progress bar, indicates the percentage of achieved badges. Each category has a different set of badges (Figure 4).

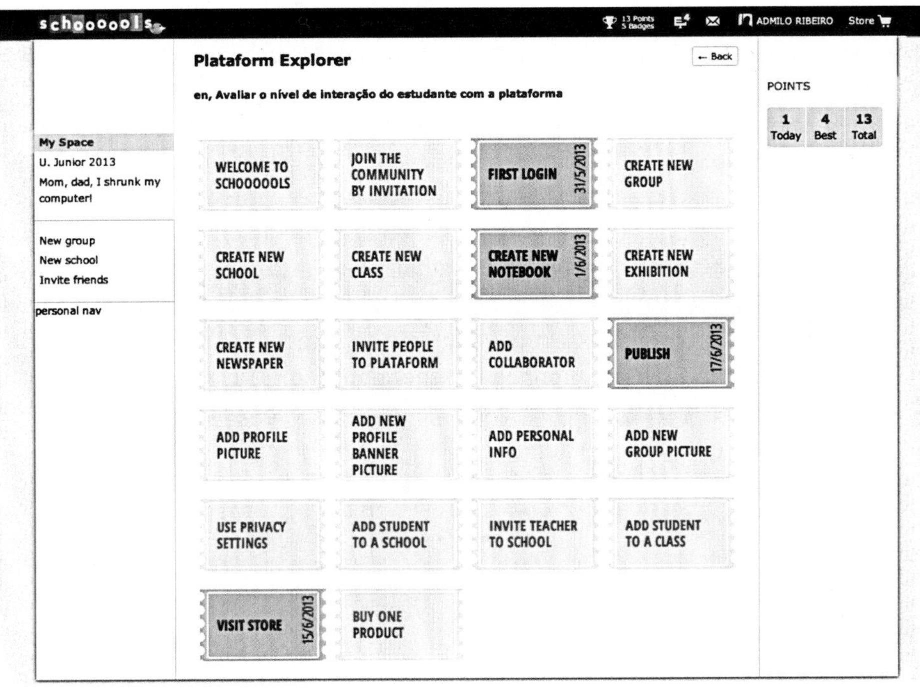

Figure 4: Schoooools.com: Badges from "Platform Explorer"

Conclusions and Future Work

Gamification is a means to design systems that motivate people to do things [Wer 12]. It applies to non-game contexts, digital or non-digital, targeting activities that people are not motivated to perform. Gamification must also be meaningful. It should aim to foster the players' intrinsic motivation and not only act on their extrinsic motivation. Target activities in a gamified system must also have intrinsic value, that is, if the game elements are removed from the system, the remaining contents must still have value. With gamification it is possible to integrate game elements with learning contents and make learning activities more attractive and engaging. Gamification has remarkable potential in education and training and can create a wide range of opportunities for research and a market for new educational tools and technological platforms.

Schoooools.com, in its current release, can be seen as a gamified system resulting form the initial SLE powered with gamification features. From the proposed architecture it has a gamification engine, an analytics engine and a player profile module. An activity manager keeps track of all the players' actions and according to a set of rules, defined in the gamification engine, the system provides feedback to the players using points and badges. A progress bar let players see how far they they have progressed in achieving all sets of badges in three different categories. Social interactions between users are facilitated through the platform's social features.

The next step will be to evaluate the gamified platform in real scenarios. In the future, it is intended to extend the digital context to the real classroom. The teacher will then be the human mediator, acting as an interface between the gamified SLE and the outside, non-digital, world, the classroom. Other system stakeholders, such as parents, should also be able to access the gamified system to view reports about their childrens' behaviour. A further step would be for teachers and parents to be players in the sense that they also need to be motivated and engaged with the system.

The proposed framework was applied to schoooools.com but it is not restricted to social learning environments. Instead, it is a general-purpose gamification framework that can be used in different non-game contexts to build gamified systems. The architecture shows how to build a gamified system and the guide is intended to help the effective use of the system in order to provide meaningful experiences.

REFERENCES

[Att 12] *Attwell, Graham (2012):* Layering Personal Learning Environments. Pontydysgu Bridge to Learning. Retrieved June 11, 2013 from *http://www.pontydysgu.org/2012/05/layering-personal-learning-environments*

[Att 09] *Attwell, Graham; Costa, Cristina (2009):* Integrating personal learning and working environment. Beyond Current Horizons. Retrieved June 11, 2013 from *http://www.beyondcurrenthorizons.org.uk/integrating-personal-learning-and- working-environments*

[Cho 13a] *Chou, Yu-Kai (2013):* Octalysis: Complete Gamification Framework. Retrieved June 7, 2013 from *http://www.yukaichou.com/gamification-examples/octalysis-complete-gamification-framework*

[Cho 13b] *Chou, Yu-Kai (2013):* Top 10 Education Gamification Examples that will Change our Future. Retrieved June 21, 2013 from *http://www.yukaichou.com/gamification-examples/top-10-education-gamification-examples*

[Csi 90] *Csikszentmihalyi, Mihaly (1990):* Flow: The Psychology of Optimal Experience. Harpers Perennial, NewYok.

[Det 11] *Deterding, Sebastian; Dixon, Dan; Khaled, Rilla; Nacke, Lennart (2011):* From Game Design Elements to Gamefulness: Defining "Gamification, Proceedings of the 15th International Academic MindTrek Conference Envisioning Future Media Environments.

[Dun 13] *Dunn, Jeff (2013):* Gamification In The Classroom: How (And Why) One Teacher Did It, Edudemic. Retrieved June 21, 2013 from *http://www.edudemic.com/2012/06/gamification-in-the-classroom-how-and-why-one-teacher-did-it*

[Har 09] *Hart, Jane (2009):* Intro to Social Learning Environments: A Social Learning Resource. Retrieved June 13, 2013 from *http://janeknight.typepad.com/socialmedia/2009/10/intro-to-social-learning-environments-a-social-learning-resource.html*

[Her 13] *Herger, Maxim (2013):* SAP Gamification Platform. Enterprise Gamification Blog. Retrieved June 6, 2013 from *http://enterprise-gamification.com/index.php/en/blog/2-news/145-sap-gamification-platform*

[Hun 04] *Hunicke, R.; LeBlanc, M.; Zubek, R. (2004):* MDA: A Formal Approach to Game Design and Game Research. Proc. AAAI workshop on Challenges in Game, AAAI Press

[Jon 12] *Johnson, L.; Adams, S.; Cummins, M. (2012):* NMC Horizon Report: 2012 K-12 Edition. Austin, Texas: The New Media Consortium. Available at *http://nmc.org/pdf/2012-horizon-report-K12.pdf*

[Jon 13] *Johnson, L.; Becker, S.; Cummins, M.; Estrada, V.; Freeman, A.; Ludgate, H. (2013):* NMC Horizon Report: 2013 Higher Education Edition. Austin, Texas: The New Media Consortium. Retrieved June 13, 2013 from *http://www.nmc.org/publications/2013-horizon-report-higher-ed*

[Lee 11] *Lee, Joey; Hammer, Jessica (2011):* Gamification in education: What, how, why bother? Academic Exchange Quarterly, 15(2):2.

[Kap 12] *Kapp, Karl (2012):* The Gamification of Learning and Instruction: Game-Based Methods and Strategies for Training and Education. San Francisco: Pfeiffer.

[Kol n.d.] *Kolsky, E. (n.d.):* Gamification Platforms vs "Gamified" Applications. Gamified Enterprise. Retrieved June 13, 2013 from *http://www.gamifiedenterprise.com/gamification-platforms-vs-gamified-applications*

[Kos 05] *Koster, R. (2005). A Theory of Fun. Paraglyph Press.*

[Kum 13] *Kumar, Janaki; Herger, Mario (2013):* Gamification at Work: Designing Engaging Business Software. Aarhus, Denmark, The Interaction Design Foundation. Retrieved June 22, 2013 from *http://www.interaction-design.org/books/gamification_at_work.html*

[Mar 12] *Marczewski, Andrzej (2012):* A Simple Gamification Framework / Cheat Sheet, Andrzej's Blog. Retrieved June 7, 2013 from *http://marczewski.me.uk/gamification-framework*

[Mar 13] *Marquis, Justin (2013):* Finding a Balance between Gamification and Education, Online Universities.com. Retrieved June 22, 2013 from *http://www.onlineuniversities.com/blog/2013/05/gblfriday-finding-a-balance-between-gamification-and-education*

[Nic 12] *Nicholson, Scott (2012):* Strategies for Meaningful Gamification: Concepts Behind Transformative Play and Participatory Museums. Meaningful Play 2012. Lansing, Michigan. Available at *http://scottnicholson.com/pubs/meaningfulstrategies.pdf*

[Ren 12] *Renfro, Adam (2012):* Gamification: Bring Gaming Mechanics Into Non-gaming Environments, GettingSmart. Retrieved June 21, 2013 from *http://gettingsmart.com/2012/06/gamification-bring-gaming-mechanics-into-non-gaming-environments*

[Sch 12] *Schoolwires (2012):* Creating a Safe Social Learning Environment To Improve Student Success, White Paper. Retrieved June 13, 2013 from *http://www.schoolwires.com/cms/lib3/SW00000001/Centricity/Domain/36/ schoolwires_whitepaper_safesociallearning_may2012.pdf*

[Sim 11] *Simões, Jorge; Aguiar, Ademar (2011):* Schooools.com: A Social and Collaborative Learning Environment for K-6, em EDULEARN11 – 3rd Annual International Conference on Education and New Learning Technologies Proceedings, Barcelona.

[Sim 12a] *Simões, Jorge; Redondo, Rebeca; Vilas, Ana (2012):* A Social Gamification Framework for a K-6 Learning Platform, Computers in Human Behavior, 28: 1 – 1, doi: 10.1016/j.chb.2012.06.007.

[Sim 12b] *Simões, Jorge; Aguiar, Ademar; Redondo, Rebeca; Vilas, Ana (2012):* Aplicação de Elementos de Jogos numa Plataforma de Aprendizagem Social. Proceedings of the II International Congress on ICT and Education – ticEduca 2012, pp 2092–2099, Institute of Education of the University of Lisbon.

[Ste 00] *Stevens, Perdita; Pooley, Rob (2000):* Using UML Software Engineering with Objects and Components, Addison-Wesley.

[Uli 11] *Ulicsak, Mary; Williamson, Ben (2011):* Computer Games and Learning: a Handbook. London, Futurelab.

[Wer 12] *Werbach, Kevin; Hunter, Dan (2012):* For the Win: How Game Thinking Can Revolutionize Your Business, Wharton Digital Press.

[Zic 11] *Zichermann, Gabe (2011):* Getting 3 Fs in Gamification. Retrieved June 6, 2013 from *http://www.gamification.co/2012/01/19/getting-three-fs-in-gamification/*

[Zic 12] *Zichermann, Gabe; Linder, Joselin (2013):* The Gamification Revolution, McGraw-Hill Education.

FIGURES

CONTACT DETAILS

Jorge Simões
Instituto Superior Politécnico Gaya
Av. dos Descobrimentos, 333
4400 – 103 Vila Nova de Gaia, Portugal
Phone: +351 (0) 223 745 730
E-Mail: *jsimoes@ispgaya.pt*

Rebeca Redondo
School of Telecommunications Engineering
University of Vigo
Campus universitario s/n. 36310 Vigo, Spain
Phone: +34 (0)986 813 469
E-Mail: *rebeca@det.uvigo.es*

Ana Vilas
School of Telecommunications Engineering
University of Vigo
Campus universitario s/n. 36310 Vigo, Spain
Phone: +34 (0)986 813 868
E-Mail: *ana.vilas@det.uvigo.es*

Ademar Aguiar
Faculty of Engineering of University of Porto
Rua Dr. Roberto Frias, s/n 4200 –465 Porto Portugal
Phone: +351 (0) 225 081 518
E-Mail: *ademar.aguiar@fe.up.pt*

Using PLEs in Professional Learning Scenarios – The Festo Case for ROLE

Maren Scheffel, Manuel Schmidt, Michael Werkle, Martin Wolpers

ABSTRACT

The competitiveness of a company depends strongly on the skills and abilities of its employees. Teachers and learners within companies often lack media competence and the ability to use self-regulated learning (SRL). The evaluations conducted in scope of the ROLE project showed that the vocational training and workplace learning providers appreciated the SRL approach and the idea of personalisation of the learning tools and content. Further, the implementation of SRL in an organisation needed the development of specific competencies by the learners, as well as guidance through the learning process from its very beginning. Thus, a learning software solution allowing a combination of curriculum-based and self-regulated learning approaches has become necessary. To address this requirement, the ROLE Project developed a Personal Learning Management System which is an OpenSocial-based Learning Management System (LMS) combining functionalities of a LMS and a PLE (Personal Learning Environment) and allowing users to construct their virtual learning environment according to their learning history, goals, and preferences. This paper describes the development of the ROLE solution from the point of view of Festo, a test bed which actively contributed to the development, testing, evaluation, and application of the ROLE approach and technology.

Note: This article has been published in the Special Edition of the eLearning Papers, Issue No. 35 "Personal Learning Environments". The link to this Special Issue is: http://openeducationeuropa.eu/en/paper/personal-learning-environments

INTRODUCTION

Over the past years, research and development in the area of intelligent and adaptive educational systems has made significant progress and the evolution of such technologies – including their psycho-pedagogical foundations – proceeds continuously. In the focus of existing approaches to intelligent and adaptive tutoring is the learning content: Adaptivity particularly refers to personalised presentation of contents and adaptive navigation through the contents. The ROLE project[1] addressed these issues specifically, focussing on enabling the individual learner as well as groups of learners

1 http://www.role-project.eu/

to adapt the learning environment to their very specific needs and, more importantly, how to enable the system to adapt its functionalities and components to the very concrete and individual demands concerning learning environment and learning strategies. The evaluation in all ROLE test beds has further underpinned the understanding that reflective and self-regulated learning is not yet an accepted and widely used learning approach. In contrast, learners as well as teachers need support in implementing this approach – provided by the ROLE project through concepts and technology. Also, when using the ROLE approach, organisations are not forced to replace their learning environment but instead are enabled to complement it with ROLE technology to provide enhanced and better learning services.

This paper presents an evaluation of one of the ROLE test beds, namely the Festo test bed[2]. The case study relates to the Festo Virtual Academy. The issues addressed here are of providing a responsive learning environment for the further education activities of a German engineering company. The target groups were employees. In summary this case study demonstrates how Festo federated and mashed-up different ROLE learning services and then compared the results with a traditional approach of having a centralised Virtual Learning Environment (VLE) Platform known as the Festo Virtual Academy. To achieve this aim, Festo effectively opened up its platforms and tools to be interoperable and "mash-upable" through the use of ROLE tools and technologies with the goal to make learning for their employees more flexible and individual. This case study, therefore, reports on how the ROLE environment can be open to a mix of (Festo-)internal learning applications alongside external ones. This is regarded as a key success factor for project ideas that emerge from developments like ROLE to influence the promotion of further education in companies and meets the overarching premise of this case study namely that it demonstrates "an internal job opportunity in a company" environment.

Background

Responsive Open Learning Environments (ROLE) was a European collaborative project with 16 internationally renowned research groups from six EU countries and China that ran from February 2009 until January 2013. ROLE technology is centred around the concept of self-regulated learning that creates responsible and thinking learners that are able to plan their learning process, search for the resources independently, learn and then reflect on their learning process and progress. The cross-disciplinary innovations of the ROLE project deliver and test prototypes of highly responsive TEL environments, offering effectiveness, flexibility, user-control and mass-individualisation. ROLE advances the state-of-the-art in human resource management, self-regulated and social learning, psycho-pedagogical theories of adaptive education and

2 *http://www.festo-lernzentrum.de/*

educational psychology, service composition and orchestration, and the use of ICT in lifelong learning. Significant benefits arise for learners, their communities, employers, TEL developers and society. The ROLE project offers adaptivity and personalisation in terms of (1) content and navigation and (2) the entire learning environment and its functionalities.

This approach permits individualisation of the components, tools, and functionalities of a learning environment, and their adjustment or replacement by existing web-based software tools. Learning environment elements can be combined to generate new components and functionalities, which can be adapted by (collaborating) learners to meet their own needs and to enhance the effectiveness of their learning. This empowers each learner to generate new tools and functions according to their needs, and can help them to establish a livelier and personally more meaningful learning context and learning experience. ROLE's generic framework uses an open source approach, interoperable across software systems and technology. Hence any tool created by an individual is available from a pool of services and tools to all learners via the internet, no matter which learning environment, operating system, or device they use, and which subject matter they learn.

The Festo Learning Centre was founded in 1994 and is an accredited institution for advanced vocational training for the Festo AG & Co.KG[3]. It offers a wide range of personnel and organisational development programmes to customers of international enterprises of all branches and institutions as well as Festo employees and private persons. The Festo Virtual Academy is the central Learning Management System (LMS) of the company. It is based on the LMS software CLIX[4] developed by IMC[5]. This bespoke LMS supports all personnel development processes and is able to deploy web-based training courses that have been designed according to didactic models in order to make their "consumption" as easy as possible for the learners. This approach also supports self-controlled learning, which means that the learners can choose what, where and when they learn from the contents of the LMS repository platform. The Virtual Academy is open for each Festo employee worldwide for their personal further education by means of the lifelong learning approach. The LMS is accessible via the internet to facilitate self-regulated learning processes for the employees (learning independent of time and place). In addition to the self-learning offers, several blended-learning modules are available. The learning processes at Festo can be described as self-controlled by the learners (employees). The users browse offered learning programmes in the catalogue of the Virtual Academy and select those they need. In the learning process itself, the learners can decide themselves what they would like to learn and which parts of the web-based training content they skip. Since the platform is available online, the learners can even access the Virtual Academy from home and participate in trainings.

3 *http://www.festo.de/*
4 *http://www.im-c.de/de/produkte/imc/software-solutions/learning-suite/entdecken/*
5 *http://www.im-c.de/*

The learners are free to define and plan what and when to learn, and how frequently to work on the web-based training offered in the catalogue. The Virtual Academy has more than 9,000 users distributed all over the world, more than 80,000 logins p.a., more than 800 learning contents in different strategic learning categories with a total learning time of approximately 2,000 hours. The contents are provided mostly in German, English and Spanish. For specific topics additional languages like Chinese, Japanese, Portuguese and Russian are also available.

Within the ROLE project, the Virtual Academy was one of the five original test beds and addressed the issue of providing a responsive learning environment within further education activities in a company. This included not only continuous technical and media-didactical possibilities of an LMS and the content within, but also the technical possibilities beyond the LMS approach. The Festo test bed focused on LMS users and especially LMS users in a company. This target group has special needs and the surrounding conditions in companies are not as flexible as those predominant, for example, in universities. In contrast to students, business learners are a very heterogeneous target group with big age differences (from 16 to 65), different educational backgrounds and previous knowledge, job-roles, learning requirements, learning preferences and learning goals. Further, the learners in business environments have primarily to fulfil their job role and learning is mostly to support them in doing so. Due to high workloads, it is often hard to learn on the job or in other words, there is no or just little time available for learning. It is often not so easy to disengage workers from their daily practices. So learners at the workplace need to be supported systematically, not only with new technology-enhanced learning solutions, but also with their development goals, the working and learning conditions in general and their work life balance.

Approach

As the Festo Learning Centre aims to meet the requirements of learning environments within a professional industry business and since the Festo Virtual Academy is effectively a real corporate learning environment, some special surrounding conditions had to be considered within the ROLE process. These special "challenges" depend on the fact that a corporate learning management system has one central main function: the further development of personnel in the company. Issues relating to these surrounding conditions are, for example: (1) the uncertain scope of openness of a corporate learning environment, i.e. how wide can a corporate learning environment be opened up, (2) the "job role" of the learner has to be in the focus of all learning processes, (3) knowledge sharing is harder to realise in the job context than in non-working life, (4) understanding learning processes during daily work and after work, and (5) system restrictions and data security. The study thus set out to address the issue of providing a more responsive learning environment within the further education activities of Festo.

From PLE and LMS to PLMS

The vision of the ROLE project was to improve especially the aspects "responsive" and "open" of the already existing learning environment of Festo – the Virtual Academy as the central Learning Management System (LMS) of the company. From Festo's point of view the main targets were to improve existing learning systems according to (1) openness and adaptivity, (2) communication with other learners, (3) facilitation of collaboration and peer-assisted learning, (4) switching between collaborative and individual work, (5) exploring ways of benefiting from the experience acquired in a company, and (6) best practice sharing. In the scope of the ROLE project, a PLE is a web-based infrastructure, where the users can access, aggregate and manipulate learning applications and resources of their preference, as well as communicate with other users sharing experiences and collaborating on projects [Vel 09]. Importantly, the ROLE PLE uses web widgets, which are small web-based software applications, to support particular learning and teaching goals or training of some specific skills.

Festo supported ideas and the development of prototypical learning widgets and mash-ups or services, which each can enhance the learning processes in corporate learning environments. Initially, the first item to be addressed during the implementation of the ROLE approach was to improve the "Openness" of the system. Thus a federated search widget was developed to enable a more focused search facility in the Festo LMS. The widget searches learning content in several external online resources and feeds results back directly to the learner within the Festo LMS. In addition, the federated search widget was also interoperable with the media-list widget. This allows users to create media lists out of the resources found with the search widget. Both widgets are featured inside the Festo Virtual Academy.

Another perspective of openness to consider in the context of this case study was the integration of user generated content as well as encouraging the possibility for learners to produce content on their own. To achieve these outcomes a commercial screen recorder facility was transformed for delivery as a widget. Thus, the resulting widget enabled learners to create their own videos. This widget bundle was given the names of "LearningTube" and "Recorder" and together both widgets provided all learners, trainers and experts with appropriate support for exchanging and communicating training content on a daily basis. The Recorder, in fact, was a tool that allowed users to create their own videos. Such videos were then uploaded to LearningTube, where they were shared with Festo colleagues worldwide. Both tools supported bite-sized learning and ensured that content could be published and distributed quickly. This style of rapid eLearning, therefore, allowed users to enhance their presentations with the addition of a voiceover and optional webcam video. The Recorder widget also provided help and support for creating resulting screenshots, enabling users to add their own commentary to PowerPoint presentations or even enabling them to emulate software simulations.

The Festo test bed examined how a PLE approach can enhance job opportunities for learners. The target was not to create a "pure" PLE but rather to combine advantages of a PLE with an existing LMS. Thus, it was not a question of replacement or substitution of an existing, traditional LMS in a company but rather an approach that enabled the enhancement of their current delivery mechanisms. It was also a question of how an existing LMS can be enriched with new information and communications technologies that accordingly enhance the end user's (i.e. the learner's) experience. This combined approach was called a "Personal Learning Management System" (PLMS) where the PLMS was comprised of the LMS and PLE together. The actual implementation of this approach, i.e. the degree to which these PLE enrichments are embedded, ultimately depended on both company-specific requirements and on the individual learning preferences as well as the anticipated learning experiences of individual learners. In general terms, however, the main targets of the PLMS approach were:

- Simplified access and advanced search of relevant content and learning materials.
- Support and improvement of the planning of learning, incorporating the reflection phases of the learning activities.
- Enabling learning motivation and promotion of self-regulated learning (SRL) as well as different forms of cooperative learning.

In order to create a software solution supporting both approaches, an OpenSocial[6] PLE has been integrated into the LMS combining functionalities of both systems. Thus, the PLMS [Sch 12] provides instructions and pre-defined learning materials allowing the users to complete learning courses as usual, but it also ensures the learning process autonomy offering personalised learning spaces, in which the users can add and use additional applications and resources.

Self-regulated Learning

Another aspect to be considered is related to the personal requirements of the learners. The learners need a set of specific skills, the so-called "self-regulated learning" (SRL) skill set. These are skills the learners must have to be able to successfully plan, conduct, and evaluate their learning activities. Some of these skills might be new to some learners, whereas others might be present and used already, but the awareness about that fact is still missing. To address this requirement, Festo initiated the "Fit for Self-Regulated Learning" initiative in the ROLE project. Various SRL learning modules were therefore implemented in the offered ROLE service. Some of the modules explicitly show that they support learners in getting SRL known as a method. Others are implicitly woven into ROLE services to make their impact on self-regulated learning visible, for example within wizards.

The OpenSocial directory of the PLMS is structured according to the phases of the self-regulated learning process described in the Psycho-Pedagogical Integration Model (PPIM) developed in the ROLE Project [Fru 10]: plan, search, learn, reflect. The PLMS is

6 *http://opensocial.org/*

divided into four learning spaces corresponding to these four steps. In order provide necessary guidance to the users, each learning space is populated with pre-defined learning widgets. Further, the PLMS contains a list of additional tools. Thus, the users may use pre-defined applications and/or supportive tools from the list arranging them in the learning spaces. This allows an efficient integration of external tools into the system respecting the interests of both the learners and the organisation. The development of the PLMS and its technical implementation focused on the personalisation, adaptivity, and user-friendliness of the PLMS making it responsive to the needs and preferences of the users. Also, it offers guidance through the SRL process and supports each phase.

Results

The concept used to evaluate the ROLE solution at Festo consisted of a combination of questionnaires, selected expert interviews, a focus group for requirement gathering purposes, a taskforce observation and interviews by project members. These various elements ensured that there were standardised frameworks for evaluation and also personal contacts to offer possibilities to clarify confusing questions and allow a little more depth. During the project, Festo carried out two main evaluation loops. The first evaluation step in the methodology was addressed when the widgets were implemented in the pilot test environment of the Festo Virtual Academy. This work was also evaluated by deploying an associated ROLE online survey. Festo also founded a small focus group of 26 colleagues to test and evaluate the ROLE technologies in the Virtual Academy from the learner's perspective. The use of the focus group meant that although the evaluation was not on a large scale, the results were of high quality. The evaluation also included a number of semi-structured qualitative interviews with learners that also had a statistical focus section with questions relating to age, gender, and experience with TEL, learning with a LMS, internet affinity as well as information collated about Web 2.0 experiences.

Evaluation Loop One

As previously described, the first step was to implement two widgets in the existing Festo Virtual Academy LMS, thus, enriching it with appropriate PLE elements. The first evaluation loop consisted of a questionnaire about the two developed widgets: the media search widget and the media list widgets. A questionnaire, asking about personal information, preferred forms of further education, daily use of the internet, affinity to web 2.0, benefit of web 2.0 and the described widgets, was created. This questionnaire was emailed to the Festo focus group; a screencast introducing the ROLE project, the ROLE approach, and the developed widgets was attached.

All responses to the questionnaire in this case study regarding the look & feel, usability and perceived usefulness were very positive concerning the applied ROLE

approach in the business context. It showed (see Figure 1) that 63% of the users liked the look & feel and 75% the usability. 19% said that that the look & feel should be improved and 13% stated that the usability should be improved. Regarding the quality of the search results, the performance and the fun factor of the widgets, 38% of the users said these issues were in need of improvement. 44% rated the quality of the search results as good, the performance got a good grade from 50% of the users, the fun factor was rated as good by 38% and even as outstanding by 13%.

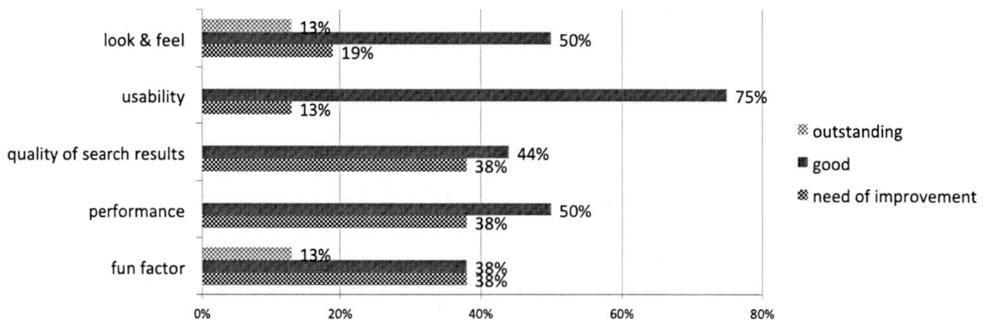

Figure 1: First impression of the prototypes

Evaluation of the benefits of the prototypes showed that most of the users saw a high or very high benefit of the offered tools. The highlights regarding the benefits were in this case the federated search feature over several knowledge resources. 50% stated a benefit and as many as 38% stated a high benefit. For the rating feature 31% stated a benefit and as many as 44% stated a high benefit. The good overall impression of the evaluation is especially reflected in the recommendation value – in total 88% of the test users would recommend the tools to their colleagues. Last but not least, perceived usefulness and effectiveness was evaluated with the question "do you think the offered services will help you to work more effectively in your job than at present?": 31% fully agreed, 50% agreed and only 6% denied that they would be more effective when working with these tools (see Figure 2). This was a very positive result for such an early prototype evaluation from Festo's point of view.

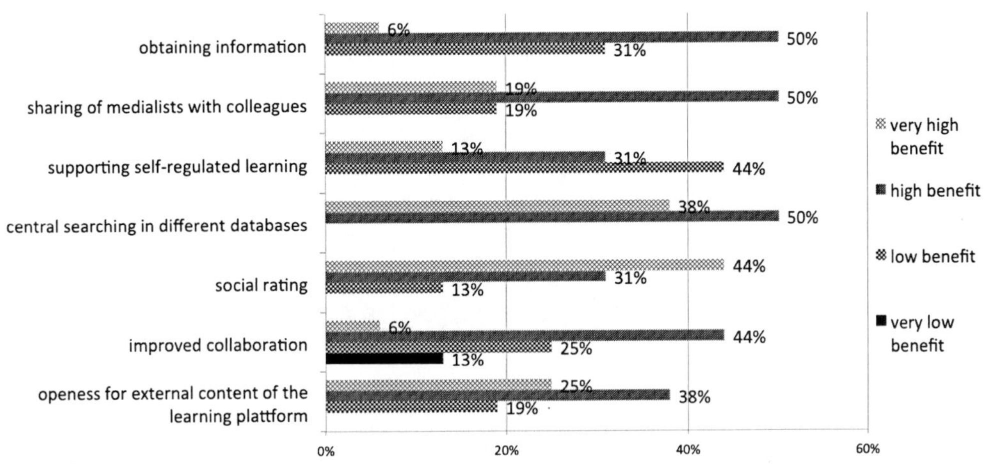

Figure 2: Benefits of the prototypes

Evaluation Loop Two

The second evaluation loop dealt with the PLMS prototype, which was developed with the goal of integrating the approaches of LMS and PLE, and thus supporting the user during self-regulated learning. The evaluation was conducted on a PLMS prototype, which was integrated into an IMC test environment. The acceptance of the learning environment was and is an essential aspect in this regard. Thus, the objective of the evaluation was to find out how well the PLMS was accepted by the employees, and which measures could be implemented to further increase its acceptance. The following usability factors were important: (1) selection and addition of widgets and navigation of learning spaces, (2) use of resources, such as wizard widgets and tutorials, (3) acceptance of the PLMS, (4) handling of the PLMS, and (5) comparisons with conventional training media and forms of learning.

Several methods were used in order to evaluate the PLMS. Observation was conducted on the one hand, and the so-called "think aloud" (TAM) or "question asking" method was used on the other. In addition, the questionnaire entitled "Perceived Usefulness and Ease of Use" (PUEU) was used in this evaluation supplementing data obtained by means of observation and the "think aloud" method. Eleven interviews were conducted with employees of the Festo Learning Centre. The employees came from different departments and had different educational backgrounds. The evaluation was allotted a duration of 45 to 60 minutes per user. To this end, the users were requested to complete a task within the PLMS. Subsequently, the test users evaluated the PLMS with regard to acceptance, system performance, required effort and user-friendliness, as well as use of and satisfaction with the application assistance. The PUEU survey consisted of two parts. Those questions which were considered as learning premise, namely those regarding age, sex and TEL experience, were presented with the PLMS test. The other part of the survey dealing with the evaluation of the product, in this case the PLMS, was conducted after the PLMS test. The evaluation supervisor was available while the questionnaire was being filled out and was able to help the test users with any questions or uncertainties. However, the test persons were initially only asked to respond to the closed questions. Then the observation started, during which time the observer took notes. If it was needed and time allowed it, the observer followed up on the open questions in order to clear up any unanswered points.

The evaluation of the PUEU questionnaire provided the following results: 82% of test users rated the learning environment PLMS as useful. 55 % indicated that they would achieve their learning goals somewhat more effectively with such a learning environment. The use of the learning environment was rated variably. 18% chose "fully correct" and 36% "rather correct" while 27% were undecided and 18% said that the use were rather not easy. There was a strong agreement of 100% that the use of the learning environment was not frustrating. But the evaluation showed that there was still a need of improvement. Almost half of the interviewees (45%) said the use of the learning environment was strenuous or rather strenuous. However, the vast majority with 72% of the respondents would use or rather use the learning environment, while only 9% said that they rather not use the tested learning technology (see Figure 3).

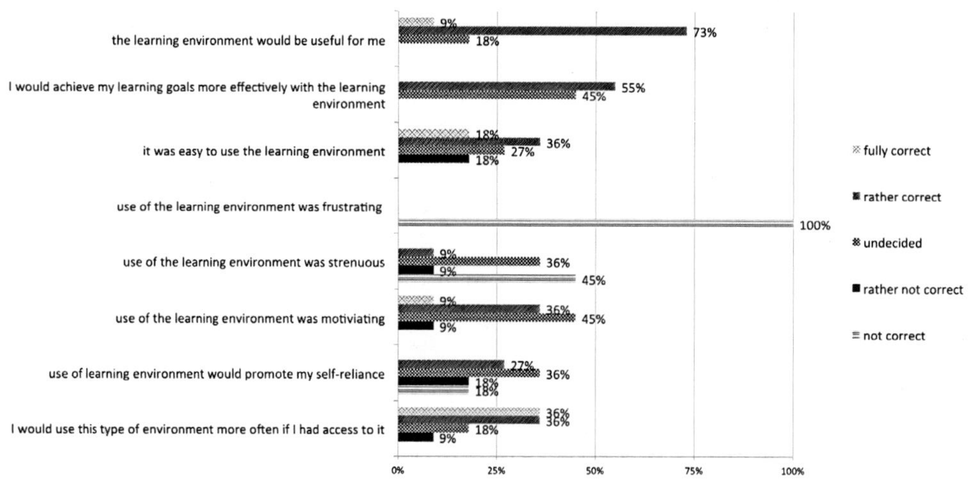

Figure 3: Results of the PUEU questionnaire

With the help of the TAM method it was possible to document positive as well as negative statements of the test users. Figure 4 represents a compendium of the most important statements, divided into the categories effort, performance and facilitation.

In conclusion, the evaluation results of the PLMS allow the following statements: (1) the use of the PLMS is deemed highly beneficial, (2) the PLMS supports the achievement of individual learning goals, (3) the PLMS would be used by the learners if access to a tool was available, and (4) usability, as well as the look & feel of the PLMS prototypes, should be improved.

Statements from the thinking aloud interviews		
How user-friendly are the PLMS and the integrated widgets? **(effort)**	Are performance and functions recognised and appreciated? **(performance)**	How well supported does the learner feel within the learning environment? **(facilitation)**
Positive: • Hardly any problems adding the widgets • Breakdown into steps promotes clarity **Room for improvement:** • Confusion upon exiting the PLMS and entering the browser • Usability of many of the widgets is faulty • The monitor is frequently overloaded with scroll bars	**Positive:** • Media lists facilitate research on the Internet **Room for improvement::** • Creation of private media lists would be desirable • Create an option for integrating well-known tools • Conventional storage media are given precedence	**Positive:** • Demo video is indispensable **Room for improvement:** • Video for the "Learn" phase is too long • Content of the wizard is not understandable at first glance • Help questions, tips and recommended tool categories do not provide enough help • It's frequently unclear when the individual learning phases are completed

Figure 4: Statements from the TAM interviews

Conclusion

From a technology perspective, success can be measured using the emergent confidence with the project progress so far, i.e. analysing the project results for the Festo test bed and the results of the different evaluation loops. All responses of the questionnaire in this case study according to the look & feel, usability and perceived usefulness are very positive regarding the applied ROLE approach in the business context. The usage of the PLE and LMS combination not only allows the personalisation of the learning process but it has also improved the learning process efficiency. The Festo project team members recognised the potential of this approach and considered it to be a useful enhancement of the learning culture at Festo for the future. In terms of challenges, however, there still appear to be some technical hurdles to overcome regarding the usability as well as look & feel of the PLMS for future implementations. These challenges relate to specific computer based issues and are all undergoing further investigation. From the pedagogical perspective, success in this case study can be measured by outlining the benefits of opening up an existing, previously closed LMS through the integration of PLE elements. There are some obvious advantages to quantify, for example, learners can choose whether the learning content within the LMS is sufficient to meet their individual learning goals or if they need to acquire additional information through the PLE part of the system. In addition, the integration of supporting ROLE-developed widgets in every phase of the PLMS prototype made it much easier for the test group to start using the environment more effectively and efficiently.

The bigger pedagogical challenge, however, remains and that is to promote this new approach to Festo learners on a large scale. For example, demonstrating the benefits of using a guided learning process within a PLMS rather than using Google to search for information needs to be resolved. In order to begin to address this issue, the initiative "Fit for Self-Regulated Learning" has been expanded and is intended to help learners acquire the skill-set they need to work successfully within a PLMS. The first results from this sub-project have included the development of a short introductory video about SRL[7]. Additionally the development of a PLMS prototype[8], which offers learning widgets for every phase of the learning process, may offer further benefits too in the future.

In the end, there were many challenges and hurdles to overcome in order for the work within this case study to commence and develop successfully. It took almost a year, for example, before the first widgets were fit-for-purpose and, therefore, could be tested by the focus group. Similarly, in a business context, there are complex requirements and restrictions. Nonetheless the feedback from the evaluation investigation remains very positive. It appears that people really liked the PLMS approach to learning tested at Festo. Additionally, and since the test phases took place, albeit on a prototype, individuals continued to ask for refinements of the system in relation to their user experience. The current vision and deployment of a PLE towards an integrated PLMS implementation with predefined learning spaces on the technical side seems to have been warmly welcomed. Evidence for the sustainability of the ROLE approach in this test bed is the fact that the LearningTube widget bundle has become an essential part of the Virtual Academy. As a result of this implementation there have been over 220 video uploads by Festo employees since July 2011, consisting mostly of screencasts and recorded presentations. These videos have been accessed over 15,000 times to date (April 2013). Additionally, the LearningTube widget bundle was acknowledged by the Comenius-EduMedia organisation and was awarded for the practical application of educational, thematic and design excellence in educational media.[9] Festo was the only industrial enterprise to receive such an award. From the learners' perspective in the company, however, it remains essential that they are able to learn in a self-regulated manner. The required technical improvements, therefore, have to be synchronised with the necessary individual development of specific SRL competences in order to meet these very real needs.

In summary, the ROLE framework enables the more targeted provision of learning support to the learner, thus enables more efficient organisational learning processes

7 *http://youtu.be/UkAkFQ5TPOI and http://youtu.be/sVTxmHokn2Y*
8 *http://role-widgetstore.eu/content/role-personal-learning-management-system*
9 *http://www.festo.com/net/sk_sk/SupportPortal/Details/250874/PressArticle.aspx*

through cheaper assembly of learning resources as the learners can do the compilation themselves, and better controlled organisational learning as the organisation can easily supervise the achievements of the learners. The ROLE results provide the opportunity to effectively support the change from a teacher-student learning paradigm to more self-regulated learning concepts. In general, the uptake of ROLE results is an on-going process that bases significantly on the understanding that ROLE technologies have the potential to ease educational practices of teachers and students by providing access to tailored learning resources that would not be available otherwise. The integration of the ROLE approach into organisational LMSs like Festo's Clix-based Virtual Academy simplifies the uptake further.

ACKNOWLEDGEMENT

The research leading to these results has received funding from the European Commission's Seventh Framework Programme (FP7/2007-2013) under grant agreement no 231396 (ROLE project).

REFERENCES

[Fru 10] *Fruhmann, K., Nussbaumer, A., Albert, D. (2010):* A Psycho-Pedagogical Framework for Self-Regulated Learning in a Responsive Open Learning Environment. In Hambach, S., Martens, A., Urban, B. (Eds.) Proceedings of the 3rd International eLBa Science Conference. Rostock.

[Sch 12] *Schanda, F., Dikke, D., Mueller, N. (2012):* Personal Learning Management Systems (PLMS): Concept, Classification, Evaluation. In Urban, B. & Müsebeck, P. (Eds.) Proceedings of the 5th International eLBa Science Conference. Rostock.

[Vel 09] *Velasco, K. (2009):* An Introduction to Personal Learning Environments. Making learning personal – using PLEs to enhance learning, retrieved June 11, 2013 from http://www.towardsmaturity.org/article/2009/11/18/introduction-personal-learning-environments.

CONTACT DETAILS

Maren Scheffel and Martin Wolpers
Fraunhofer Institute for Applied Information Technology FIT
Schloss Birlinghoven, 53754 Sankt Augustin, Germany
{maren.scheffel, martin.wolpers}@fit.fraunhofer.de

Manuel Schmidt and Michael Werkle
Festo Lernzentrum Saar GmbH
Obere Kaiserstraße 301, 66386 St. Ingbert-Rohrbach, Germany
{mans, werk}@de.festo.com

Investigating teachers' perception about the educational benefits of Web 2.0 personal learning environments

Ebrahim Rahimi, Jan van den Berg, Wim Veen

ABSTRACT

Implementing personal learning environments (PLEs) in educational settings is a challenging and complex process. Teachers as the main agents of change in their classroom settings need support in designing and implementing these new learning environments and integrating them into the educational process. In this paper, we propose a model to implement Web 2.0 PLEs in educational settings based on the conceived objectives of PLEs namely (i) enhancing the students' control in educational process and (ii) supporting and empowering students to build and deploy their PLEs. In addition, we develop a technological prototype based on the model, and report and analyze the perceptions of a group of teachers regarding the potential of the prototype to improve the educational process. The results suggest that the implementation of the model can contribute to the development of a student-centric learning environment and improvement in the teachers' technological, pedagogical, and content knowledge (TPACK).

Note: *This article has been published in the Special Edition of the eLearning Papers, Issue No. 35 "Personal Learning Environments". The link to this Special Issue is: http://openeducationeuropa.eu/en/paper/personal-learning-environments*

Introduction

In recent years, the concept of personal learning environments (PLEs) has attracted the attention of researchers and practitioners in the educational technology domain [Att-07b] says:

> *"important concepts in PLEs include the integration of both formal and informal learning episodes into a single experience, the use of social networks that can cross institutional boundaries and the use of networking protocols (Peer-to-Peer, web services, syndication) to connect a range of resources and systems within a personally-managed space."*

The main feature of PLEs that distinguishes them from other sorts of technology-based learning initiatives lies in their emphasis on the role of students as the manager and developer of their learning environments. In this regard, [Att 07a] defines Web 2.0 PLEs

as activity spaces, consist of loosely coupled Web 2.0 tools and learning resources collected by students to interact and communicate with each other and experts in order to address their heterogeneous learning requirements, the ultimate result of which is the development of collective learning. Along similar lines, [Dre 10] and [Väl 10] define the development of PLEs as a student-driven learning process and an important learning outcome constructed by students. Implementing the PLE concept in educational settings is a complex process that consists of several challenges. Firstly, it requires redefining the commonly accepted roles of teachers and students in the educational settings. The traditional procedures of teaching assume students as not sufficiently knowledgeable individuals to take full control over their learning. This assumption strengthens the role of teacher as the main controller of the educational practices with the main goal of transferring predefined content to the students [Dro 06] resulting in too much teacher's control in the educational process and leading to poorly tailored learning experiences, students' boredom and demotivation [Gar 87]. Residing too much control with the teacher is in stark contrast to the conceived objective of PLEs to transfer control of learning from teacher to students and can diminish mutual communication as well as opportunities for students to construct meaning and knowledge [Att 07a], [Buc 12].

Secondly, generally speaking, teachers, as the main agents of change in their classrooms, are resistant to adopt technological and pedagogical innovations [Ert 10]. [Hop 97] wrote, teachers basically have to contend with two factors with technology adoption being (i) the psychological effect of change and (ii) learning to use technology. Nonetheless, the PLE concept has introduced the third challenging factor to teachers: rethinking their pedagogical approach to facilitate more students' control in the educational process using Web 2.0 tools and technologies.

Thirdly, beyond some technologically oriented approaches, there are not clear references and well-established pedagogical models of PLE-based teaching and learning as well as practical advices to support it available. In this regard, as asserted by [Fie 11], while there is an intense focus on issues of re-instrumentation of teaching and learning practices in the PLE literature, enhancing students' control as the main objective of PLE remains largely untouched and ignored. Therefore, teachers do not have clear perception about the PLE concept, and its technological and pedagogical implications and benefits, which makes them hesitant to accept and adopt the concept.

Research has shown that the new technology or pedagogy adoption decisions are mainly influenced by teachers' individual attitudes towards the technology or pedagogy, which in turn are formed from specific underlying personal beliefs about the consequences of the adoption [Sug 04], [Ma 09]. Therefore, they must be personally convinced of the feasibility and benefits of the new technology or pedagogy before adoption and integration occur [Lam 00]. Research has suggested that one of the best ways to convince and motivate teachers to adopt a new technology or pedagogy is by providing opportunities for them to witness and perceive the benefits of these changes. In this regard, [Ert 10] asserted that observing examples and models of a technology integration or a pedagogical approach by teachers can increase their knowledge, change their belief system and, convince them to adopt the new technology or pedagogy by helping them to understand what looks like the approach or tool in practice and to make judgment about whether that approach or tool (i) is relevant to their goals, (ii) enables them to meet student needs, and (iii) addresses important learning outcomes.

In this paper, we sought to develop a model to support building and deploying PLEs and to investigate teachers' perceptions regarding the impact of PLEs on improving educational practices. In this regard, first we develop a pedagogically oriented model for PLE-based teaching and learning. Then we build a technological prototype based on this model to be used as an example for introducing and presenting the PLE concept. Afterwards in order to examine how the prototype can contribute to improving the educational practices, we report the results of the conducted interviews with a group of teachers in the context of a secondary school. Finally, we propose design principles and guidelines to improve the next version of the prototype.

Research Methodology

In order to develop a model to support building and deploying PLEs, a design-based research for one iteration approach was used comprising four broad phases, as illustrated in Figure 1 [Ma 09]. Design-based research focuses, simultaneously, on practice and theory through finding and solving practical problems and providing design principles. To do so, it starts with (i) identifying and analyzing a complex real world educational problem in the research context and (ii) generating a solution based on reviewing existing theories and consulting with practitioners, (iii) evaluating the solution by gathering empirical data, and (iv) reflecting on the design experience to refine the solution and construct theoretical knowledge [Ree 05].

Design-based Research: A Process for One Iteration

Analysis of Practical Problems by Researchers and Practitioners 1
Review the literature to determine the significance of the problem 1.2
Identify a practical problem 1.1

Development of Solutions with a Theoretical Framework 2
Develop a prototype that serves the research purpose 2.5
Identify development methods 2.4
Identify the purpose and research questions for a development iteration 2.3
Determine the role of research in developing the solution 2.2
Conceptualize a solution within theoretical framework 2.1

Evaluation and Testing of Solutions in Practice 3
Draw conclusions and determine research findings 3.3
Gather and analyze data to answer research questions 3.2
Identify research methods 3.1

Documentation and Reflection to Produce "Design Principles" 4
Synthesize guidance for concluding design-based research 4.2
Synthesize design principles for developing the proposed solution 4.1

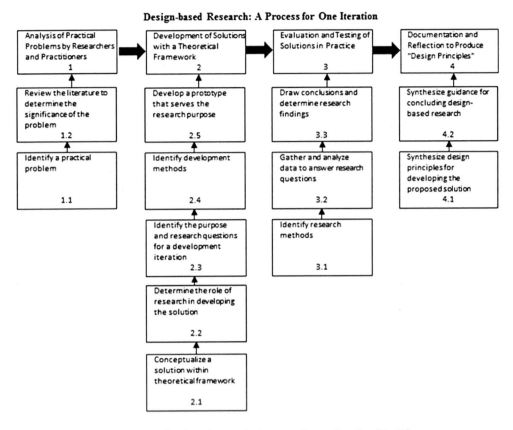

Figure 1: Design-based research: A process for one iteration [Ma 09]

Analysis of a practical problem

The context of this research is a secondary school. Seeking the ways to take advantage of the PLE concept, Web 2.0 tools and social software to enrich teaching and learning processes, and to improve pedagogical and technological competencies of teachers and students are the main drivers for this school. Following design-based research, we started our research by identifying a problem within this context.

Identify a problem

Although the school's teachers have been trying to adopt a PLE-based pedagogical approach, there was not a model available to support teachers and students to develop and deploy their PLEs. As a result, the teachers did not have a clear conception and understanding of the PLE concept, and its benefits and implications for their educational practices, which affected their willingness to adopt and apply this concept in their classrooms.

Determine the significance of the problem

In the e-learning domain, PLEs are increasingly attracting the attentions of educational researchers and practitioners as an effective pedagogical approach to addressing issues of personalization and student's control. A problem with supporting the conceived objectives of PLEs has been that, while there is a large and increasing number of suitable Web 2.0 tools and learning resources, a comprehensive pedagogical and technological framework as well as practical advice on how to construct Web 2.0 PLEs is unavailable. Affected by this gap, educators at different educational levels are forced to adapt and rethink their teaching approaches in conjunction with the advent of new Web 2.0 PLEs without having a clear perception of PLEs and a roadmap for attending to students' various needs [Kop 08], [Fie 11].

Development of a solution with a theoretical framework

To address the identified problem we decided to develop a pedagogical model and technological prototype based on this model. There are two main conceived objectives of PLEs that can be used to outline a model for developing and deploying PLEs in educational settings, being (i) enhancing the students' control in educational process, and (ii) supporting and empowering students to design and develop their PLEs [Att 07a], [Joh 08], [Dre 10], [Val 12]. To support these objectives, several learning theories and principles should be involved in order to define the main components of the model and their interactions.

Student's control in educational process is concerned with the degree to which the student can influence and direct their learning experiences and it relates to several aspects of the educational process [Gar 87]. Firstly, the theory of transactional control [Dro 07] suggests that control is concerned with choices. Based on this theory, an indicator for a "mature learner" is her ability for making relevant and effective choices in her learning journey. Hence, providing students with proper technological, pedagogical, and social choices to define their learning aims and methods is a prerequisite step for them to achieve control over their learning by moving from a "state of dependence to one of independence", and has the potential to enhance the student's feeling of ownership and control. According to [Buc 11], there are different sorts of choices for students in PLEs including technological choices (i.e. learning tools), pedagogical choices (i.e. learning objectives, learning content, learning rules and, learning tasks), and social choices (i.e. learning community).

Secondly, developing and applying PLEs requires flexible pedagogical approaches and technological activity spaces to allow students to construct and manipulate their learning environments by defining their learning goals, choosing tools, joining or starting communities, and assembling resources [Att 07a]. Providing flexibility in pedagogical approaches or technological aspects has the potential to improve students' control over their learning process. As asserted by [Buc 12] there is a strong relationship between students' control and their feeling of ownership over learning with (perceived) possibilities to manipulate their learning environments.

Thirdly, according to [Joh 08], any attempt for developing PLEs should focus on the personal development of students as an inherent aspect of PLEs. Reflection has been asserted as the core source of personal development [Sch 83] by enhancing the effectiveness of learning and promoting metacognition, learning to learn and self-regulation [Ver 12]. Accordingly, any model aims to support the development of PLEs, should provide opportunities and triggers for students to reflect on their learning practices. Contextual information on the learning process has been proven to support the students' reflection by stimulating the students' engagement in collaborating process, raising their awareness about the learning environment and triggering their reflection about acquired competences [Gla 07]. In a PLE-based learning scenario, an important part of contextual information encompasses past or current activities or events occurred in the learning environment through deploying web tools by the students. Collecting and presenting these information can provide possibilities for students to observe each other learning behavior, reflect on their learning process and progress by comparing aspects of their learning experience with other students, and collaborate with peers by sharing and receiving material and providing feedback [Ver 12], [Val 12].

Fourthly, according to [Joh 12], there is a bidirectional and feedback relationship between the learning environment and the student's personal agency in a way that the things that students do are transformative of the environment within which they operate, and vice versa.

According to [Rah 13a], in PLE-based learning both teachers and students should be assumed as learners. Indeed, the teachers in order to improve their teaching practices have an unceasing need to learn how to teach with technology, while the students need to learn how to learn by managing technology. From this perspective, the teacher and students are partners in the educational process [Cla 05] and as noted by [Ho 03], "teaching is not the art of filling the student with knowledge in the way one would fill and empty receptacle. Teaching is a two-way learning process in which the student and teacher help each other to learn by sharing their insights and difficulties with each other." From the PLE perspective, it can be argued that any attempt for enhancing student's control should recognize and corroborate the role of students in this feedback mechanism.

Figure 2 depicts the proposed implementation of the model, built upon the mentioned learning theories and principles. The model consists of two main parts, namely parts A and B, to address the two above-mentioned objectives of PLEs, respectively. Part A aims to enhance students' control in educational process. Derived from the mentioned learning principles, this part has four main components, being (i) choices, (ii) personal activity spaces, (iii) aggregated information, and (iv) feedback system. The teacher seeds the learning environment by providing appropriate technological, pedagogical, and social choices. The students can access and use these choices in their personal activity spaces to perform learning activities and support their learning requirements. Appropriate information pertains to these learning activities then can be

aggregated to be used to support reflection and collaboration among the students. The feedback system aims to encourage the students to discover and introduce the learning affordances of the provided choices and other sorts of learning resources based on the ways that they perceive and operationalize them in their learning process. The teacher can use this insight for reseeding and reshaping the learning environment.

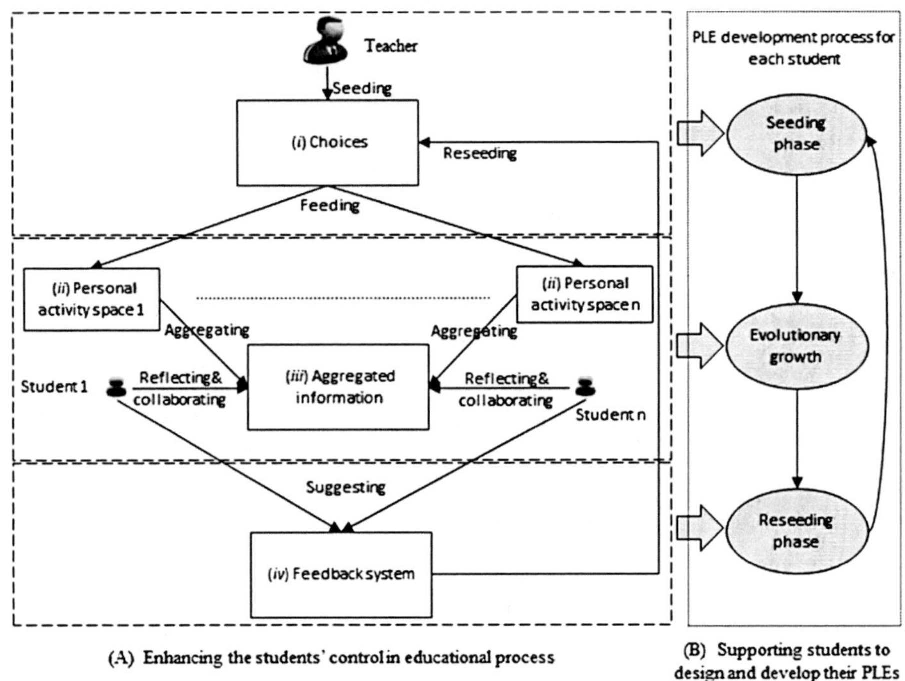

Figure 2: The proposed model consists of two parts to support the main objectives of PLEs

Part B illustrates how the model supports students to design and develop their PLEs. The model follows an iterative end-user development (EUD) approach [Fis 98] for designing and building PLEs. The EUD concept was originally developed in the field of computer science and Human-Computer-Interaction aiming at allowing and empowering end users of software applications as "owners of problems" to act as designers to engage actively in the continuous development of their environments. [Fis 98] introduced the seeding, evolutionary growth, and reseeding (SER) process model to operationalize this concept by encouraging designers to conceptualize their activity as meta-design, thereby supporting end users as the developers of their environment rather than restricting them to passive consumers. From this perspective, a PLE can be envisioned as a learning environment seeded by the teacher, as designer, with an initial set of relevant technological, pedagogical, and social choices (seeding phase). Then it is

flourished and evolved by adding new learning resources through active participation of the teacher and students as a community of learners (evolutionary growth). The PLE will be reseeded through the feedback mechanism in order to add new choices or remove the current choices (reseeding phase).

Determine the role of research in developing the solution

The role of this research is to develop a first-iteration design of a model for constructing PLEs.

Identify the purpose and research questions for a development iteration

The purpose of this research is to implement a technological prototype based on the model and next to examine the perceptions of teachers about the potential of the prototype to improve the educational process. The following research question guides the research:

How do the teachers perceive the PLE prototype as a means to improve the educational process?

Identify development methods

Several issues pertaining to the implementation of the prototype need to be addressed, including (i) choosing an appropriate technological platform, (ii) identifying the tools to develop the prototype, (iii) providing technological choices to seed the prototype, (iv) determining the specifications of the PLE interface and, (v) supporting the reseeding phase.

Recent advances in computing, multimedia, communication, and web technologies have provided unprecedented opportunities for the educational institutions and learners to pursue and enrich their teaching and learning activities. Taking advantage of these advances, cloud computing is becoming a main paradigm in addressing the requirements of the web-based teaching and learning initiatives. Cloud computing supports SaaS architecture (i.e. the capabilities of software applications are exposed as services) and provides reliable, assured, and flexible service delivery while keeping the users isolated from the underlying infrastructure. As a result, "cloud computing makes it possible for almost anyone to deploy tools that can scale on demand to serve as many users as desired" without bickering about technical expertise and maintenance issues [Al-Z 09].

Google apps for education is an appropriate cloud-based platform providing numerous technological possibilities for developing the prototype. It allows students to access thousands of available gadgets or build their own to fulfill their heterogeneous learning needs and provides several possibilities to support online collaboration and social learning. For instance, Google Docs and Spreadsheets allow the creation of documents and spreadsheets with more collaborative capacity and enable students to communicate around content. Also, Google Calendar lets students and teachers to set their personal or class-wide learning goals, plan the educational events, and monitor their learning process. Moreover, Google sites allows student to create their own private or public websites to publish and present their thought and findings.

The interface of the PLE prototype for each student can be divided into two parts: a personal part and a social hub. The personal part provides the student's access to a gadget container comprising of thousands gadgets. The student has full control over her personal part and can use it as an activity space to support her learning purposes by accessing, using, adding, customizing, sharing or removing gadgets. The social hub is a shared place between all PLEs where the students' activities and experiences in different tools are aggregated using aggregation software and presented to be used as a source of reflection and collaboration. It also contains a set of common tools seeded by the teachers to support the main educational process of the school, namely orientation, execution and evaluation processes.

Google sites supports developing a specific type of start page consisting of two parts including public and private parts, accessible via a unique URL. The public part is manageable by the admin of the page and is visible for all of the allowed users, while the private part is visible and manageable only by the users. These functionalities define the start page as an appropriate option to build the PLE interface by using the public part of the start page to develop the social hub of the PLE interface and the private part for the personal part of the PLE interface.

To support the reseeding phase, the functionalities of Google spreadsheets and Google sites, along with HTML, can be used to implement a feedback mechanism. This mechanism allows the students to introduce and share their preferred web tools and learning resources based on a defined structure, explain the learning benefits and affordances of tools, and rate them based on some defined criteria such as ease of use or learning usefulness.

Develop a prototype that serves the research purpose

After having identified and chosen the development methods, the next step was to implement the prototype. Figure 3 shows the PLE interface for each student consisting of a social hub and a personal part. The social hub provides the following functionalities: (a) Seeding the PLE with appropriate choices in terms of web tools, useful links and relevant people: (c) Providing links to the students and teachers' websites and blogs; (d) Presenting teacher's announcements; (e) Aggregating learning activities and experiences of students accomplished in different tools by using a feed aggregation software (i.e. FriendFeed); (f) Managing class-wide activities by using a calendar widget. The personal part provides students a flexible activity space to manage their learning activities and develop their PLEs by exploring and exploiting the learning affordances of the provided choices and a rich set of the available gadgets.

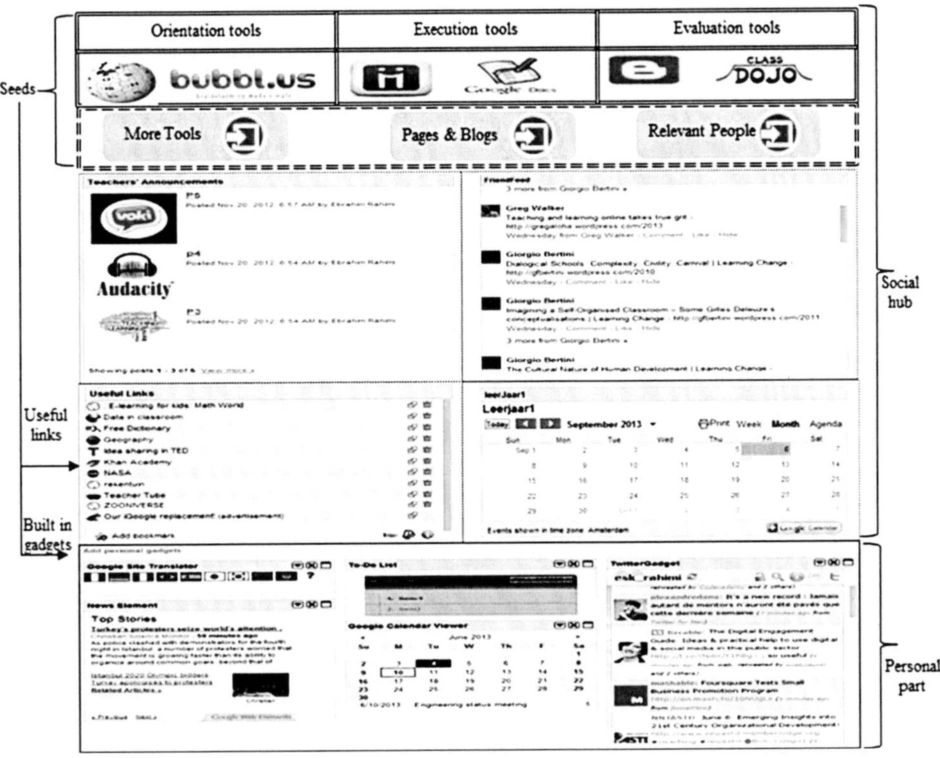

Figure 3: The interface of PLE for each student

For each web tool seeding the PLE, an introduction page illustrates the tool and its educational usages, as shown in Figure 4. Also, the students are asked to evaluate the tool and explain its learning affordances based on their personal experiences with the tool. This information then can be used by teachers to reseed and retool the learning environment and design appropriate learning tasks.

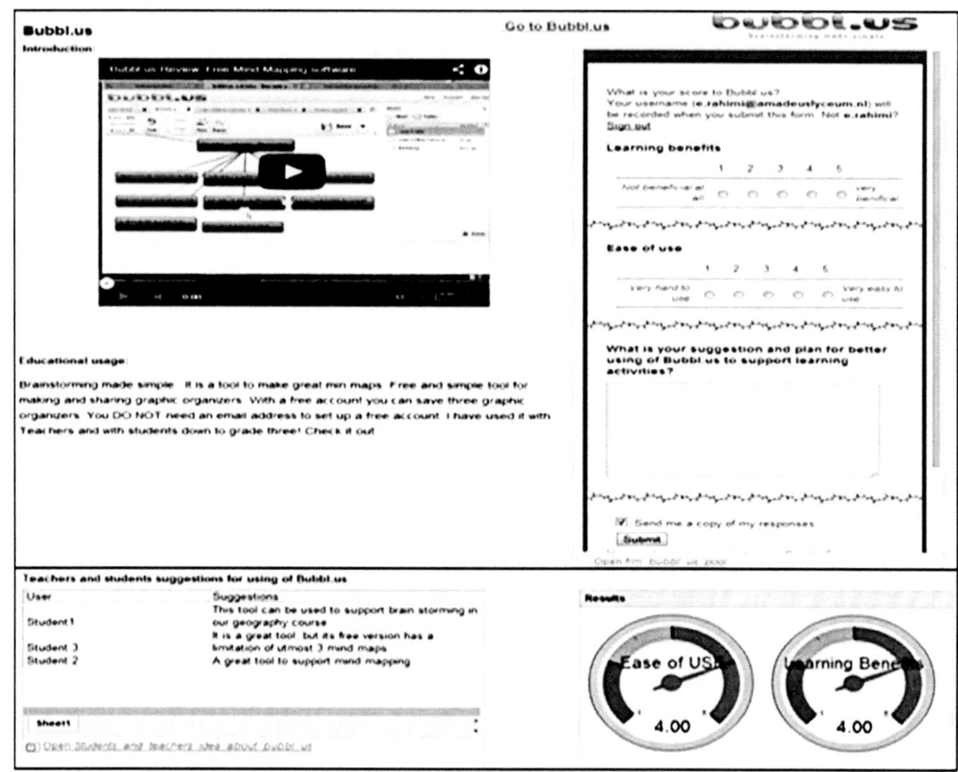

Figure 4: A page for introducing each web tool and receiving students' feedback about the tool

As a part of the reseeding phase, as shown in Figure 5, the students are encouraged to introduce new learning resources they have found useful to be used to reseed the PLE.

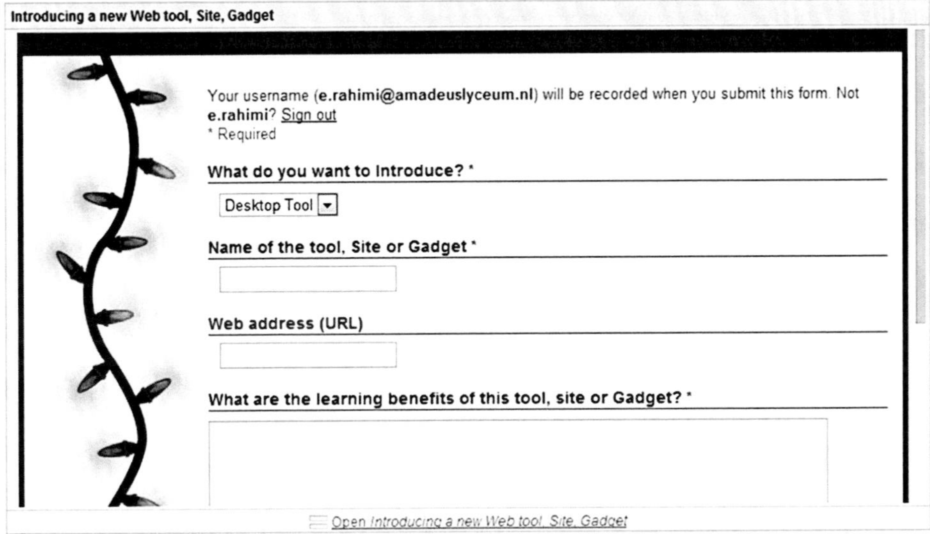
Introducing a new Web tool, Site, Gadget

Your username (**e.rahimi@amadeuslyceum.nl**) will be recorded when you submit this form. Not **e.rahimi**? Sign out

* Required

What do you want to Introduce? *

Desktop Tool

Name of the tool, Site or Gadget *

Web address (URL)

What are the learning benefits of this tool, site or Gadget? *

Open Introducing a new Web tool, Site, Gadget

Introduced Tools by teachers and students

USER	TYPE	Name	Web Address	Learning Benefits
e.rahimi@amadeuslyceum.nl	A Web Site (i.e. Twitter, Hyves)	Twitter	www.twitter.com	1- Networking 2- Group working 3- Connecting to the world
e.rahimi@amadeuslyceum.nl	A Web Site (i.e. Twitter, Hyves)	hyves	www.hyves.nl	a social networking site
e.rahimi@amadeuslyceum.nl	A Web Site (i.e. Twitter, Hyves)	bbc learning english	www.bbc.com/learni	a lot of movies in english
e.rahimi@amadeuslyceum.nl	Gadget	Word of the day		Gadgets exist for all different types of words - SAT/GRE/ACT words of the day, or foreign language words of the day, or just general words from a dictionary. These words could perhaps be used in a writing warm-up activity Explore this type by entering 'Word of the da[illegible] or 'Daily word' into the gadget directory searc[illegible]

Figure 5: A page for introducing new learning resources by students

Evaluation and testing of the solution in practice

Identify research methods

Due to the exploratory nature of this research, we chose qualitative research methods to support data gathering and analysis processes [Yin 08]. Yin identified six possible sources of evidence including: documentation, physical artifacts, interviews, direct observations, participant-observation, and archival records. For the purpose of this study, we selected the interview as the main method to collect data. We adopted a purposeful sampling technique [Pat 02] to select teachers with a variety of background and disciplines, and with a different amount of experience related to using web tools to support their teaching process.

Gather and analyze data to answer research question

After having identified the research methods, we started to collect and analyze data. For data collection, six interviews with ten teachers were conducted. We used the following procedure to conduct each interview: A few days before each interview an account to access to the prototype was created and sent to the interviewees along with a brief description of the PLEs concept. Due to the unfamiliarity of the most of the interviewees with this concept, we asked the interviewees to explore the prototype before the interview meetings to gain an initial perception of the PLEs concept and prototype. Each interview lasted between one to two hours. During each meeting we first started by introducing and explaining the PLEs concept and then receiving their reactions and feedback about the concept and prototype based on their previous experiences of using web tools in their classrooms. As stated by [Ma 09], linking the topic of discussion to the past experience of interviewees can mentally prepare them to use their experiences to evaluate conceptual models and prototypes. In the second part of interview, we described the different functionalities of the prototype. We presented different scenarios to explain how these functionalities can support their teaching practices as well the learning process of students. After this part, we asked the interviewees about their final thoughts, perceptions, expectations and reactions to the prototype.

The collected data then were analyzed by using Atlas.ti software. The analysis procedure included transcribing audio data, entering data into Atlas.ti, coding data, reading the transcripts organized by codes, writing memos, recoding and merging similar codes as necessary, grouping codes into categories, creating network diagrams by establishing relationships or links between codes, and writing up conclusions.

Draw conclusions and determine research findings

Figure 6 presents the results of the analysis phase describing the teachers' perceptions about the ways that the prototype can contribute to improving the educational process. In this figure, the first number between parentheses indicates groundedness (that is, the number of times mentioned in the interviews), the second number indicates density (that is, the number of codes to which it has a relationship).

Participants remarked that the personal part of PLE (7 mentions, Figure 6) can help teachers to realize the ways that students learn with web tools (12 mentions, Figure 6) and in turn it can support the design of appropriate technology-based learning tasks (18 mentions, see Fig.6) resulting in the adoption of a student-centric learning approach. Furthermore, the personal part of PLE can increase the encouragement of students to find/share learning resources (12 mentions, Figure 6), resulting in the improvement of teacher's TPACK, i.e. the knowledge that the teacher needs to know in order to be able to teach with technology [Mis 06]. As remarked by participants, one of the main issues to adopt the PLE-based teaching approach by teachers is their estimation about the required changes in their teaching process (7 mentions, Figure 6) which can be improved

by the improvement of teacher's TPACK, which in turn can increase the tendency of teacher toward technology (4 mentions, Figure 6).

As remarked by participants, the social hub of PLE (4 mentions, Figure 6) is useful to identify students' and teachers' preferred web tools and learning resources (4 mentions, Figure 6) and can facilitate the exchange of good practices (4 mentions, Figure 6) with regard to the teaching and learning usage of web tools. As a result, the social hub of PLE can assist teachers in identifying the usefulness and learning values of web tools (23 mentions, Figure 6). As remarked by participants, identifying the usefulness and learning values of web tools has an enviable position in improving educational process (9 mentions, Figure 6) and increasing the teachers' tendency toward technology and teacher's TPACK. Furthermore, identifying the usefulness and learning values of web tools can support teachers in the selection of appropriate web tools (20 mentions, Figure 6), resulting in the design of appropriate technology-based learning tasks.

Participants asserted that the combination of the personal part of PLE and social hub of PLE can support the creation of an interactive learning environment (6 mentions, Figure 6) by providing opportunities for students to enrich their learning experiences by using digital tools and collaborate with each other around the content and technology.

The teachers also remarked that not only students but also other teachers should be able to share their experiences, good practices, and success stories regarding integration technology as well as the learning values and benefits of web tools by using the prototype. One teacher emphasized this requirement as below:

Teachers have always some ongoing educational activities and projects. They have an unceasing need to know about tools to support these activities. The social hub of PLE should provide a place for teachers to share their tools and the ways that they use them. These information can be very helpful for other teachers with same needs and projects.

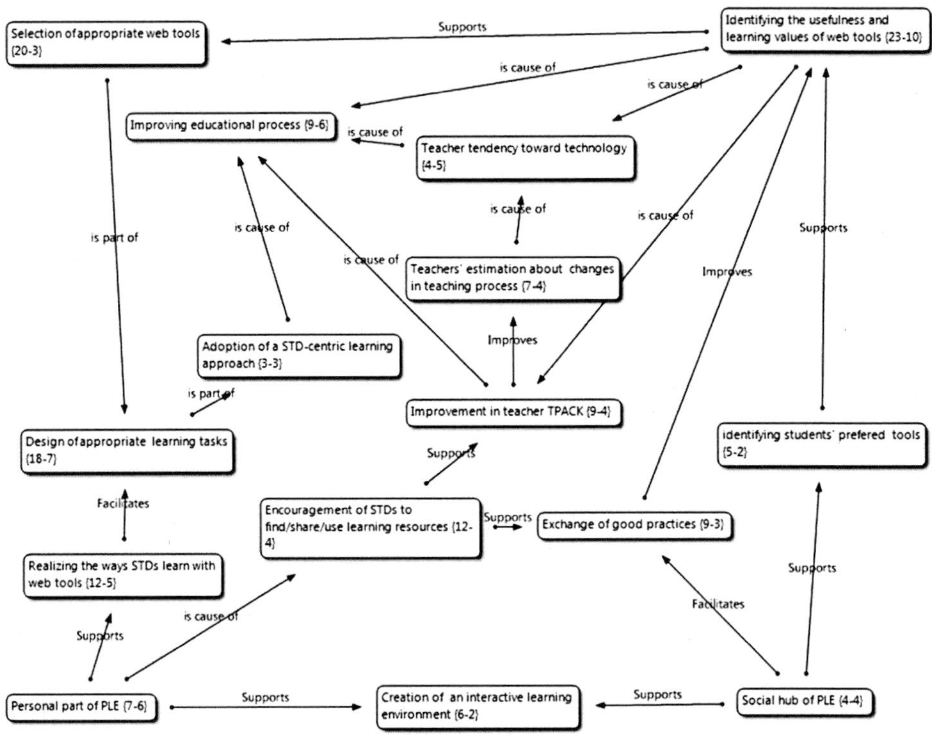

Figure 6: The perceptions of the teachers regarding the impact of the prototype on educational process

Documentation and reflection to produce design principles for the proposed solution
The results have revealed the main sorts of knowledge, skills, and support teachers require to facilitate PLE-based teaching and learning including: (a) Identifying the students' web tools preferences; (b) Realizing the ways that students use and learn with web tools; (c) Identifying the usefulness and learning values of web tools; (d) Defining clear criteria to assess, evaluate, and introduce the learning affordances and benefits of web tools by students and teachers; (e) Selecting appropriate web tools to support different phases of teaching and learning process; (f) Designing appropriate learning tasks by using selected web tools; (g) Encouraging students to choose and use web tools, reflect on their learning values, and share their learning values; (h) Getting aware of other teachers' practices and success stories with web tools.

Addressing these requirements can improve the educational process not only by helping teachers to establish a student-centric learning environment, but also by supporting the "situated professional development" of teachers. Situated professional development addresses teachers' specific needs within their specific environments by

allowing them to gain "new knowledge that can be applied directly within their classrooms" [Ert 10]. In this regard, Kennedy in [Ert 10] noted that the most important feature of a professional development approach is a strong focus on helping teachers understand how students learn specific content, and how specific instructional practices and tools can support student learning outcomes.

This approach to the teachers' professional development conforms with the recently emerged paradigms in teaching theories that emphasize teaching and learning are intertwined and state "teaching practices and theories of teaching should be based on knowledge and theories of how students learn" [Ver 99]. From the PLEs perspective, learning is a student-driven self-regulated knowledge constructing process. In this regard, as stated by [Tur 08], the organization of learning resources by students at a PLE into meaningful learning activities toward achieving learning goals can be considered as act of instructional design, corresponding to the forethought phase of Zimmerman's self-regulated learning model. Accordingly, this calls for theories of teaching that are based on an analysis of students' learning process ongoing throughout their PLEs.

We derived the following design principles from the research findings to guide developing the next version of the prototype:

- Teachers need to know students' technological preferences and the ways they use web tools in order to implement a student-centric teaching and learning approach and support their professional development process. Addressing this requirement needs adding a monitoring and analyzing functionality to the prototype to observe the personal parts of students, trace their use of each tool, and provide appropriate information about the usage pattern of web tools.
- The personal part of PLE should provide students with appropriate technological choices. The level and scope of these choices is an important factor influencing the students' control. While a restricted personal part can lead to poorly tailored learning experiences and students' boredom and demotivation, a limitless freedom will lead to the teachers' loss of control on the students' interaction with technology. In this situation dialogue between teacher and students is the best solution to make decision about the scope of students' technological choices.
- The results of this study indicate that the adoption of PLE-based learning by teachers strongly depends on the teachers' estimation of the required changes in their teaching process. According to [Gus 95], the amount of change individuals are asked to make is inversely related to their probability of making the change. Hence following a step-by-step technology integration approach by focusing on teachers' immediate needs and facilitating small changes within teaching and learning practices appears to be an effective long-term strategy to implement PLEs. Also, presenting inspiring models of PLE and describing how they can support different teaching and learning scenarios can improve the teachers' tendency toward the adoption of the PLE-based learning.

- The PLE prototype should provide opportunities for teachers to share their examples of "good teaching" that include the integration of technology. These examples can help teachers to develop confidence by hearing about or observing other teachers' successful efforts. As asserted by [Ert 10], "observing successful others can build confidence in the observers who tend to believe if he/she can do it, then I can too."

Summary

In this paper, a new implementation and deployment model to develop PLEs in educational settings has been proposed. The model aims to put students in a higher level of control in the educational process by acknowledging and corroborating their role as active learners, contributors, and designers. The results of this research indicate that the teachers' perceptions regarding the potential of the technological prototype, built upon the model, to improve the educational process is positive. Also, the results provide the sorts of knowledge, skills, and support teachers require in order to facilitated PLE-based teaching and learning. Based on these findings, the research offers design guidelines to improve the next version of the prototype. Further research is supposed to be needed to apply these guidelines, and test and evaluate the modified version of the prototype from the teachers' and students' perspectives.

Acknowledgements

The authors want to thank to the teachers, staff, and students of the Amadeus Lyceum secondary school in Vleuten, Netherlands for their valuable participation in this research. In addition, the authors would like to express their appreciation to Graham Attwell for his comments on this paper. The authors also want to express their gratitude to the Ministry of Science, Research, and Technology (MSRT) of the Islamic Republic of Iran for their financial support.

REFERENCES

[Al-Z 09] *Al-Zoube, M. (2009). E-Learning on the Cloud. Int. Arab J. e-Technol.,1(2), 58–64.*

[Att 07a] *Attwell, Graham (2007a):* Personal Learning Environments-the future of eLearning? eLearning Papers, 2(1), 1–8.

[Att 07a] *Attwell, Graham (2007b). The Social impact of Personal Learning Environments, Retrieved October 10, 2013, from* http://www.pontydysgu.org/2007/11/the-social-impact-of-personal-learning-environments

[Buc 11] *Buchem, Ilona; Graham Attwell; and Ricardo Torres (2011):* Understanding Personal Learning Environments: Literature review and synthesis through the Activity Theory lens. Proceedings of the second PLE Conference,(pp. 1–33). Southampton, UK.

[Buc 12] *Buchem, Ilona. (2012):* Psychological Ownership and Personal Learning Environments: Do sense of ownership and control really matter? Proceedings of the 3th PLE Conference, Aveiro, Portugal. Retrieved from: *http://revistas.ua.pt/index.php/ple/article/view/1437/1323*

[Cla 05] *Clayson, Dennis E.; and Debra A. Haley (2005):* Marketing models in education: students as customers, products, or partners. Marketing Education Review, 15(1), 1–10.

[Dre 10] *Drexler, Wendy (2010):* The networked student model for construction of personal learning environments: Balancing teacher control and student autonomy. Australasian Journal of Educational Technology. 26(3), 369–385.

[Dro 06] *Dron, Jon (2006):* Social software and the emergence of control. Sixth International Conference on Advanced Learning Technologies, IEEE, 904–908.

[Dro 07] *Dron, Jon (2007):* Control and constraint in E-Learning: Choosing when to choose. Idea Group Publishing.

[Ert 10] *Ertmer, Peggy A., and Anne T. Ottenbreit-Leftwich (2010):* Teacher technology change: How knowledge, confidence, beliefs, and culture intersect. Journal of Research on Technology in Education, 42(3), 255–284.

[Fie 11] *Fiedler, Sebastian, and Terje Väljataga (2011):* Expanding the concept of learner control in higher education: consequences for intervention design. In:11th IEEE International Conference on Advanced Learning Technologies (ICALT), 262–264.

[Fis 98] *Fischer, Gerhard, and Eric Scharff (1998):* Learning technologies in support of self-directed learning. Journal of Interactive Media in Education, 1998(2).

[Gar 87] *Garrison, D. Randy, and Myra Baynton (1987):* Beyond Independence in distance education: The concept of control. The American journal of distance education, 1(3).

[Gla 07] *Glahn, Christian, Marcus Specht, and Rob Koper (2007):* Smart indicators on learning interactions. In: Creating new learning experiences on a global scale. Springer Berlin Heidelberg, 56–70.

[Gus 95] *Guskey, Thomas R (1995):* Professional development in education: In search of the optimal mix. In T. R. Guskey & M. Huberman (Eds.), Professional development in education: New paradigms and practices. New York: Teachers College Press. 114–131.

[Ho 03] *Ho, Wai Luen (2003):* 60 Strategies to Inspire Creativity: The Secret to Unleashing Creative Energy and Awakening the Genius Within!. Pearson Education Asia.

[Hop 97] *Hope, Warren C. (1997):* Resolving teachers' concerns about microcomputer technology. Computers in the Schools,13 (3-4), 147–160.

[Joh 08] *Johnson, Mark; and Oleg Liber (2008):* The personal learning environment and the human condition: From theory to teaching practice. Interactive Learning Environments, 16, 3–15.

[Joh 12] *Johnson, Mark William, and David Sherlock (2012):* Beyond the Personal Learning Environment: attachment and control in the classroom of the future. Interactive Learning Environments, (ahead-of-print), 1–19.

[Kop 08] *Kop, Rita; and Adrian Hill (2008):* Connectivism: Learning theory of the future or vestige of the past? International Review of research in open and distance learning, 9(3).

[Lam 00] *Lam, Yvonne (2000):* Technophilia vs. technophobia: A preliminary look at why second-language teachers do or do not use technology in their classrooms. Canadian Modern Language Review, 56 (3), 390–420.

[Ma 09] *Ma, Yuxin; and Stephen W. Harmon (2009):* A case study of design-based research for creating a vision prototype of a technology-based innovative learning environment. Journal of Interactive Learning Research, 20(1), 75–93.

[Mis 06] *Mishra, Punya, and Matthew Koehler (2006):* Technological Pedagogical Content Knowledge: A framework for teacher knowledge. Teachers College Record, 108(6), 1017–1054.

[Pat 02] *Patton, Michael Quinn (2002):* Qualitative research and evaluation methods (3rd ed.). Thousand Oaks, CA: Sage Publications.

[Rah 13a] *Rahimi, Ebrahim, Van den Berg, Jan. & Veen, Wim (2013a):* A framework for designing enhanced learning activities in web2.0-based Personal Learning Environments. In: Proceedings of World Conference on Educational Multimedia, Hypermedia and Telecommunications 2013. Chesapeake, VA: AACE, 2222–2231.

[Rah 13b] *Rahimi, Ebrahim; Van den Berg, Jan; and Veen, Wim (2013b):* Investigating teachers' perception about the educational benefits of Web 2.0 personal learning environments. eLearning Papers, 35.

[Ree 05] *Reeves, Thomas C.; Jan Herrington; and Ron Oliver. (2005):* Design research: A socially responsible approach to instructional technology research in higher education. Journal of Computing in Higher Education,16(2), 96–115.

[Sch 83] *Schön, Donald A (1983):*The reflective practitioner: How professionals think in action, Vol. 5126. Basic books.

[Sug 04] *Sugar, William, Frank Crawley, and Bethann Fine (2004):* Examining teachers' decisions to adopt new technology. Educational Technology & Society, 7(4), 201–213.

[Tür 08] *Türker, Mustafa Ali; and Stefan Zingel (2008):* Formative interfaces for scaffolding self-regulated learning in PLEs. eLearning Papers, 14.

[Väl 10] *Väljataga, Terje; and Mart Laanpere (2010):* Learner control and personal learning environment: a challenge for instructional design. Interactive Learning Environments, 18(3), 277–291.

[Ver 99] *Vermunt, Jan D.; and Nico Verloop (1999):* Congruence and friction between learning and teaching. Learning and instruction, 9(3), 257–280.

[Yin 08] *Yin, Robert K. (2008):* Case study research: Design and methods, Vol. 5. SAGE Publications, Incorporated.

[Val 12] *Valtonen, Teemu; Stina Hacklin; Patrick Dillon; Mikko Vesisenaho; Jari Kukkonen; and Aija Hietanen (2012):* Perspectives on personal learning environments held by vocational students. Computers & Education, 58(2), 732–739.

[Ver 12] *Verpoorten, Dominique; Wim Westera; and Marcus Specht (2012):* Using reflection triggers while learning in an online course. British Journal of Educational Technology, 43(6), 1030–1040.

FIGURES

CONTACT DETAILS

Ir. Ebrahim Rahimi, M.Sc.
E-Mail: *e.rahimi@tudelft.nl*

Prof. Dr. Jan van den Berg
E-Mail: *j.vandenberg@tudelft.nl*

Prof. Dr. Wim Veen
E-Mail: *w.veen@tudelft.nl*
Delft University of Technology
The Faculty of Technology, Policy and Management,
The Netherlands

Personal learning environments: a conceptual landscape revisited

Sebastian H.D. Fiedler, Terje Väljataga

ABSTRACT

This paper reports on a renewed attempt to review and synthesise a substantial amount of research literature on Personal Learning Environments published in recent years. Earlier comprehensive review efforts had attested considerable conceptual differences within the research community. If and how these differences have qualitatively changed since 2010, is the focus of an ongoing literature review project. Some provisional findings and insights are reported and discussed.

Note: *This article has been published in the Special Edition of the eLearning Papers, Issue No. 35 "Personal Learning Environments". The link to this Special Issue is:* http://openeducationeuropa.eu/en/paper/personal-learning-environments

Introduction

In 2010 we carried out a rather comprehensive review of the contemporary literature on Personal Learning Environments (PLEs) published in English. Our aim was to document, discuss and interpret the range of interpretations and conceptualisations that had surfaced in the ongoing debates and exchanges in the wider research community. We presented the results of our effort at first at the PLE 2010 conference in Barcelona and later published the paper titled "Personal Learning Environments: Concept or Technology?" in a special issue of the International Journal of Virtual and Personal Learning Environments (IJVPLE) in 2011 [Fie 11]. In this first broader literature review we identified two fundamentally different conceptions that heavily influenced and limited the unfolding discourse on Personal Learning Environments. We suggested that a large group of proponents of PLEs almost exclusively addressed issues of digital instrumentation and re-instrumentation of learning activity in predominantly formal educational contexts [God 09], [Tar 09], [Zub 08]. Furthermore, authors within this strand of research and development discussed these issues in relation to the existing state of the Web as the leading medium of our times in general [Gie 02], and to personalisation, selection, modification and adaptation of tools and interfaces by (potential) users in particular. Personal Learning Environments were basically portrayed as concrete technical systems or tool collections.

In contrast to this rather technically oriented conceptualisation of Personal Learning Environments we had also identified a second major strand of research and practice in the literature. Authors that belonged to this strand of research tended to be concerned with how individuals or collectives could gain control over significant elements of their overall learning activity and its instrumentation [Att 07], [Dow 07], [Joh 08]. Apparently they interpreted the notion of Personal Learning Environments rather as a concept or approach to the development and maintenance of "environments for/of personal learning".

[Buc 11] who carried out another comprehensive review of literature on PLEs in 2011, seem to confirm the applicability of this distinction within the overall PLE research literature. In their review framework [Buc 11] made an explicit attempt to apply concepts that had been developed within the Helsinki school of Cultural-Historical Activity Theory (CHAT) [Eng 87], [Eng 10]. While this exercise apparently helped the authors to produce a variety of rather useful descriptive elements, their initial argumentation for operationalising "the constituting elements of PLEs as activity systems" [Buc 11: 7], turned out less convincing from our perspective. Initially, [Buc 11] acknowledge that "capturing the individual activity, or how the learner uses technology to support learning, lies at the heart of the PLE concept" [Buc 11: 1]. However, they do not follow through with this idea of "individual activity". Instead they turn to Engeström's [Eng 87] notion of Activity System which by default conceptualises the subject as a "collective subject". This fact is actually pointed out by the authors themselves within their text. Their claim that Personal Learning Environments "can be viewed as complex activity systems" [Buc 11: 1] thus seems questionable in various regards. We would argue instead that the PLE concept rather embraces all the perceived elements that an individual can turn into instruments for mediating her actions while realising a particular learning activity. Thus, the PLE cannot be the activity (or activity system) itself. It is rather a concept that indicates instruments (or potential instruments) for mediating actions in the context of learning activity. In addition, the subject of individual (learning) activity is the individual. If individual (learning) activity can, and should be, described as an "activity system" in the first place requires some more in depth discussion from our point of view, in particular if one makes explicit references to Engeström [Eng 87] notion of activity systems formed by collective subjects. While we certainly welcome all efforts to produce more comprehensive and potentially integrative reviews of the literature on PLEs, we would have liked [Buc 11] to provide a more critical analysis of their conceptual starting point and possible contradictions between Engeström's Activity System concept and the notion of individual learning activity and its personal environments. Nevertheless, we would like to stress that the literature review by [Buc 11] delivered relevant insights into the breadth of instrument mediation that is discussed within the wider PLE literature. To our knowledge their work also marks the most recent comprehensive literature review in this regard.

From our perspective the ongoing proliferation and differentiation of the notion of Personal Learning Environments calls for a renewed effort of targeted, comprehensive

review and analysis. In particular, we are interested in analysing if the conceptual differences within the research community that we had attested in 2010 have actually undergone any traceable, qualitative changes in the meantime. For this purpose we put our analytical focus on how different contributions in this area tend to employ explicit or implicit boundary judgements to construct their particular object(s) of research and potential change [Fie 12], [Mid 00], [Ull 10].

By reviewing, analysing, and commenting on the current landscape of expanding research, its potential direction, and fields of applications, we fundamentally hope to support the ongoing discourse on personal learning environments within the wider research community. However, it should be made clear at this point that this paper is merely reporting on a work in progress which we outline in more detail in the following section.

Methodic approach

Building a literature base for review

Given our limited resources we applied an iterative approach for building and systematically expanding the literature base for our review project. Initially we conducted an online search for "personal learning environment(s)" and "PLE(s)" with a focus on academic publications in English in the period from 2010 to 2013 of the following types:

- peer reviewed journal articles
- peer reviewed conference and workshop proceedings
- reports issued by academic institutions.

Mainly for research economic reasons we refrained from including more informal texts published on the Web (such as Weblogs, Wikis, and so forth) at this point in time. We then compared our initial findings with the list of resources that had been published by [Buc 11] and added all items that fitted our defined publication period and publication types and had not shown up in our own search efforts. While we started the review process with this initial set of items we manually reviewed the reference sections of each article for further candidates for inclusion. Our attempts to retrieve full archives of the PLE conference proceedings from 2010 and 2011 were severely hindered. We are currently still missing various items from these proceedings. It appears that the original hosts of these archives have taken them offline. We think that the research community needs to address this issue and either insist on a more responsible and long-term provision of conference proceedings on the side of the organising and hosting entities, or find and promote more durable, independent archiving solutions elsewhere.

Altogether we have been able to include 82 papers in our literature base so far. While we cannot and do not want to claim comprehensiveness with this selection, it seems fair to expect that it represents a considerable slice of the recent, international, academic research literature that explicitly references the Personal Learning Environment concept. Since we have not completed our iterative review process entirely we see room for the inclusion of additional publication items as we proceed.

Review process, analytical framework and other instruments

We took inspiration from a comparative, methodological study of the systems of inquiry and change promoted by a selection of educational research approaches by one of the author [Fie 12] to develop a preliminary analytical framework for our literature review.

Since the conceptual variability and its partial incommensurability in the research literature on Personal Learning Environments has been established in earlier reviews (see for example [Buc 11], [Fie 11], we decided to focus our analytical effort this time on how the various contributions under review outline essential boundaries and elements of their respective inquiry approach and its use of the PLE concept.

We thus concentrated on tracing the following elements within our analytical framework:

1. how is the overall *object of inquiry* constructed?
   - any *problem description*?
   - any *change objective(s)* stated?
   - any explicit *definition of the PLE concept*?
   - any specific *context/setting/field of application*?
2. what *inquiry methods & instruments* are employed?
   - any empirical work in the field?
   - any intervention into existing practice?
   - any development of technical or conceptual instruments?

To support our structured analysis we made use of the generic text generating and organising software Scrivener that allows for manual de-constructing, excerpting, categorising, sorting and writing in an integrated interface. Though Scrivener supports the initial work with texts rather well and even allows for the limited use of custom meta-data, we are still pondering feeding elements of our analysis into a database application or a dedicated qualitative data analysis software in a later stage of the project.

Following our preliminary analytical framework, we have so far managed to review 57 papers out of the 82 papers that currently make up our (still expanding) literature base. While the review is not completed and further publications are still on our retrieval list awaiting their inclusion, we nevertheless want to take the opportunity to report, highlight, and comment on some provisional findings and insights to support the ongoing discourse and reflection on the PLE concept within the wider research community.

Provisional findings and insights

In search for conciliation

Currently our preliminary literature review shows that the mainstream PLE research is still predominantly concerned with the digital instrumentation of teaching and studying activity in formal higher education. This dominant group of researchers acknowledges contradictions between the current institutionalised technology provision (such as learning management systems, virtual learning environments, etc.) and a growing number of freely accessible networked tools and services (often referred to as Web 2.0 approach). The Web 2.0 approach as explained, for instance, by Soumplis, Chatzidaki, Koulocheri, & Xenos [Sou 11] "is about the active participation of users, not as passive content consumers but as active content creators. It is also about the ability of applications to be flexible enough to adapt rapidly to the user's individual needs" [Sou 11: 346]. The self-controlled, digital instrumentation, which gives people control, ownership and freedom to customise and personalise their own environment (of tools) is seen as the main contradiction to the dominant institutional provision of digital instruments that "fails to adapt to the Web 2.0 attitude" [Sou 11: 346], thus constraining and setting numerous barriers for developing students' digital practice [Con 11], [Oli 10]. Furthermore, some authors claim, e.g. [Cas 10], that students nowadays are demanding the use of these new technologies when they enter educational establishments. Therefore, according to [Moc 12] and many others there is a growing need in the context of formal higher education "to respond to the trend of learners increasingly consuming web tools and sharing contents" [Moc 12: 1].

In consequence the main problem in the field of PLE research from this perspective is to bring the Web 2.0 approach into the formal higher education context by providing a set of networked tools and services that students can use to create their own PLEs. As pointed out by [Moc 12] among many others, institutionalised technology provision "cannot be simply excluded from the learning environment landscape or replaced by PLEs" [Moc 12: 2]. Marrying what is currently implemented in institutions with what is available outside of formal higher education is thus seen as the primary solution. And here the dominant group of PLE researchers talk about the partial re-instrumentation of teaching and studying activity with a set of networked tools and services. The lack of learner control, ownership and personalisation as the perceived drawback of monolithic institutional technology, is assumed to be corrected through the projected re-instrumentation with more loosely-coupled networked tools and services. It must be noted here that in this group of PLE literature the concepts of learner control, ownership and personalisation are mainly presented on a very general level without making any explicit connections to the respective strand of research in adult and higher education.

We interpret this kind of focus of PLE research as an attempt to reconcile the dominant institutional technology provision with more distributed, networked landscapes of digital instruments. Our claim is explained and clarified in the following paragraphs.

A sizeable group of researchers works on how to integrate and build bridges amongst institutional technology and "PLEs" from a rather broad and general perspective (see for example [Cas 10], [Gar 11], [Mil 11], [Moc 11], [Moc 12], [Pet 10], [Whi 11a], [Whi 11b], [Whi 10]. Thus, the term *institutionalised personal learning environment* has emerged. For instance, the University of Southampton has carried out a thorough study regarding their current institutional virtual learning environment (VLE) and related practices in order to find "a replacement for parts of the existing technology infrastructure" [Whi 11a: 2]. They are interested in finding ways to enable "...the learner to operate within a consolidated environment where they intermix their own chosen environments with others which have functions to perform in support of the processes of learning" [Whi 10: 4]. The solution is to develop an iPLE "within which students and teachers can select the tools they wish to use" [Whi 11a:15].

A similar approach is taken by [Mil 11] who suggest that "the power and value of the institutional personal learning environment resides in the 'technology affordances' which enable users to customise and personalise the system in a socially useful and educationally constructive manner" [Mil 11:1]. In comparison to [Whi 11a], [Whi 11], [Whi 10] these authors emphasise, however, co-design with students and staff and ambitious enterprise-level integration. The declared aim of [Mil 11], for example, "is to provide an infrastructure that can act as the basis for an evolving digital teaching and learning environment, loosely coupled legacy systems, and provide support for the social and community aspects of the institution (including pre-registration students and alumni)" [Mil 11: 1]. Furthermore, [Pet 10] present a "first step that shows the technical feasibility as well as the principles of the integration of the personal and institutional spaces through the aggregation of services" [Pet 10: 4]. For them "PLEs are an *ad hoc*, opportunistic aggregation of Web 2.0 services built to support a specific learning goal" [Pet 10: 1].[Cas 10] have also chosen to address institutionally powered personal learning environments. Their vision is to apply Web 2.0 tools (blogs, wikis, starting pages), services (del.icio.us, Flickr, YouTube) and data sharing (social networking, learn-streaming) in an integrated manner. [Cas 10] understand iPLE as "an attempt to build a PLE from the point of view of the university, so that every institutional service can be integrated, but flexible enough to interact with the wide range of service learners could consider important during their life-long learning"[Cas 10: 297]. This iPLE constitutes the single interface window for users to merge both personal and institutional spheres.

[Gar 11] consider it "necessary to develop the LMS by integrating it with contexts that include new technological trends and are focused on the student" (p. 1223) and refer to this as Personalized Learning Environments. Their possible solution is a web service-based framework, which consists of Moodle as the institutional environment, and a (Wookie) widgets container as the informal and personalised component. It uses web services, and interoperability specifications to communicate between both environments [Gar 11].

Unlike the previously presented authors, the purpose of Moccozet et al. [Moc 12] is not to provide an institutional PLE but rather an extension of it: a "PLE enabler". Such a PLE enabler aims to bridge personal, institutional and worldwide resources, thus enabling collaborations between co-learners and the sharing of resources [Moc 12: 2]. Their PLEs include two intersecting components: a Personal Web Tools (PWT) component gathers the web tools that learners use for performing learning actions. A Personal Learning Network (PLN) component refers to the network of people and resources that learners generate and organise during the realisation of both formal and informal learning activity. The idea of "personalisation" is presented as "an environment that provides a personalised interface to University data and services and at the same time exposes that data and services to a student's personal tools" [Moc 12: 2]. They claim that "the resulting iPLEs scheme can be viewed as a student centric self-directed collaborative didactic dashboard, clearly distinct from a VLE" [Moc 12: 2].

Based on out current level of analysis we have identified a number of more specific problems that are addressed within this general *search for conciliation.*

Managing assessment

While the presented examples of integrating PLEs into an institutional technology landscape are approached on a rather general level, some researchers are especially concerned with the management and assessment of learning success in such settings. "Any Personal Learning Environment natively lacks any assessments feature in order to assist teachers in the processes of grading the learning outcome of any activity and whether or not the learning outcome is consistent and sufficient for the scope of any course" [Sou 11: 347]. [Sou 11] attempt to design a learning assessment method within the scope of PLEs making use of rubrics. [Con 11] is focusing on "interoperability scenarios to allow the assessment of the personalized informal activity, and in this way, obtain measurable information about the advantages of personalization in learning" [Con 11: 801]. From their perspective the actions carried out in the PLE should be reported to the institutional environment as a way to measure the "informal" activity [Con 11]. [Pet 10] acknowledge that "PLEs seem ideal for the support of a socio-constructivist approach" [Pet 10: 2] but lament that they are not *a priori* suited for formal learning (i.e., having an assessment of the new knowledge). Thus their "aim is to design an infrastructure enabling the integration of a set of services and information sources and to combine them to define a learning environment suitable for the learners as well as the teachers" [Pet 10: 2].

Recommender systems

Another, smaller group of researchers focuses on supporting students to manoeuvre within these hybrid institutional-personal systems. They develop recommender systems for students while implementing PLEs. [Ebn 11], for example, investigate four possibilities to apply recommender systems within PLEs (a study path, a widget, a peer student and a hybrid recommender system), while [Mik 11a] and [Mik 11b] focus on recommending potential 'study-buddies', with whom learners share common competencies, goals, and resources.

Mash-ups

The attempt to provide students with a selection of web-based tools and services, in turn, creates yet another set of problems. A considerable amount of research is done to find ways to deal with the enormous number of Web 2.0 applications, which allegedly overwhelm teachers and students alike [Ebn 10]. The paper from Ebner & Taraghi [Ebn 10] can serve as a good example from this group. These authors pose the question: "how can a Personal Learning Environment for Higher Education look like? Especially if the MashUp principle will be an appropriate possibility to enhance learning and teaching" [Ebn 10: 1159]. From their perspective the idea of PLE emerged in order "to overcome the challenge of various distributed resources and the customization of the services" [Ebn 10: 1159]. They understand PLEs as a technical concept because "it describes the functionalities that a system should have to actively support personalized learning on the Web" [Ebn 10: 4]. A PLE is basically a client-side environment (a "Rich Internet Application") that "comprises a mashup of different small independent web applications and services selected by the user" [Ebn 10: 7]. For instance, the TU Graz PLE represents "a web portal that students can fully adjust to their personal needs by adding and removing widgets as well as modifying widget preferences" [Ebn 10: 9]. It thus acts as a widget container to integrate the distributed resources, services and applications into the learning environment [Ebn 10]. Their PLE instantiation follows the W3C specifications, "a standard that can be used as basis for all PLE and e-learning applications. Thereby the problem of interoperability would be solved and a worldwide exchange of widgets will be possible" [Ebn 10: 1164].

Another example of an interoperability mash-up framework comes from [Gov 11]. [Gov 11] are in the process of developing a responsive PLE in which responsiveness is defined "as the ability to react to the learner needs" [Gov 11: 2]. Their mash-up framework provides a common technical infrastructure to assemble widgets and services in Personal Learning Environments [Gov 11: 1]. Similarly, [Ull 10] interpret a PLE as a mashup of "learning services". They claim that "the idea behind PLE is that learners can assemble their own learning environments from existing services" [Ull 10: 271]. In their research these authors made pre-build PLEs accessible to students. Concluding their own field experience they somewhat paradoxically suggest that "PLE usage is still only for teachers who feel comfortable with and are proficient in technology" [Ull 10: 277].

Synopsis

We found strong indication that in general researchers in the PLE arena tend to agree that higher education institutions should move away from one-size-fits-all models of technology provision. However, the previously presented extractions from PLE research

papers represent rather technologically oriented change objectives. We can witness that institutional technology provision is currently searching for conciliation by integrating more networked tools and services, but the core of the debate still focuses on the role of institutions as an infrastructure provider. The main effort seems to be put on developing an "effective PLE" which is seen as "a space where students can use the tools they want" [Con 11]. The presented group of researchers seems to believe that PLEs should have some sort of institutional provision incorporated. Such institutional infrastructure initiatives, however, also run the risk to sabotage and undermine personal autonomy and freedom despite of the ritually evoked argument that higher education should move towards student-centric concepts, learner control and personalisation.

"Personalisation" in particular is approached from a very technical point of view. For instance, personalisation for [Whi 11a: 14] means "the user can change the layout and choice of widgets" in iPLE or [Ebn 11: 1] "personalisation is seen in merging contents, services and applications from multiple websites in an integrated, coherent way, therefore, PLEs offer a new form of personalized learning". The concern doesn't seem to be whether PLEs should remain the sole domain of the learner or in what way an institutional personal learning environment remains personal, but rather how to keep control over students and their environments. From our point of view the aforementioned examples demonstrate quite clearly a rather careless and uncritical use of the terms "personal" and "personalised" which often results in the provision of rather limited degrees of learner control over a relatively narrow range of instrument choices thus essentially creating an "illusion of choice" well documented in the literature on learner control and self-direction in education [Gei 76].

It is obvious that this kind of approach does not really shift the control from a teacher to a learner in any comprehensive way [Väl 10]. The guiding idea seems to be supporting and extending the established activity system of teaching and studying in formal higher education with new digital tools. The systematic experimentation with the values and practices that these very instruments promote or simply carry along are largely left aside. As pointed out by Feenberg [Fee 10], when one chooses to use a particular technology one doesn't simply render an existing way of life more efficient. One often chooses a different way of life. This different way of life brings about changes in our behaviour, our beliefs and practices, and our wider social norms and structures. Or to sum it up with the words of Tripathi [Tri 06: 7]: "Technology transfer without appropriate cultural transfer is not sufficient".

In search for emancipation

While going through the current PLE literature we have also come across a few studies, which take a decidedly different perspective. For instance, [Val 12] and Castaneda and Soto [Cas 10] seem to interpret the notion of PLEs predominantly as an educational concept. Their understanding of PLEs certainly goes beyond mere digital instrumentation of activity.

From the point of view of [Val 12: 34] PLEs concretise "several attributes of learning (personalisation, ownership, control, responsibility, collaboration) by allowing students to choose the methods and software for their learning. From this perspective, PLEs are seen as an ICT based pedagogical approach or model rather than a technological platform". Similarly to the studies presented in the previous section [Val 12] consider personalisation, student control, self-direction and ownership as important concepts connected to PLEs. For them "personalised learning" is "where students are encouraged to bring their unique ideas and backgrounds to the learning situation as resources... and where students take decisions about their learning in a certain self-managed way [Val 12: 733]. In their theoretical grounding they make an effort to connect the PLE as a concept with research in self-direction, ownership and collaboration. [Val 12] study has been the only one in our literature base so far which has focused on vocational students and their PLEs. The authors are especially interested in "what kind of personal learning environments would students produce, for what purposes and functions?" [Val 12: 732] and what challenges would occur.

A somewhat similar study was carried out by [Cas 10]. Their understanding of a PLE relates to a set of tools, information sources, connections and "activities-experiences" a person uses to learn [Cas 10]. It means that a PLE of a person includes: "the sources he use for founding information, the relationship he has with this information, as well as relationships between this information and other sources consulted...people who he use as a reference, the connections between those and himself, and the relationships between those people and others..." [Cas 10: 10]. In addition, a PLE also includes "the mechanisms that help him to rework and rebuild information and knowledge, both in the phase of individual reflection and recreation, as phase in which other people help us reflecting for its reconstruction" [Cas 10: 10]. The main focus of their study is to provide students with "some mechanisms and tools to develop their own PLE in the future" [Cas 10: 24]. The rationale for introducing students to the concept of PLE and related techniques lies for the authors in professional development which "has to include basic competences to continue learning in the current –even the future- rapidly changing world [Cas 10: 10]. Thus, the emphasis in addition to (re-)instrumentation of activity is also on understanding and modelling one's learning activity in a broader sense and its potential supporting environment.

Although the majority of authors tend to make a connection to self-direction either as a required competence for developing one's PLE or as a disposition that is developed through the process of creating a PLE, so far we have come across very few papers that put an explicit focus on aspects of self-direction.

[Kra 12] consider self-regulated learning (SRL) and its requirements as a viable conceptual basis for promoting PLEs. They write that "a good SRL solution should be personalized and adaptive, providing a right balance between the learner's freedom and guidance, in order to motivate the learner, but also to support his or her when needed" [Kra 12: 711]. They stress the importance of variety of individual approaches and

dependencies from different contexts. From their point of view "students are in charge of their learning process, emphasizing meta-cognition in learning" [Kra 12: 710]. In addition, a PLE consists of "tools, communities, and services that constitute the individual educational platforms that learners use to direct their own learning and pursue educational goals" [Kra 12: 710].

[Dab 12] also describe the connection between self-regulated learning, PLE and social media. They follow Zimmerman's concept of self-regulated learning [Zim 00] and develop a pedagogical framework for social media use that aligns with the three phases of Zimmerman's self-regulated learning model. The goal of their framework is "to inform college faculty and instructors how to engage students in a transformative cycle of creating PLEs that support self-regulated learning [Dab 12: 6]. Apparently their starting point is the notion of learners who constantly seek and share information by using digital and networked technologies and who become active co-producers of content. Their critique towards the use of LMSs is related to lack of pedagogical affordances of social media. [Dab 12] perceive PLEs "as both a technology and a pedagogical approach that is student-designed around each student's goals or a learning approach" [Dab 12: 4]. They continue that "PLEs can be considered as a promising pedagogical approach for the deliberate or intentional integration of formal and informal learning spaces" [Dab 12: 4].

While the majority of studies are concerned with students [Sha 12] acknowledge the different roles of teachers in relation to PLEs as an important and necessary research focus within the overall research in the field. They start their paper by questioning traditional teaching competencies in learner-controlled PLE settings. [Sha 12] carry out an in-depth literature review on teachers' competencies and roles required to provide tasks and guidance to students in settings that make use of PLEs. Their study concludes that the "PLE construction process requires equal participation of both students and the teachers, hence, a teacher may not necessarily perform all the roles, but, rather, she interacts with students in general. Yet, in any case, teacher's required competencies depend not only on the role being performed, but, also on the nature and complexity of the tasks they are supposed to carry out" [Sha 12: 30].

Synopsis

So far our review and analysis shows that since 2010 published research that is predominantly concerned with how individuals or collectives could gain control over significant elements of their learning activity and its instrumentation is simply dwarfed by the technologically oriented research that focuses on the reconciliation of the institutional provision of digital instruments in higher education. It seems fair to attest that this type of research is rather marginalised in the overall PLE arena. This is a somewhat unfortunate development from our point view, since this strand of research actually engages in intervention studies in the field that are focused on particular developmental objectives, while the more technically oriented strand limits its empirical efforts mostly to feasibility and usability studies of prototypes. Much of the latter type of work reminds us of how Selwyn [Sel 10] aptly described some of the shortcomings of mainstream educational technology research: "The pretext of much academic work in the field is that technology is set inevitably to change educational contexts for the better. Thinking along these lines, it follows that the main task of educational technology analysts is to identify the impediments and deficiencies that are delaying and opposing the march of technological progress" [Sel 10: 69]. A considerable amount of contemporary PLE research seems to be driven by these implicit assumptions and takes educational "ends" as a given. Thus, it doesn't really surprise that the dominating strand of research focuses on technical developments, while this second strand of research is more concerned with the further development of personal dispositions and the gradual emancipation of learning activity and its self-directed instrumentation.

Concluding remarks

We are well aware of the limitations that go along with reporting from an analytical work in progress. However, our provisional findings seem to indicate that the general conceptual differences between two major strands of PLE research [Fie 11] are still in place and well alive. On the basis of the literature that we have been able to review so far, it appears however that they have found new foci of interest. The first strand of research is now predominantly concerned with marrying the PLE concept with institutional landscapes of tools and services. The second strand of research is engaging more and more in empirical intervention studies in the field that apply the PLE concept in the context of personal development of dispositions that are deemed to be necessary for the independent pursuit of learning activity beyond the constraints of formal education.

Amidst these recent developments we still maintain our view that the notion of personal learning environments is best treated as an intermediate concept that allows for the systematic, further development of learning activity and its digital instrumentation. We have thus integrated it in our work "as an additional conceptual instrument to analyse and model the resources (and their digital representation and mediation) that an individual is aware of and has access to in the context of an educational project at a given point in time. This understanding emphasises the individually perceived nature of a personal learning environment (and its potential instruments) in relation to a specific personal learning project. It is thus rather used as a subjective, mental construct and not as a concrete manifestation of particular sets of instruments" [Fie 12: 26]. It should be emphasised that this understanding also allows for its application outside the boundaries of formal educational systems.

From this perspective many authors regularly commit a sort of pars-pro-toto fallacy whenever they proclaim that this or that particular Web-based instrument "is" the PLE of a particular person. First of all, it makes little sense to make such claim without any description of the learning activity or particular learning project that a person is

trying to carry out. Second, in most cases it is a rather fancy and unconvincing claim that any learning activity of a certain level of complexity and seriousness is exclusively mediated by a single digital instrument, or even instrument collection alone. We think that this manner of speech is potentially detrimental to the notion of increasing control over one's personal learning activity and its creative instrumentation over time and in between contexts.

We will continue our ongoing review project and hope to report a more differentiated analysis of our still expanding literature base in the near future. So far we have only been able to emphasise some main demarcation lines and visible directions in the field. However, it will require a sustained, collective effort to pay justice to the overall variability and more subtle differences in this expanding field of research and development.

Acknowledgement

This research was funded by Estonian Ministry of Education and Research targeted research grant No. 0130159s08 and Mobilitas/ESF.

REFERENCES

[Att 07] *Attwell, Graham (2007). Personal learning environments - future of eLearning? eLearning Papers, 2(1), 1-7.*

[Buc 11] *Buchem, Ilona; Attwell, Graham; Torres, Ricardo (2011). Understanding personal learning environments:* Literature review and synthesis through the Activity Theory lens. PLE Conference 2011. Retrieved from *http://journal.webscience.org/658/1/PLE_SOU_Paper_Buchem_Attwell_Torress.doc*

[Cas 10] *Casquero, Oskar; Portillo, Javier; Ovelar, Ramón; Benito, Manuel; Romo, Jesús (2010):* iPLE network: An integrated elearning 2.0 architecture from a university's perspective. Interactive Learning Environments, 18(3), 293-308.

[Cas 10] *Castaneda, Linda; Soto, Javier (2010). Building personal learning environments by using and mixing ICT tools in a professional way. Digital Education Review, 18, 9-25.*

[Con 11] *Conde, M. A., Garcia-Penalvo, F. J., & Alier, M. (2011):* Interoperability scenarios to measure informal learning carried out in PLEs. In F. Xhafa, L. Barolli & M. Köppen (Eds.), Proceedings of Third IEEE International Conference on Intelligent Networking and Collaborative Systems. Los Alamitos: IEEE Computer Society, 801-806.

[Dab 12] *Dabbagh, N., & Kitsantas, A. (2012). Personal learning environments, social media, and self-regulated learning:* A natural formula for connecting formal and informal learning. Internet and Higher Education, 15, 3-8.

[Dow 07] *Downes, Stephen (2007). Learning networks in practice. Emerging technologies for learning, 2, 19-27. Retrieved from http://partners.becta.org.uk/index.php?section=rh&catcode=_re_rp_02&rid=13768*

[Ebn 11] *Ebner, Martin; Schön, Sandra; Taraghi, Behnam; Drachsler, Hendrik; Tsang, Philip (2011). First steps towards an integration of a personal learning environment at university level. In R. Kwan, C. McNaught, P. Tsang, F. L. Wang & K. C. Li (Eds.), Enhancing Learning Through Technology. Education Unplugged:* Mobile Technologies and Web 2.0. Berlin: Springer-Verlag, 22-36.

[Ebn 10] *Ebner, Martin; Taraghi, Behnam (2010). Personal learning environment for higher education - A first prorotype Proceedings of World Conference on Educational Multimedia, Hypermedia and Telecommunications 2010, 1158-1166. Chesapeake, VA:* AACE.

[Eng 87] *Engeström, Yrjö (1987):* Learning by expanding. Helsinki: Orienta-konsultit.

[Eng 10] *Engeström, Yrjö; Sannino, Annalisa (2010):* Studies of expansive learning: foundations, findings and future challenges. Educational Research Review, 5(1), 1-24.

[Fee 10] *Feenberg, Andrew (2010). Ten paradoxes of technology. Techne, 14(1).*

[Fie 10] *Fiedler, Sebastian H. D. (2012). Emancipating and developing learning activity:* Systemic intervention and re-instrumentation in higher education. Turku: Painosalama.

[Fie 11] *Fiedler, Sebastian H. D.; Väljataga, Terje (2011). Personal learning environments:* concept or technology? International Journal of Virtual and Personal Learning Environments, 2(4), 1-11.

[Gar 11] *Garcia-Penalvo, Francisco J.; Conde, Miguel A.; Alier, Marc; Casany, Maria J. (2011). Opening learning management systems to personal learning environments. Journal of Universal Computer Science, 17(9), 1222-1240.*

[Gei 76] *Geis, George L. (1976). Student participation in instruction:* student choice. The Journal of Higher Education, 47(3), 249-273.

[Gie 02] *Giesecke, Michael (2002). Von den Mythen der Buchkultur zu den Visionen der Informationsgesellschaft:* Trendforschung zur aktuellen Medienökologie. Frankfurt a. M: Suhrkamp.

[God 09] *Godwin-Jones, Robert (2009). Emerging technologies:* personal learning environments. Lanuage Learning and Technology, 13(2), 3-9.

[Gov 11] *Govaerts, Sten; Verbert, Katrien; Dahrendorf, Daniel; Ullrich, Carsten; Schmidt, Manuel; Werkle, Michael et al. (2011). Towards responsive open learning environments:* The ROLE interoperability framework. In C. D. Kloos, D. Gillet, R. M. C. Garcia, F. Wild & M. Wolpers (Eds.), Towards Ubiquitous Learning. Proceedings of 6th European Conference onTechnology Enhanced Learning. Berlin: Springer-Verlag.

[Joh 08] *Johnson, Mark; Liber, Oleg (2008). The personal learning environment and the human condition:* from theory to teaching practice. Interactive Learning Environments, 16(1), 3-15.

[Kra 12] *Kravcik, Milos; Klamma, Ralf (2012). Supporting self-regulation by personal learning environments. In I. Aedo, R.-M. Bottino, N.-S. Chen, C. Giovannella, D. G. Sampson & Kinshuk (Eds.), Proceedings of 12th IEEE International Conference on Advanced Learning Technologies. Rome:* IEEE Computer Society, 710-711.

[Mid 00] *Midgley, Gerald (2000). Systemic intervention:* philosophy, methodology, and practice. New York: Kluwer Academic/Plenum Publishers.

[Mik 11] *Mikroyannidis, Alexander (2011). Evolving e-learning ontologies for personal and cloud learning environments. In K. Yetongnon, R. Chbeir & A. Dipanda (Eds.), The Seventh International Conference on Signal Image Technology & Internet-Based Systems. Dijon:* IEEE Computer Society, 32-37.

[Mik 10] *Mikroyannidis, Alexander; Lefrere, Paul; Scott, Peter (2010). An architecture for layering and integration of learning ontologies, applied to personal learning environments and cloud learning environments. In M. Kemni, Kinshuk, D. Sampson & J. M. Spector (Eds.), 10th IEEE International Conference on Advanced Learning Technologies. Los Alamitos:* IEEE Computer Society, 92-93.

[Mil 11] *Millard, David E.; Davis, Hugh C.; Howard, Yvonne; McSweeney, Patrick; Yorke, Chris; Solheim, Heidi et al. (2011). Towards an institutional PLE. PLE Conference 2011. Retrieved from http://eprints.soton.ac.uk/192861/*

[Moc 12] *Moccozet, Laurent (2012). Introducing learning performance in personal learning environment. In I. Aedo, R.-M. Bottino, N.-S. Chen, C. Giovannella, D. G. Sampson & Kinshuk (Eds.), Proceedings of 12th IEEE International Conference on Advanced Learning Technologies. Rome:* IEEE Computer Society.

[Moc 11] *Moccozet, Laurent; Benkacem, Omar; Ndiaye, Bineta; Ahmeti, Vjollca; Roth, Patrick; Burgi, Pierre-Yves (2011). An exploratory study for the deployment of a techno-pedagogical staff learning environment. PLE Conference 2011. Retrieved from http://ple.unige.ch/Documentation/pleconf2011.pdf*

[Moc 12] *Moccozet, Laurent; Benkacem, Omar; Platteaux, Hervé; Gillet, Denis (2012). An institutional personal learning environment enabler. In I. Aedo, R.-M. Bottino, N.-S. Chen, C. Giovannella, D.*

G. Sampson & Kinshuk (Eds.), *Proceedings of the 2012 12th IEEE International Conference on Advanced Learning Technologies. Rome:* IEEE Computer Society, 51-52.

[Oli 10] *Oliveira, Lino; Moreira, Fernando (2010). Personal learning environments:* Integration of Web 2.0 applications and content management systems. In E. Tome (Ed.), Proceedings of 11th European Conference on Knowledge Management, 2, 1171-1177.

[Pet 10] *Peter, Yvan; Leroy, Sabine; Lepretre, Eric (2010). First steps in the integration of institutional and personal learning environments. Retrieved from http://www.lifl.fr/~petery/PeterLeroyLepretre-2010.pdf*

[Sel 10] *Selwyn, N. (2010). Looking beyond learning:* Notes towards the critical study of educational technology. Journal of Computer Assisted Learning, 26 (1), 65-73.

[Sha 12] *Shaikh, Zaffar A.; Khoja, Shakeel A. (2012). Role of teacher in personal learning environments. Digital Education Review, 21, 23-32.*

[Sou 11] *Soumplis, Alexandros; Chatzidaki, Eleni; Koulocheri, Eleni; Xenos, Michalis (2011). Implementing an open personal learning environment. In P. Angelidis & A. Michalas (Eds.), Proceedings 2011 Panhellenic Conference on Informatics. Los Alamitos:* IEEE Computer Society, 345-349.

[Tar 09] *Taraghi, Benham; Ebner, Martin; Till, Gerald; Mühlburger, Herbert (2009). Personal learning environment - a conceptual study. International Journal of Emerging Technologies in Learning, 5, 25-30.*

[Tri 06] *Tripathi, A. K. (2006). Reflections on the philosophy of technology culture of technological reflection. Retrieved from http://ebookbrowse.com/v7i29-tripathi-pdf-d185134342*

[Ull 10] *Ullrich, Carsten; Shen, Ruimin; Gillet, Denis (2010). Not yet ready for everyone:* An experience report about a personal learning environment for language learning. In X. Luo, M. Spaniol, L. Wang, Q. Li, W. Nejdl & W. Zhang (Eds.), Advances in Web-Based Learning - ICWL 2010, 269-278.

[Väl 10] *Väljataga, Terje (2010):* Learner control and responsibility: expanding the concept of self-direction in higher education, 946. Tampere: Tampere University of Technology.

[Val 12] *Valtonen, Teemu; Hacklin, Stina; Dillon, Patrick; Vesisenaho, Mikko; Kukkonen, Jari; Hietanen, Aija (2012):* Perspectives on personal learning environments held by vocational students. Computers & Education, 58, 732-739.

[Whi 11a] *White, Su; Davis, Hugh (2011a). Making it rich and personal:* crafting an institutional personal learning environment. International Journal of Virtual and Personal Learning Environments, 2(3), 1-18.

[Whi 11b] *White, Su; Davis, Hugh (2011b). Rich and personal revisited:* Translating ambitions for an institutional personal leraning environment into a reality. PLE Conference 2011. Retrieved from *http://eprints.soton.ac.uk/272140/*

[Whi 10] *White, Su; Davis, Hugh; Morris, Debra; Hancock, Pete (2010). Making it rich and personal:* Meeting institutional challenges from next generation learning environments. PLE Conference 2010. Retrieved from *http://eprints.soton.ac.uk/271327/*

[Zim 00] *Zimmermann, Barry J. (2000). Attainment of self-regulation:* A social cognitive perspective. In M. Boekaerts, P. Pintrich & M. Zeidner (Eds.), Self-regulation: Theory, research, and applications. Orlando: Academic Press, 13-39.

[Zub 08] *Žubrinić, Krunoslav; Kalpić, Damir (2008). The Web as personal learning environment. International Journal of Emerging Technologies in Learning, 3, 45-58.*

CONTACT DETAILS

Dr. Sebastian H.D. Fiedler
Tallinn University
Centre for Educational Technology
Narva mnt. 29,
10120 Tallinn, Estonia
Phone: +372 (0)6409 355
E-Mail: *fiedler@tlu.ee*

Dr. Terje Väljataga
Tallinn University
Centre for Educational Technology
Narva mnt. 29,
10120 Tallinn, Estonia
Phone: +372 (0)6409 355
E-Mail: *terje.valjataga@tlu.ee*

Beyond books: The librarian, the research assignment, and the PLE

Alison Hicks

ABSTRACT

Using the example of an Antarctic Studies seminar, this paper explores the design of an alternative research assignment that is based on the principles of PLEs. Analysis of blog posts and reflective surveys explore the overlap with information literacy and demonstrate the importance of building partnerships with librarians.

Introduction

The teaching of research is one of the cornerstones of undergraduate education [Fis 09]. Being able to evaluate or frame an argument around sources is seen as core for scaffolding disciplinary thinking and practice [Biz 87] and is increasingly sought after by employers [Hea 12]. Notwithstanding, the process is often centred around the research paper, essay or final project. While this can give students the space to explore a theme in depth, faculty are often disappointed by the results, particularly the frequent lack of critical engagement with sources.

Librarians have seen the teaching of information literacy (IL) skills as a way to combat these issues. Yet, the concept of information literacy, which lies at the heart of lifelong learning and is defined by the Alexandria Proclamation as a way to empower "people in all walks of life to seek, evaluate, use and create information effectively to achieve their personal, social, occupational and educational goals" has not always been seen in this light [UNE 05]. It is often reduced to focusing on a "rote mastery of functional skills" or being seen as overtly library centric [Coo 11].

Recognising these problems, a group of librarians has started to explore new approaches to the development of student research capacities. These include a greater emphasis on the place of critical pedagogy and critical information studies within IL. However, while the development of a more responsive pedagogical stance is important, it is clear that the inherent nature of the research paper still stands in the way of student inquiry. In this way, the need to develop alternative research assignments has driven librarians to explore approaches from other fields. The personal learning environment (PLE), with its focus on scaffolding personal learning capacities as well as modern learning environments, is seen as a potential framework to scaffold these research competencies.

Accordingly, the author of this short paper will explore an undergraduate capstone History research assignment that was redesigned around PLE concepts. Focusing on

introducing students to the collaborative and participatory nature of historical research, the assignment was also designed to help students gain research experience that would serve them for academic, work and personal environments. Accordingly, the author will start by providing an overview of typical challenges associated with research papers before moving on to explore how PLEs can be used as a framework for scaffolding student research capacities. The author will finish the paper by reflecting on the growth of PLEs across campus, as well as the value of engaging varied faculty, including librarians.

Research Assignments

The research paper or essay is a common assignment for undergraduate classes. Yet, while it is designed to introduce learners to academic discourse and disciplinary research models, librarians and faculty are increasingly starting to criticise this traditional model of engagement [Elm 06]. On one hand, this is because the research paper structure often fails to let students engage critically with sources. By focusing on the number or type of sources students need, we fail to scaffold student engagement with authority. Furthermore, by making it sound like the point of the assignment is to locate sources, we fail to engage students with the collaborative and participatory nature of research [Fis 11]. On the other hand, the traditional model of research papers also fails to engage students with broader and more flexible information environments. By focusing on finding the formal final products of scholarship such as articles or books, we ignore systems of informal scholarship and the broader research process [Lec 96]. And, by typically concentrating on scholarly or subscription sources, we deny the development of a student's personal information seeking strategies and informal or lifelong learning habits. Just like complaints about the VLE, research is perceived as bounded and static. It is small wonder that the research process is seen as confusing for students and frustrating for faculty.

Librarians have typically tried to address flaws in the research assignment through IL tutorials. Rejecting IL standards and practice that often seem to reflect print-based realities, librarians have started to draw from the field of critical pedagogy and critical information studies in order to develop critical information literacy, a more responsive approach to teaching and learning. While critical information literacy (CIL) can be hard to define, it can be characterised as a disposition towards learning that centres around the learner, and importantly, the interrogation of information systems and landscapes. In this way, CIL questions "the social construction and cultural authority of knowledge; the political economies of knowledge ownership and control; [or] the development of local communities' and cultures' capacities to critique and construct knowledge" among other things [Luk 99]. In the information age, these questions are more important than ever, especially when they impact core librarian values of preservation, privacy and equal access. Notwithstanding, while critical information literacy provides a valuable approach to scaffolding student inquiry, it does not provide a robust structure or framework for scaffolding the information environment. The paper will now turn to exploring how the PLE can build upon this progressive IL thinking in order to scaffold learner information landscapes.

Personal Learning Environments and Critical Information Literacy

A close examination of PLE principles demonstrates that there is significant overlap with and support of the research process. Firstly, it is obvious that the research process is messy and non-linear. PLEs are built to recognize the diverse yet chaotic nature of information interactions. Secondly, the research process draws upon a broad range of sources, including the informal network of scholarship and filters that academics have spent years cultivating. The PLE aims to scaffold a broad learning environment that covers a wide range of "tools, artefacts, processes and physical connections" [Cou 10]. Thirdly, the research process sees learner creation or production as a way to break down academic boundaries and position research as a conversation that the learner can enter. The PLE too recognises the value of student participation, encouraging the learner to form and be part of a network. Lastly, one of the overarching goals of the research assignment is to integrate learners into disciplinary discourse. The PLE too is characterised as the "spaces in which people interact and communicate" and, as such, can be seen as a way "to immerse yourself into the workings of a community" [Dow 10]. From these brief observations, it is clear that the PLE and the research process align well together. In this way, the PLE may offer an alternative approach to the goals of the research paper. More importantly, the PLE's strength in scaffolding information environments complements the CIL focus on developing the researcher disposition. In this way, it would seem that by combining the PLE framework with the CIL disposition, librarians can develop a richer and more valuable approach to engage students in questions about research and inquiry.

Accordingly, the librarian drew from this literature to design a new research assignment that would meet learner needs as well as starting a conversation about research literacies in knowledge societies. The assignment consisted of several stages. Firstly, students were asked to present several of the core resources they found on their topic on the course blog. This had to include at least 1 journal, 1 professional association, 1 expert and 1 informal source (for example a blog or Twitter account). In this way, the assignment drew from the PLE structure to engage students with the broad array of information sources. At the same time, it draws from CIL by exposing students to research in context, or informal scholarly habits. This helps break down barriers, and enables learners to see research as a conversation that they can enter. Secondly, students had to provide an in depth analysis of these sources on the class blog. This included an

analysis of how they found the source and why they chose it for the assignment. The PLE structure guides students to track "clues" in the scholarly conversation and gain a wider sense of the connections and conversation within their topic, the network of people and ideas. At the same time, the CIL focus on a contextual evaluation of sources, as opposed to a teacher-driven prescribed checklist, allows students to develop a more critical stance within information environments. Thirdly, students had to reflect periodically on their research process and progress. This integrated both the PLE and CIL focus on developing self-regulated learning. Guided questions, such as "Who can publish on a topic?" also helped students reflect about the norms and conventions of the Antarctic research community, an important part of CIL. Lastly, students remixed and synthesised sources in their final paper to make their own contributions to the conversation. This draws upon both PLE and CIL aims to create authentic learning experiences and where participation is more valued than the final product. In sum, the librarian drew from PLE literature to establish a framework that enabled navigation in and the creation of an information environment. She also drew from CIL literature to encourage the development of the learner's critical disposition, by reflecting on scholarly practice and global information flow. And, through combining both PLE and CIL principles, she created a research assignment that aimed to make the research process more meaningful in academic practice and beyond.

HIST492: History of the Antarctic Treaty System

In Spring 2013, the librarian integrated the new research assignment into HIST492, Capstone Seminar: History of the Antarctic Treaty System. As a capstone seminar class, enrollment was low with only nine senior students (four female, five male) of which eight consented to participate in this study. In this way, the librarian hoped to test this theoretical background with a small group of students as a pilot study. As part of the class, students had to choose a research topic that was focused on an aspect of Antarctic politics. This included various domestic and international topics such as Japan and Antarctica or Antarctica and the Third World. While the collaboration with the professor was driven by personal interest, Antarctic Studies proved to be a perfect environment for this type of exploratory assignment design. As a new field of study, much relevant material is available online, yet it is scattered around the web in government documents, data sets, archives, blogs and even ice-core samples. In addition, the interdisciplinary and contested nature of Antarctica means that research is under-developed; yet it also forms an ongoing, international and participatory conversation.

At the end of the semester, the assignment responses and the reflective surveys were coded and analyzed by both the professor and the librarian to examine the effect of the assignment on student learning. The reflective surveys gave an interesting snapshot of student attitudes to academic research. At the beginning of the semester, students showed several misgivings about research, including the belief in "right" and "wrong" sources and failing to recognise the part this plays in investigation and inquiry: "The questions that I have about my topic are whether or not I am taking the correct approach to my argument". By mid-class, however, when students completed their blog posts, students appeared to have gained more confidence with the research process and highlighted various changes they made to their original approach. Notwithstanding, critical analysis was still fairly basic. While students readily modeled textbook answers about scholarly credibility, for example, responses often failed to show a thoughtful engagement with what this meant: "I trust all of my information simply for the fact that the search engines I have used were scholarly". In addition, students seemed unable to apply these criteria to other situations, for example non-scholarly sources. By the end of the semester though, students were starting to question these information environments more: "Is [their research] all from second hand materials or are they actually on the ground doing field work?". Students also demonstrated a broader understanding of authority: "I've learned that casual sources (blogs, websites, etc.) can be useful sources and that I don't just have to use journals and books, so long as I address the questions concerning bias and credibility of the author."

These findings were also backed up in the research assignment responses. As a whole, students posted highly appropriate and interesting sources on the blog. In addition, source evaluation was extensive and showed an engagement with broad concepts of credibility and the subsequent contribution to their argument: "It may also provide a counter to my thesis, as having a twitter account is not very isolated from the rest of the world." Students also showed a growing awareness of the interconnected nature of research, and the networked conversation: "This will be able to contribute to my paper because it will help with narrowing down which authors to particularly look at when it comes to Antarctica."

Obviously, this project was not without limitations and flaws. Firstly, the class on which this assignment was tested was very small, consisting of eight students. Further research should test this framework on a larger class, as well as outside of the field of history to examine its potential away from the guided seminar setting. Furthermore, no control group or comparison group was established. As such, it is impossible to say whether the assignment irrevocably improved final papers or student learning. Nonetheless, students indicated that they greatly enjoyed and valued the worth of the assignment, which indicates some level of success. Future research should try and parse the worth of this assignment out more fully. Lastly, the assignment was limited to the class blog, due to the professor's reluctance to introduce another new technology to the students. As such, the librarian plans to build on this research in order to explore further iterations of assignments that use the PLE framework. This could include the use of Diigo or Storify as tools to engage learners in bigger questions about knowledge and inquiry.

Summary

In summary, the author has demonstrated that the PLE forms a viable framework for creating alternative research assignments that are suited to the demands of the changing information landscape as well as learner needs. Student reflection and assignment responses demonstrate an engagement with the networked world of information, which was generally perceived as being very helpful for the future. Students also praised the assignment in the separate end of semester evaluation. While the study shows several shortcomings, this pilot-study indicates that broader application and testing would be worthwhile.

PLEs have been nurtured with the field of educational technology. However, in this paper, the author shows that PLEs are also increasingly valuable across campus, and for a variety of purposes. In addition, the author demonstrates that while traditional information literacy feels outdated, many librarians are starting to develop a more critical approach to information literacy that intersects with many of the guiding principles of the PLE. This could add a useful critical voice that has been missing from the literature so far. Ultimately, this confluence of interest can only expand interest and acceptance of PLEs, and encourage the creation of broad and holistic educational practice across campus.

REFERENCES

[Biz 87] *Bizzell, Patricia, Herzberg, Bruce (1987):* Research as a Social Act. In: The Clearing House, 60,7, 303–306.

[Coo 11] *Coonan, Emma (2011):* A new curriculum for information literacy: Theoretical background. Retrieved June 2014 from *http://arcadiaproject.lib.cam.ac.uk/docs/theory.pdf*

[Cou 10] *Couros, Alec (2010):* Developing personal learning networks for open and social learning, *In George. Veletsianos (Ed.), Emerging Technologies in Distance Education. Athabasca. Athabasca University Press, 109–128.*

[Dow 10] *Downes, Stephen (2010):* Pedagogical foundations for personal learning. Retrieved June 2014 from *http://www.slideshare.net/Downes/pedagogical-foundations-for-personal-learning*

[Elm 06] *Elmborg, James (2006):* Critical information literacy: Implications for instructional practice. In:The Journal of Academic Librarianship, 32, 2, 192–199.

[Fis 11] *Fister, Barbara (2011):* Sources of Confusion. Retrieved June 2014 from *http://www.insidehighered.com/blogs/library_babel_fish/sources_of_confusion*

[Fis 09] *Fister, Barbara (2009):* Fostering Information Literacy through Faculty Development. In: Library Issues Briefings for Faculty and Administrators, 29, 4, 1–4.

[Hea 12] *Head, Alison (2012):* How College Graduates Solve Information Problems Once They Join the Workplace. Retrieved June 2014 from *http://projectinfolit.org/pdfs/PIL_fall2012_workplaceStudy_FullReport.pdf*

[Lec 96] *Leckie, Gloria (1996) Desperately seeking citations:* Uncovering faculty assumptions about the undergraduate research process. In: Journal of Academic Librarianship 22, 3, 201–208.

[Luk 99] *Luke, Allan & Kapitzke, Cushla (1999):* Literacies and libraries: Archives and cybraries. In: Pedagogy, Culture and Society, 7, 3, 467–491.

[UNE 05] *UNESCO National Forum on Information Literacy (2005). Alexandria Proclamation on Information Literacy and Lifelong Learning. Retrieved June 2014 from http://archive.ifla.org/III/wsis/BeaconInfSoc.html*

CONTACT DETAILS

Alison Hicks
University of Colorado, Boulder 184 UCB, 1720
Pleasant Street
Boulder, 80309, USA
Phone: +1 (0)303 6787155
E-Mail: *alison.hicks@colorado.edu*

Reflecting the Learning Process Using LAMA

Helena Dierenfeld, Agathe Merceron

ABSTRACT

This paper introduces the LAMA tool and shows how to use it to analyze usage data stored by Learning Management Systems. For example it is possible to have information on how forums are used by readers and writers, or on how specific learning resources are accessed. Because LAMA is independent of any particular LMS, we believe that it could be adapted to other software used in PLEs that also store usage data.

Introduction

A great variety of software combined with almost permanent Internet connections allows students and teachers to arrange their own personal learning environment, which opens the way for novel teaching and learning experiences. We believe that this trend will continue in the cities of the future. As an example [Buc 12] reports on a project in which six virtual teams of students dispersed in six physical locations of two countries, Germany and Israel, had to develop a prototype of an educational software for mobile phones. To communicate [Buc 12] used Web 2–0 software such as wiki, blog, twitter and adobe connect. [Kil 12] describes the use of reputation software to teach collaborative software development, and so to emphasize the social aspects of learning as well as the personal self-organization of students. These new ways of teaching and learning bring about new questions: How do teachers and students use their Personal Learning Environment (PLE)? Can we identify types of PLE users? Are there PLE usages that are more beneficial to learning?

Most computer based learning systems used in PLEs are storing user interaction data in log files or databases. Thus it is possible to analyze these interaction data and get information on how PLEs are used. Analyzing the usage data can give information that fosters reflection and helps improve the teaching and learning experience. For example [Har 09] analyses how students organize their personal information space and identify four types of students according to the folder structure they choose, flat or deeply nested or some in between combination. [Par 12] investigate learning and performance from a social network perspective. Starting from discussion forums used by full-time industry worker professionals engaged in an online post-graduate program, they built corresponding social networks and add a measure called Richness Content to take into consideration the quality of the messages. Students are divided in groups. There are group forums accessible solely to the group and a general forum accessible to all students. [Par 12] find support for several hypotheses regarding learning, in particular that Richness Content is positively correlated with a strong engagement in the group forum as opposed to a strong engagement in the general forum. [Sie 12] goes much further and propose to provide different stakeholders in education with a variety of dashboards visualizing learning. The analytics dashboard of a student for example would include diagrams depicting the social network of co-learners in a course.

In this contribution we show how usage data in learning management systems (LMSs) can be analyzed with the LAMA tool (Learning, Analytics, Mining and Adaption). LMSs are not exactly PLEs, they are rather personal teaching environments for teachers. However they contain forums, wikis and also can be seen as repositories of learning resources. Thus, they have many similarities with software used in PLEs. Therefore, we believe that analysis techniques for LMSs can be transferred to PLEs.

Analyzing such data is promising to improve the learning and teaching experience, because this could help answering several interesting questions strartin with fairly easy questions like "How many students use the forum?", moving to more complex ones like "Is there a connection between completing a task and the learning success?" to even very complex ones like "Are students adopting different learning strategies, and if yes, which ones?". In the last few years a strong learning analytics community was formed. A number of works focus on the development of warning systems, detecting students in danger (analyzing data to obtain information on lack of social connections, irregular system usage, or problems with specific learning tasks) to provide early interventions incorporated in the learning management system (see [Ess 12] or [Sig 13] for examples of such works).

Our approach is to develop a tool focusing rather on analyzing the data of users with the intention of identifying trends within the usage. The aim of our tool LAMA is to allow different stakeholders (teachers, administrators, researchers and providers of learning material) to analyze usage data by themselves looking for information interesting to them, e.g. getting knowledge on students' communication within a course or on students' interaction with resources that could help identifying shortcomings in the material's structure.

In the next section we give a short overview of the LAMA tool. We follow with a case study and finish with conclusions.

The LAMA Tool

LAMA works platform independent, this allows comparing the usage of different learning systems and, may be more important, to merge data stored by different learning systems. This is useful for teachers who teach courses with different learning systems. Unfortunately the structure of stored log files differs between learning systems. In addition not every learning system stores the same kind of data and often most of the

data is only important for system administration. Therefore, we are extracting useful data from log files or databases stored by LMS to a data model that we developed, see [Krü 10] and further enhanced in [For 13]. Technically what is needed is a connector that extracts usage data from a specific learning system and imports them in the data model. Presently connectors are implemented for the LMSs Moodle and Clix, and for the learning portal ChemgaPedia. This approach can be used for PLEs too. Data stored in a wiki and in a blog for instance could be combined in the data model of LAMA.

LAMA is structured into three levels to support different needs and abilities of stakeholders: The first level is creating text files with useful data for analysis. Anonymisation allows for complying with privacy laws in vigor in many European countries. Only anonymous data can be kept for a long span of time. Comparing several successive cohorts of students does require keeping the data for a longer time than usually allowed for non-anonymous data. The stakeholder gets a table containing anonymised user interaction data. The table describes who interacted at which time with which part of the learning system. This allows stakeholders to analyze the data using external tools. In [Die 12] we showed how to use the Pivot Tables from Excel to analyze these text files. For working with these Pivot Tables we are providing two different kinds of text files. The first file focuses on interaction frequency while the second focuses on usage and learning success (measured by grades) in dependency of learning material usage. This level is convenient for stakeholders that are IT-affine and want to explore usage data by themselves in some depth.

The second level is a collection of internal analysis methods to get a quick idea of the data. Therefore we provide tables and figures interesting for the stakeholders and showing key indicators, e.g. user interactions with specific material or interactions by date. However, it is a challenging task to define which analysis methods are the informative ones for as many stakeholders as possible, so the tool has to provide a set with which one can compose a personal dashboard. This level is convenient for example for teachers who just want to check quickly key-figures such as: are all the online-resources used, or how are forums used?

The third one is also a collection of internal analysis methods, but it supports more complex analysis tasks. Here we are giving hints for those complex analysis tasks like defining learning types, mentioned in the beginning of this paper. To answer these questions, we are relying on different data mining techniques such as clustering. The implementation of the third level is not started yet. This level is meant for stakeholders that have some familiarity with data mining and can understand and interpret results returned by data mining algorithms.

Case Study

Many learning/teaching scenarios involve that students and teachers communicate via a forum. Looking at the forum itself does not give a good overview of how it is used: do students read it? Do they keep accessing it even if no post has been made? A simple histogram as shown in Figure 1 gives keys to answer such questions. Figure 1 shows access to a forum over time in an online-course taking place in summer semester 2013 focusing on the six weeks period from March, 18 till April, 30. The online-course has been taught using the LMS Moodle. Data have been extracted from Moodle and imported into the LAMA data model. A vertical bar indicates the number of writing/reading accesses per day to the forum. A reading access is written in the legend as "view discussion" while a writing access is mentioned with "add discussion". At a glance one notices that the forum is much more accessed for reading than for writing. This is a common observation also made by others, see for example [Cob 12]. One notices the big pick on March 27, which coincides with the first online meeting and the real start of the course. One notices the weekly picks that match the weekly online conferences. One notices also the decrease in the use of the forum over the first month after the start. The last posting was on April 16 but reading accesses to the forum still continued after that date. In that case this access-pattern corresponds to the expectations of the teacher: important issues were raised and answered in the forum in the first 2 weeks of the course.

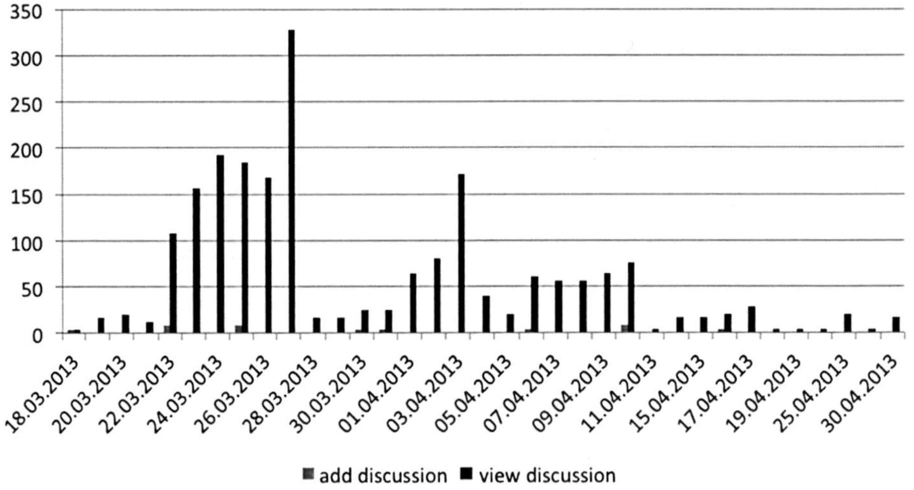

Figure 1: Writing and reading accesses to a forum over time

Figure 2 shows access over time to two specific resources called "exercises" and "exercises with solutions". The teacher keeps updating these two specific resources and

is interested to check whether students keep accessing them. Figure 2 shows the total number of accesses to these two resources per day. The higher number of accesses coincides with an update.

These analyses are made using pivot-tables on the tables given by the first level of the tool. They also correspond to diagrams that could be added to the dashboard in the second level, thus allowing the teacher to quickly check whether the intended teaching scenario works out. The histogram on forum-access could be adapted to an individual student by showing own reading and writing accesses against the ones of the others, allowing to reflect about own participation in the forum.

[Die 12] shows to build a histogram of all uploaded learning objects of a course sorted by number of accesses with the very same table. At a glance it is possible to grasp which learning objects are frequently accessed and which ones are barely used. [Die 12] shows also how it is possible to check whether the average mark on some assignment of students that have used some selected learning object is better than the general average. This possibility allows teachers to investigate whether the use of some material might have impact on success. Templates of Pivot tables have been created for these analyses and can be used by others. Stakeholders just need to upload the files produced by the first level of LAMA into the given templates [LAM 13].

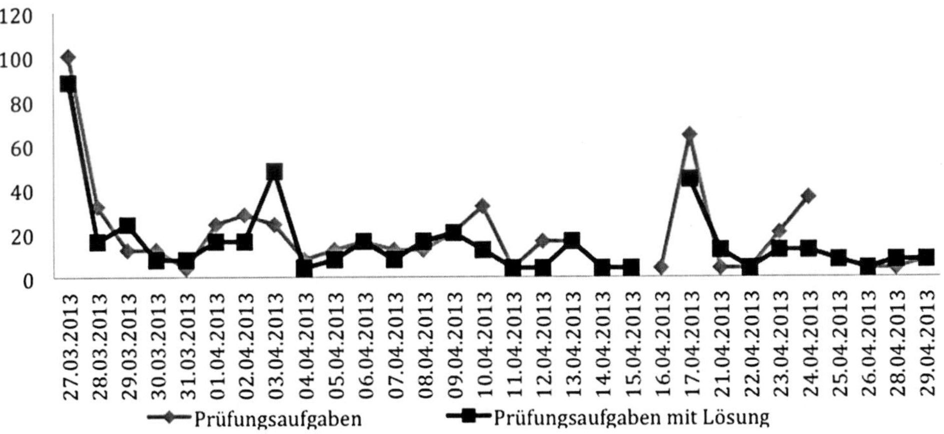

Figure 1: Accesses to two specific learning resources over time

LAMA and PLEs

The above case study takes the perspective of the teacher who has provided or made mandatory the LMS Moodle as one component of the personal learning environment of the learners enrolled in the course. LAMA can easily be extended to the perspective of the learner and show his / her own accesses only, or his / her own accesses together with the accesses of the rest of the cohort.

Because of the fundamental independence between learning systems and LAMA, usage data can be in principle extracted from the different tools that a learner has chosen in her Personal Learning Environment and combined into the single data model of LAMA. Looking at learner's own accesses only, a learner can obtain a summary of own overall activity over a chosen timespan. Because data is stored anonymized in the data model, activities of all users can be visualized as well, and a learner can be aware of the activity of all learners using the same tools. We believe that such information can bring better awareness of own learning attitude and support reflexive learning.

Conclusions

In this contribution we have introduced the tool LAMA. Primary aim of LAMA is to support different stakeholders in their analysis of usage data stored by learning management systems. Three different levels are foreseen in LAMA to adapt better to different needs and types of stakeholders. In particular the second level with dashboard can provide a kind of flexible warning system for the teacher to check whether the intended learning scenario works out. LAMA is platform independent. It has its own data model. Connectors import data from the database or log files of a learning management system into the data model of LAMA. Learning management systems have components such as forums, wikis, chats, repositories that are found in PLEs. Therefore LAMA could also be used with PLEs since they utilize similar components though in a flexible way. Connectors have to be implemented to import usage data stored by systems such as forums, blogs, wikis or repositories. In this paper we have shown how LAMA can support awareness on how a forum is used over time. The same can be done with another collaborative tool such as a wiki or a blog. A limitation of the approach is the availability of the data. Students organize themselves and share using social networks like Facebook. If students use some environment that is completely decoupled from the teaching institution, data might not be accessible and therefore cannot be analyzed. Currently we conduct experiments with different stakeholders to match the tool better their needs, especially in view of the development of the third level of LAMA.

Acknowledgement

This work is partially supported by the "Berlin Senatsverwaltung für Wirtschaft, Technologie und Forschung" with funding from the European Social Fund. We thank colleagues for their collaboration in analyzing usage data of their courses.

REFERENCES

[Buc 12] *Buchem, Ilona (2012):* Managing Diversity in internationalen Projektteams an der Hochschule. In Gross, M. & von Klinski, S. (Eds.). Angewandte Forschung zur Stadt der Zukunft - Aktuelle Forschungsarbeiten zu urbanen Technologien und Infrastrukturen sowie urbanem Leben: Logos Verlag Berlin, 93-95.

[Cob 12] *Cobo, German; Garcia, David; Santamria, Eugenia; Moran, Jose Antonio; Melanchon, Javier; Monzo, Carlos (2012):* Using Agglomerative Hierarchical Clustering to Model Learner Participation Profile in Online Discussion Forums. In: Buckingham Shum, Simon; Gasevic, Dragan; Ferguson, Rebecca (Eds.) Proceedings of the 2nd International Conference on Learning Analytics and Knowledge. (Vancouver, Canada, April 29 – May 2). ACM, 248-251.

[Die 12] *Dierenfeld, Helene; Merceron, Agathe (2012):* Learning Analytics with Excel Pivot Tables. Proceedings of the 1st Moodle Research Conference. S. Retalis & M. Dougamias (Eds.). Chernia, Creete, 115- 121. Retrieved May 2014 from *http://research.moodle.net/pluginfile.php/140/mod_resource/content/2/Full%20Proceedings.pdf*

[Kno 75] *Dierenfeld, Helene; Merceron, Agathe (2012):* Learning Analytics with Excel Pivot Tables. Proceedings of the 1st Moodle Research Conference. S. Retalis & M. Dougamias (Eds.). Chernia, Creete, 115- 121. Retrieved May 2014 from *http://research.moodle.net/pluginfile.php/140/mod_resource/content/2/Full%20Proceedings.pdf*

[Ess 12] *Essa, Alfred; Ayad, Hanan (2012):* Student Success System: Risk Analytics and Data Visualization using Ensembles of Predictive Models. In: Buckingham Shum, Simon; Gasevic, Dragan; Ferguson, Rebecca (Eds.) Proceedings of the 2nd International Conference on Learning Analytics and Knowledge. (Vancouver, Canada, April 29 – May 2). ACM, 158-161.

[For 13] *Fortenbacher, Albrecht; Beuster, Liane; Elkina, Margarita;, Kappe, Leonard; Merceron, Agathe; Pursian, Andreas, Schwarzrock, Schwarzrock; Wenzlaff, Boris (2013):* LeMo: a Learning Analytics Application Focussing on User Path Analysis and Interactive Visualization. In Proceedings of the 7th IEEE International Conference on Intellingent Data Acquisition and Advanced Computing Systems: Technology and Application (IDAACS'2013), Berlin (Germany), September 12-14 2013, ISBN 978-1-4799-1426-5, 748-753.

[Har 09] *Hardof-Jaffe, Sharon; Hershkovitz, Arnon; Abu-Kishk, Hama; Ofer Bergman; Nachmias, Rafi (2009):* How do Students Organize Personal Information Spaces? In Barnes, T., Desmarais, M., Romero, C., Ventura, S. (Eds.) Proceedings of the 2nd International Conference on Educational Data Mining. (Cordoba, Spain, July 1-3), EDM'09, 250-258.

[Kil 12] *Kilamo, Terhi, Hammouda, Imed; Chatti, Mohamed Amine (2012):* Teaching collaborative software development: a case study. In: Glinz, M., Murphy, G. & Pezzè, M. (Eds.) ICSE 2012 Proceedings of the 2012 International Conference on Software Engineering, IEEE Press Piscataway, NJ, USA, 1165-1174.

[Krü 10] *Krüger, Andre, Merceron, Agathe; Wolf, Benjamin (2010):* A Data Model to Ease Analysis and Mining of Educational Data. In: Proceedings of the 3th International Conference on Educational Data Mining, Pittsburg, USA, 131-140.

[LAM 13] *LAMA. (2013):* Learning – Analytics – Mining – Adaptation, Veröffentlichungen & Downloads, retrieved May 2014 from *http://wissen.beuth-hochschule.de/datamining/*

[Par 12] *Paredes, Walter Christian; Chang, Kong Shin Kenneth (2012):* Modeling Learning & Performance: A Social Networks Perspective. In: Buckingham Shum, Simon; Gasevic, Dragan; Ferguson, Rebecca (Eds.) Proceedings of the 2nd International Conference on Learning Analytics and Knowledge. (Vancouver, Canada, April 29 – May 2). ACM, 34-42.

[Sie 12] *Siemens, George; Gasevic, Dragan;, Haythornthwaite, C., Dawson, S., Buckingham Shum, Simon; Ferguson, Rebecca; Duval, Eric; Verbert, Katrien; Baker, Ryan S.J.d. (2012):* Open Learning Analytics: an integrated & modularized platform Proposal to design, implement and

evaluate an open platform to integrate heterogeneous learning analytics techniques. Retrieved May 2014 from *http://solaresearch.org/OpenLearningAnalytics.pdf*

[Sig 13] *Signals. (2013):* Stoplights For Student Success, retrieved June 8, 2013 from *http://www.itap.purdue.edu/studio/signals/*

FIGURES

CONTACT DETAILS

Prof. Dr. Agathe Merceron
Beuth Universty of Applied Sciences
Department Computers Science and Media
Luxemburger Street 10
13353 Berlin
Phone: +49 (0)30 4504 5105
E-Mail: *merceron@beuth-hochschule.de*

PLE as an Assessment for Learning Tool in Teacher Education

Carmen Arbonés, Isabel Civera, Neus Figueras, Cristina Montero, Salvador Rodríguez, Theresa Zanatta

ABSTRACT

This paper presents the results of an action research study on the implementation of a Personal Learning Environment (PLE) as a tool for assessment for learning in teacher education at the Universitat de Barcelona. Preliminary findings show that the use of the PLE as an assessment tool not only improves students' learning outcomes but also provides a research tool to assess, and a vehicle to promote, the role of reflection in initial teacher education.

Introduction

This study is derived from the project 2012PID-UB/099 "L'entorn personal d'aprenentatge: una eina per a la reflexió metacognitiva i per a l'avaluació formativa a la menció de llengües estrangeres dels graus d'educació infantil i d'educació primària" ("The Personal Learning Environment: a tool for metacognitive reflection and assessment for learning in the English Specialty for the undergraduate degrees for Infant and Primary Education") (Universitat de Barcelona, 2012–2013). The aims of the project were backed by the authors' familiarization with prior research in the three areas targeted: pre-service teacher training, assessment, and the use of new technologies, most specially Personal Learning Environments (PLE). This section briefly reviews the issues identified in the relevant literature which informed and helped put together the teaching programme and the project itself.

Issues related to pre-service teacher training

Trainee teachers are often described as seeing "the world of the classroom from a centre lying within themselves" [Dia 91], drawing on their own learning experience and the beliefs constructed during their years as students at school. The objective of pre-service teacher training is to help trainees deepen and widen their understanding of education and of educational ideas and principles, and to become students of their own teaching, going beyond skill training. In an era where it has become impossible to know everything, [Tra 09] "connectivism", where each learner builds his/her own network of knowledge sources to be able to access them whenever he/she needs them, is an approach which in the digital era can empower trainees to extend their knowledge. Tracey argues, however, that connectivism should be understood in relation to previous approaches such as the one prevalent in the 1980s, instructivism, and the one that is still present in our classrooms, constructivism; there is no one pedagogy superseding the other, rather a gradient or continuum that shows how different approaches can be integrated.

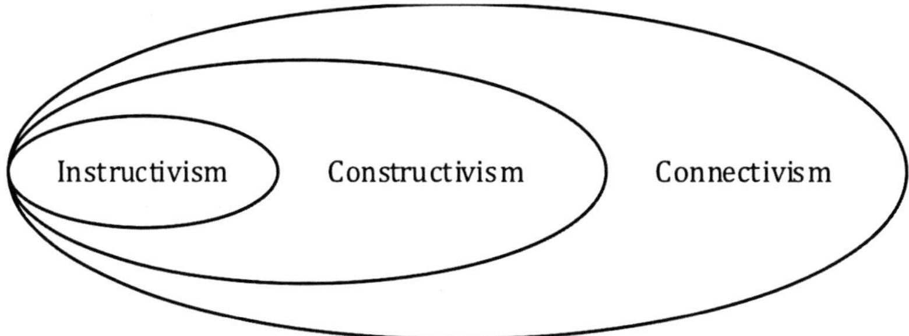

Figure 1: Gradient in pedagogies [Tra 09]

The present project aims at integrating the three pedagogies at different phases and with different purposes, as will be described in the following sections.

Issues related to assessment

The project's approach to assessment drew on the work by researchers like Paul Black and Dylan Wiliam in the UK and David Boud in Australia who have attempted to define how assessment for learning can take place in the classroom. [Bla 09] highlighted the roles that different actors in the classroom can and should play (teachers, students as self and peers) in the various assessment stages along the three key processes in any teaching-learning event, by providing directions and feedback on (a) where students are (their present abilities), (b) where they need to go (the learning target), (c) how to get there (the processes and the content to develop to achieve the learning target).

The limitations of the present article do not allow for a full discussion of [Bla 09] proposed framework for assessment for learning, but due to the relevance of the framework's five main strategies for the project, they are listed below.

1. Clarifying learning intentions and criteria for success.
2. Engineering effective classroom discussions and other learning tasks that elicit evidence of student understanding.
3. Activating students as instructional resources for one another.
4. Activating students as the owners of their own learning.
5. Providing feedback that moves learners forward.

In the following sections, instances of these strategies will be described whilst presenting the development of the project.

Issues related to the uses of the Personal Learning Environments (PLE)

The idea of Personal Learning Environments only emerged in 2006 [Att 07] and the literature on their development and use is mostly *on line*. The open nature of the PLE, its focus primarily on the learner [Sch 08] and the new approach to using technologies it presented would provide the ideal structure to integrate the different objectives we aimed at. [Pre 01] argues that many of the skills that have fostered new technologies, such as parallel processing, graphics awareness or random access, which have profound implications for student learning, are usually ignored by teachers. PLEs can emphasize these skills by facilitating simultaneously different ways of processing information as well as providing a space for reflection on metacognition and self-regulated learning. Students' reflections on the role of PLEs in initial teacher training as well as a longlife learning instrument [Ade 10] will be presented in following sections.

Approach and methodology

The project has been conducted during the fourth (and last) year of the Infant and Primary Teacher Education degrees at the *Universitat de Barcelona* and involves over 80 students intending to teach in primary and infant schools in Catalonia. The content of the modules that the students were enrolled in ranges over various subjects on teaching and learning English as a foreign language at primary and infant level such as *Language Teaching Methodology*, *Storytelling* and *Teaching Practice*.

One of the main aims of the course was to improve the quality of the trainees' learning behaviour by facilitating reflection as a core element of their development and raising their awareness of the benefits of reflective and self-regulated learning. This comprised the adoption of the following elements: (a) a PLE, as the medium for implementing the formative assessment strategy. This also presented the opportunity for students to make links between different modules; (b) a self and peer assessment methodology, as the basis for formative assessment associated with each core task of the module; (c) a weekly logbook in which students consider how they perceived their own progress throughout the course.

According to [Tra 09], initial sessions were organized in which students were "instructed" on a selection of Web 2.0 tools to search and filter resources and information. They were followed by input and face-to-face sessions in which the concept of PLE and SymbalooEDU were introduced and intentions were shared and clarified in classroom discussions. Students invited teachers to their PLE and teachers gave feedback. Reflection accompanied the knowledge "construction" process from the beginning by means of the individual weekly logbook entries and joint reflection after the tasks carried out in class which facilitated the development of tools and skills for self-assessment and peer assessment. At the same time, the social dimension of the PLE allowed students to share their thoughts, and provided a space for introspection and shared analysis or, in other words, for metacognition. This aspect was reinforced by the creation of a collaborative blog in which, in addition to sharing information, ideas, knowledge and resources, students published their tasks undertaken in groups and conducted an informal peer assessment.

Since it is the first time the module was implemented, it was agreed that action research was the most appropriate design, due to its ability to support a process of change in which the researchers would be active participants. [Ste 75] in his seminal text, "An Introduction to Curriculum Research and Development", relates the usefulness of the action research method for educators and it remains one of the most effective ways of bringing about change in educational settings. The project would also be subjected to on-going development throughout its implementation. [Bas 98]'s approach was considered to be the most appropriate because of the detailed structure it provides: 1. Define the enquiry; 2. Describe the situation; 3. Collect evaluation data and analyse it; 4. Review the data and look for contradictions; 5. Tackle a contradiction by introducing change; 6. Monitor the change; 7. Analyse evaluative data about the change; 8. Review the change and decide what to do next.

Three data-gathering procedures were established to obtain information throughout the project: (1) Students' reflections on their experience by means of a weekly logbook entry and a final essay; (2) Observation of the screenshots of the students' PLE, who were asked to send a screenshot of their PLEs in SymbalooEDU which was linked to the module in Moodle; (3) Interviews with the course lecturers and with some students. This procedure was applied so as to triangulate data.

Results

The data collected is still being processed, and so far only the students' personal accounts and the screenshots of their PLE have been analysed. The accounts show students' personal and professional involvement in the project, also made explicit in the wealth of resources included in their PLEs.

PLEs contributed to the development of the students' ICT and metacognitive skills. To be able to create their PLE, students had to have some basic skills in ICT in order to find, collect and file relevant information. At the same time, they needed to think about the elements that would constitute their PLE in accordance with their objectives. Therefore, students were able to evaluate the quality and reliability of information available to them as well as decide the most suitable tool for the different tasks they were required to complete. This process is reflected in the following quote from one of the students' personal account:

"It is not difficult to create a Symbaloo webmix, but it is not easy to fill it with meaningful tiles. While building my PLE, I understood that it makes no sense to add tiles indiscriminately. At the beginning I added things just to increase my collection, but in less than a week I erased everything because I realised I was not creating my personal learning environment but a chaos. Thus my PLE has been built consciously, serenely, through a deep thinking". (AP's PLE Report, January 2013)

The social dimension of the PLE contributed to the students' metacognitive skills development. They had to be able to analyze and discuss their peers' performance, request feedback from colleagues about their work and integrate aspects of these opinions or criticism in order to improve their future actions [Wil 09]. Another dimension to consider was the ability of students to negotiate with classmates tools, roles and procedures to be followed during group work. This is seen in the following reflection:

"The idea of creating a PLE was difficult to understand at first. So, I would have needed some more instructions because I have felt a little bit lost sometimes. On the other hand, I'm really proud of myself and my colleagues because we have created a social network through different mediums to solve our problems, doubts or opinions, working together to improve our skills". (MA' s PLE Report, January 2013)

The quality of the students' reflections on the learning process, and on the self-assessment of their achievements is seen in the quotes included below.

"At the beginning of this subject, when I heard the term PLE I got a bit lost because I didn't know what to do. Then, when I investigated a bit more about the topic I realized that to create a Personal Learning Environment I had to be responsible for my learning process and that scared me. Before doing this subject the teacher used to tell us what to do and how to do it, and it was difficult for me to change my way of working". (NL's PLE Report, January 2013)

"I have discovered my limitations, my mistakes, and I found different ways to solve these mistakes". (AB's PLE Report, January 2013)

"My PLE has been a great tool to realize how my knowledge has been changing and my Symbaloo changed with it". (IB's PLE Report, January 2013)

"This is my PLE and it is called Good Steps. I decided to call it like this because it really shows what I understand when I think about the education process and my PLE". (EC's PLE Report, January 2013)

Summary

The analysis of the data shows that the potential of the PLE as an assessment for learning tool has been confirmed. Teachers and students shared learning intentions and criteria for success from the start, and continued discussion and feedback amongst students and between students and teachers through the weekly logbook entries made the use of additional assessment instruments unnecessary. Learning and assessment were fully integrated in the learning process, as this final quote from a student expains:

> *"To conclude with my learning process I have to admit that it has been very complex. After creating my own PLE I have a satisfactory feeling because I think I have done it well". (NL's PLE Report, January 2013)*

A key aspect of the students' PLE was the establishment of their learning goals together with the decisions they made throughout the process in order to achieve them. Their PLE should include the set of tools, information, connections, storage, and the knowledge resulting from the interaction of these components. An example can be seen in the following excerpt taken from the final account of one of the students in the course:

> *"Chinese balloons do not fly at the first moment. There is a meticulous procedure to follow: They need the inflammable material, the fire, someone to set fire to them and someone to hold them. Then, with this mixture the balloons grow and grow and finally, when their structure is big and strong enough, they fly away [...] My PLE follows a similar path. I need different inputs, such as the practice hours, the theory, professional talks, the debates, my classmates' presentations, their different points of view... and all this together builds a new me..." (MP's PLE Report, January 2013).*

Another remarkable aspect that can be observed in most of the students' personal accounts is the transfer to their future classroom practice of their awareness of the benefits of reflective, self regulated learning:

> *"My conclusion: I would like to support now the use of PLE since it follows the methodology that I want to teach my future students: the idea that the process is more important than the mere transmission of knowledge, that the pupils are the real protagonists, the idea that every child is different from each other and every child learns at a different pace, the idea that we should start teaching by considering students' interests and motivations. Also, I like the idea that it would help children to relate school context to their personal lives." (JG's PLE Report, January 2013)*

From these conclusions, we see how the PLE provided four concrete opportunities for assessment for learning in teacher education:

1. Throughout the process, teachers and students shared in the development of learning objectives, intentions and criteria for success.
2. The PLE provided a framework to bring together and organise individual student learning goals as well as make visible the decisions that were taken throughout this process.
3. As a result of the two previous aspects, assessment and learning were fully integrated in the process.
4. Students developed confidence which will allow them to transfer their awareness of the benefits of reflective, self-regulated learning to their future classroom practice.

To conclude, the use of a PLE as an assessment for learning tool seems to have fostered students' reflection on their learning and provides new insights into using it in Higher Education.

REFERENCES

[Ade 10] *Adell, Jordi; Castañeda, Linda (2010):* Los Entornos Personales de Aprendizaje (PLEs): una nueva manera de entender el aprendizaje. In Roig Vila, Rosabel; Fiorucci, Massimiliano (Eds.) Claves para la investigación en innovación y calidad educativas. La integración de las Tecnologías de la Información y la Comunicación y la Interculturalidad en las aulas. Stumenti di ricerca per l'innovaziones e la qualità in ámbito educativo. La Tecnologie dell'informazione e della Comunicazione e l'interculturalità nella scuola.Alcoy: Marfil – Roma TRE Universita degli studi

[Att 07] *Attwell, Graham (2007):* Personal Learning Environments – the future of eLearning? In: eLearning papers, Vol. 2. Retrieved May 2012 from *http://www.elearningpapers.eu/*

[Bas 98] *Bassey, Michael (1998):* Action Research for Improving Educational Practice. In: Halsall Robert (Ed): Teacher Research and School Improvement. Milton Keynes, UK. Open University Press, 167–178.

[Bla 09] *Black, Paul; Wiliam, Dylan (2009):* Developing the theory of formative assessment. In: Educational Assessment, Evaluation and Accountability (formerly the Journal of Personal Evaluation in Education), 21 (1), 5–31.

[Dia 91] *Diamond, C.T.Patrick (1991):* Teacher education as transformation: A psychological perspective. Milton Keynes, UK. Open University Press.

[Pre 01a] *Prensky, Marc (2001a):* Digital natives, digital immigrants. In: On the Horizon 9 (5): 1–6. Retrieved May 2014 from *http://www.marcprensky.com/writing/Prensky%20-%20Digital%20Natives,%20Digital%20Immigrants%20-%20Part1.pdf*

[Pre 01b] *Prensky, Marc (2001b):* Digital natives, digital immigrants, part 2: Do they really think differently? In: On the Horizon 9 (6): 1–6. Retrieved May 2014 from *http://www.marcprensky.com/writing/Prensky%20-%20Digital%20Natives,%20Digital%20Immigrants%20-%20Part2.pdf*

[Sch 08] *Schaffert, Sebastian; Hilzensauer, Wolf (2008):* On the way towards Personal Learning Environments: Seven crucial aspects. In: elearning Papers, Vol. 9. Retrieved May 2012 from *http://www.elearningpapers.eu/*

[Ste 75] *Stenhouse, Lawrence (1975):* An Introduction of Curriculum Research and Development. London. Heineman.

[Tra 09] *Tracey, Ryan (2009):* Instructivism, constructivism or connectivism? Retrieved June 2011 from *http://ryan2pointo.wordpress.com/2009/03/17/instructivism-constructivism-or-connectivism/*

[Wil 09] *Wild, Joanna; Wild, Fridolin; Kalz, Marco; Specht, Marcus; Hofer, Margit (2009):* The Mupple Competence Continuum. In: Second International Workshop on Mashup Personal Learning Environments, 4th EC-TEL Conference. Nice. France.

FIGURES

CONTACT DETAILS

Carmen Arbonés
Departament de Didàctica de la Llengua i la Literatura
Facultat de Formació del Professorat
Universitat de Barcelona – Campus Mundet
P. de la Vall d'Hebron 171
08035 Barcelona
Phone: +34 (0)934 035 079
E-Mail: *carbones@ub.edu*

Isabel Civera
Departament de Didàctica de la Llengua i la Literatura
Facultat de Formació del Professorat
Universitat de Barcelona – Campus Mundet
P. de la Vall d'Hebron 171
08035 Barcelona
Phone: +34 (0)934 035 079
E-Mail: *icivera@ub.edu*

Neus Figueras
Departament de Didàctica de la Llengua i la Literatura
Facultat de Formació del Professorat
Universitat de Barcelona – Campus Mundet
P. de la Vall d'Hebron 171
08035 Barcelona
Phone: +34 (0)934 035 079
E-Mail: *neusfigueras@ub.edu*

Cristina Montero
Departament de Didàctica de la Llengua i la Literatura
Facultat de Formació del Professorat
Universitat de Barcelona – Campus Mundet
P. de la Vall d'Hebron 171
08035 Barcelona
Phone: +34 (0)934 035 079
E-Mail: *cristina_montero@ub.edu*

Salvador Rodríguez
Departament de Didàctica de la Llengua i la Literatura
Facultat de Formació del Professorat
Universitat de Barcelona – Campus Mundet
P. de la Vall d'Hebron 171
08035 Barcelona
Phone: +34 (0)934 035 079
E-Mail: *srodriguezalm@ub.edu*

Theresa Zanatta
Departament de Didàctica de la Llengua i la Literatura
Facultat de Formació del Professorat
Universitat de Barcelona – Campus Mundet
P. de la Vall d'Hebron 171
08035 Barcelona
Phone: +34 (0)934 035 079
E-Mail: *theresazanatta@ub.edu*

Personal Learning Environments for Inquiry-Based Learning

Alexander Mikroyannidis, Alexandra Okada, Peter Scott

ABSTRACT

Personal Learning Environments (PLE) have recently emerged as a novel approach to learning, putting learners in the spotlight and providing them with the tools for building their own learning environments according to their specific learning needs and aspirations. This approach enables learners to take complete control over their learning, thus supporting self-regulated and independent learning. This paper introduces a new European initiative for supporting and enhancing inquiry-based learning through Personal Learning Environments consisting of personal and social inquiry tools. This approach aims at supporting students in developing self-regulated learning skills by conducting scientific inquiries in collaboration with peers.

Introduction

Personal Learning Environment (PLE) is a facility for an individual to access, aggregate, manipulate and share digital artefacts of their ongoing learning experiences. The PLE follows a learner-centric approach, allowing the use of lightweight services and tools that belong to and are controlled by individual learners. Rather than integrating different services into a centralised system, PLEs provide learners with a variety of services and hands over control to them to select and use these services the way they deem fit [Cha 07], [Fie 10], [Wil 08].

Self-regulated learning (SRL) comprises an essential aspect of the PLE, as it enables learners to become "metacognitively, motivationally, and behaviourally active participants in their own learning process" [Zim 89]. Although psycho-pedagogical theories around SRL predicate the advent of the PLE, SRL is a core characteristic of the PLE. SRL is enabled within the PLE through the assembly of independent resources in a way that fulfils a specific learning goal. In this way, the PLE allows learners to regulate their own learning and reach their learning outcomes more efficiently and effectively [Ste 06].

Inquiry-Based Learning (IBL) follows the SRL paradigm by enabling learners to take the role of an explorer and scientist as they try to solve issues they came across and that made them wonder, thus tapping into their personal curiosity. IBL supports a meaningful contextualization of scientific concepts by relating them to personal experiences. It leads to structured knowledge about a domain and to more skills and competences about how to carry out efficient and communicable research. Thus, learners learn to investigate, collaborate, be creative, use their personal characteristics and identity to have influence in different environments and at different levels (e.g. me, neighbourhood, society, world).

Learners can go through IBL workflow processes at various levels of autonomy and complexity, consequently with various degrees of support [Taf 80]. At the highest level, called 'Open Inquiry' they are only guided by self-reflection, reason and they make sense of phenomena individually or collaboratively, organize and orchestrate their (shared) activities and construct and disseminate knowledge. At the lowest level, they are completely guided by the teacher when defining a problem, choosing a suitable procedure (method) and finding a solution.

weSPOT (Working Environment with Social, Personal and Open Technologies for Inquiry Based Learning; http://wespot-project.eu) is a new European project, aiming at propagating scientific inquiry as the approach for science learning and teaching in combination with today's curricula and teaching practices. weSPOT aspires to lower the threshold for linking everyday life with science teaching in schools by technology. weSPOT supports the meaningful contextualization of scientific concepts by relating them to personal curiosity, experiences and reasoning. In short, weSPOT employs a learner-centric approach in secondary and higher education that enables students to: (1) Personalize their IBL environment via a widget-based interface; (2) Build, share and enact inquiry workflows individually and/or collaboratively with their peers.

This paper presents the weSPOT approach for supporting and enhancing inquiry-based learning through PLEs consisting of personal and social inquiry tools. This paper is structured as follows: Section 2 provides an overview of existing IBL models, as well as the IBL model that the weSPOT project has developed. Section 3 introduces the PLE-driven approach of IBL in weSPOT, followed by an inquiry scenario in Section 4. Finally, the paper is concluded in Section 5 and the next steps of this work are outlined.

Inquiry-Based Learning Models

Inquiry workflows can be described by graphical representations, whose aim is to help users visualize and orchestrate their inquiry projects. These representations are a key to personal as well as social IBL. Learners can link diverse steps of their investigation and represent their scientific reasoning by integrating graphically their questions, hypothesis, concepts, arguments and data. Inquiry workflows play an important role as visual strategy and mediating tools in scientific reasoning. As a knowledge mapping strategy, they enable users to connect and make their conceptual and procedural knowledge explicit. As a reflective aid, they provide visual guidance for users rethinking and reasoning through their graphical representations. As a visual language, they support users to make their argumentation clear for generating a coherent document outline.

The literature of Inquiry-based Science Education presents several approaches, which can be considered as templates or models for IBL. Based on John Dewey's philosophy that IBL begins with the curiosity of learners [Dew 38], several authors [Bru 02], [Whi 98] suggest a 5-step cycle of inquiry, as shown in Figure 1.

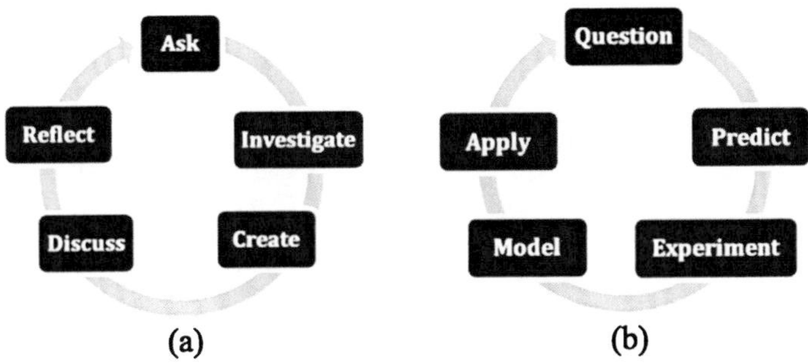

Figure 1: Five-step models by (a) [Bru 02] and (b) [Whi 98]

These steps comprise a continuous cycle for asking questions and making predictions; investigating solutions through experiments; creating new knowledge and models; applying and discussing discoveries and experiences; and reflecting on newfound knowledge and/or starting new question.

A slightly different approach proposed by [Lle 04] is a 6-step inquiry cycle (Figure 2): generating a question; brainstorming; stating a hypothesis; choosing a course of action and carrying out the investigation; gathering data for appropriate conclusions; and communicating the findings.

Figure 2: Six-step model by [Lle 04]

There is also a significant number of approaches originating from a variety of learning contexts, such as collaborative or individual inquiry; real or simulated environment;

curriculum guided or not. [Mur 07] proposes 7 steps of inquiry for implementation in groups and integration of investigation to the curriculum (Figure 3).

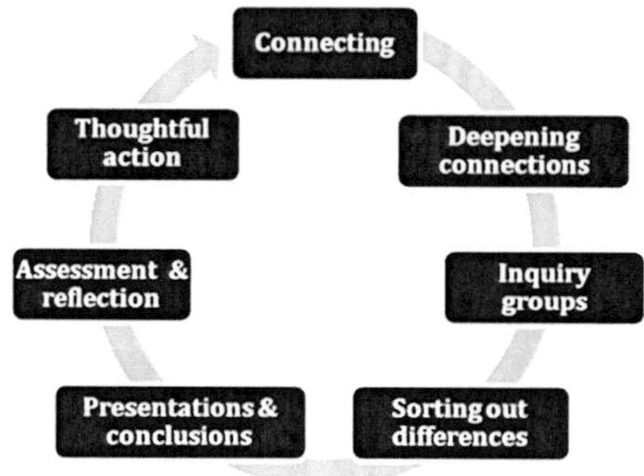

Figure 3: Seven-step inquiry cycle by [Mur 07]

[Mul 2012] highlight the inquiry cycle based on an 8-phase model, comprised by initial topic selection, communication of findings and reflection upon the method of inquiry (Figure 4).

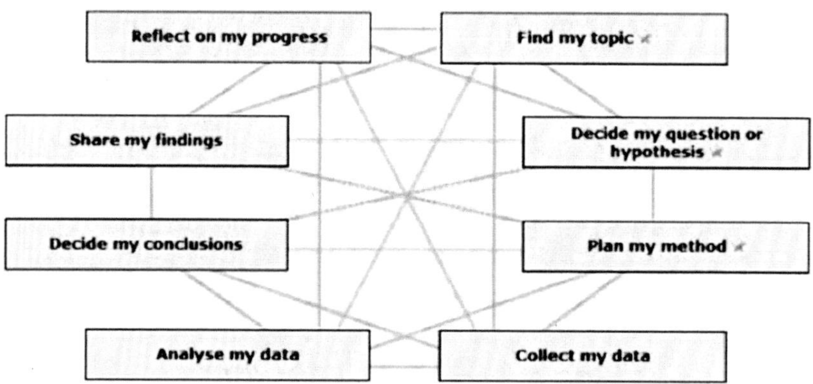

Figure 4: Eight-phase inquiry model by [Mul 12]

The weSPOT IBL model (Figure 5) moves on from the simplistic cyclical models as it aims to model the complete scientific inquiry process. The weSPOT model is based on the steps required for good research, such as data collection, data analysis, hypothesis forming, communication and dissemination of findings etc. It also shares some of the phases that [Mul 12] describe in their model, such as create a question or a hypothesis, collect data, analyse data etc., but it is more elaborate regarding the sub-phases,

providing a detailed description of tasks that teachers and students should consider when performing an inquiry [Pro 13].

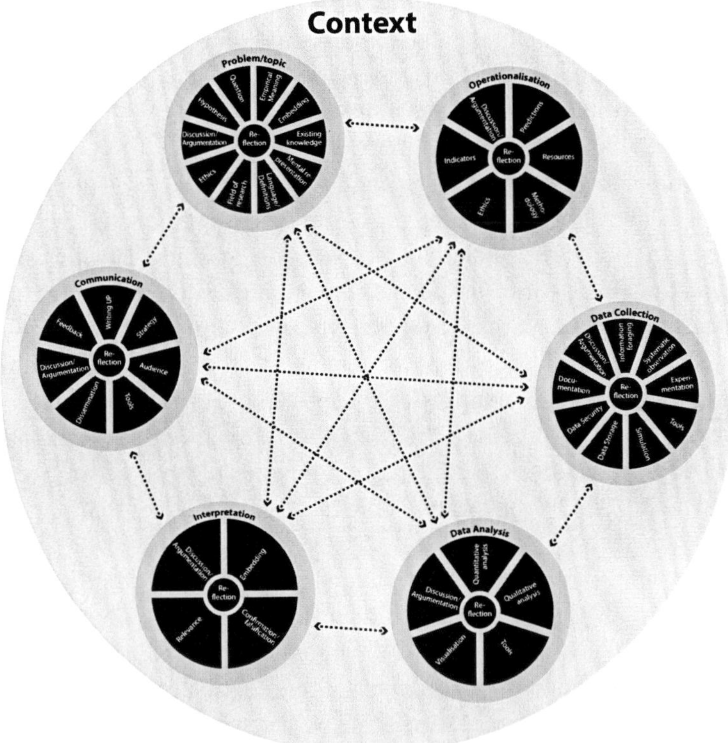

Figure 5: The weSPOT IBL model [Pro 13]

Personal and Social Inquiry in weSPOT

As we have learned from the European project ROLE (Responsive Open Learning Environments; www.role-project.eu), what is often missing from the PLE is not the abundance of tools and services, but the means for binding them together in a meaningful way [Mik 12]. weSPOT will address this issue by providing ways for the integration of data originating from different inquiry tools and services. Most importantly though, weSPOT will enable the cognitive integration of inquiry tools by connecting them with the student's profile, as well as her social and curricular context. Individual and collaborative student actions taking place within different inquiry tools will update the learning history and learning goals of the student, thus providing them and their tutors with a cohesive learning environment for monitoring their progress.

The Web 2.0 paradigm offers new opportunities for social learning by facilitating interactions with other learners and building a sense of connection that can foster trust and affirmation [Wel 09]. Social learning, according to [Hag 10], is dictated by recent shifts in education, which have altered the ways we catalyse learning and innovation. Key ingredients in this evolving landscape are the quality of interpersonal relationships, discourse, personal motivation, as well as tacit over explicit knowledge. Social media offer a variety of collaborative resources and facilities, which can complement and enrich the individual's personal learning space.

weSPOT will provide students with the ability to build their own IBL environment, enriched with social and collaborative features. Smart support tools will be offered for orchestrating inquiry workflows, including mobile apps, learning analytics support, and social collaboration on scientific inquiry. These offerings will allow students to filter inquiry resources and tools according to their own needs and preferences. Students will be able interact to with their peers in order to reflect on their inquiry workflows, receive and provide feedback, mentor each other, thus forming meaningful social connections that will help and motivate them in their learning. From a learner's perspective, this approach will offer them access to personalized bundles of inquiry resources augmented with social media, which they will be able to manage and control from within their personal learning space.

It should be noted though, that there is a significant distinction between the user-centric approach of the Web 2.0 paradigm and the learner-centric approach of weSPOT. This is because a social learning environment is not a just a fun place to hang out with friends, but predominantly a place where learning takes place and it does not take place by chance but because specific pedagogies and learning principles are integrated in the environment. Quite often, what students want is not necessarily what they need, since their grasp of the material and of themselves as learners, is incomplete [Shu 10].

In order to transform a Web 2.0 environment into a social learning environment, students need to be constantly challenged and taken out of their comfort zones. This raises the need of providing students with the affirmation and encouragement that will give them the confidence to proceed with their inquiries and investigations beyond their existing knowledge. weSPOT will address this issue through a gamification approach, by linking the inquiry activities and skills gained by learners with social media. In particular, this approach will define a badge system that will award virtual badges to students upon reaching certain milestones in their inquiry workflows. Students will then be able to display these badges in their preferred social networks. This approach will enhance the visibility and accrediting of personal inquiry efforts, as well as raise motivation, personal interest and curiosity on a mid-term effect.

PLEs for Inquiry-Based Learning: A Scenario

In this section, we present an IBL scenario in order to illustrate the personal and social approach of the weSPOT project. This scenario is concerned with the domain of microclimates, which is used within a secondary education context [Oka 08]. Microclimates are areas where the normal temperature and conditions are slightly different from the surrounding areas. The weSPOT inquiry environment is shown in Figure 6 and can be accessed at http://inquiry.wespot.net. It is has been built using the Elgg social networking framework (http://www.elgg.org). Elgg allows users to create accounts, connect with other users, work with widgets, collaboratively author content, create and join groups, as well as participate in discussion forums.

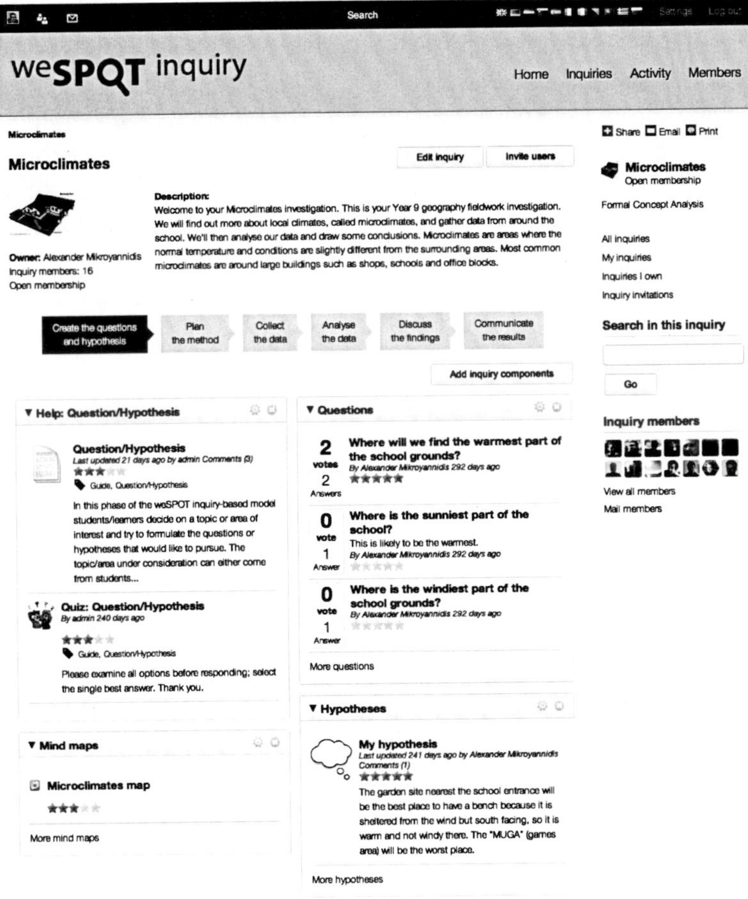

Figure 6: The weSPOT inquiry environment populated with inquiry components for the Microclimates scenario

In order to perform the Microclimates inquiry in this environment, the teacher first creates the inquiry space shown in Figure 6. By default, the inquiry space is structured according to the 6 phases of the weSPOT IBL model [Pro 13]. These phases are:

1. Question/Hypothesis
2. Operationalisation
3. Data Collection
4. Data Analysis
5. Interpretation
6. Communication

Each phase is pre-populated with a set of inquiry components, displayed as widgets. The teacher can customise each phase by adding or removing inquiry components. The available inquiry components are tailored for a particular inquiry-related task corresponding to a sub-phase of the weSPOT IBL model, e.g. data collection, data analysis, hypothesis forming, reflection, etc.

The students can then join the space that the teacher has created and start performing the inquiry by interacting with the inquiry components in collaboration with each other. The aim of the Microclimates inquiry is to find the best place to install a new bench inside the school premises. The initial hypothesis is that the best place is the garden site nearest the school entrance because it is sheltered from the wind but south facing, so it is warm and not windy there. Other places to be considered are the car park, the canteen, the games area and the reception.

As shown in Figure 6, the scientific questions proposed by the teacher are:

- Where is the windiest part of the school grounds?
- Where is the sunniest part of the school? This is likely to be the warmest.
- Where will we find the warmest part of the school grounds?

Therefore, the inquiry is based on 4 measurements: speed of wind, sunny periods, temperature and humidity. For each possible location in the school premises, the students collect data (e.g. photos) by using mobile devices that feed the collected data back to the corresponding inquiry components. The students then use the inquiry components to analyse their data (e.g. by creating graphs) and discuss their findings in discussion forums in order to reach a conclusion. The conclusion reached in this inquiry is that the reception is the best place to have a bench at the school because it is very sunny, very warm and not windy.

Conclusion

The weSPOT project is investigating IBL in secondary and higher education, in order to support students in their scientific investigations through a personal and social inquiry approach. This approach enables students to build their widget-based PLE with support from their teacher and then use this PLE collaboratively in order to perform scientific investigations together with their peers. As the project is still in its early stages, the research and technological work presented in this paper will be continued towards lowering the threshold for linking everyday life with science teaching and learning. The specific added value in lowering this threshold will be investigated through a variety of pilots in real-life learning settings within secondary and higher education, starting with the scenario presented in this paper.

Acknowledgement

The research leading to these results has received funding from the European Community's Seventh Framework Programme (FP7/2007-2013) under grant agreement N° 318499 – weSPOT project.

REFERENCES

[Bru 02] *Bruce, Bertram C.; Bishop, Ann P. (2002):* Using the Web to Support Inquiry-based Literacy Development, Journal of Adolescent and Adult Literacy vol. 45, no. 8, pp. 706–714.

[Cha 07] *Chatti, Mohamed Amine; Jarke, Matthias; Frosch-Wilke, Dirke (2007):* The future of e-learning: a shift to knowledge networking and social software, International Journal of Knowledge and Learning, vol. 3, no. 4/5, pp. 404–420.

[Dew 38] *Dewey, John (1938):* Logic – The Theory Of Inquiry, New York, USA, Henry Holt and Company.

[Fie 10] *Fiedler, Sebastian; Väljataga, Terje (2010):* Personal learning environments: concept or technology? In: Proceedings of PLE Conference, Barcelona, Spain.

[Hag 10] *Hagel, John; Seely Brown, John; Davison, Lang (2010):* The Power of Pull: How Small Moves, Smartly Made, Can Set Big Things in Motion, New York, Basic Books.

[Lle 04] *Llewellyn, Douglas (2004):* Teaching High School Science Through Inquiry: A Case Study Approach, 1st ed., Corwin Press.

[Mik 12] *Mikroyannidis, Alexander; Connolly, Teresa (2012):* Introducing Personal Learning Environments to Informal Learners: Lessons Learned from the OpenLearn Case Study. In: Proceedings of PLE Conference, Aveiro, Portugal.

[Mul 12] *Mulholland, Paul; Anastopoulou, Stamatina; Collins, Trevor; Feisst, Markus; Gaved, Mark; Kerawalla, Lucinda; Paxton, Mark; Scanlon, Elleen; Sharples, Mike; Wright, Michael (2012):* nQuire: technological support for personal inquiry learning. In: IEEE Transactions on Learning Technologies, vol. 5, no. 2, pp. 157–169.

[Mur 07] *Murdoch, Kath (2007):* A basic overview of the Integrated Inquiry planning model. Date Accessed: 31/01/2013, *http://www.inquiryschools.net/page10/files/Kath Inquiry.pdf*.

[Oka 08] *Okada, Alexandra (2008):* Scaffolding School Pupils' Scientific Argumentation with Evidence-Based Dialogue Maps. In: Knowledge Cartography: Software tools and mapping techniques, Alexandra Okada, Simon Buckingham Shum and Tony Sherborne, Eds., London, UK Springer, pp. 131–162.

[Pro 2013] *Protopsaltis, Aristidis; Hetzner, Sonia; Held, Paul; Seitlinger, Paul; Bedek, Michale; Kopeinik, Simone; Rusman, Ellen; Firssova, Olga; Specht, Marcus; Haimala, Fotini; Kikis-Papadaki, Kathy; Okada, Alexandra; Mikroyannidis, Alexander; Scott, Peter (2013):* Pedagogical and Diagnostic Framework. In: weSPOT project deliverable.

[Shu 10] *Shum, Simon Buckingham; Ferguson, Rebecca (2010):* Towards a social learning space for open educational resources. In: Proceedings of 7th Annual Open Education Conference (OpenED2010), Barcelona, Spain, November 2–4.

[Ste 06] *Steffens, Karl (2006):* Self-Regulated Learning in Technology-Enhanced Learning Environments: lessons of a European peer review. In: European Journal of Education, vol. 41, no. 3/4, pp. 353–379.

[Taf 80] *Tafoya, Estelle; Sunal, Dennis; Knecht, Paul (1980):* Assessing Inquiry Potential: A Tool For Curriculum Decision Makers. School Science and Mathematics, vol. 80, no. 1, pp. 43–48.

[Wel 09] *Weller, Martin (2009):* Using learning environments as a metaphor for educational change. On the Horizon, vol. 17, no. 3, pp. 181–189.

[Whi 98] *White, Barbara; Frederiksen, John (1998):* Inquiry, Modeling, and Metacognition: Making Science Accessible to All Students. Cognition and Instruction, vol. 16, no. 1, pp. 3–118.

[Wil 08] *Wilson, Scott (2008):* Patterns of personal learning environments. Interactive Learning Environments, vol. 16, no. 1, pp. 17–34.

[Zim 89] *Zimmerman, Barry (1989):* A Social Cognitive View of Self-Regulated Academic Learning. Journal of Educational Psychology, vol. 81, no. 3, pp. 329- 339.

FIGURES

CONTACT DETAILS

Dr. Alexander Mikroyannidis
Knowledge Media Institute, The Open University
Milton Keynes MK7 6AA, United Kingdom
E-Mail: *A.Mikroyannidis@open.ac.uk*

Prof. Peter Scott
Knowledge Media Institute, The Open University
Milton Keynes MK7 6AA, United Kingdom
E-Mail: *Peter.Scott@open.ac.uk*

Dr. Alexandra Okada
Knowledge Media Institute, The Open University
Milton Keynes MK7 6AA, United Kingdom
E-Mail: *A.L.P.Okada@open.ac.uk*

New Potentials of Hypermedia Video for Gathering and Providing of Procedural 'Knowledge' in Industrial Environments

Robert Strzebkowski, Alexander Schulz-Hyen, Sven Spielvogel, Sebastian Riedel

ABSTRACT

In this paper we describe the idea and the current development of the running project VIWITRA – visually based knowledge transfer – short title. In the scope of this project, a collaborative media platform for documentation and instruction of procedural/implicit knowledge for technician staff in service and construction working areas in the industry field will be implemented. The aim is to provide for this target group a media tool and platform for most possible easy usage and self-production of interactive video-based and with multimedia content hyperlinked instructions. This paper outlines main reasons, approaches and current developments of the project.

Background and Requirements

We have been experiencing for years many changes in the industry and services sector caused by the increasing speed in the innovation process and still higher frequency by the appearance of new technical solutions, machines and engines models, in the introduction of new work concepts as well as due to the use of the modern communication technologies and infrastructures [Tid 09]. The national and world wide process of globalization of product manufacturing, sales and services are building the second important aspect of modern industry and services [Mar 12]. This development leads to a higher frequency of exchanges of industry goods by customers because of new or updated machine/engine models, parts and technical solutions.

Customers worldwide estimate the same goods from the same company and as possible fast service for changing, installing or repairing of technical systems. Through the common use of a wide range of Internet based services in the private as well as in the business sector, customers expect transparent and fast services.

Consequently the manufacturers of industry goods require a global network of service staff with most fast possible reaction to the service demands of the customer.

This challenge requires in turn as fast as possible training and knowledge acquisition of the service staff in the global service network [Cog 99]. The service and construction tasks are mostly action-oriented activities, in which the processes of assembling, disassembling and reassembling of engines and technical modules are mostly required. For the accomplishment of such action-oriented tasks the availability of so called 'procedural' knowledge is required[Der 90]. This kind of knowledge can be best acquired directly in the task situation, when performing task activities and most effectively with the help of an experienced colleague, who can coach and support the learning process with some hints if needed [McL 96]. This is so long the most ideal situation for the acquisition of procedural knowledge. In the time of increasing diversity of products and technologies as well as the speed of their changes there is (a) still less time and money for such 'ideal' training situations with the presence of a coaching 'master/wizard colleague' and (b) the difficulty to know exactly each engine part and each 'move' for assembling/disassembling due to the increasing range of products and their parts.

The industry-oriented services have been using for several years increasingly electronic and online documents and instructions or manuals to help the technicians onsite with the service tasks [Lan 13]. But there is a problem with the 'traditional kind' of documentation: it is not very appropriate for the instruction for action-oriented tasks, in particular for quite complex assembling and disassembling activities. The problem is in the two-dimensional and still-picture based presentation of the service activities. For someone who has ever tried to master the quite easy assembling task with a piece of IKEA furniture, it is easy to understand the problem of recognition of the right parts and the right view angle of the furniture piece.

There is needed a very special kind of instructional pictures, which have to be produced by graphic designers, and tested at high cost. Additionally by the high frequency of technical changes, such traditional print-based instructions are probably no more up to date by the time of their availability. Good pictographic instruction, like IKEA is 'profitable' if the company is selling thousands of pieces with the same instruction or the instruction belongs to a complex engine or system which is again expensive and is changing rather slowly, e.g. airplanes or ships. There still remains the question if the still-picture based instruction is the appropriate instruction method for the industrial tasks with focus on construction, installation and repair of engines and machines.

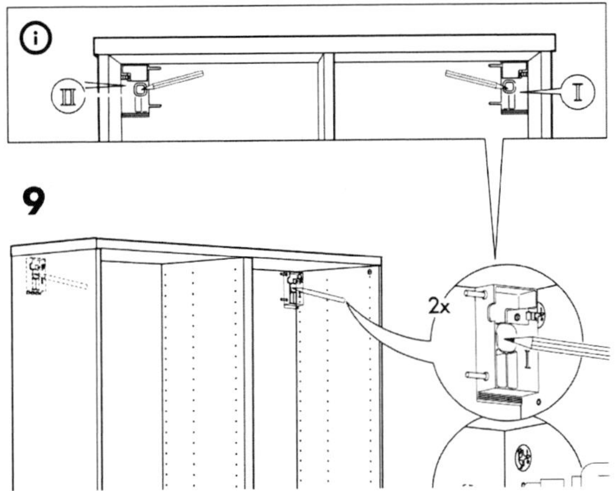

Figure 1: A part of a current IKEA assembling instruction © IKEA [IKE 13]

It is quite obviously that motion pictures are well suited for the presentation of action-oriented tasks [Zha 05]. Motion pictures can show activities as coherent action scenes without interruption. Through the presentation of different points of view, perspectives and close-ups they can substitute the three-dimensional view as well as the eye and head movements [Sal 94] Imagine at this point a small future situation, in which the exemplary IKEA assembling instruction is placed not on paper or traditional PDF document but on a kind of flexible OLED screen and the assembling scenes are video filmed. Do you think it could help with the assembling procedure?

On the Internet, e.g. YouTube, but also in different hardware stores (e.g. BUAHAUS in Germany), there is increasing number of professional and private made instructional videos for installation and repair activities for a wide range of different objects, e.g. cars repairs, house or flat construction, exchange of bath/kitchen appliances and furniture etc.

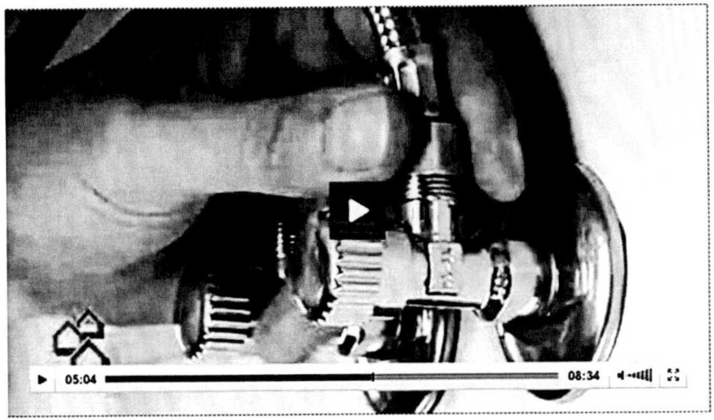

Figure 2: Screenshot from an installation video for bath objects © www.bauhausinfo.de [Bau 13]

On the other hand, there is a well known result from the multimedia research that only video based presentation is not sufficient for instruction of tasks like assembling and installation of complex machines or engines with many different mechanically parts. What is needed are exact descriptions and numbers of parts, interfaces and their parameters. Despite of the great possibilities of a video picture, focus points like arrows or oval shapes are needed to guide the look of the user to the right place and the right object on the screen. This presentation and information requirements leads more in the direction of a multimedia system, but with video as a major presentation format. A so called 'complementary' presentation forms cause most effective information perception and processing [Sch 94].

Nowadays we have been experiencing an enormous change in the possibilities to get a video online or take it mobile with us. But also to record a video sequence or take a photograph as well as to make some easy editing of media. Each smartphone today provides this functionality. But also the new video or photo cameras, which are available in a very handy size, can take both picture formats and do some editing. Especially with the new mobile media and computer equipment like smartphones, tablets or small laptops there are new possibilities for easy and fast production of media.

The number of people, which are active using the built in media functionalities of their mobile devices are exponentially growing [BIT 13].

Figure 3: iMovie™ video editing Application on Apple's iPhone™ [App 13]

Hence, there is also growing an important experience not only for use of the new media devices but often also to manage the media data in different offline or online media editing or database applications like iPhoto™, Picassa™, YouTube™.

The service staff have been increasingly using mobile devices for electronic documentation like PDF. Most of them are using additionally mobile devices in the private time to make private media – photographs or video. If we combine those device and

media skills, there is a new possibility to produce video and photograph-based documentation and instruction by the construction and service staff themselves.

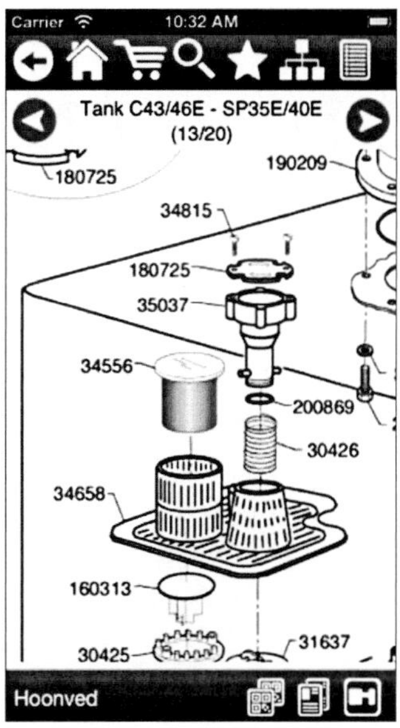

Figure 4: Left – Screenshot from the iPhone App 'Hoonved – Service Manual' [Hoo 13]

Very often such installing and repairing process knowledge will be taken from a company with the moment of the retirement of employees. And it is still difficult to 'safe' this knowledge. Furthermore there are also some constraining aspects of producing instructional media or to safe the procedural knowledge through an externally producer or video team: the production costs, the production time, the understanding of the knowledge domain and the fastest possible availability of such media documents. The majority of document and instruction systems or software do not allow to complement and to modify media directly at the appropriate place inside the document through the staff themselves. But through the availability of the mobile devices with their multimedia production tools there is a great opportunity for completion and updating of the existing documents with pictures, video sequences, text or audio.

The exponential growth and availability of broadband infrastructure allows more and more to provide access of such updated documents and media files online. Also the modifications made by the employees themselves on-site can be integrated immediately after the modification is made into the company's media and documentation system or network. Thereby the service technicians could work with newest and updated state of the documentation and instruction. At this point, an enormous motivation effect can be expected if the employees can produce and modify the instructional content or documented work activities by themselves. One can speak in this case about a 'collaborative documentation and instruction' process.

The available broadband network whether per WiFi or per UMTS/LTE let the employees also stream live video and voice either to the help desk or to an another service colleague which is not on-site to share and discuss the current problem and the possible solutions like per Skype™. The 'video conferencing' possibility is already saving time and money in the traditional business. Those advantages can be also expected.

Approach(es)

The project is titled: *"Development of a web based software framework for the production of multimedia and didactically correct instructions for visually knowledge transfer in the industry – ViWiTra"*. The platform will provide tools and functionalities for the production as well as for the online and offline presentation of video based step-by-step instructions for construction, installing and service tasks.

The most important requirement is the simplicity in the functionality of the platform and the integrated tools, so that the employees can use it in a very simple and intuitive manner. Therefore we are focusing on the presentation side on the usage of tablet devices, which can be controlled easily with the Single- & Multi-Touch technique with one or two fingers. The media platform VIWITRA will provide a wide range of functionalities, with aspects and approaches, which are related to the above mentioned requirements.

The Interactive Motion Picture Approach

As mentioned above, the main presentation form in the VIWITRA system is video. The video sequences show the assembling or dissembling activities and they are divided into short steps, so each particular action could be fast and easy realised, understood and reproduced.

The segmentation of the whole installation process in particular steps brings also the advantage of easy navigation and play functionality. The user does not need to care about the problem with pause, stop and seek for replay the needed part of the video, what is the common usage pattern by the traditional video players and portals like YouTube or also by the specialized portals like hardware stores.

The step-based interactivity is also necessary for the choice of the right branch in the video sequences because the engines can be configured with different parts or modules like a car with different engines and interiors.

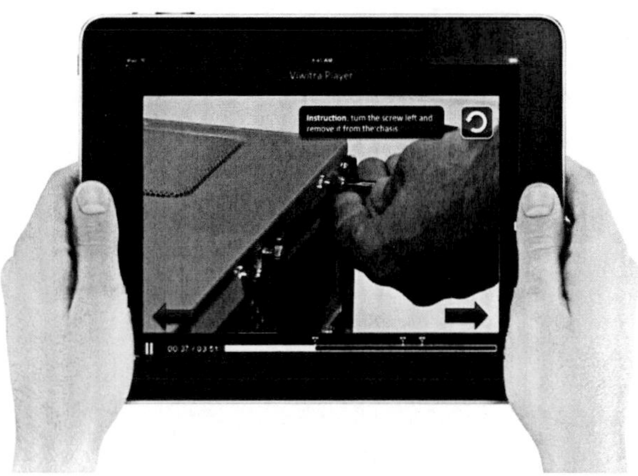

Figure 5: Draft of the VIWITRA player with work instructions

The Safety Approach

Despite the choice of the right parts and the right related video sequence there is implicit associated the safety for preserving damage of the given engine, but above all to preserve the employees from health or body damages.

Figure 6: Draft of the VIWITRA player with the danger information and confirmation functionality for removing the power cable

There are lot of dangerous work situations during installation, construction or repair activities in an industrial environment, which could be caused by electric power, heat, moving parts or aggressive chemical substances etc. For the whole service activity as well as in particular in each step there will be indicated the possible dangerous reasons and there will be presented appropriate protective activities as well as cloths like gloves or glasses to avoid any human damage. At this point we have the possibility to provide the next video sequence in conditional manner first by confirmation through the employee e.g. for wearing the required protective cloths.

The Self-Production of Media and the Collaboration Approach

One of the main goals of the VIWITRA media system is the possibility for the employees in the installation and service work area to produce the interactive video-based instructional material on their own. This approach should lead to a much faster production time of instructional media and much more up-to-date content. Other aspects include the direct transfer of procedural knowledge and the production 'from specialist to novice' an important one. Probably this leads to more authenticity of the content and reduces the 'knowledge transformation gap' between the experienced technician, the media producer and hence the new specialist as user.

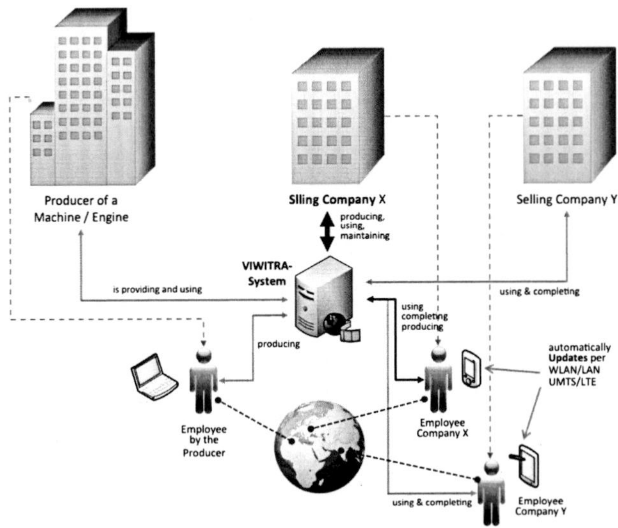

Figure 7: The collaboration approach of the VIWITRA platform

The production chain can be very different. Usually or ideally should the producer of a machine or engine produce the original installation and service instruction material. If such media do not exist, the selling or installing/service company could produce the video-based instruction.

The VIWITRA platform will allow the registered users (e.g. employees) from different companies, to complete, extend or to improve the existing instruction. The collaborative work especially trough the modification and updating of the content could foster the installation or service processes, because the missing information could be fast completed.

The important aspect is again to provide tools for comments and completions in most simple way like with a photo or video accomplished with an audio comment or short text.

Figure 8: Draft of the collaborative made completions and notices

The self-production approach brings an additionally important aspect of a more conscious reflection on the work process. There is a well-known phenomena: during the preparation of training or educational material a strong reflection processes about the learning material takes place. This reflection activity could reveal eventually existing problems of the installation or reparation processes. The detected difficulties in the work processes could flow back to the engineers of the product to improve the technology or just the placing of the parts within a system. The produced video sequences could help the engineers of the machines get access to a great 'experience base' with filmed installation or service activities how the technician colleagues in the service are dealing with the constructional guidelines and circumstances. In this way a collaborative 'Knowledge Base' about the work processes, problem issues and appropriate tools, machine parts could be established .

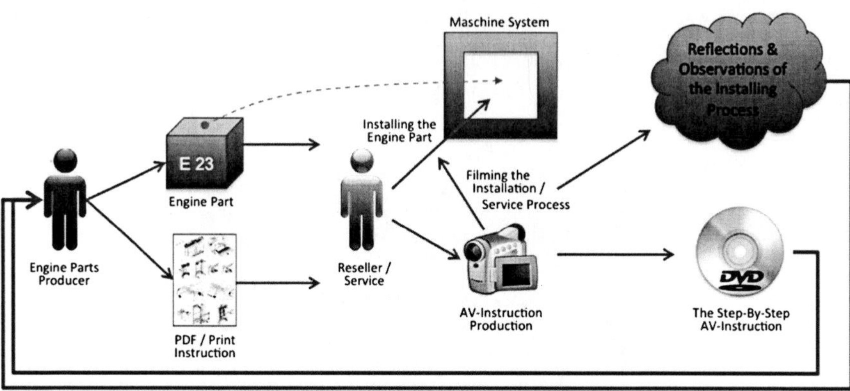

Figure 9: The reflecting and feedback process during the media production phase and through the visualized work steps

The collaboration approach is referring also to the real-time video-based communication for the collaborative solution finding. Here a technician can communicate on-site via video streaming, show live the problem point at the machine and share this moving picture either with a central help desk or with a colleague. It is foreseen, that the collaboration participants can draw on the video picture to point the 'problem' areas, like a 'video-based white board'.

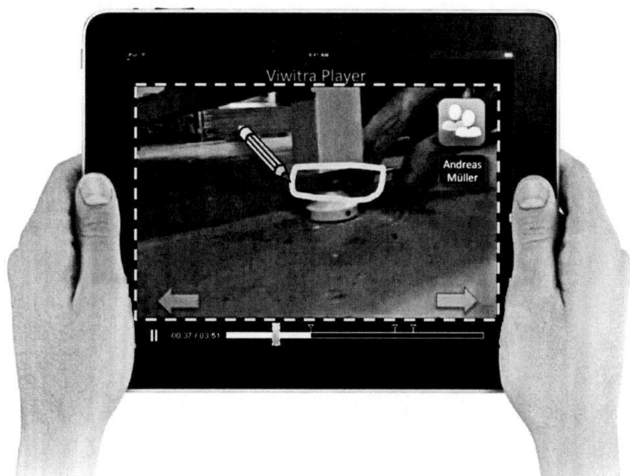

Figure 10: Draft of the live video streaming based collaboration in which two employees observe the same video picture and can draw on it

The Hypermedia Approach

The hypermedia approach is quite old. However, with the availability of the newest technologies implemented by the mobile devices and the very easy user interface based on finger gestures, this approach could experience a renaissance of interest and application. Like mentioned above there is need for additional media presentation form despite the video sequences like PDF documents, zoom-able high resolution pictures for small details, still pictures and text for example for the collaborative completions.

This additional information and content objects correspond to each video and activity step. Some few of them with crucial information or with conditional confirmations are overlaying the video picture but the most additional content is placed around the video screen to not disturb the user by viewing the video.

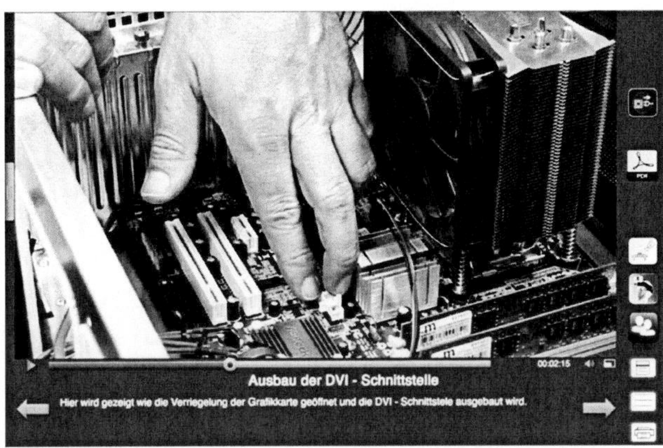

Figure 11: Hypermedia player with additional documents and information related to the current work step on the right side of the screen

The hypermedia approach should simplify the access to all needed documents and presentations of a certain work step at one place at one screen without the constraints to use of more than one media device or additionally printed documents. Every required information should be in the distance of a 'finger touch'.

The 'Didactic Template' Approach

Because the technical employees are not educated for the preparation of didactical materials like multimedia instructions, they need an effective help for this task. The VIWITRA system takes this aspect very seriously and will provide several techniques to support the technician staff. On the one hand, the VIWITRA system provides special editing tools, which should work as intuitive as possible – see the part about the 'Intuitive Tools Approach' later in this text. Especially for the production process of

the instructional material a 'template approach' will be used. It means that prepared 'instructional frameworks' will guide the production staff by the scripting and editing process of the interactive and hypermedia video. There will be two main templates: (a) for the installation and assembling process of new systems, and (b) for the service tasks which consist of disassembling, repair and reassembling activities.

For these both major processes different start points of work process will be provides, e.g. in a new installation, the environment for the machine and identification of the parts there should be first prepared; in the service/repair processes the first step should be the separation from the electric power connection etc.

The template engine will be work both: by the composition of the instruction script and by the assembling of the already made video sequences as well as directly by the filming the process activities.

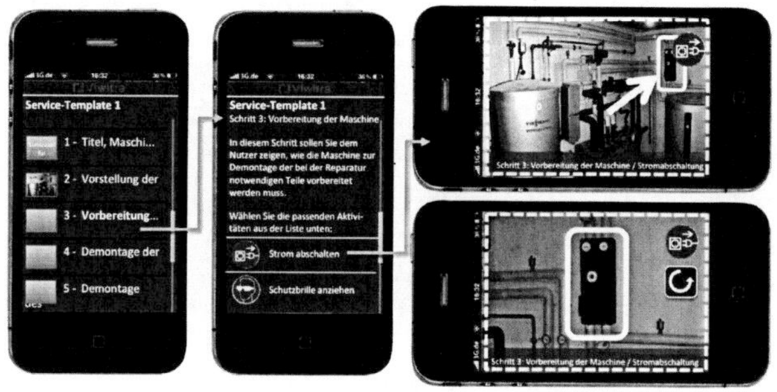

Figure 12: Draft of the Template-guided filming and assembling of a service process with the suggested steps and content sequence

Like shown in the figure above, there are not only didactic guiding steps but also the 'filming app' should support the technician employees by the choice of the right camera shot position and size. Furthermore with a VIWITRA Video-App tool, it should be easy to use – just like on the smartphone – to make the video sequences, without having to learn to handle a video camera with lot of new functionalities. Most of the employees are quite familiar with video filming with a smartphone. The VIWITRA System provides extra didactic and essential film techniques instructions for the technical employees to help them by the process of planning and compositing of the interactive and hypermedia video instructions.

The Simple and Intuitive Tool Approach

The most essential part of the VIWITRA production and presentation system for interactive hypermedia instructions is the set of editing tools to plan, edit and assemble the instruction. These tools should be as easy and as intuitive as possible, because the technical employees don't have time to learn complex tools. Therefore it is necessary in

the scope of our project to build such media production application because the existing known video editing tools like Adobe Premiere or Apple Final Cut and also the quite easy tool iMovie are often still to complex in the usage and regarding the functionality and work process not prepared for the requirements of step-by-step hypermedia instructions in the industry field.

There are four editing modules in the VIWITRA System: (a) the clip & timeline editor, (b) the sequence editor, (c) the overlay and asset editor, and (d) the player module. These tools are integrated in one application. The main approach of the editing tools is to provide all the necessary information by the creation process most possible seamless at the same place, but also with the flexibility to focus on certain tools and information more than on others.

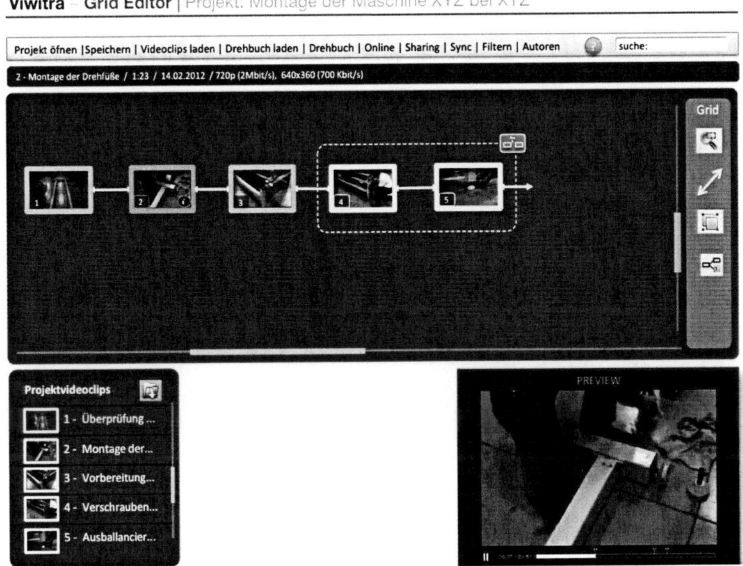

Figure 13: Example of the tool 'Sequence (Grid) Editor' with the asset manager and the video player

One of the most interesting tools is the 'sequence editor', which allows arranging video clips in a specific order and also with conditional branches with the very intuitive drag & drop technology (Figure 13).

Results

The VIWITRA project is still work in progress. All main editing tools are realised in the basic functionality. Because of the development status the usability evaluation process is now starting.

There have been discussions with some industry and vocational education companies and all of them see a very promising solution to produce and use video based interactive instruction content as well as to preserve the implicit activity-based knowledge with such easy to use tools.

Conclusions

Because of the current development status of the project without evaluation of the usage of the system, we can only provide a hypothetic conclusions at this time. Based on the experience and the theory background in following areas: usage of modern mobile devices, video as an appropriate presentation format for procedural and implicit knowledge, the need for instruction support in the installation and service area, for providing easy to use and supportive, guiding editing tools, for providing instructional information in easy steps with hypermedia linked information and for supplying collaboration, the VIWITRA platform should lead to a very helpful authoring as well as instructional environment for multimedia instructions for action-based implicit knowledge.

Acknowledgements

This project was initiated from the company docuserve GmbH in Hamburg (under the former company's leadership until September 2012 and the initiative of Robert Moeller) and is being now realized in cooperation with the company Modern Learning GmbH from Berlin. The Project is funded by the German Federal Ministry of Economics and Technology in the scope of the funding program ZIM (Central Innovation Program for the Mid Tier).

REFERENCES

[App 13] *Apple iMovie. Retrieved Mai 2013 from: http://www.apple.com/de/apps/imovie*

[Bau 13] *Bauhaus. Retrieved Mai 2013 from: http://www.bauhaus.info/interaktiv/bauhaus-tv/montage-eines-waschbeckens/index.html*

[BIT 13] *BITKOM (2013):* Smartphones werden zur Urlaubskamera, Retrieved Mai 2013 from: *http://www.bitkom.org/files/documents/BITKOM_Presseinfo_Urlaub_Kamera_17_06_2013.pdf*

[Cog 99] *Cogburn, Derrick L. (1999):* Globalization, Knowledge, Education and Training in the Information Age: *http://www.unesco.org/webworld/infoethics_2/eng/papers/paper_23.htm*, Mai 2013

[Der 90] *Derry, S. (1990):* Learning Strategies for Acuiring Useful Knowledge. In: Jones, B.F.; Idol, L. Dimensions of Thinking and Cognitive Instruction. The North Central Educational Laboratory, Lawrence Erlbaum Associates, Inc., Hilsdale, NJ., p. 347–379

[Hoo 13] *Hoonved App, Apple App Store. Retrieved Mai 2013 from: https://itunes.apple.com/de/app/hoonved-service-manual/id605755720?l=en&mt=8*

[IKE 13]: *IKEA. Retrieved Mai 2013 from: http://www.ikea.com/ms/de_DE/customer_service/assembly_instructions/assembly_instructions_splash.html*

[Lan 13] *Landgraf, Evelyn; Kluger, Reinhard (2013):* Fit for Mobile: Anlagendokumentation mit Windows und Android. Retrieved Mai 2013 from: *http://www.elektrotechnik.vogel.de/engineering-software/articles/391158*

[Mar 12] *Marsh, Peter (2012):* The New Industrial Revolution: Consumers, Globalization and the End of Mass Production. Yale University Press Publications.

[McL 96] *McLellan, Hilary (1996):* Situated Learning Perspectives. Educational Technology Publications, Englewood Cliffs, NJ.

[Sal 94] *Salomon, Gavriel (1994):* Interaction of media, cognition and learning. New Jersey, Lawrence Erlbaum Associates.

[Sch 94] *Schnotz, Wolfgang; Kulhavy Raymon W. (1994):* Comprehension of Graphics. Advances in Psychology, 108. Amsterdam, Elsevier Science B.V.

[Tid 09] *Tidd, Joe; Bessant, John (2009):* Managing Innovation: Integrating Technological, Market and Organizational Change. John Wiley & Sons Ltd., Chichester.

[Zha 05] *Zhang, Dongsong; Zhou, Lina; Briggs, Robert O.; Nunameker, Jay F. (2005). Instructional video in e-learning:* Assessing the impact of interactive video on learning effectiveness. Elsevier B.V., Retrieved Mai 2013 from *www.sciencedirect.com*, *http://www.qou.edu/arabic/researchProgram/eLearningResearchs/instructional.pdf*

CONTACT DETAILS

Prof. Dr. Robert Strzebkowski
Beuth University of Technology Berlin
Luxemburger Straße 10, 13353 Berlin (Germany)
Phone: +49 (0)30 4504 5212
E-Mail: *robertst@beuth-hochschule.de*

Alexander Schulz-Hyen
Beuth University of Technology Berlin
Luxemburger Straße 10, 13353 Berlin (Germany)
Phone: +49 (0)30 4504 2282
E-Mail: *a.schulzheyn@gmail.com*

Sven Spielvogel
Beuth University of Technology Berlin
Luxemburger Straße 10, 13353 Berlin (Germany)
Phone: +49 (0)30 4504 2282
E-Mail: *spielvogel@beuth-hochschule.de*

Sebastian Riedel
Beuth University of Technology Berlin
Luxemburger Straße 10, 13353 Berlin (Germany)
Phone: +49 (0)30 4504 2282
E-Mail: *sebastian.riedel@outlook.com*

Personal Information Spaces are the students' first and foremost PLE

Sharon Hardof-Jaffe, Rafi Nachmias

ABSTRACT

Personal Learning Environment (PLE) is a term that usually describes a tailor-made environment, software or concept, for students. In this paper we would suggest that while users manage personal information items in various personal information spaces, they are tailoring their own PLE using many tools, environments and spaces. We present findings on the role of personal information spaces in students' learning tasks and the relationships between the different tasks and the personal information space characteristics.

Introduction

Today, information access has become a centric interaction in our everyday lives. Increasingly, mobile tools allow us to retrieve and use our information items anytime and anywhere. People find, save and organize various information items in their own personal information spaces during work, learning and leisure tasks [Jon 08]. Personal information management is a term which describes all the activities users perform in order to organize their personal information items, in order to retrieve them later in time [Ber 03]. PIM, as it was later defined, "is intended to support the activities that we, as individuals, perform in order to structure our daily lives through the acquisition, organization, maintenance, retrieval, and sharing of information" [Tee 06]. Personal information spaces are varied collections of information items which the user saves and organizes over the years [Bru 05]. These spaces are personal, not merely by virtue of them belonging to one specific person, but also because they are personal and the organizational principals of personal information spaces are highly subjective. The users' subjective approach to personal information management suggests and shows evidence that users manage personal information items based on three subjective principles: the relevance of the items, the project to which they relate, and the context [Ber 03] [Ber 08]. In the learning context, personal information space is the place where students save and manage their learning material and tasks, and create continuously growing personal information archive of information items which are related to learning the subject matter. In a previous pilot study we suggested that PIM activities have the potential to become a continuous process of knowledge construction which requires sorting, naming, classifying and categorizing skills [Har 11]. In this paper we

show that personal information spaces are the centric environment of learners' lives today and we present findings about the functional, cognitive and affective roles of the personal information space in learning tasks.

Background

Personal Information Management

PIM is a research field that emerged at the end of the 20 century and over the last ten years it has moved to the forefront of information science research interest, since the users' challenges are continuously expanding and many difficulties have emerged as a result of the many PIM tools and PIM solutions that are available for organizing and storing personal information items on PCs, laptops, mobiles and on the web e.g. Dropbox Google docs, *box.com*, Copy [Jon 07]. Personal Information Management (PIM) is the activity by means of which users save and organize information in order to retrieve it at another time [Ber 03]. PIM supports users in organizing everyday information activities – saving, collecting, categorizing, retrieving and sharing [Bar 95], [Lan 95], [Bel 02], [Tee 06], [Jon 07]. There are three main actions that take place in PIM: Saving – all activities performed by users in order to keep new information items, Retrieving – all activities users perform in order to find and re-find information items, and Meta-level actions – cultivating and organization activities e.g. filing, classifying and categorizing, naming and deleting.

At first PIM studies examined activities in various collections, E-Mails, files, images and favorites in order to reveal PIM users' goals, PIM behavior, PIM strategies and the personal information spaces structures [Mal 83], [Whi 96], [Abr 98], [Fis 06]. Later on, PIM was examined in wider contexts using crosstools, and the first studies to apply crosstools exposed the difficulties of PIM users, PIM strategies, and PIM organization principals, as well as the main appreciation that PIM is totally different from information organization in libraries or other public archives [Boa 04], [Ber 03; 08]. The PIM organization principals are based on subjective parameters. The user-subjective approach puts forward three attributes of personal information management: the Project Attribute, which is a user-subjective classification based on the user's projects; the Importance Attribute, which is the organization of items according to their importance and relevance to the user; and the Context Attribute where a user saves and retrieves his information items according to the context in which he uses them. The same item can be used by different users in several contexts [Ber 03], [Ber 08]. Today, PIM is becoming a more and more complex activity, since new tools and technologies appear keep appearing, thus enabling PIM to be used with cloud computing and mobile devices. Users manage much more than three collections and, in addition to their information items, they have to manage many tools and applications. These new tools, add more complexities to the personal information space structure, and studies have shown that the challenges regarding the new tools continuously grow [Berg 12], [Kim, 12]. Kim suggests a new approach to PIM – the Behavioral approach – this approach places the emphasis on teaching and guiding users – instead of solving their problems – using new and better tools.

Users organize their personal information items for various purposes: work, studies or leisure [Boa 04]. Users also manage personal information items in order to create a legacy, to share resources, to confront fears and anxieties, as well as for identity construction [Kay 06]. Moreover, users utilize the folder structure in order to understand their project and its components [Jon 05] and to help make decisions and acquire a sense of ownership [Pra 06]. Another new term that has arisen over the past three years is the personal information curation, in the sense of art curation [Whi 11]. Users do not just save, organize and retrieve; they also keep the information for long periods of time, and make an effort to organize them in useful ways so that they will be able to exploit them in the future. The information exploitation is the result of the saving and organizing activities. The shift in the term from personal information consumption to personal information curation highlights two trends in the use of personal information: the first is saving and organizing information items with no specific use – users keep information items which are interesting or might be useful to a future project, or they have some importance to them. The second trend is sharing activities – more and more users permit others to access their personal information items, and expose and share information items; sharing has become an important consideration in PIM organization strategies and tools [Mar 06], [Whi 11]. Personal information curation includes the goal of presenting the information in the same way as presenting art works at exhibitions. Curation includes saving, maintaining and adding value information by metadata which describes the item [Dar 08], [Eip 10]. It also means that the users give an interpretation and value to the items he chooses to keep or share.

Studies indicate that PIM requires a great deal of time and effort [Klj 04], and involves cognitive aspects [Lan 88], [Whi 96], [Jon 05]. PIM activities also have an affective aspect: users' feelings: guilt, frustration and dissatisfaction, alongside a sense of confidence, satisfaction and a sense of ownership [Bel 00], [Boa 04], [Mar 06], [Jon 08]. One's PIM characteristics are influenced by many factors: the context, the tasks types, the tools, item contents etc. [Bar 95], [Boa 04], [Gwi 07].

Personal information learning spaces

Personal information spaces are collections of information items that users save and organize over the years [Bru 05]. Personal information space contains information items, tools, and applications. On the other hand [Jon 08] defines personal information as: information which is owned by the user, information about the user, information that is directed at the user, information that is sent by the user, information the user uses or any information that is relevant or useful to him. Personal information space includes not only information that is controlled by the user but also information

that is about the user and controlled by others. For example, health information or information about bank accounts. In the learning context, a good example would be the student's grades. This information is related to the user and he can access it via a user name and password, but he cannot manage the space where the information is located. Personal information space is a collection of complex varied information items where each collection has common denominators, such as the item format, item subject, goals, environment, etc. For example, the collection of correspondence is in the E-Mail, the learning items are in the laptop folders, the items from the collaborative assignments are in Google drive, or in the drop box, the picture collection is in Picasa. These collections are islands of personal information where users have control over what they contain and how they are organized [Jon 08]. Today, thanks to cloud computing technologies and mobile devices, personal information spaces are available to users anytime and anywhere. We can distinguish three types of personal information spaces: 1. the personal information space on the user's PC, 2. personal information spaces on the web, which the user can access and control from any device through a user name and password, and 3. the mobile space, the information items in the Cellphone (iPhone) and tablets (e.g. iPad). In personal mobile information spaces users not only keep information items from SMS and contacts but also links and application of personal web spaces (e.g. Dropbox). Personal information spaces are characterized by continuous growth, they keep growing over time, and the habit of deleting_cannot keep up with the habit of adding information [Fis 06]. Many collections and the unlimited accessibility to them have led to changes in personal information management challenges: synchronize issues, loss_of items, feelings of loss of control over the personal items, and the need to deal with constantly new arrivals of information, even when the user is not available to deal with this new information [Ber 04], [Jon 07], [Ber 12].

Hierarchical organization tools are the most common tools used in PIM applications, e.g. desktop systems. This allows users to create personal information archives in varied information structures, according to their subjective categorization. Folders and files are arranged in a hierarchical tree structure, i.e., each item (except for the root) has a link to one parent item – with branches (folders) and leaves (files); visualizing this structure reveals the relationship between elements and groups within the repository [Mul 95], [Shn 97], [Mar 03]. Although hierarchical information structures have been criticized, mainly because of their single-inheritance principle, they have two main advantages: a) the information items are categorized into meaningful groups; b) easy retrieval – the user is able to track his location in the archive during navigation [Dou 00], [Nie 00]. Today, the strengths of the hierarchical structure are once again appreciated and new methods of automatic organization of information items suggest the benefits of categorization and convenient navigation of search results of other information structures [Yee 03], [Kak 05], [Hea 06], [Xin 08]. Users create different hierarchical structures which differ according to the depth and width of the tree, folder size and pile size. In a study that was conducted on a personal information space that was allocated to students at university, four methods of organizing information structures for personal servers were found: piling – keeping most of the files in the root directory; one folder filing – filing most of the items in one folder; small folder filing – organizing the personal information items in many small folders; and big folder filing – a combination of filing most of the documents in different folders, but still maintaining one subfolder which contains many files, i.e., a hidden pile [Har 09]. In another previous study, it was found that users prefer wide and shallow structures and that this preference is reasonable since retrieval from these structures is quicker [Ber 11].

Students' Personal Information Spaces

PIM is one of the new cornerstones of the reciprocal ever-changing processes between humans and information, a change which is characterized by the abundance of available information, information spread, hyper textual information, multiple information and multiple formats of information items [Sal 00]. [Mio 09] claimed that PIM is one of the new literacies the learner needs to acquire today [Mio 09]. They defined PIM as the process by which an individual stores his\her information items in order to retrieve them later on, and they specify the required PIM skills: giving meaningful names to information items and folders, avoiding creating folders with too few or too many information items, avoiding creating folders with too many depth hierarchal folders, putting shortcuts to information items of high relevancy to the user on the desktop, and avoiding clustering folders with irrelevant information items. [Cha 08] found that students had specific needs such as backup problems and version management. As part of their studies, the students preferred the use of "list" and "detail" over "icons" and "tiles", and relied on item names which reflected the contents. They also found two strategies in relation to the time of creating a new folder: pre-builders – students who create new folders which are planned before they produce any new item, and post builders – students who create new folders after a certain number of items have been collected. [Rob 10] found that students find that PIM is getting more complicated over time due to the rapidly changing digital formats, and that they need to adopt broad strategies to cope with their electronic and traditional print-based resources, and to integrate other emerging information formats, of personal interactions with peers, via social networking websites (Tweets, RSS, Facebook, etc.).

Furthermore, PIM activities require a cognitive process in which students create, manage and construct information archives, and acquire knowledge through a process whereby learners actively integrate new information with existing information [Har 11]. In this process the students create a personal information archive or database or, as we named it – the personal information learning items space. In personal information spaces, as time passes, the information changes according to the context of the work – items are added, items change their position and other items are deleted [Kri 04]. The personal information learning items space functions as a mediation space between the vast amount of information in the web space and the limited capacity of the human

mind [Har 11]. In a previous article we drew three information spaces with which the students interact: 1) The Public Information Space – includes information spaces on the web; these information spaces are accessible to all, or at least to many people. 2) The Inner Information Space – the information items that the student already knows, and this space includes the information items that were added to the cognitive systems as a result of the learning process. 3. The Personal Information Space – in this space the user keeps the information items that he collects from the public space as well as the information he creates from the inner space. The personal information space is the mediation space between the vast amount of information in the web space and the limited capacity of the human mind (Figure 1).

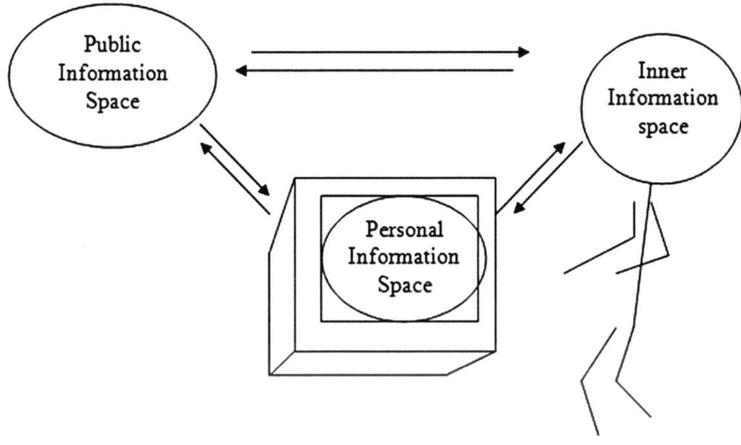

Figure 1: The information spaces in the learning process

We would like to suggest that the personal information space is the student's PLE, and it functions as mediation and a reflection of his learning activities and progress.

PLE – as a description of concepts and a software application of personal learning environments – aims to present the wide nature of PLE and its role in the learning process. The software approach goals are to offer technological solutions in terms of architecture, functionalities and services to the learner. The concept approach goals are to develop a better understanding of the nature of PLE, and to offer systematic analyses of PLE and solutions to the type of learning for which they are intended [Hen 10]. Therefore we found personal information management and the behavioral approach thereof to be of the utmost importance to any concept or tools which are developed for PLE. This study suggests examining personal information spaces as a learning environment, PLE, and to find out what the relationships are between different learning tasks and the activities the students perform in their personal information space during these tasks.

In order to understand PIM activities in learning tasks we set two main research questions: What is the role of personal information spaces in the learning process? What is the relationship between the learning environment characteristics and the students' PIM characteristics?

Methodology and results

A qualitative phenomenology method was used in this study to enable the examination of phenomena in their contexts. The study examined the phenomena as it takes place in the students' life and in their perceptions, in the way they value and experience it [Cre 98]. A phenomenology study is examining the way thing are themselves, with the aim of creating meaning out of the subjective descriptions [Wil 01]. 41 students participated in the study: 10 high school students, 15 undergraduate students and 16 postgraduate students. All the students participated in in-depth interviews in front of their personal computer. The interview included three stages: the first – focused on the history of the phenomena, the second, on details of the experience, and the third on the interviewer's reflection on the meaning of the phenomena [Sie 91]. The students described their personal information space organization and management, explaining how they managed their personal information items and showed their PIM activities from previous learning tasks.

In addition, the students demonstrated their PIM activities from 80 learning tasks. These tasks were categorized according to their types – research work, analyses, comparative work on summaries, drills and creative pieces (art, music etc.). In order to examine the students' actual activities in their personal information space data files, the list describing the files and folders (full paths) for 25 users were collected. This data was collected using a script that was written for the study. These data files included raw data describing 199,776 files and folders, of which 37,932 related to learning tasks. The data presented the personal information space sizes, structures, file numbers, folder numbers, items formats, hierarchy depth, average file per folder and the maximum and minimum number of files per folder.

The students' personal information spaces

Most of the students in the study had folders which were dedicated to their learning items; those who did not have folders were all high school students. The graduate students and the post graduate students used folders with meaningful names_(e.g. "methodology" and "contracts"), and most files were named and divided into subfolders. The students used three PIM strategies: Piling – no folders or subfolders and files were heaped on a growing pile; Filing by course – files were organized according to the course they belonged to; and Filing by subject – where files were organized according to the learning contents. 13 students (31.7 %) used the piling strategy, 18 students

(43.9%) organized their learning items in folders by courses, 10 students (24.4%) organized learning items by subjects (in addition to the filing by course strategy) and in this strategy the folder names were connected to the contents and purpose of the information items that were contained in them.

Table 1: PIM strategies by groups

	N	PILING	FILING BY COURSE	FILING BY SUBJECT
High school students	10	90% (9)	0% (0)	10% (1)
Undergraduate students	15	13.3% (2)	80% (12)	6.3% (1)
Postgraduate students	16	12.5% (2)	37.5% (6)	50% (8)
Sum	41	31.7% (13)	43.9% (18)	24.4% (10)

Most students organized their personal information learning items in one central place, others separated their items in a few spaces, knowing which different items and projects they had in each (e.g. discs, Dropbox) and only a few organized their spaces in a roundabout structure, where they separated the items in many spaces but kept a control centre – a place from where they could reach each item of information. These students had a high level of metacognitive activities in their personal information space organization, since they had classified not only the information items but they had classified their information spaces.

The role of personal information spaces in the learning task

We found that personal information spaces and the management activities play a central role in the learning process. The personal information space is the place where students are able to manage their learning material and tasks on a daily basis: "... I come home after studying...". Students organized information items from previous tasks and previous courses and their personal information spaces form an inseparable part of their learning and become a learning archive which is constructed during their years of studies. The academic students in the study attributed great importance to their personal information spaces: "I bought a computer when I was 21, since then the hard-disk goes everywhere with me... it has become my first and foremost tool" (28 year old postgraduate student). The personal information space constitutes a mediation space between the public information and their knowledge. For the students it is the place of knowledge integration: "It is like a clean piece of paper that you write on...everything comes together". It provides a place where they can interact peacefully with their information items, in a place where they know what information items they have, they own the content items and they can add and delete as they please – everything is under their control. This is a safe place, away from the density and overload of information that many students feel in public information spaces (e.g. digital archives, sites, and digital libraries). We found that personal information spaces play an affective role in learning activities; we found that they provide a sense of control and ownership over the information and the studies, and over assignments: the final submitting of assignments: "I prepare myself before the semester starts (he collects files and creates folders for the courses)", "I feel it (the files) belongs to me", "here is everything I have".

Finally, we found that personal information spaces have a cognitive role as the place which reflects the student learning contents; what he collects, what his fields of interest are: "here I do the brainstorming", "here I sort" "categorized" "it shows me my research stages". The personal information space is the place where new items are connected to previous ones, and it is the students' map of the main concepts of his study contents and tasks. Therefore, we find that over and above the functional use, the personal information space constitutes a place where the students interact with new knowledge, sort it, evaluate it and integrate it into their existing personal information archives. This is the place where students work on their learning assignments, store their information resources and integrate them into new ideas.

To sum up, we have found three main roles of personal information spaces and management in learning: 1) a learning management role, 2) a cognitive role – an archive space which reflects the learning process and facilitates thinking about the learning contents and connections of contents through metadata attributes such as file names, folder names, tags and structures, and 3) an affective role – because personal information spaces are archives over which the students feel a sense of ownership and control as well as over the organization of learning information in them.

The relationship between learning activity characteristics and PIM

We found that there are differences between the various learning tasks and their PIM characteristics; this relationship reveals differences in the number of information items (Table 2), in the information organization strategy items (Table 3) and in the importance attributed to them, as well as in the cognitive and affective aspects of PIM activities (Table 4). The prominent variable which was found to relate to the students PIM activities was the nature of the assignments. When it came to research assignments (seminars, theses etc.), students collected more information items and made more of an effort to organize the task information space: "any course and its characteristics". The students managed their personal information items differently in different learning environments according to the type of the learning tasks, the nature of interaction between the student peers and instructors, and the type of learning items. In inquiry assignments, many information items from the web, such as: articles, document links, correspondence, images, etc. were kept in particular folders, and, in some

cases, together with subfolders. In courses, which had a final test, only a few files (less than 10) appeared in the students' personal information space, since the students did not keep any digital information items relating to these courses in their computers: "courses with no assignments do not exist here".

Table 2: Number of item by task types

FREQUENCY (% from all learning tasks)	**1 ITEM**	**2–5 ITEMS**	**6–10 ITEMS**	**MORE THAN 10 ITEMS**	**MORE THAN 20 ITEMS**	**TASK TYPE**
51 (63.8%)	9 (17.6%)	13 (25.5%)	7 (13.7%)	13 (25.5%)	9 (17.6%)	Inquiry
12 (15%)	2 (16.7%)	8 (66.7%)	1 (8.3%)	1 (8.3%)	0	Analysis, comparison and summary
11 (13.8%)	1 (9.1%)	5 (45.5%)	0	5 (45.5%)	0	Test and practice/tutoring
6 (7.5%)	1 (16.7%)	3 (50%)	0	1 (16.7%)	1 (16.7%)	Creation
80 (100%)	13(16.25%)	29 (36.25%)	8 (10%)	20 (25%)	10 (12.5%)	All

Table 3: PIM goals by task types

FREQUENCY (% from all learning tasks)	**SHORT TERM FUNCTIONAL GOALS**	**LONG TERM FUNCTIONAL GOALS**	**COGNITIVE GOALS**	**TASK TYPE**
51 (63.8%)	10 (19.6%)	31 (60.8%)	10 (19.6%)	Inquiry
12 (15%)	0	11(91.7%)	1 (8.3%)	Analysis, comparison and summary
11 (13.8%)	0	11 (100%)	0	Test and practice/ tutoring
6 (7.5%)	0	6 (100%)	0	Creation
80 (100%)	10 (12.5%)	59 (73.8%)	11 (13.8%)	All

Table 4: PIM strategy by task types

FREQUENCY (% from all learning tasks)	PILING	FILING BY COURSE	FILING BY SUBJECT	TASK TYPE
51 (63.8 %)	16 (31.4 %)	26 (51 %)	9 (17.6 %)	Inquiry
12(15 %)	5 (41.7 %)	7 (58.3 %)	0	Analysis, comparison and summary
11 (13.8 %)	2 (18.2 %)	9 (81.8 %)	0	Test and practice/ tutoring
6 (7.5 %)	2 (33.3 %)	4 (66.7 %)	0	Creation
80 (100 %)	25 (31.3 %)	46 (57.5 %)	9 (11.25 %)	All

Another environment characteristic which was found to be linked to PIM behavior was collaborative tasks. When the students had to submit an assignment together, in a cooperative or in a collaborative learning process, they adjusted their PIM activities to the collaborative process and to their peers, as they needed to find common organization principals in order to share and use the same items. The wide range and diversity of PIM activities used by one student across different learning assignments, indicates that the characteristics of the learning environment have a major influence on PIM activities. This factor should be taken into consideration when planning assignments and choosing tools in the environment to work on the shared files.

Conclusions and implications

Personal information spaces are very important places that students create in order to narrow the gap between their limited capabilities – to process information and to acquire knowledge (as talented as they are) – and the wide range of information items available to them on web spaces. The research findings show that personal information spaces on laptops, DiskOnKeys, cloud spaces such as Dropbox, or Google drives, are the main personal digital environment in learning processes. These spaces play a central role in the learning process as they support functional, cognitive and affective aspects which are of great importance in learning. These spaces are becoming inseparable parts of the users today, particularly in students' everyday lives; they allow students to reflect on, evaluate, analyze and categorize the information items they have collected and to integrate them into new themes. Managing personal information spaces requires skills and these skills vary from student to student and from task to task. It is one of the most essential literacies users need nowadays, and its acquisition is vital for almost every aspect of life, e.g. work, academic life, and even leisure.

As a result of these research findings and discussions we would suggest that students choose or create a main space for their personal information management. This space will be the focal point and will function as a control center for all the personal and shared information spaces. From this center the student manage and reach all his personal spaces on the laptop, PC, discs, and on the web, and make efficient use of the varied spaces in which he collects, organizes and shares his personal information space. This main PLE center will serve all of the user's assignments and projects in formal and informal learning, and in work and leisure projects. It will provide him with a simple and controlled way of creating varied links (and passwords), and leave the choice of the organization structure, folder tags or piles to the user himself. A central place will enable students to organize and access through any device, but, more importantly, it will give students as well as their teachers a sense of the structure of their information archives and therefore a sense of the structure of the learning contents in their subjective interaction, and they will be able to use their information spaces so these spaces are a reflection of the learning process they are going through – a learning process of continuous construction of their own knowledge base.

REFERENCES

[Abr 98] *Abrams, David, Ron Baecker, Mark Chignell. (1998). Information archiving with bookmarks:* Personal web space construction and organization. Proceedings of the SIGCHI Conference on Human Factors in Computing Systems, 41-48.

[Bar 95] *Barreau, Deborah, Bonnie A. Nardi. (1995). Finding and reminding:* File organization from the desktop. ACM SigChi Bulletin, 27(3), 39-43.

[Bel] *Bellotti, Victoria, Ian Smith. (2000). Informing the design of an information management system with iterative fieldwork. Proceedings of the 3rd Conference on Designing Interactive Systems:* Processes, Practices, Methods, and Techniques, pp. 227-237.

[Ber 12] *Bergman, Ofer. (2012). The User-Subjective Approach to Personal Information Management:* From Theory to Practice. In Human-Computer Interaction: The Agency Perspective, 55-81). Springer Berlin Heidelberg.

[Ber 03] *Bergman, Ofer, Ruth Beyth-Marom, Rafi Nachmias. (2003). The User Subjective Approach to Personal Information Management Systems. Journal of the American Society for Information Science, 54(9), 872-878.*

[Ber 08] *Bergman, Ofer, Ruth Beyth-Marom, Rafi Nachmias. (2008). The user subjective approach to personal information management systems design:* Evidence and implementations. Journal of the American Society for Information Science and Technology, 59(2), 235-246.

[Ber 04] *Bergman, Ofer, Richard Boardman, Jacek Gwizdka, William Jones. (2004, April). Personal information management. In Chi'04 extended abstracts on human factors in computing systems, 1598-1599). ACM.*

[Ber 11] *Bergman, Ofer, Steve Whittaker, Mark Sanderson, Rafi Nachmias, Anand Ramamoorthy. (2011). The effect of folder structure on personal file navigation. Journal of the American Society for Information Science and Technology (JASIST), 61(12), 2300-2310.*

[Boa 04] *Boardman, Richard, M. Angela Sasse. (2004). Stuff goes into the computer and doesn't come out:* A cross-tool study of personal information management. Proceedings of the SIGCHI Conference on Human Factors in Computing Systems, 583-590.

[Bru 05] *Bruce, Harry. (2005). Personal, anticipated information need. Information Research, 10(3), 10-13.*

[Cre 98] *Creswell, John W. (1998). Qualitative inquiry and research design:* Choosing among five traditions. Sage Publications, Inc.

[Cha 08] *Chang, S., & Ko, M. (2008). Behaviors of PIM in context of thesis and dissertation research. CHI 2008 Workshop.*

[Dar 08] *Darlington, M., Steve J. Culley, Yuyang Zhao, Simon A. Austin. (2008). Defining a framework for the evaluation of information. International Journal of Information Quality, 2(2), 115-132.*

[Dou 99] *Dourish, Paul, W. Keith Edwards, Anthony LaMarca, Michael Salisbury. (1999). Presto:* An experimental architecture for fluid interactive document spaces. ACM Transactions on Computer–Human Interaction (TOCHI), 6(2), 133-161.

[Eip 10] *Eipert, Sue. (2010) Curated information:* what it means for researchers. FUMSI Magazine, 35, 9-14.

[Fis 06] *Fisher, Danyel, A. J. Brush, Eric Gleave, Marc A. Smith. (2006). Revisiting Whittaker & Sidner's "email overload" ten years later. Proceedings of the 2006 20th Anniversary Conference on Computer Supported Cooperative Work, 309-312.*

[Gwi 07] *Gwizdka, Jacek, Chignell, Mark H. (2007). Individual differences. In Jones, William, Jaime Teevan (eds.). Personal Information Management, 206-220. University of*

[Har 09] *Hardof-Jaffe, Sharon, Arnon Hershkovitz, Hama Abu-Kishk, Ofer Bergman, Rafi Nachmias. (2009). Students' organization strategies of personal information space. Journal of Digital Information.*

[Har 11] *Hardof–Jaffe, Sharon, Rafi Nachmias. (2011). Personal information management and learning. International Journal of Technology Enhanced Learning, 3(6), 570-582.*

[Hea 06] *Hearst, Marti A. (2006). Clustering versus faceted categories for information exploration. Communications of the ACM 49, 4 (Apr. 2006), 59-61.*

[Hen 10] *Henri, France, Bernadette Charlier. "Personal learning environment:* A concept, an application, or a self-designed instrument?."Information Technology Based Higher Education and Training (ITHET), 2010 9th International Conference on. IEEE, 2010.

[Huc 01] *Hutchins, Edwin. (2001). Cognition distributed. In Smelser, Neil, J. Paul B. Baltes. (eds.). International Encyclopedia of the Social and Behavioral Sciences, 2068-2072. Amsterdam:* Elsevier.

[Jon 08] *Jones, William. (2008). Keeping found things found:* The study and practice of personal information management. Burlington MA: Morgan Kaufmann.

[Jon 07] *Jones, William. (2007). Personal information management. Annual Review of Information Science and Technology, 41(1), 453-504.*

[Jon 05] *Jones, William, Ammy Jiranida Phuwanartnurak, Rajdeep Gill, Harry Bruce. (2005). Don't take my folders away!:* Organizing personal information to get things done. CHI'05 Extended Abstracts on Human Factors in Computing Systems,1505-1508.

[Kay 06] *Kaye, Joseph'Jofish, Janet Vertesi, Shari Avery, Allan Dafoe, Shay David, Lisa Onaga, Ivan Rosero, Trevor Pinch. (2006). To have and to hold:* Exploring the personal archive. Proceedings of the SIGCHI Conference on Human Factors in Computing Systems, 275-284.

[Kak 05] *Käki, Mika. (2005) Findex:* Search result categories help users when document rankings fail. In Proceedings of ACM SIGCHI. Portland, OR, 2005.

[Kos 00] *Kosala, Raymond, Hendrik Blockeel. (2000). Web mining research:* A survey. SIGKDD Explorations, 2(1), 1-15.

[Kim 12] *Kim, Jinyoung. (2012). Guiding users to improve personal information management. Retrieved on December 2012 from http://pimworkshop.org/2012/pdf/kim_2012_guiding.pdf*

[Klj 04] *Kljun, Matjaž, David Carr. (2004). Piles of Thumbnails – Visualizing document management. Proceedings of the 27th International Conference on Information Technology Interfaces (ITI2005), Cavtat, Croatia, 20-23.*

[Lan 88] *Lansdale, Mark W. (1988). The psychology of personal information management. Applied Ergonomics, 19(1), 55-66.*

[Mal 83] *Malone, Thomas W. (1983). How do people organize their desks?:* Implications for the design of office information systems. ACM Transactions on Information Systems (TOIS), 1(1), 99-112.

[Mar 03] *Marsden, Gary, David E. Cairns. (2003). Improving the usability of the hierarchical file system. Proceedings of the 2003 annual research conference of the South African institute of computer scientists and information technologists on Enablement through technology, 122-129.*

[Mar 06] *Marshall, Catherine C., William Jones. (2006). Keeping encountered information. Communications of the ACM, 49(1), 66-67.*

[Mio 08] *Mioduser, David, Rafi Nachmias, Alona Forkosh-Baruch. (2008). New literacies for the knowledge society. In Voogt, Joke, Gerald Knezek. (eds.). International Handbook of Information Technology in Primary and Secondary Education (pp. 23-42). New York:* Springer.

[Mul 95] *Mullet, Kevin, Darrell Sano. (1995). Designing Visual Interfaces. SunSoft Press, Mountain View, CA, 1995.*

[Nie 00] *Nielsen, Jakob. (2000) Designing Web Usability:* The Practice of simplicity. New Riders Publishing, Indiana.

[Pra 06] *Pratt, Wanda, Kenton Unruh, Andrea Civan, Meredith M. Skeels. (2006). Personal health information management. Communications of the ACM, 49(1), 51-55.*

[Rob 10] *Robinson, Sara P. (2010). Personal information management strategies in higher education. BOBCATSSS 2010 symposium, Parma.*

[Sal 00] *Salomon, Gabriel. (2000). Technology and education in the age of information. Zmora-Bitan, Israel:* Haifa University Press. (In Hebrew)

[Sei 06] *Seidman, Irving. (2006). Interviewing as qualitative research:* A guide for researchers in education and the social sciences. New York: Teachers College Press.

[Shn 97] *Shneiderman, Ben. (1997), Designing the User Interface:* Strategies for Effective Human-Computer Interaction. 3rd. Addison-Wesley Longman Publishing Co., Inc.

[Sie 06] *Siemens, George. (2006). Knowing knowledge. Lulu.com. CA.*

[Tee 06] *Teevan, Jaime, William Jones, Benjamin B. Bederson. (2006). Personal information management. Communications of the ACM, 49(1), 40-43.*

[Whi 11] *Whittaker, Steve (2011). Personal information management:* from information consumption to curation. Annual review of information science and technology,45(1), 1-62.

[Whi 96] *Whittaker, Steve, Candace Sidner. (1996). Email overload:* Exploring personal information management of email. Proceedings of the SIGCHI Conference on Human Factors in Computing Systems: Common Ground, 276-283.

[Wil 01] *Willis, Peter. (2001). The "things themselves" in phenomenology. Indo-Pacific Journal of Phenomenology, 1(1). Retrieved on December 2012 from http://www.ajol.info/index.php/* ipjp/article/viewFile/65726/53414

[Xin 08] *Xing, Dikan, Gui-Rong Xue, Qiang Yang, Yong Yu. (2008). Deep classifier:* automatically categorizing search results into large-scale hierarchies. In Proceedings of the International Conference on Web Search and Web Data Mining.

[Yee 03] *Yee, Ka-Ping, Kirsten Swearingen, Kevin Li, and Marti Hearst. (2003). Faceted metadata for image search and browsing. In Proceedings of the SIGCHI Conference on Human Factors in Computing Systems, 401-408.*

FIGURES

CONTACT DETAILS

Sharon Hardof-Jaffe
Tel Aviv University
School of education
Israel
E-Mail: *Sharonh2@tau.ac.il*

Rafi Nachmias
Tel Aviv University
School of education
Israel
E-Mail: *Nachmias@post.tau.ac.il*

Case-based Workflow Modeling in Support of Automation the Teachers' Personal and Social Behavior

Malinka Ivanova, Mirjam Minor

Abstract

One part of teachers is very active participant in virtual social space forming Personal Learning Networks (PLNs) with the aim to receive and share knowledge, taking the role of a tutor or a learner. Their time and effort could be optimized if they utilize some functions for automation of important and often repeated activities. The paper explores several possibilities for performance support of teachers when they use their PLNs. The workflow technology of business informatics is applied to model activity structures that could be recommended for following by teachers. This could shorten the distance among learning, effectiveness and time.

Introduction

Nowadays, teachers receive a wide range of knowledge using social networking sites, looking for suitable contacts and appropriate content. They spend less or much time in the networked world performing different activities to search, interact, share, like/dislike, group, etc. Their time and effort can be optimized if they utilize some functions for automation like: group people, group messages, prioritize activities, or if they use tools for searching on a given criterion, filtering, recommending, etc. On the other side, the previous research shows that Personal Learning Network (PLN) has potential to facilitate the development of given personal and professional skills and abilities. PLN can be used for learning through active participation or through observation of others' activities. The teachers' behavior during the PLN utilization can also be optimized through different techniques for automation to shorten the distance among learning, effectiveness and time.

For the purposes of this exploration we use the gathered data from the previous study [Iva 12] and several scientific reports, e.g. Twitter in EFL education [Mor 09], Graasp for collaborative learning [Li 12], social media for engineering communication [Meh 10]. Current research papers are related to the typical activities performed by teachers and learners when they use social networking sites. These activities are not structured in any criterion. One interesting example for activities grouping in time (weekly) is presented in [Wan 12]. The authors perform an exploratory study about the Facebook utilization as a learning management system to facilitate teaching and learning in two elective courses (formal education). For this purpose a special Facebook group is created. The activities from the teacher side include: information announcement with integrated hyperlinks, pictures and videos; course recourses sharing in format of text, PowerPoint and PDF. The event function is used to organize course content in weeks; two type of discussions are managed: through received feedback after the event announcement and through usage of default discussion function; link to an external survey is created; journaling and monitoring of the students' activities is done. Learners reflect on a topic and share opinion and resources, receive feedback from other participants, and manage contacts. The findings point that learners like Facebook wall used as a notice board and as a journal of activities and content, structuring the activities in weeks, possibilities for communication and interactions. They see the potential of Facebook as a tool for learning management in spite of the existing constrains and limitations. In this example the tutor goes further and groups learning activities in time (weekly) and students appreciate that.

The identified teachers' activities in social networking sites are following: share, communicate, collaborate, comment, give opinion, announce event, announce results, moderate discussion, search, add contacts, upload files, read. We are going further not only to select the activities, but also to ascertain the logically arranged sequences of activities. Modeling of workflows is performed from two perspectives for automation: (1) functional – using the main functions of social media to support teachers (e.g. add comment, add people, upload file, like), (2) operational – considering the personal preferred operations in the process of automation.

The methodology of case-based adaptable workflows is applied to structure the activities of teachers in social networks and to adapt to their personal needs. Case-based reasoning [Aam 94] is related to a collection of cases that record performed activities. These gathered cases could be used to: (1) recommend the most suitable case to support teacher's behavior or (2) to form a new case based on the existing cases and emerging new situation [Min 14].

The aim of the paper is to explore the possibilities for automation of several regularly repeated activities of teachers when they use their Personal Learning Networks and to develop structured case-based workflows. This will be a base and first step for software development. In this work several workflows are created, describing some typical activities for teachers.

Related work

When we refer to the effectiveness of teachers' activities, we take into consideration previous research related to people and content searching, filtering and recommending. In this section several examples showing facilitation of social networks' users through available automated functions are explored. These examples are used for better understanding user needs and existing technical solutions.

Automation techniques

- A method for *selection of social media content* (Twitter) is proposed in [DeC 11]. The selection criteria are based on the different weights for a wide variety of content attributes. The content diversity is quantified then through applying the information theoretic measure entropy. The result set includes minimum distortion on a given topic.
- A system that *tracks conversations* on social platforms (Facebook and Twitter) is developed to identify and *prioritize posts and messages* that are related to a given topic (enterprises). An agent is created with functions facilitating the processes of monitoring, tracking and responding to customers [Ajm 13]. Different messages are connected to different weights to be prioritized. For example, messages with complaints have high priority and stimulate discussion and active participation.
- The problem about *influential users and passive users* on Twitter is treated in [Rom 11]. The authors present an algorithm that identifies who is an active participant and influences others and who is a passive user (does not read messages or ignores them, follows many people, re-tweets rarely). User activity related to posts forwarding is tracked and is a base for algorithm calculation. The algorithm can filter content that is most rated and liked.
- Personalized item recommendation widget is presented in [Guy 10]. Recommendations are done after *collecting the relationships among people, tags and items.* The recommender system is evaluated and the results point that a hybrid people-tag-based recommender has several advantages than recommendations based on people work.
- Another recommender system based on *user-model* is developed in [Set 08]. The software learns user's preferences about the received knowledge, predicts the usefulness of given messages for him and recommends suitable ones. The proposed solution is evaluated using social networking website Orkut and results are promising according to the authors.
- A framework with a possibility to *summarize Twitter stream messages*, retirement of messages and their reconstruction around a given topic is presented in [Yan 12]. An algorithm detects evolutionary events between two different intervals of time. The authors wish to understand how user interests change and evaluate and how topics are trending.

Types of Users in Social Networks

The types of Social Networking Sites (SNS) users according to their performed activities and level of participation are examined in [Bra 11]. The authors divide users in five groups: sporadic, lurkers, socialisers, debaters and actives. The data are gathered after a survey and users' typology is verified after quantitative and qualitative analysis.

An empirical study and analysis about the activities and contributions of users in online social networks are analyzed in [Guo 09]. The findings point that user behavior

is related to daily and weekly contributions through posting, but their participation time cannot be described with exponential distributions. The authors propose models describing how users create links and how their networks progress in time.

The factors that are important for lifetime forming in online social networks are researched in [Lan 11]. They divide lifetime to active and passive according to users' activities and behavior. The prerequisites for passive lifetime are two: received activity and undirected activity among friends of a user. Authors have five recommendations contributing to stimulation of active behavior: encouragement for friendships, making friendships not only with popular users in the network, encouragement for communication, friendly attitude to new users, and encouragement for frequent posting.

For the purposes of our research we divide users of social networking sites to passive and active in their time of usage. They can be characterized by different level of activeness in different time of their learning sessions according to their learning priorities and goals. The users learn by observation or through participation and possess favorite activities. The learning of these users could be optimized if recommendations with structured activities are supposed. Figure 1 presents a model showing the criterion and procedure for structured workflows generation. The software gathers data and understands the favorite activities of a SNS user; creates a user model with preferences; classifies this user in the category of passive or active for the current learning session; generates workflow with structured activities to satisfy or motivate for participation the passive user and to satisfy the active one.

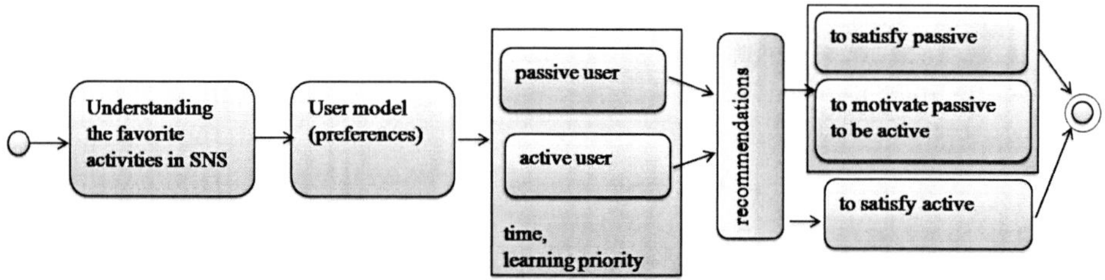

Figure 1: Criterion and procedure for generation of structured workflows

We created two different sets with activities typical for passive and active users. Under passive user we understand a person who prefers to learn alone without getting advantages of participation and communication. Passive users learn through observation: read the shared knowledge, accept or not friendships, follow people, monitor activities, track activity stream, use applications with special purposes, search. The activity set of active users consists of activities that contribute to enrichment of the network knowledge: add comments, publish content/opinion, share link/file, like/dislike, join/create groups, use chat, communicate via direct messaging or other applications, extend contacts, make friendships.

Serendipity, Accidental and Intentional Learning

Usually, learning in social networks occurs accidentally and in a serendipitous way and it depends on the specificity of created Personal Learning Network. Every individual teacher sees different messages and unique information stream. This fact has an impact on learning curiosity and changing learning needs. [Kop 12] argues that emerging applications such as recommenders, RSS aggregators and microblog platforms are effective because they can facilitate serendipitous learning on open online networks. Teachers have control on their PLNs organization, but also they are in touch with unexpected information sources. At this moment serendipity is not automated, just serendipitous content and contacts could be recommended.

On the other hand, PLNs are created intentionally according to the teachers' interests and future plans. This suggests that they strive to be connected to people who are sources of topic related content. In spite of the intentional disposition of PLNs, we find many serendipitous events and processes. In this aspect our supposition in the paper is that teachers respond to serendipitous events in intentionally topic-driven PLNs (Figure 2).

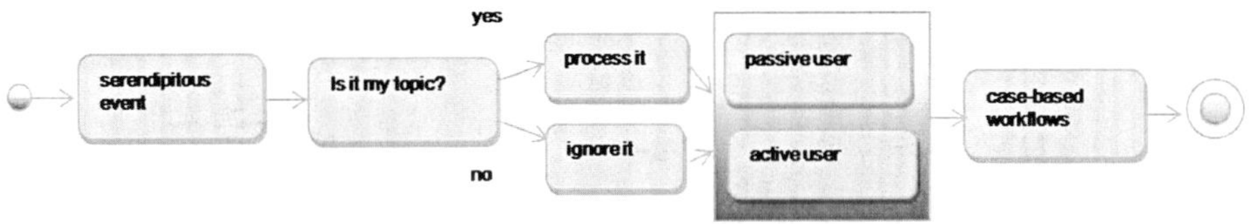

Figure 2: Serendipitous events in intentionally topic-driven PLNs

Research methods

The research design of this paper follows the design-oriented paradigm of business informatics [Hev 04]. It aims at conducting a feasibility study on whether workflow technology is applicable in order to partly automate the work of teachers in PLNs and to increase the reusability of this work. Following a build-and-evaluate cycle as proposed in [Hev 04], a workflow model for learning procedures within PLNs is created (during the build phase) and its technical feasibility is tested by deriving a couple of workflow instances from the activities observed in recent PLNs (during the evaluate phase). The results of this technical feasibility study are a prerequisite for our future work. The two main research questions are: *Q1 Representation:* How can activities of teachers in social networks be represented and structured in a workflow model? *Q2 Applicability:* Can the workflow model be populated by cases (workflow instances) for different learning scenarios and user types?

The representation is developed by creating a workflow model following recent technical standards for workflow design, and the applicability is tested by modeling a set of diverse workflow samples.

Modelling workflows

Traditionally, workflows are "the automation of a business process, in whole or part, during which documents, information or tasks are passed from one participant to another for action, according to a set of procedural rules" [WFM 99]. Recently, a broader notion is emerging, where a workflow describes any flow of activities. This notion includes the activities of a learner during the use of a PLN for a particular learning task. For instance, a learner might prepare a course on a novel topic and use the PLN for identifying the most important issues and for collecting teaching and examination material.

A workflow consists of a control flow and a data flow. A set of activities combined with control-flow-structures like sequences, parallel or alternative branches, and loops forms the control flow. In addition, activities consume resources and create certain products, which both can be physical matter (such as paper books) or information. The data flow describes the interaction of activities with resources and products.

Workflows can be executed automatically by a Workflow Management System (WfMS). The WfMS enacts the workflow and controls its execution. There are two types of activities: manual activities and automated activities [Wes 12]. Manual activities are performed by human beings who might use software systems during execution or who might perform the activity without any software, for instance, by reading a book. Automated activities do not involve a human user; they are executed by a software service, for instance, by a Twitter analysis tool. The WfMS triggers the activities in the order that is specified by the control flow. In case of an automated activity, it calls according to the software service. In case of a manual activity, it informs the user via a work list (a kind of interactive to-do-list) what is to do, which tools and data are available, and whether there is a deadline until when the activity has to be finished. When an activity has finished execution, the WfMS receives the results of the activity via the return values from a service or by a click on the completed button of a work list. Then, the WfMS triggers the next activity or activities.

In this work, several workflows are created, describing some activity structures for teachers in their active timeline and passive timeline. Here are shown the workflows in Business Process Modeling Notation (BPMN) [Wes 12] related to: the process of getting to know a new item from the topic, getting feedback for slides and how to discover an expert for a topic.

Workflow 1: Getting to know a new subtopic from the topic

Workflow 1 for a passive user

W1 describes the process of getting to know a new subtopic from the topic (Figure 3). The first step in the workflow is to receive a serendipitous message. If this message contains intriguing information in the area of the teacher' interests, then the user can go further clicking on the link. Then the software could suggest this teacher to subscribe to the information source (if a RSS feet exists) or/and to follow the person who share this information. Also, the software could recommend a search to be performed for finding the similar information sources or resources. The received knowledge should be summarized in different forms (note taking, passing quiz, game playing, etc.).

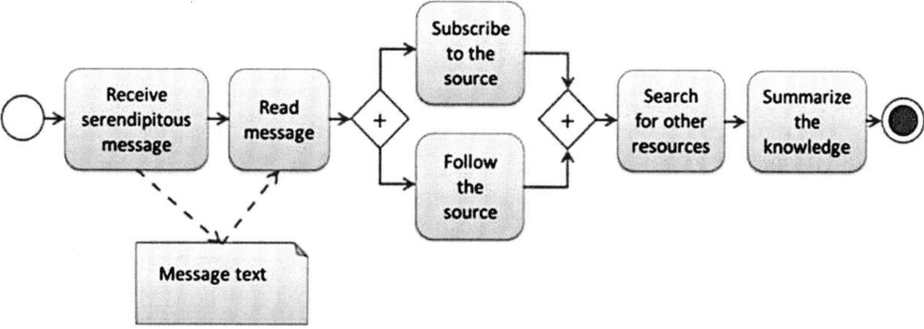

Figure 3: Workflow 1 for a passive user

Workflow 1 for a passive user with an intention to be activated

The aim of this workflow is not only to suppose future activities, but also to stimulate participation of a passive user (Figure 4). After receiving a message and reading its content, at the beginning the person acts as a passive user subscribing to the source or/and following the person who shares this information. Then, the software recommends to post opinion or/and communicate with the human information source. At the final step, the knowledge has to be summarized using different methods.

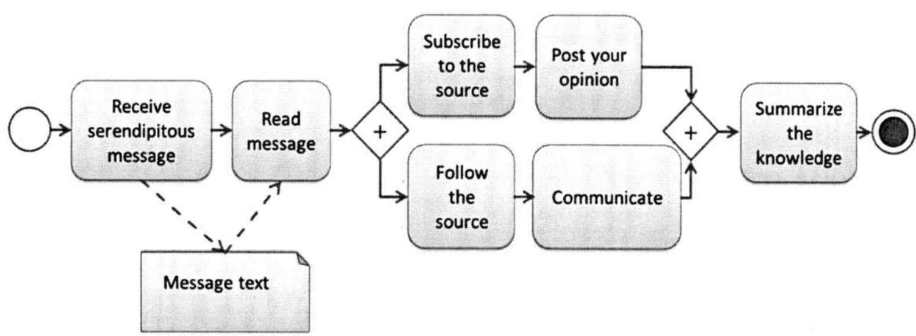

Figure 4: Workflow 1 for a passive user who could be activated

Workflow 1 for an active user

The suitable activities for an active user after reading the content of a message could be to comment/like/share content, search for other resources that could again be commented/liked/shared, etc (Figure 5). The last step is related to drawing of conclusion about the reached knowledge.

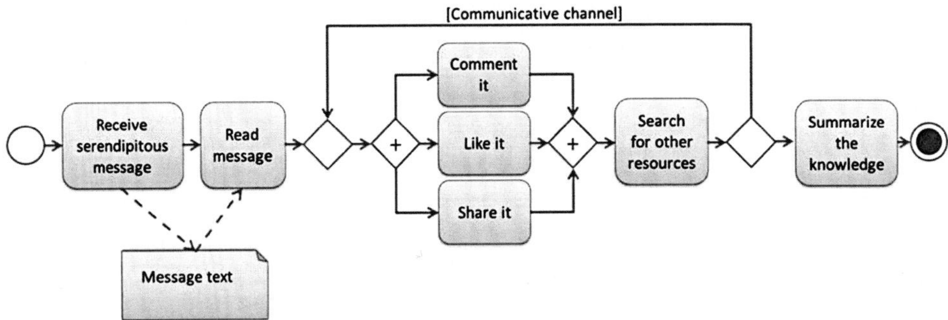

Figure 5: Workflow 1 for an active user

Workflow 2: Getting feedback for slides

Workflow 2 for an active user

W2 describes how to get feedback for slides (Figure 6). W2 is suitable for an active user who is sociable and should publish the content. In the first step the slides should be put on SlideShare. Then the slides could be announced in the social networks and the link could be shared. The user goes further with performing activities such as: to describe the presentation or a separate slide, to ask questions related to the presented topic and to organize a discussion through replaying the received answers. At the end the feedback is collected and summarized.

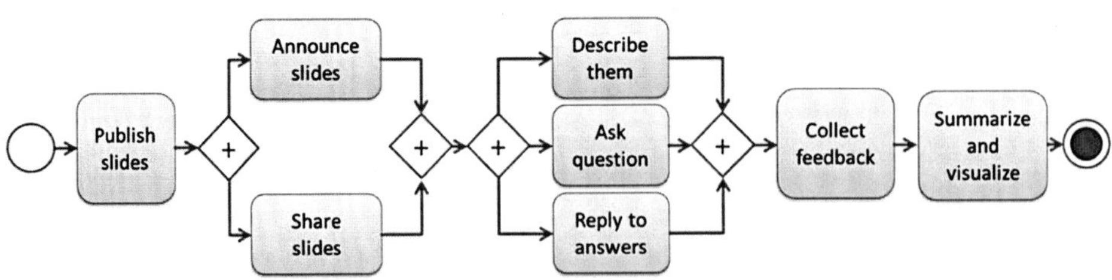

Figure 6: Workflow 2 for an active user

Workflow 3: Discover an expert for a topic

Workflow 3 for a passive user

W3 shows how to discover an expert for a topic (Figure 7). First, the user should be interested in the content of a message and should read it. Then the user could perform content/people search through the Twitter/Facebook stream. The received results should be selected that should lead to the finding of a person with an advanced knowledge about the given topic. In the subsequent step the user could subscribe to the information source or follow the found expert.

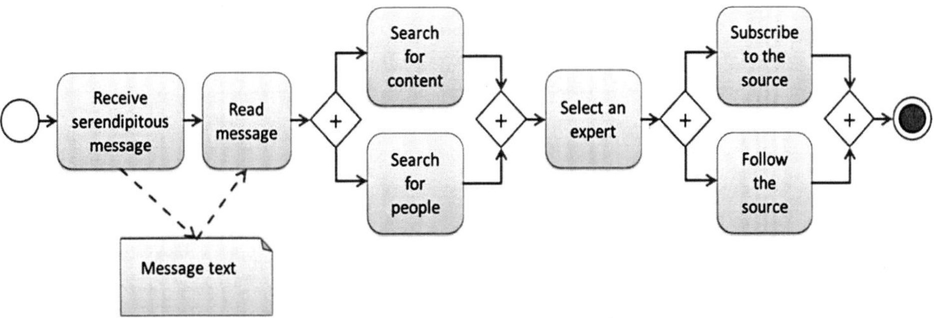

Figure 7: Workflow 3 for a passive user

Workflow 3 for a passive user with an intention to be activated

This workflow is modeled for a passive user who can be activated (Figure 8). In this case as a subsequent step is suggested an active action like communication with the found expert.

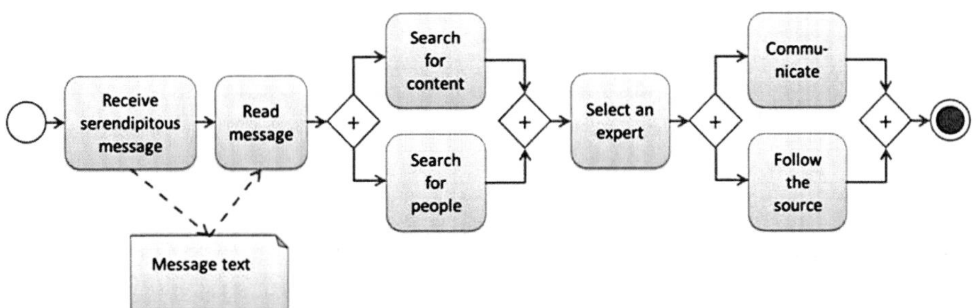

Figure 8: Workflow 3 for a passive user who could be activated

Workflow 3 for an active user

When a user is active and he is looking for an expert, then he could perform several activities: to join a specific group, to connect and communicate with people, to follow them and their messages (Figure 9). Then the user could select the best person fitting his interests.

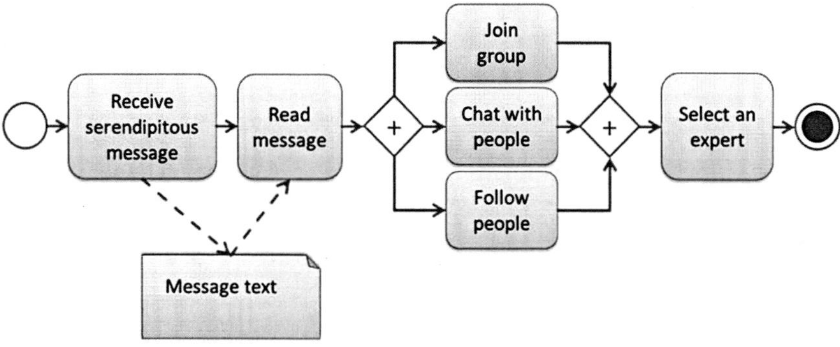

Figure 9: Workflow 3 for an active user

Conclusions

The paper presents models of structured activities in time and according to the learning priority and learning needs utilizing case-based workflow technology. The workflows originate from serendipitous events and they are categorized according to the user type. These workflows describe important cases of activities performed during the PLNs organization and utilization. They will support teachers through recommendations and guidance giving, making their learning more effective. The created workflows are the first step in the process of software development. They figure the main functions for activities' automation and semi-automation facilitating the teachers' personal and social behavior. We think that the automation of typical activities is a crucial prerequisite leading to the achievement of improved learning quality.

REFERENCES

[Aam 94] *Aamodt, Agnar, Plaza, Enric (1994):* Case-based reasoning: Foundational issues, methodological variations, and system approaches. AI communications, 7 (1), 39–59.

[Ajm 13] *Ajmera, Jitendra, Ahn, Hyung-il, Nagarajan, Meena, Verma, Ashish, Contractor, Danish, Dill, Stephen, Denesuk, Matthew (2013):* A CRM system for Social Media [Challenges and Experiences]. Proceedings of the 22nd international conference on World Wide Web, 49–58.

[Bra 11] *Brandtzaeg, Petter, Heim, Jan (2011):* A typology of social networking sites users. International Journal of Web Based Communities, 7 (1), 28–51.

[DeC 11] *De Choudhury, Munmun, Counts, Scott, Czerwinski, Mary (2011):* Identifying Relevant Social Media Content: Leveraging Information Diversity and User Cognition. Proceedings of the 22nd ACM conference on Hypertext and hypermedia, 161–170.

[Guo 09] *Guo, Lei, Tan, Enhua, Chen, Songqing, Zhang, Xiaodong, Zhao, Yihong (2009):* Analyzing Patterns of User Content Generation in Online Social Networks. Proceedings of the 15th ACM SIGKDD international conference on Knowledge discovery and data mining, 369–378.

[Guy 10] *Guy, Ido, Zwerdling, Naama, Ronen, Inbal, Carmel, David, Uziel, Erel (2010):* Social Media Recommendation based on People and Tags. Proceedings of the 33rd international ACM SIGIR conference on Research and development in information retrieval, 194–201.

[Hev 04] *Hevner, Alan, March, Salvatore, Park, Jinsoo, Ram, Sudha (2004):* Design Science in Information Systems Research. MIS Quarterly, 28 (1), 75–105.

[Iva 12] *Ivanova, Malinka, Holotescu, Carmen., Grosseck, Gabriela (2012):* Analysis of Personal Learning Networks in Support of Teachers Presence Optimization. The PLE Conference 2012 Proceedings, Aveiro, Portugal, 11–13 July, 2012. Retrieved May 2014 from *http://revistas.ua.pt/index.php/ple/article/view/1439*

[Kop 12] *Kop, Rob (2012):* The Unexpected Connection: Serendipity and Human Mediation in Networked Learning. Educational Technology & Society, 15 (2), 2–11.

[Lan 11] *Lang, Juan, Wu, Felix (2011):* Social Network User Lifetime. International Conference on Advances in Social Networks Analysis and Mining, 25–27 July, 2011, 289–296.

[Li 12] *Li, Na, Helou, Ingram-El, Gillet, Denis (2012):* Using Social Media for Collaborative Learning in Higher Education: A Case Study. 5th International Conference on Advances in Computer-Human Interactions, Valencia, Spain, 30 January -4 February, 2012. Retrieved May 2014 from *http://infoscience.epfl.ch/record/170400/files/ACHI2012_React.pdf*

[Meh 10] *Mehlenbacher, Brad, McKone, Sarah, Grant, Christine, Bowles, Tuere, Peretti, Steve, Martin, Pamela (2010):* Social media for sustainable engineering communication. Proceedings of the 28th ACM International Conference on Design of Communication, 65–72.

[Min 13] *Minor, Mirjam, Bergmann, Ralph, Görg, Sebastian (2014):* Case-based Adaptation of Workflows. Journal Information Systems, 40, 142–152.

[Mor 09] *Mork, Cathrine-Mette (2009):* Using Twitter in EFL Education. Jaltcall journal, 5 (3), 41–56.

[Rom 11] *Romero, Daniel, Galuba, Wojciech, Asur, Sitaram, Huberman, Bernardo (2011):* Influence and Passivity in Social Media. Proceedings of the 20th international conference companion on World Wide Web, 113–114.

[Set 08] *Seth, Aaditeshwar, Zhang, Jie (2008):* A Social Network Based Approach to Personalized Recommendation of Participatory Media Content. International conference on Weblogs and Social Media. Retrieved May 2014 from *http://www.cse.iitd.ernet.in/~aseth/modelv3.pdf.*

[Wan 12] *Wang, Qiyun, Woo, Huay, Quek, Choon, Yang, Yuqin, Liu, Mei (2012):* Using the Facebook group as a learning management system: An exploratory study. British Journal of Educational Technology, 43 (3), 428–438.

[Wes 12] *Weske, Mathias (2012):* Business Process Management Concepts, Languages, Architectures. 2nd edition 2012. Berlin, Heidelberg: Springer Berlin Heidelberg, *http://dx.doi.org/10.1007/978-3-642-28616-2.*

[WFM 99] *WFMC – Workflow Management Coalition. (1999):* Workflow Management Coalition Glossary & Terminology, 1999. Retrieved May 2014 from *http://www.wfmc.org/standars/docs/TC-1011_term_glossary_v3.pdf.*

[Yan 12] *Yang, Xintian, Ghoting, Amol, Ruan, Yiye, Parthasarathy, Srinivasan (2012):* A Framework for Summarizing and Analyzing Twitter Feeds. Proceedings of the 18th ACM SIGKDD international conference on Knowledge discovery and data mining, 370–378.

FIGURES

CONTACT DETAILS

Assoc. Prof. Malinka Ivanova
Technical University of Sofia
College of Energy and Electronics
Blvd. Kl. Ohridski 8
1000 Sofia
E-Mail: *m_ivanova@tu-sofia.bg*

Prof. Mirjam Minor
Johann Wolfgang Goethe-University Frankfurt am Main
Institute for Computer Science
Robert-Mayer-Straße 10
D-60325 Frankfurt am Main
E-Mail: *minor@informatik.uni-frankfurt.de*

A theoretical analysis of the socio-material entanglement of Personal Learning Environments and its methodological and pedagogical implications

Sabine Reisas

ABSTRACT

This paper elaborates the role of the socio-material entanglement of PLEs by discussing two common conceptualizations of context: an individual-centered approach and an activity-oriented view. Furthermore the author outlines how learning is conceptualized according to each concept to identify possible impacts on PLE research, pedagogical consequences and implications for designing learning environments (e.g. e-learning, face-to-face) that aim to encourage students to reflect on existing PLEs as well as to adjust to current and future knowledge working and learning situations.

Introduction

In current knowledge working and learning situations people are often separated in different environments. This means that people are working on the same topics, but maybe not at the same time and place. The availability and use of resources may differ from colleagues of other institutions or disciplines, which in turn can influence modes of working and learning. Each working and learning process may demand specific artefacts to foster development and problem solving. These artefacts act as mediators that transform working and learning practices, because according to its affordances it can help to gain new insights into a phenomenon, problem, and the underlying mechanisms. An artefact can be changed, reworked and negotiated and is therefore constantly evolving. This implies that artefacts inherent an emergent nature and historicity and develop through highly diverse contextual practices. These practices and artefacts can differ according to each workplace. Knowledge workers like students or researchers often work in diverse teams and are confronted with varying and emerging resources and practices. Modern working situations demand new ways of thinking and learning to facilitate students not only to apply common knowledge and practices, but rather to co-create, generate, negotiate and adapt knowledge and the accompanying practices to upcoming needs and therefore to transform their personal learning environments. Especially in distance- and e-learning environments this could foster development and learning and an understanding how to connect with an evolving conglomerate of mediating artefacts.

A literature review on Personal Learning Environments (PLEs) of submissions for the PLE Conference in 2011 (Southampton, UK) and 2012 (Aveiro, Portugal) shows that there is an increasing awareness of those issues and an interest on creating tools that foster students to transform their PLEs and to help them to overcome those aforementioned issues of current working and learning situations. From the literature review current research questions can be deduced and categorized as follows:

- Research on usefulness and usage of tools to foster learning and building PLEs, e.g. [Sal 11], [Mar 12], [Arr 12].
- Research on requirements for designing tools and platforms that foster productivity, and participation as well as requirements that support personal goals and needs, e.g. [Wol 11], [Iva 12], [Gar 12].
- Research on user experiences and perceived control over tools and online platforms, e.g. [Buc 12].
- Research on how PLEs are managed by the individual, e.g. [Cas 12].
- Research on tools and platforms and their means for enabling social learning and informal interactions, e.g. [Att 12], [Höl 12], [Pai 12].

The categorization above shows two important research strands on PLEs: On the one hand a large number of case studies focus on existing tools and platforms. Those resources are being evaluated from a user-centered or in other words individual-centered perspective. On the other hand research questions regarding social and epistemic issues become more and more important in PLE research. A deeper analysis of the literature shows that the theoretical foundation of PLE studies are increasingly based on social perspectives on learning. Frameworks like the socio-historical activity theory by Vygotsky (1978), "Communities of practice" by [Lav 08] as well as knowledge building by [Sca 03] and the concept of shared spaces for emerging relationships (BA) by [Non 97] come into focus of researchers. It can also be observed that some authors [Att 07], [Fie 10], [Rav 11], [Mir 12], [Rei 12b] challenge the common notions of a PLE by pointing out cultural, social and epistemic dimensions and their possible impacts on developing teaching and learning environments.

Although the theoretical foundation of research is more often based on a social perspective on learning, there is no consistent definition of a PLE. [Buc 11] identified a dichotomy of a technology-oriented view and a pedagogical-oriented view on PLEs. This dichotomy is still visible in the implementation of current research studies. If we compare the underlying definition of a PLE with the theoretical foundation of research studies it becomes visible that a social and epistemic grounding does not lead per se to an exploration of the role of social relations and interactions.

In this sense the author starts from the assumption that not only a specific theoretical framework sets the scope on PLE research, but also the frame or conceptualization of a PLE. Furthermore it can be stated that selecting research methods, interpreting research results, deducing requirements for instructional design and pedagogical

concepts as well as developing platforms and technologies are influenced by the underlying assumptions of a PLE and its relation or (depending on the perspective) embeddedness in contextual aspects. Luckin [Luc 10] also states that people's intention and meaning is embedded in the context of a learning activity, therefore context can be seen as an important factor for personal learning environments (PLEs). Because of this it is essential to gain an understanding of common underlying conceptualizations, their applicability in the scope of PLE research and the pedagogical consequences for developing approaches and educational practices. Such an understanding can help to identify the means and issues for research and to question the taken-for-granted. Considering the awakening interest by the PLE community in a dynamic and emergent perspective on PLE this understanding might also help to explore means for developing new approaches and to gain new insights for broadening the research frame, the interpretation and appraisal of research results.

Approach

Based on the aforementioned remarks, this paper examines the role of the socio-material entanglement by analyzing the notion of context within two common conceptualizations: At first an individual-centered perspective is discussed, which separates context from the individual. The second perspective – the socio-historical activity theory – shows that context is not described as an outer shell, but has a more complex view on context and its socio-material entanglement. The paper elaborates each concept successively by reviewing the perspectives on context. For each concept the author has a closer look at possible impacts on PLE research and its pedagogical consequences. The paper aims to provide insights that can be taken into consideration when framing PLEs as well as planning PLE research and developing new approaches for current and future knowledge working and learning situations.

Conceptualizations of context & the social interwoveness of PLEs

In the following the mechanistic view of context will be introduced and then distinguished from the activity theory as an alternative conceptualization of context. The differences between each theory and the means for PLEs are subsequently deduced.

The mechanistic view

The individual-oriented view has its origins in the mechanistic view – developed over centuries, e.g. by René Descartes, John Locke and Isaac Newton. The mechanistic view proceeds on the assumption that context can be viewed as a container for a learning situation surrounding an individual. Therefore context is seen as independent and can be explained in "a unique and permanent way" [Fig 06], because it is defined as an objective machine that holds the (scientific) truth and determinate human reasoning

[Ham 96]. [Fig 06] describe it as follows: "[...] there is a reality out there that is independent from our thoughts and beliefs about it. This reality, tangible or immaterial, holds a degree of stability that makes it potentially knowable and explainable by immutable laws, whatever its complexity." From Descartes' point of view this means that only through the separation of mind and body exploring the scientific truth becomes possible [Des 79]. This dichotomy of internal and external or individual and social is a guiding premise and leads to the argument that it is necessary to subordinate outside influences to reason, because the body and its imperfect senses can deceive epistemic processes [Fig 06]. Learning is defined as a process where an individual learner creates knowledge through the interpretations of an outer situation by breaking down the problem into small solvable subquestions. At first a learner explores general aspects and simple questions, based on previous knowledge the learner is then able to solve more and more complex problems, which leads him to become an expert. Descartes follows that each and every problem is solvable by this process [Des 79]. John Locke stated that the human mind can be seen as a "tabula rasa" – a clean slate that can be inscribed by those outer forces of objective context conditions [Loc 79]. This also intends the notion that knowledge can be directly transferred from one person to another [Loc 79]. The surrounding environment (e.g. classroom) or scales (e.g. local vs. global) affect the individual but both exist independently. Therefore context is stated as a container for an individual at the center who is influenced by what is given by the surrounding scales and forms the environment as well as the content of what can be learned. Learning as discerning the truth and constructing meaning is therefore an individual process based on reasoning and not based on exploring activities and is only achievable through the outer environment that provides the content and objective basis of valuation [Des 79]. The learner identifies the truth by mistrusting the material environment and therefore also social relations and language, which might contain wrong or misleading aspects. In this sense the mechanistic view rejects the notion of a reciprocal relation between the individual and the environment or in other words social relations [Des 79].

[Ham 96] states that this perspective reached its peak in behaviorist paradigms, where a stimulus-response model describes the components of learning as input (context) and output (observable behavior) and do not focus on the learning process itself, but rather on outer objects that change human behavior. Even today models of instructional design – this includes not only behaviorist approaches, but also approaches that are theoretical based on the cognitivist praradigm as well – are based on the underlying mechanistic perspective in the sense of the dichotomy of mind and body [Ase 96]. For a broader discussion on convergent aspects in cognitivist and behaviorist paradigms [Per 11], [Cas 84]. [Fig 06] point out that the mechanistic perspective is still widely distributed in current educational systems "Unfortunately, however, the mechanistic vision of learning as the 'delivery of content' still dominates to a large extent the educational processes of the present day" [Fig 06].

In the scope of the derived perspective a PLE can be defined as something that surrounds the individual and consists of an aggregation of components or variables building the notion of context. These components are seen as objective objects (e.g. learning spaces, learning content, tools, requirements, social aspects, methods etc.) and if carefully selected by course developers or teachers and evaluated by researchers they will influence the individual by changing their behavior in an expected way. The goals and meanings are deduced through individual reasoning about the given environment.

In research this definition of a PLE becomes visible by evaluating the usage of existing tools or by developing adequate requirements to cause specific behaviors. Research questions from this point of view would be interested in efficiency and productivity (e.g. faster problem solving) of learners induced by context conditions as well as in exploring requirements for developing adequate environments that provide functionalities where learners are enabled to perceive a platform or a tool as the "objective" PLE. The idea of continuity or in other words the transmission of knowledge based on the cartesian view allows for a transmission of PLEs: Providing an adequate PLE – this also includes providing specific tools, the "right" software, delivering the "right" content and introducing the "right" methods as well as providing adequate social forms of learning (e.g. small learning group) and feedback – leads to individual reasoning and therefore learning, because it is assumed that those context conditions shape and strengthen behavior [Per 11]. This also includes the aspect of generalization that means that those PLEs, which inherit the notion of "scientific truth" can also be adapted by other people. If we consider pedagogical approaches within the scope of a mechanistic view this would mean to provide an incremental instructional design, where the individual can deduce the PLE by analyzing the components of context through learning task that become increasingly more difficult.

This argumentation has a critical consequence for PLE research as well as developing pedagogical concepts within the scope of the mechanistic view: the research frame as well as research methods need to be challenged continuously, because they could be too narrowly defined or based on traditional assumptions, which may lead to wrong interpretations of research results. Another important aspect should be mentioned: Approaches based on the mechanistic view only allow for inquiring a static image of attributes and do not explore processes of learning in time. If we consider PLEs as something dynamic it would be necessary to rethink the underlying paradigm. Furthermore inquiring only partial aspects of a problem (e.g. specific functionalities of a platform) should be checked if they are sufficient and if a joint consideration of those partial aspects would lead to holistic results on PLEs.

In the following an alternative perspective – activity-oriented view – is discussed that contributes to educational research in a different way by offering also social and cultural perspectives on learning.

The activity-oriented perspective and additional notions

In contrast to the mechanistic view activity-oriented approaches do not differentiate between those aforementioned ecologies which separate the individual from context, but rather see the subject and its environment as well as the resources as mutually entangled [Luc 10], [Orl 07]. This paper complements the activity-oriented view with Orlikowski's practice-oriented notion of an "constitutive entanglement" [Orl 07] of activity, materiality and social relations. For an elaborated discussion on practice-oriented approaches [Fen 11], [Ghe 09], [Orl 07]. The grounding concept of socio-materiality assumes that the activity is initiated by the individual itself, but rather forced by the socio-material entanglement between an individual or a group and the technology or resource, which makes an activity possible [Fen 11]. The idea that practices are negotiated and reshaped by human beings through the usage of tools binds PLEs – which are understood as activity systems – to practices [Rei 12b]. Furthermore the author argues that tools offer the possibility to gain "experiences with practices in contexts" and "PLEs as activity systems serve as a vehicle to articulate these practices." [Rei 12b].

The process of a socio-material "becoming" in emerging and dynamic connections and relations is also an important factor for the activity-oriented perspective. Knowledge is generated through ongoing interactions with artefacts in activities: "To know is to be able to participate with the requisite competence in the complex web of relationships among people, material artefacts and activities [Ghe 01]. Acting as a competent practitioner is synonymous with knowing how to connect successfully with the field of practices thus activated" [Ghe 09]. Each activity is therefore constituted through social and cultural aspects that are embedded in context and in turn shaping the notion of a dynamic context.

Activity Theory

The socio-historical activity theory (AT) model developed by Vygotsky, Leont'ev as well as Luria in the 1920s and 1930s focuses not on an individual, but rather on an activity where a subject constitutes an object through the mediation of artefacts. The terms artefacts and tools are used synonymously in this paper and are defined not only as materials or technologies, but also conceptual frameworks, mental models, heuristics, speech etc. For a more elaborated description [Tes 99]. This paper wants to point out that a techno-deterministic view of artefacts is rejected from an activity-theory lense. The framework was further developed by [Eng 07], who extended the model by adding three more components that are formed by an activity: Rules, community and division of labour. To understand the notion of context and the ensuing role of social factors. [Tes 99] point to some first guiding principles that are important to consider: The authors argue that if analyzing an activity it is important to consider not only the components, but also the relations between them, which rules and norms emerge between the people who are participating in that activity as well as getting an understanding about goals and intentions, which objects are central to the activity and what kind of

outcomes can be identified [Tes 99]. To fully understand the meaning of context and its implication for inquiring and developing PLEs the paper outlines at first the mechanisms that constitute an activity and how goals and motives are generated within the scope of AT. In the following paragraphs the paper elaborates the aforementioned questions about how learning takes place, which role social and individual factors as well as artefacts (tools) play. Gradually, it follows a discussion what constitutes context and what does this mean for PLEs.

To understand the motives of an activity, analyzing an activity system starts with the central component – the (learning) object – that allows to distinguish between different activities and is constituted by a subject through the mediation of tools [Nar 97]. The object inhabits the motives for conducting an activity, which consists of diverse actions and operations that are influencing an outcome. It has to be noted now that the origin of an object and therefore its motives are defined as social. [Tes 99] state that actions or chains of actions are performed consciously, with time and practice, those actions can transform to (unconscious) operations. Actions are always goal-oriented, where operations depend on those conditions [Tes 99]. Furthermore the authors point out that activities can become actions and also operations through the process of internalization. When those conditions change operations can "return to the level of conscious action" [Kuu 97]. The reverse process also reveals that an activity is a dynamic system where it is possible that operations can become conscious again (e.g. through analyzing or reflecting operations and actions). The aspect of consciousness allows to argue that people and things are not seen as equivalent in the scope of AT. Motives and consciousness are only inherent in humans, because consciousness is defined by Vygotsky as "a phenomenon that unifies attention, intention, memory, reasoning, and speech." [Nar 97]. The explained dynamic process is also an important premise for identifying routines and questioning the taken-for-granted that might become essential for developing concepts that create opportunities for analyzing existing PLEs.

As a consequence of this argumentation context considers not only objects and people as constituting, but also underlying motives and goals as well as artefacts. The following paragraph discusses how learning and development take place and extend this notion of context with the concept of internalization and contradictions:

How learning takes place

In the sense of Vygotsky (1978) learning is a dialectical process of internalization and externalization, where internalization is defined as the "internal reconstruction of external operations". Those processes of internalization and externalization are realized through the concept of mediation, where a mediator (e.g. tool, rules and division of labor) enables a subject to reconstruct those higher mental processes [Luc 10]. These higher functions are at first interpersonal – thereof rooted in culture – and are transformed through internalization to intrapersonal functions. Learning takes place where diverse activities proceed simultaneously and often hindering or fostering each other, because those contradictions allow for analyzing activities that are mostly unconscious [Rei 12b].

Considering contradictions and the social origin of the subject a learning activity is always social in the way that it is a shared activity and as a consequence it is bounded by conditions of interactions, communications and cooperation [Gie 06]. Furthermore knowledge is generated and motivation and goals can change through social interactions and negotiation [Gie 06] during a learning activity. Contradictions in the sense of an enabler of change and learning also challenge people to question their existing PLEs within the process of negotiating learning and working practices. Therefore social factors are important to consider in PLE research, if we keep in mind that personal experiences and practices are always at play. Furthermore the concept of contradictions raises new questions for developing teaching and learning environments in the scope of PLEs as well as how to act in concrete teaching and learning situations (for example): How are contradictions regarding PLEs perceived by students? What kind of interventions induce contradictions that foster students to reflect and adapt their PLEs? How are contradictions influencing negotiation and creation of new practices? How and why do PLEs change?

In the frame of the aforesaid conditions of how learning takes place, context can be extended by the notion of being an emerging system through contradictions, which enable processes of learning and development. The following paragraph discusses the role of the subject and its consequences for an individual. It extends the notion of context with the concept of social and cultural entanglement.

The role of the individual and its socio-material entanglement

It should be noted that from Vygotsky's point of view the subject is not an individual per se, but rather individual learners that are entangled in the social and cultural environment. Hence, [Gie 06] refers to an "overall pedagogical subject" that interlocks those social relations. Especially from a pedagogical point of view (e.g. for e-learning, course or curricula development) as well as from a research perspective when analyzing PLEs and their underlying activities this aspect should be considered very carefully, because this demands not only reflective researchers, but also reflective practitioners and students that are engaged in those educational interactions. Within these processes of educational interactions, which are challenged by contradictions, the subject is seen as the initializing force of an activity, who facilitates development in the sense of changing itself to shared goals and actions to meet cultural and social requirements [Gie 06]. Giest states, that a shared goal of a learning activity lies in the development of personality and not in executing specific learning tasks [Gie 06]. Therefore an overall pedagogical subject and its learning activity as well as development (in general) are always interwoven with the cultural and social environment. As a consequence pedagogical concepts from the activity-oriented view should not only focus on the individual mind, but rather on creating spaces and opportunities that induce dissonance

(contradictions) as well as facilitating cooperation and collaboration between people who are involved, so that learning and development can take place. Following this, it also raises the issue about the idea of control over those learning processes and outcomes, especially from the point of view that those processes are socially shared and negotiated and where personal "interests are constantly at play" [Fen 11]: From the activity-oriented view people are not only simply participating in a working and learning situation, they are actively renewing and co-producing their practices and therefore their PLEs and in the same time influencing the practices and environments of others through interaction and cooperation. Furthermore it becomes visible that if people are in control of those processes they also should be aware of their responsibility regarding others. Even if PLEs seem to be personal, this shows that through the social and cultural entanglement those practices and decisions made by people are never autonomously, they are always influencing others. If we want to design learning opportunities and technology from an activity-oriented view, people should be aware that they play an important role within the social entanglement of an "overall pedagogical subject". This means for lifelong learning that a PLE is also a dialectical process of learning and developing one's own PLE as well as influencing others.

It can be said that the Activity Theory framework provokes new questions: For example it raises questions about the relations of an activity as well as between diverse activity systems. It asks about the context and its historicity, about how mediation takes place and which role artefacts play in this process and how they develop over time and space. The framework is interested in pedagogical interactions, personal experiences, meanings and tools.

It was stated before, that context is an emerging system, which holds the aspect of a process. From the arguments above it can be deduced that this dialectical process of learning and development is also socially and culturally entangled. The following paragraph discusses the role of mediators, especially artefacts, which facilitate internalization and externalization. It also elaborates the interdependency of activity and context.

Role of mediators

The interdependency of activity and context emerges through the concept of mediation. From the perspective of AT artefacts facilitate processes of internalization through shared activities, because on the one hand artefacts are dynamic enablers of communication and on the other hand results of those shared activities [Gie 06]. In the scope of pedagogogical interactions the "overall pedagogical subject" is never detached from artefacts, because artefacts are shaped by cognition and culture and in turn this shapes the artefacts and therefore those tools are never neutral [Rei, 12b]. Considering PLEs this means that artefacts are shaped in practices as well as they are changing PLEs through their role as mediators and the means they provide. Analyzing the historicity of artefacts can be seen as a valuable insight in human development for identifying contradictions within and beyond multiple activity systems. This implies

also studying the way how artefacts are used and if the intended function or ways of using them differ from the ways people actually use and integrate them in practices (abuse/misuse). Tools as mediators and their affordances create means for concretisation in a process of negotiating with people during an activity and implies the possibility to gain experiences with practices in contexts [Rei 12b]. Consequently, reflecting existing PLEs seems to be an important activity for students, teacher and researcher, because it allows them to actively explore existing artefacts and their social and cultural historicity to take advantage of their qualities they inhabit as well as the means they provide. This could enable people to actively create and develop their practices and artefacts more responsibly and to get a better understanding of a shared object or in other words, those ill-structured problems they are engaged in. Because of that developing PLEs can be seen as a highly social and epistemic process, which helps to gain new insights through exploring artefacts in activity to activate contradictions that foster learning and a "becoming" within the socio-material entanglement. Considering that developing a PLE can be defined as an emergent and dynamic learning practice. As a consequence, a simple transmission of PLEs is not possible in the sense of AT. Re-thinking and co-producing PLEs need opportunities that foster active engagement, so that developing PLEs can become an inherent part of everyday working and learning activities. Moreover the individual is then enabled to detect its role within this social and cultural epistemic process of "collaborative transformative practices" and to take over responsibility in creating PLEs not only in institutional situations but also understanding it as a lifelong learning process. This also shows that the construction of meaning is not only an individual process, but rather embedded in artefacts and their histories as well as culturally and socially dependent. Considering PLEs it can be said that materials (as artefacts) are playing a dynamic role as well as the social dimensions and its underlying components like motives of activities and goals of objects. It follows that for selecting adequate methods for inquiring PLEs the following aspects should be considered: meanings negotiated in those social epistemic processes as well as perspectives, experiences and social and cultural embeddedness of people. For example ethnography can play an important role if we want to investigate the boundaries of activities and overlapping systems where contradictions as opportunities arise, which can foster developing PLEs. Another aspect for inquiring PLEs are those shared objects and the mediating artefacts that are used. Examining those overlapping activity systems might gain new insights about how people change their PLEs in practices as time goes by.

As a consequence, from the activity-oriented perspective it can be said that context is not an environment, but rather constituted through the activity itself and is seen as a dynamic process, where an overall social and cultural entangled subject is re-producing and constructing context through overlapping activity systems by negotiating contradictions that emerge between the constituting and interwoven components of those activity systems.

Conclusions

The paper compared an individual-centered and an activity-oriented view of context to identify the role of social factors and the means for PLEs. From the individual-centered perspective context was identified as an aggregation of components that surround an individual. This dichotomy of mind and body leads to a separation of the individual from social relations. Learning is only possible through a mono-directional relationship between the environment and the mind, where mistrust towards the surroundings helps to interpret and identify the truth. From this perspective the paper argued that PLEs are seen as something outside the individual. They can be designed in a specific way, which would enable a learner to shape its behaviors. For developing PLEs this would mean that a transmission of PLEs are possible in the sense that providing an adequate environment would lead students to adopt it as their own. An incremental instructional design were identified as a pedagogical approach, which could foster learning in the sense of the mechanistic view. The paper also mentioned that individual-centered research do not focus on the learning process, but rather explores static images such as efficiency or productivity of those outer learning environments for improving existing tools and platforms.

From the activity-oriented perspective the focus of inquiry lies on the relations between those components of an activity as well as to identify those contradictions to gain an understanding not only about how people cooperate, but also to understand why they are doing it and how new practices emerge through the mediation of artefacts. AT also refers to consider the historical and cultural embeddedness of tools to explain learning and development [Fen 11). Moreover it can be argued that practices are produced and refined by human beings through the usage of materials that ties PLEs intrinsically to practices [Rei, 12b]. Developing PLEs from an activity-oriented perspective was defined as a highly social epistemic process. This socio-material entanglement rejects the separation of a technological-oriented and the pedagogical-oriented view of PLEs, which has an important impact of selecting adequate research methods.

Summarizing it can be said that the mechanistic view on learning and development focus on static images of context conditions as existing or given components (e.g. social factors) that influences individual learning, while an activity-oriented perspective addresses learning processes that are seen as constitutively entangled with socio-materiality. For inquiring PLEs and developing learning opportunities (e-learning and face-to-face scenarios) to address the demands of a knowledge society rethinking the underlying paradigms can help to ask new questions and to gain a better understanding of the dynamic aspects of PLEs. PLE research should rethink traditional research methods, results and interpretations continuously to broaden the research frame. Adequate research methods that accept teaching and learning situations as complex "networks of connections-in-actions" [Ghe 09] could be considered as well as long-term studies to get new insights about PLEs as a lifelong learning process.

REFERENCES

[Arr 12] *Arrufat, Mª Jesús Gallego; Sánchez, Vanesa Gámiz (2012):* Steps to reflect on the Personal Learning Environment: Improving the learning process? In: PLE Conference Proceedings 2012. Aveiro, Portugal. Retrieved September 2013 from *http://revistas.ua.pt/index.php/ple/article/viewFile/1430/1316*

[Ase 96] *Asendorpf, Jens B. (1996):* Psychologie der Persönlichkeit: Grundlagen. Berlin, Heidelberg. Springer.

[Att 07] *Attwell, Graham (2007):* Personal Learning Environments – the future of eLearning? Retrieved June 2014 from *http://senior.googlecode.com/files/media11561-1.pdf*

[Att 12] *Attwell, Graham; Deitmer, Ludger (2012):* Developing Work based Personal Learning Environments in Small and Medium Enterprises. In: PLE Conference Proceedings 2012. Aveiro, Portugal. Retrieved September 2013 from *http://revistas.ua.pt/index.php/ple/article/viewFile/1432/1318*

[Buc 11] *Buchem, Ilona; Attwell, Graham; Torres, Ricardo (2011):* Understanding Personal Learning Environments: Literature review and synthesis through the Activity Theory lens. In: Proceedings of the The PLE Conference 2011. Southampton, UK, 1–33. Retrieved March 2012 from *http://journal.webscience.org/658/1/PLE_SOU_Paper_Buchem_Attwell_Torress.doc*

[Buc 12] *Buchem, Ilona (2012):* Psychological Ownership and Personal Learning Environments. Do sense of ownership and control really matter? In: PLE Conference Proceedings 2012. Aveiro, Portugal. Retrieved September 2013 from *http://revistas.ua.pt/index.php/ple/article/viewFile/1437/1323*

[Cas 84] *Case, Robbie; Bereiter, Carl (1984):* From behaviourism to cognitive behaviourism to cognitive development: Steps in the evolution of instructional design. In: Instructional Science, 13, 2, 141–158.

[Cas 12] *Castañada, Linda; Adell, Jordi (2012):* Future Teachers Looking for their PLEs: the Personalized Learning Process Behind it all. In: PLE Conference Proceedings 2012. Aveiro, Portugal. Retrieved September 2013 from *http://revistas.ua.pt/index.php/ple/article/viewFile/1440/1326*

[Des 79] *Descartes, René (1979):* Abhandlung über die Methode. In: Erkenntnis- und Wissenschaftstheorie, 2, 4. ed., Münster, 16–24.

[Eng 07] *Engeström, Yrjö (2007):* Activity theory and individual and social transformation. In: Engeström, Yrjö; Miettinen, Reijo; Punamäki, Raija-Leena (Eds.): Perspectives on activity theory. Cambridge: Cambridge University Press, 19–38.

[Fen 10] *Fenwick, Tara (2010):* Re-thinking the “thing”: Sociomaterial approaches to understanding and researching learning in work. In: Journal of Workplace Learning, 22, 1/2, 104–116.

[Fen 11] *Fenwick, Tara J.; Edwards, Richard; Sawchuk, Peter (2011):* Emerging approaches to educational research. Tracing the sociomaterial. 1st ed. Milton Park, Abingdon, Oxon, New York. Routledge.

[Fie 10] *Fiedler, Sebastian; Väljataga, Terje (2010):* Personal learning environments: concept or technology? In: The PLE Conference. Barcelona, Spain. Retrieved March 2012 from *http://pleconference.citilab.eu/wp-content/uploads/2010/07/ple2010_submission_45.pdf*

[Fig 06] *Figueiredo, António Dias de; Afonso, Ana Paula (2006):* Context and Learning: A Philosophical Framework. In: Figueiredo, Antonio Dias; Afonso, Ana Paula (Eds.): Managing learning in virtual settings: The role of context. Hershey, PA. Information Science Pub., 1–22.

[Gar 12] *Garcia, Iolanda; Gros, Begoña; Mas, Xavier; Noguera, Ingrid; Sancho, Teresa; Ceballos, Jordi (2012):* Just4me- functional requirements to support informal self-directed learning in a personal ubiquitous environment. In: PLE Conference Proceedings 2012. Aveiro, Portugal. Retrieved September 2013 from *http://revistas.ua.pt/index.php/ple/article/viewFile/1446/1332*

[Ghe 09] *Gherardi, S. (2009):* Introduction: The Critical Power of the 'Practice Lens'. In Management Learning, 40, 2, 115–128.

[Gie 06] *Giest, Hartmut (2006):* Lernen – betrachtet aus tätigkeitstheoretischer Perspektive. In: Lernen und Neue Medien. Potsdam. Univ. Potsdam, Zentrum für Lehrerbildung.

[Ham 96] *Hampden-Turner, Charles (1996):* Modelle des Menschen: Dem Rätsel des Bewusstseins auf der Spur. Weinheim. Beltz, PsychologieVerlagsUnion.

[Höl 12] *Hölterhof, Tobias; Nattland, Axel; Kerres, Michael (2012):* Drupal as a Social Hub for Personal Learning. In: PLE Conference Proceedings 2012. Aveiro, Portugal. Retrieved September 2013 from *http://revistas.ua.pt/index.php/ple/article/viewFile/1453/1339*

[Iva 12] *Ivanova, Malinka; Grosseck, Gabriela; Holotescu, Carmen (2012):* Analysis of Personal Learning Networks in Support of Teachers Presence Optimization. In: PLE Conference Proceedings 2012. Aveiro, Portugal. Retrieved September 2013 from *http://revistas.ua.pt/index.php/ple/article/viewFile/1439/1325*

[Jon 99] *Jonassen, David H.; Tessmer, Martin; Hannum, Wallace H. (Eds.) (1999):* Task analysis methods for instructional design. Mahwah. NJ. L. Erlbaum Associates.

[Kuu 97] *Kuutti, Kari (1997):* Activity Theory as a Potential Framework for Human-Computer Interaction Research. In: Nardi, Bonnie A. (Ed.): Context and consciousness. Activity theory and human-computer interaction. Third printing. Cambridge, Mass. MIT Press, 17–44.

[Loc 79] *Locke, John (1979):* Über den menschlichen Verstand. In: Erkenntnis- und Wissenschaftstheorie. 4. ed., Münster, 24–30.

[Luc 10] *Luckin, Rosemary (2010):* Re-designing learning contexts. Technology-rich, learner-centred ecologies. New York. Routledge. [Kindle Edition]

[Mar 12] *Marin, Victoria; Salina, Jesús; de Benito, Bárbara (2012):* Using SymbalooEDU as a PLE Organizer in Higher Education. In: PLE Conference Proceedings 2012. Aveiro, Portugal. Retrieved September 2013 from *http://revistas.ua.pt/index.php/ple/article/viewFile/1427/1313*

[Mir 12] *Mirza, Mahrukh; Chaterjee, Arunangsu (2012):* The impact of culture on personalization of learning environments. Some theoretical insights. In PLE Conference Proceedings 2012. Aveiro, Portugal. Retrieved September 2013 from *http://revistas.ua.pt/index.php/ple/article/viewFile/1436/1322*

[Nar 97] *Nardi, Bonnie A. (Ed.) (1997):* Context and consciousness: Activity theory and human-computer interaction. Third printing. Cambridge, Mass. MIT Press.

[Non 97] *Nonaka, Ikujiro; Takeuchi, Hirotaka; Mader, Friedrich (1997):* Die Organisation des Wissens: Wie japanische Unternehmen eine brachliegende Ressource nutzbar machen. Frankfurt/Main. Campus-Verlag.

[Orl 07] *Orlikowski, W. J. (2007):* Sociomaterial Practices: Exploring Technology at Work. In Organization Studies, 28, 9, 1435–1448.

[Pai 12] *Pais, Fátima; Santos, Carlos; Pedro, Luís (2012):* Sapo Campus Schools: Network Learning, Teaching and People. In: PLE Conference Proceedings 2012. Aveiro, Portugal. Retrieved September 2013 from *http://revistas.ua.pt/index.php/ple/article/viewFile/1462/2302*

[Per 11] *Perera, Nishan C. (2011):* Cognitivist vs. Behaviourist Paradigms: Points of Convergence and Divergence. Retrieved September 2013 from *http://nishancperera.com/2011/01/31/cognitivist-vs-behaviourist-paradigms-points-of-convergence-and-divergence-by-nishan-perera/*

[Rav 11] *Ravenscroft, Andrew; Attwell, Graham; Blagbrough, David; Stieglitz, Dirk; (2011):* 'Jam Hot!' Personalised radio ciphers through augmented social media for the transformational learning of disadvantaged young people. In: Proceedings of The PLE Conference 2011. Southampton, UK. Retrieved September 2013 from *http://journal.webscience.org/557/, checked on 10/16/2013*

[Rei 12a] *Reisas, Sabine (2012):* Exploration of concepts to facilitate diverse knowledge practices and personal learning environments. In: Proceedings of the Fourth Annual Teachers College Educational Technology Conference. New York. Columbia University, 54–55.

[Rei 12b] *Reisas, Sabine (2012):* Diverse Knowledge Practices through Personal Learning Environments – A theoretical Framework. In: PLE Conference Proceedings 2012. Aveiro, Portugal. Retrieved September 2013 from *http://revistas.ua.pt/index.php/ple/article/viewFile/1463/1349, checked on 9/2/2013*

[Ric 13] *Richter, Christoph; Allert, Heidrun (2013):* Making Use of Artefacts in Design Practice. 8th International Conference: Researching Work and Learning. Symposium: Materials (& Meaning) in the Making. Sterling, United Kingdom.

[Sal 11] *Salinas, Jesús; Marín, Victoria; Escandell, Catalina; (Keine Angabe); (Keine Angabe); (Keine Angabe) (2011):* A case of institutional PLE: integration of VLE and e-portfolio for students. In: Proceedings of the The PLE Conference 2011. Southampton, UK. Retrieved September 2013 from *http://journal.webscience.org/585/*

[Sca 03] *Scardamalia, Marlene; Bereiter, Carl (2003):* Knowledge Building. In: Encyclopedia of Education, 2nd ed., New York. Macmillan Reference, 1370–1373. Retrieved September 2013 from *http://ikit.org/fulltext/2003_knowledge_building.pdf*

[Tes 99] *Tessmer, Martin; Rohrer-Murphy, Lucia (1999):* Activity Theory. In: Jonassen, David H.; Tessmer, Martin; Hannum, Wallace H. (Eds.): Task analysis methods for instructional design. Mahwah, NJ. L. Erlbaum Associates, 159–172.

[Tol 07] *Tolman, Charles W. (2007):* Society versus context in individual development: Does theory make a difference? In: Engeström, Yrjö; Miettinen, Reijo; Punamäki, Raija-Leena (Eds.): Perspectives on activity theory. Cambridge. Cambridge University Press, 70–86.

[Vyg 78] *Vygotsky, Lev Semyonovitsch (1978):* Mind in society: The development of higher psychological processes. Cambridge. Harvard University Press. [Kindle Edition]

[Wen 08] *Wenger, Etienne (2008):* Communities of practice. Learning, meaning, and identity. 16th ed., Cambridge. Cambridge Univ. Press.

[Wen 10] *Wenger, Etienne; McDermott, Richard; Snyder, William M. (2010):* Cultivating communities of practice: A guide to managing knowledge. Boston, Mass. Harvard Business School Press.

[Wol 11] *Wolpers, Martin; Friedrich, Martin (2011):* Widget User Interface considerations for ROLE widgets. In: Proceedings of the The PLE Conference 2011. Southampton, UK. Retrieved September 2013 from *http://journal.webscience.org/654/1/S5-Wolpers-Friedrich-u2x-4-ple.pdf*

CONTACT DETAILS

Sabine Reisas, M.A.
Christian-Albrechts-Universität zu Kiel
(Kiel University)
Department of Media Education/Educational
Computer Sciences,
Olshausenstraße 75,
24098 Kiel, Germany
Phone: +49 (0)431 880 5572

Do you want to connect? Recommendendation strategies for building Personal Learning Networks

Kamakshi Rajagopal, Jan van Bruggen, Peter B. Sloep

ABSTRACT

Recommender systems on social networking sites make users of these sites aware of various resources and people that otherwise they may have missed. In Personal Learning Networks, recommendation is used to create new connections by creating opportunities for interaction and conversation between learners. This article describes the outcomes of a workshop held at the PLE Conference 2013 on the design of recommender systems and on the concepts that determine how they work.

Introduction

Recommender systems on social networking sites (SNS) make users of these sites aware of various resources and people that otherwise they may have missed. These systems are increasingly used for educational purposes, to connect learners with suitable learning resources, peers and tutors [Man 12]. In Personal Learning Networks (PLNs), recommendation can be used to create new connections between learners in order to support their continuous non-formal learning. The challenge in PLNs is to create opportunities for interaction and conversation between learners [Raj 12], [Tin 09].

As recommender systems shape our interactions on SNS, users of these systems need to understand the concepts that determine how they work. In this article, we describe the outcomes of a workshop held at the PLE Conference 2013 that focussed on the concepts behind recommender systems, in particular tag-based user profiles and two matching methodologies for extending PLNs through an interactive exercise.

We will first give some background on the use of recommender systems for learning, looking at both the recommendation of learning objects and of people. Then we will flesh out the aspects of matching people for learning and make a case for looking for dissimilarity (rather than similarity). Next, we will look at the workshop and the outcomes of the workshop. We will end with some considerations stemming from the workshop and clues for further research.

Recommender Systems for Learning

The use of recommendations is widespread on the Internet, especially on social networking sites. Ranging from the next item to buy on Amazon, or the next book to read on Goodreads to the next person to connect to on LinkedIn, recommender systems determine much of how each of us experiences the web. A high level of personalisation has become the norm on the web, where we expect to see links to the things or people that matter to us. This only seems to increase with the advent of Big Data, that allow technologists to create more complete profiles of users on the Internet. However, many users are oblivious to just how far-reaching this profiling goes and how it affects the objects they get to see (or not to see) and the people they get to meet online (or not to meet). For lifelong learners, who use the Internet as a source of information and for knowledge building, this aspect of recommender systems is problematic. To understand why, we need to look closer at the way recommendation works online. All recommender systems conceptually consist of three components (i) a user profile to characterise an individual user, (ii) a matching algorithm to determine which users should be recommended to each other, and (iii) a user interface, to introduce users to their recommended match.

The quality of the recommendations will depend on how well the learner can be profiled and how a good match is defined. Current recommender systems for learning broadly follow the same strategies as recommenders in other environments. Strategies such as collaborative filtering and content-based recommendation follow a principle of similarity: when the user has indicated an interest in some way, the recommending system looks for items that match that interest or people who share that interest.

For learning purposes, this principle of similarity is flawed. Individuals learn in diverse groups, where people from different backgrounds come together [Mor 13], [Pes 14]. And people seek out differences when making contacts with strangers [Raj 12b]. So, there is a need for dissimilarity: looking for people who share certain things, but also critically differ in some meaningful way. The difference opens up the scope for interest and for potential learning [Pes 14], [Raj XX].

Workshop Setup

In our workshop, we aimed to get the participants to work out the nitty-gritty details of the calculations according to two recommendation algorithms: one based on similarity and one based on dissimilarity. The participants were asked to create user data, gather and categorise this user data and finally match one's own data individually with the others in the group. By working manually and following all the steps involved, participants could experience how their data is transformed and used to make decisions regarding their interests and expertise.

The workshop setup guided this through a series of group and individual exercises. This workshop is an adapted version of the workshop conducted at the eTwinning conference, based on the Connect the Dots! Reflection Exercise [Raj 12a]. The aim of the workshop was to replicate the recommendation methods employed in [Raj XX]. The workshop was interactive with individual activities, in-pair activities and small-group work.

1. First, the participants seated at a same table were asked to introduce themselves to the others at the table. They were also asked to make a mental note on who they would want to meet up with later in the conference.
2. Next, they were asked to write down 10 tags on cards – one tag per card – that describe their work and the topics they found important in the PLE conference.
3. Per table, the participants then pooled all the tags in the centre of the table and compared them. Similar tags were stapled together in a pile, and one marker tag was chosen to mark each pile. For example, tags such as *create*, *creativity* and *creation* belong to the same pile, with as marker tag *create*.
4. Using all the marker tags on the table, the participants then indivdidually needed to make tagsets, by writing down marker tags that belong together according to them.
5. In the next step, one-to-one matches were made with everyone at the table:
   (A) first on similarity, looking at the number of common tags as a fraction of the total number of tags created
   (B) then on dissimilarty, looking at the product of i) the number of overlapping tagsets as a fraction of the total number of tagset matches and ii) the 10-log[1] of the total number of tagset matches.
6. Finally, the participants were asked to reflect on who came out as the best match on both similarity and dissimilarity from the calculations. Also, they considered if these outcomes were in line with their prior 'gut' feeling?

Results

Five people attended the workshop: three with a technical background (P1, P2, P5) and two with an educational practitioners background (P3, P4). Two of the three technical participants were colleagues of each other (P1 and P2). This select group allowed the discussions to go deeper and further than otherwise would have been possible. The matching exercise resulted in two matching tables, one for similarity and one for dissimilarity (Table 1 and Table 2).

1 The 10-log was used to reduce the magnitude of the resulting number to a matching score between 0 and 1, in order to make it comparable with others.

Table 1: Similarity matrix of matching scores (with marker tags): this matrix is symmetrical due to how similarity is calculated

SIMILARITY					
	P1	P2	P3	P4	P5
P1		0.105	0.053	0.053	0
P2			0.050	0.050	0
P3				0.150	0
P4					0
P5					

Table 2: Dissimilarity matrix of matching scores (with tag sets): this matrix is symmetrical due to how dissimilarity is calculated

DISSIMILARITY					
	P1	P2	P3	P4	P5
P1		0.29	0.19	0.28	0.33
P2			0.09	0.36	0.36
P3				0.18	0.21
P4					0.33
P5					

Table 3 groups the results of the matches, in terms of who is the best match for whom. From the table, it is clear that the similarity matrix is symmetric. P is as similar to P' as P' is to P; this is a consequence of the way similarity is calculated and the number of shared tags in this small group. In the group of five participants, one participant (P5) remains without a match, whereas the other two matches were to be expected: the technical people are grouped together as are the educational practitioners. In contrast, matching on dissimilarity results in directional matches, where every person has a best match in the group. In this instance, the difference between the two methods is largely due to the number of shared marker tags that skews the similarity matching method. In larger groups with more marker tags, similarity might also result in directional matches.

Table 3: Results of matching

SIMILARITY	DISSIMILARITY
P1-P2	P1≥P5
P3-P4	P2≥P4; P2≥P5
P5!	P3 ≥P5
	P4≥P2
	P5≥P2

Discussion

Although the participation at this workshop was quite low, from a design point of view the participants' reactions to how they were matched was interesting. It also gave the authors the opportunity to observe discussions in one group closely. Regarding the differences between the matching methods, it was interesting to see that even in the select group of participants, we could see very different types of matches emerging by using the different methods. In particular, matching on similarity indicated a huge difference between one participant (P5) and the rest of the group. As a result, this person did not have a recommended match. However, the same participant emerged as the best match for three participants in the group when matching on dissimilarity. The group agreed that the method of dissimilarity needs to be further researched. Of particular interest is how the two methods perform in groups of different sizes.

Regarding the process of calculating matches, it was remarkable how the participants quickly brought in other, more intelligent steps to improve the marker tags in the third step of the exercise. Examples of these improvements included intelligent interpretation of tags (such as through synonyms, part-whole categorisation etc.), reformulation and clarification, etc. For the exercise, the participants were therefore repeatedly instructed to keep to the simple method of gathering based on common stems of the words used. From a design point of view, implementing this type of intelligence would involve more complex natural language processing techniques and a memory-heavy lexicon and/ontology. However, it is not clear if these more complex techniques to create the marker tags would necessarily improve recommendations. More research is needed to investigate the benefits of more complex techniques in recommendation

Finally, when asked to reveal if the matches followed their own initial impressions on which contact to pursue, the participants revealed it was difficult to make such a decision after initial contacts (although some did indicate initial preferences). However, through increased interaction throughout the exercise, they did see which contacts might be more valuable than others. In these, it was clear that such choices were dependent on a whole range of things, from professional to personal to other.

Summary

In summary, the workshop brought to light the seeming shortcomings of recommendation on the basis of similarity in online applications. The method of dissimilarity offered a first step for further research. The discussions also indicated how the technical aspects of recommendation online are quite restrictive in the data they have access to, whereas learners in face-to-face environments have many more opportunities and considerations to connect.

Acknowledgements

The work presented at this workshop is partly based on Kamakshi Rajagopal's doctoral studies and follows on the work conducted in the Language Technologies for Lifelong Learning (LTfLL) project.

REFERENCES

[Man 12] *Mansouelis, Nikos; Drachsler, Hendrik; Verbert, Katrien; Santos, Olga C. (Eds.) (2012):* Proceedings of the 2nd Workshop on Recommender Systems for Technology Enhanced Learning (RecSysTEL 2012). Published by CEUR Workshop Proceedings, 2012, Vol. 896.

[Mor 13] *Moreland, Richard L.; Levine, J. M.; Wingert, M. L. (2013):* Creating the ideal group: Composition effects at work. In: Understanding group behavior 2, 11–35.

[Pes 14] *Peschl, Markus. F.; Fundneider, Thomas (2014):* Designing and Enabling Spaces for collaborative knowledge creation and innovation : From managing to enabling innovation as socio-epistemological technology. In: Computers in Human Behavior. doi:10.1016/j.chb.2012.05.027.

[Raj 12] *Rajagopal, Kamakshi; Joosten-ten Brinke, Desirée; Van Bruggen, Jan; Sloep, Peter B. (2012):* *Understanding personal learning networks: Their structure, content and the networking skills to optimally use them.* In: First Monday, 17(1), 1–12.

[Raj 12a] *Rajagopal, Kamakshi, Van Bruggen, Jan, & Sloep, Peter B. (2012):* Working Format: Connect The Dots! Reflection Exercise. Heerlen, The Netherlands: Open Universiteit in the Netherlands (CELSTEC, TELLNet). *http://hdl.handle.net/1820/4513*

[Raj 12b] *Rajagopal, Kamakshi; Verjans, Steven; Costa, Cristina; Sloep, Peter B. (2012):* *People in Personal Learning Networks: Analysing their Characteristics and Identifying Suitable Tools.* In: Proceedings of the Eighth International Conference on Networked Learning 2012, 252–259.

[Raj XX] *Rajagopal, Kamakshi; Van Bruggen, Jan; Sloep, Peter B. (20XX):* "I connect with people who think differently from me": People Recommenders that Match on Dissimilarity (submitted).

[Tin 09] *Tinsley, Ron; Lebak, Kimberley (2009):* Expanding the Zone of Reflective Capacity: Taking Separate Journeys Together. In: Networks, 11(2). Retrieved from *http://journals.library.wisc.edu/index.php/networks/article/view/190*

CONTACT DETAILS

Dr. Kamakshi Rajagopal
Open Universiteit
Valkenburgerweg 177
6419 AT Heerlen
E-Mail: *kamakshi.rajagopal@gmail.com*

Dr. Jan van Bruggen
Open Universiteit
Valkenburgerweg 177
6419 AT Heerlen
E-Mail: *jan.vanbruggen@ou.nl*

Prof. Dr. Peter B. Sloep
Open Universiteit
Valkenburgerweg 177
6419 AT Heerlen
E-Mail: *peter.sloep@ou.nl*

PLEs and epistemological practice – The meaning of Self organization competency for PLE based learning

David Kergel

ABSTRACT

An effective use of PLEs for learning processes requires the capability of self-organization. The integrative use of different Web 2.0 applications needs to be accompanied by a reflexive approach which stresses epistemological and media-theoretical aspects of PLEs: The article discusses two issues: (a) to what extend such a reflexive approach towards the use of PLEs can be considered as an epistemological practice, and (b) how is it possible to optimize the individual epistemological process of knowledge construction via the combination of different Web 2.0 applications?

Introduction

Within the discussion of the possibilities and limitations of e-learning 2.0 the question of organising Web 2.0 based applications becomes relevant. How and by which strategies can these applications be used in formal learning contexts? This paper's basic thesis is that according to conceptions of the PLE, the use of Web 2.0 applications requires a high degree of self-determination and critical self-reflection from the learning individual. This thesis makes it necessary to consider the following issues: (a) implications of Web 2.0 based discussions for media theory, (b) the historical/ societal context of e-learning 2.0, (c) the meaning of critical self-reflection for PLEs. This strategy makes it possible to outline keystones for a didactic development of PLEs.

Implications for media theory

The link between communication structures and learning paradigms actualises more or less explicit media-theoretical issues such as learning paradigms determine relations of media (e.g. Montessori materials) and individuals (e.g. a child) within learning contexts. With reference to McLuhan's maxim that 'the media is the message', the communicated content is inextricably linked with the media and its structure. One could propose the thesis that not only the content is bound to the media, but also the individual who uses the media. Subsequently media have a 'subjection impact' on the individual. Subjections 'shape' the individual and the individual's self-reflexivity, self-conception and self-consciousness [But 97]. This point unfolds within the

use of media: Uni-directional media like Web 2.0 applications address the receiver in a passive way. The receiver possesses a receptive function within uni-directional media based communication processes. Poly-directional media structure the sender-receiver dichotomy dynamically. The receiver of a piece of information can react almost instantly by creating a piece of content and thus promptly transforms himself into a sender: When a blog entry is posted the reader can instantly react to this entry via a commentary and creates a new text. This new text includes blog entry and commentary: "Social software offers the opportunity to narrow the divide between producers and consumers. Consumers themselves become producers, through creating and sharing" [Atw 07: 1]. The consequences which emerge out of this process for the media are far-reaching. The text loses its linear, enclosed structure and receives hypertextual structures. The function of an 'author' is not linked to one specific individual. The author as producer of a text is constituted during a text production which is – at least theoretically – infinite: each comment can be followed by another comment or a new blog entry which in turn initiate new reactions. The meaning of a text changes constantly. From the point of view of media theory, one could analyse the process as follows: the structure of a medium prefigures the communication process between individuals and subsequently the way they interact with each other. A media-theoretical interpretation of Deleuze's position that "(...) Modes of life inspire ways of thinking; modes of thinking create ways of living" [Del 04: 66), shows that newly emerging communicative processes enable new social practices. As a political example, the Facebook Revolution in the course of the Arab Spring reveals how a resistance movement can de-centralize itself through the use of Web 2.0 based social software. These new Web 2.0 based communication possibilities need to be reflected upon and conceptualised. The technical innovations which constitute Web 2.0 mean also a challenge for e-learning. Due to their medial structure the communicative innovations and the scope of their possibilities present a significant challenge to the individual and his or her self-organisation within learning processes. With reference to Deleuze one could say that 'Modes of Web 2.0 based learning inspire ways of thinking and create ways of learning.' In the course of the discussion and conception of an appropriate approach, the possibility of a paradigm change in learning is discussed [Gai 08: 5]. Mason and Rennie stress that Web 2.0 based e-learning is connected with constructivist theories [Mas 10: 98].

Web 2.0 based learning in a historical context

The theoretical conception of conventionalised pedagogical practice is historically bound. The way in which these practices are discursively framed depends on the specific historic situation out of which pedagogical practice and theory develop. A medieval pedagogy bases itself on another paradigm such as the pedagogy of ancient city-states [Ter 09]. Pedagogic conceptions are based – more or less explicitly – on anthropological conceptions. Although educational science is still discussing the relevance, meaning of constructivist learning theories [Ber 04]. The epistemological basis of these theories can be traced back discursively to the constitution processes of civil society. In contrast to feudal society, which legitimated itself through God as the point of origin for meaning and structures of meaning, the upcoming bourgeoisie favoured a secularistic, rationally based world-view. For an example for this rationalism one could refer to Kant's epistemological concept. According to Kant, the subject with its transcendental competence is the only valid authority for knowledge. Working from this premise, Kant developed an epistemological model which Jäger calls the basic thesis of constructivism [Jäg 98: 147]. Adorno and Horkheimer [Ado 97: 106] stress that this epistemology corresponds to the self-conception of civil society due to its emphasis on the active individual.

The relationship between constructivist learning paradigms and Kant's epistemology is addressed by various educational researchers [Sie 99]. Because Kant's epistemological concept set an insurmountable difference between the experience of the world and the objective world, the subject constructs meaning in the course of epistemological processes [Sie 99: 52]. With this epistemological scepticism towards a normative realism, an alternative perspective on the learning individual emerged. Instead of a deficit-orientated approach which analyses what the learning individual does not yet know, constructivist theories focus on the individual attempting to give meaning to the world and thus creating knowledge.

The concept of knowledge acquisition is based on an epistemological scepticism which is based on a societal self-understanding. This understanding is in turn embedded in specific historical contexts. From this point of view it may be interesting to ask whether the shift of the latest constructivist approaches away from the single individual towards more interactionistic-constructivistic perspectives is based on societal dynamics. Does the interactionistic-constructivistic approach mirror social processes?

With reference to Foucault, Ariès [Ari 75] developed the thesis that education is a practice of bourgeois self-assurance: The bourgeois individual needs rationally based guidance in order to be accepted into civil society. This socialising process has to be ensured by education which focuses on the single individual. The educational focus on the single individual corresponds to the epistemological model which considers the autoreferentiality of a single individual to be a valid point of origin for knowledge creation. Interactionistic-constructivistic approaches, however, focus on collective, inter-individual processes of knowledge creation. With reference to post-modern sociological theories one could identify some societal reasons for this change. These reseans include (a) an increasing decentralisation of work processes, decentralisation of (urban) private life [Stä 11], and a decentralisation of life-planning. From this perspective it can be said that changes in the labour market and prevailing crises make life planning increasingly difficult [Hep 09].

The increasing relevance of such positions and their societal acceptance also manifests itself in the learning paradigm of interactionistic-constructivism. This learning paradigm reacts to such a cultural change:

"But cultural change, with an increase of pluralism, diversity, cultural and migration differences, entails the necessity to educate and nurture this sensitivity for all observers." [Rei 07: 13]

The increase of pluralism has an effect on interactionistic processes in which the individual is involved, in which the individual unfolds him/herself via interactionistic processes. One can locate Reich's approach of interactionistic-constructivism within the context of these socio-cultural tendencies:

"Since the contents of learning are always embedded in and communicated through lived relationships with others, relationships themselves have become a primary concern of education. At the same time the space and liberty of interpretation has grown in our culture. The different versions of reality constructions that are present in any communicative situation demand social open-mindedness. We cannot rely on traditions or rituals the way other generations did. In responding to unambiguity and ambivalence we must balance out our more complex communication and an open attitude by changing in our observations between the inner and outer views." [Rei 07: 14]

Valid meaning is created within collective negation processes (e.g. Wikipedia could be considered as an example of such a collective process of knowledge construction). With regard to a focus on practical learning via Web 2.0 based applications, it is possible to extend the model of interactionistic-constructivism and integrate aspects related to media theory. The construction of meaning takes place within communication processes. With reference to Web 2.0 applications, the individual is embedded in a specific context, which a social software application provides. The individual is confronted with specific expectations within this context: applications like Twitter or Facebook provide normative spaces with specific horizons of expectation, specific language codes etc. Within this normative space the individual performs/ constructs themselves through communication strategies. Just as truth is, according to pragmatic conceptions, situationally bound, identity construction via (self-) narratives through communication strategies depends on the communication code of a social software application. These narratives, the way an individual participates in communication processes, depend on the normative presets of Web 2.0 based social software applications. The interactionistic dynamic within which the individual articulates themselves is prefigured by these applications. For a learning paradigm which adequately theorises the possibilities of Web 2.0 applications for e-learning, this communication processes has to be analysed appropriately.

From the perspective of learning paradigms one could set the following condition: An interactionistic-constructivistic approach which theorises the interactive dimensions of Web 2.0 for learning processes appropriate, has to take into account phenomena like Web 2.0 based knowledge creation (e.g. the potential infinity of a weblog or Wikipedia). The typical and constitutive aspects for this knowledge creation via Web 2.0 based technology (the UGC which requires the production of content and a communicative, poly-directional orientation) have to be discussed from a perspective of learning theory. Web 2.0 applications are mostly used in informal learning processes which are embedded in an interactionistic, supraindividual dynamic: on the one hand Web 2.0 applications are popular and can provide a high degree of motivation for the learner. On the other hand the individual can easily vanish within the context of this collaborative communication process.

PLEs enable an integration of constructivist approaches which stress the importance of the single individual as a point of origin for valid knowledge creation and learning processes in interactionistic dynamics. PLEs are located within this tensioned relationship – collaborative learning processes and knowledge creation versus the single individual as point of origin in construction processes.

Critical self-reflection as a constitutive part of PLEs

Zingle and Türker point to the aspect that PLEs need pedagogical added value to ensure that PLEs are not reduced to a purely functional "management system" [Zin 08: 1]. Schaffert et al. locate this added value within the pedagogical re-definition of the learner [Sch 08: 16]. A similar position is formulated by Attwell when he states:

> *"The development and support for Personal Learning Environments would entail a radical shift, not only in how we use educational technology, but in the organisation and ethos of education." [Atw 07: 5]*

This 'new ethos' requires a high degree of self-reflection from the learner in course of using Web 2.0 applications for formal learning processes. This high degree of self-reflection can be described with the epistemological terms of the '*subject*' and the '*self*'. From an epistemological point of view the *self* can be considered the 'effect' when the individual reflects about him*self*. Due to '*self*'-reflection the individual as subject becomes his own object, conceptualises his own needs and develops a *self*-image. The subject, represented in the '*I*', reflects about him*self* through the construction of the '*self*'. *Self*-organization can in turn be understood as an auto-referential organization of the '*I*'. In course of interaction with the environment the '*I*' develops a cognitive and emotive representation which can be conceptualised with the notion *se*lf-organization. Mead used the notions 'I' and 'Me': 'The "I" is the response of the organism to the

attitudes of the others; the "me" is the organized set of attitudes of others which one himself assumes. The attitudes of the others constitute the organized "me", and then one reacts toward that as an "I"' [Mea 55: 175]. This interaction with the environment, in which the '*self*' as an effect is constructed, is bound to the media. A – more or less explicit – basic premise of PLEs consists in the thesis that the 'I' developed a self-concept which manifests itself in the self-confident use *of* Web 2.0 applications for learning processes. According to these reflections one could formulated: Why does which media are used, and the way they are used for learning, depend on the self-assessment of the 'I' in the course of learning processes. The training of such reflection-strategies can be understood as the pedagogical added value of PLEs.

The establishment of such *self*-reflectively based PLEs requires media pedagogical considerations. From a didactic point of view it is relevant to develop learning scenarios which mediate reflection strategies. These strategies should enable the learner to reflect about themselves in the course of interaction with the Web 2.0 environment.

Keystones for a didactic development of PLEs

The relationship of the '*I*' to him*self* and to his environment can be reflected in the process of producing a text [Fre 00]. Experiences can be reflected and categorised through a written text.

The "'I'-'self'-'environment'" relationship can be reflected in the course of text production. The text is thus a metonymical manifestation of this reflection process.

With regard to the use of social media in learning contexts one could use the following guiding question for a text: In which way do I use which social media software? Such a question requires one to position oneself within the '*I*'/'media use' relationship. With reference to learning processes via Web 2.0 based applications one can specify this guiding question: In which way do I use media for learning processes? How do I understand my own position (role) during the use of the media? The use of Web 2.0 based applications is (mostly) connected with communication processes, so that one must clarify whether the application is used '*more productively or more receptively*'? And further: Why do I prefer to use more productive or more receptive applications?' Such a narrative-orientated reflection of media use ensures according to [Dan 02] the appropriate reflection of media use in the course of learning processes.

E-Portfolios as spaces for reflections on media pedagogy

In addition to this position it is important to provide action strategies for the learner so that s/he is able to make appropriate use of Web based 2.0 media and thus construct a PLE (from this perspective PLEs are in turn metonymical manifestations of *self*-reflection). Such action strategies have to provide spaces for reflection so that the learner can think about his or her learning-related media use critically. The construction of such spaces requires a meta-level which enables written reflection on media use and the position of the subject in the course of this specific media use. For instance: How do I understand myself/ my role in course of web-blogging? Or in more epistemological terms: Which kind of (implicit) self-conception accompanies my web-blogging? Such initial questions might lead from a reflection of concrete media use to media use on a more abstract level: Which media do I use for which purposes? Where can I optimise my media use for learning? E-portfolios can be used as a forum and e-learning tool to practice such thinking strategies. An e-portfolio allows the learner to collect artifacts produced in the course of learning processes. It is also possible to collect notes which reflect learning processes. [Arn 11: 255] point out that e-portfolios could be used as a forum for reflection on individual competency development. The learner can address open questions or his/her artifacts and insights or review the learning strategies used and their outcomes in relation to the learning targets etc. Conceived thus, an e-portfolio reveals the relevant connection between the theory and practice of media use: a sovereign media use, which is central for PLEs, requires critical reflection on the relationship of the '*I*' to the use of media. This relationship will be addressed in the following discussion of a possible conception which leads from reflections of media use within e-portfolios to the construction of PLEs. E-portfolios provide a frame which can be used to reflect the implementation of Web 2.0 applications in the course of an individual learning process. Such use of e-portfolios makes it possible to gradually open up the reflection of the learning process to the construction of PLEs.

The central question is how to implement such a use of e-portfolios in pedagogical practice?

With reference to Mason and Rennie one could cite the didactic, action-orientated strategy to establish a mix of normative impulses (the learning individual *has* to reflect on the use of Web 2.0 applications) and observational learning (in the broader sense of this concept). Mason and Rennie recommend, for instance, that the teacher should introduce a weblog to aid his teaching [Mas 10: 104]. In a second step, the learner should develop their own weblog which addresses a "(...) subject that interests them and is relevant to theories of the course." [Mas 10: 104]. According to Mason and Rennie, this action-orientated learning has to be accompanied by normative impulses: *"Setting formative or graded assessments that require students to read (and comment upon) each other's blog sites (...)"* [Mas 10: 104]. This approach can be supported by implementation of e-portfolios, enabling the individual learner to practice reflecting about the learning process and the action-orientated use of Web 2.0 based applications. The use of Web 2.0 applications in formal learning contexts and the *self*-understanding in the course of this use can be reflected within e-portfolios: What knowledge was I able to gain through the use of the Web 2.0 application x? Which difficulties had to be mastered during this process? How did I master these difficulties? How did I experience myself in the course of this learning process?'

From E-Portfolios to PLEs

Initially, a certain degree of practice has to be attained in reflection regarding media use in learning processes. Later, the teacher could require a concept of an integrative collocation of different Web 2.0 applications from the learner. Such a strategy makes it possible to realize an essential feature for PLEs – "The idea of a Personal Learning Environment is also based on being able to aggregate different services" [Atw 07: 5] – successively by the learner themselves. The teacher could formulate a content-orientated learning task and connect this task with aspects of media pedagogy. If, for instance, a group of students are asked to give a presentation on the history of education, the Web 2.0 as an action-orientated learning area could be implemented as follows: The presentation could be produced in the form of a podcast. Alongside the preparation of the content (which could involve the reception of Web 2.0 applications like podcasts, blogs etc.) the students would need to make themselves familiar with podcasting software such as Audacity. Communication processes between the group members could be organised (and documented) via weblogs (the use of a weblog in turn requires the writer to familiarise with themselves with weblog providers such as Wordpress). Google Docs could be used for collaborative text production. As an accompanying task, the students could reflect on the experience of the Web 2.0 based preparation of a presentation within their e-portfolio (aspects of group dynamic and self-experience could be addressed explicitly). The e-portfolio has the advantage of providing a space for reflection detached from the group for the individual learner. The self-reflection makes it possible to locate the individual's own personality within the context of the group dynamic in the course of the collaborative learning process: Which kind of media usage is preferred and why? Do asynchronous media offer security within the group's work or does this kind of medium destroy collaborative dynamics?As soon as the use of Web 2.0 based applications are practised and organised (e.g. with different presentations in different groups), the individualised use of integratively organized Web 2.0 applications for learning processes can be fostered. The individual learner could formulate a learning target and develop strategies for a Web 2.0 based learning process in which the learner gained the required knowledge: What do I want to achieve with which use of media?

PLEs in formal learning contexts can be understood as the integrative and systematic use of Web 2.0 based applications within learning processes. This kind of integrative, and systematic use of media can be ensured by reflective strategies. The reflection process addresses the possibilities of knowledge creation through the use of a specific medium: Which kind of knowledge can I gain through which medium? Beyond this, the reflection process addresses the individual's own *self*-understanding in the course of the media usage.

Conclusion

The emphasis on *self*-reflexivity is a reaction to discourse formations and a media-environment which are becoming increasingly complex. Every individual is embedded within these discourse formations and media-environment. Critical examination and evaluation of the use of the media-environment enable the individual to establish a *self*-determined usage of media. The PLE is a manifestation of this kind of a *self*-determined media usage. In an ideal scenario, PLEs and *self*-reflection are deeply linked and interrelated with each other, so that the '*I*' expresses itself through a sovereign use of media. This type of sovereign media usage is becoming relevant with regard to an increasingly complex and increasingly media-defined living environment. A didactic operationalisation seeking to guide the learner towards a PLE therefore has to consider aspects of media pedagogy as well as the acquisition of specialist technical knowledge.

REFERENCES

[Ado 97] *Adorno, Theodor W., Horkheimer, Max (1997):* Dialektik der Aufklärung. Frankfurt am Main: Suhrkamp.

[Ari 75] *Ariès, Philippe (1975):* Geschichte der Kindheit. München: Hanser.

[Arn 11] *Arnold, Patricia, Thillosen, Anne, Zimmer, Gerhard (2011):* Handbuch e-Learning. Lehren und Lernen mit digitalen Medien. Bielefeld: Bertelsmann.

[Atw 07] *Atwell, Graham (2007):* The Personal Learning Environment – the future of eLearning? In *eLearning Papers*, Vol. 2. Retrieved 05.09.2008 from URL: *http://www.elearningeuropa.info/files/media/media11561.pdf.*

[Ber 04] *Berzbach, Frank, (2004):* Die Ethikfalle. Pädagogische Theorierezeption am Beispiel des Konstruktivismus. Bielefeld: Bertelsmann.

[But 97] *Butler, Judith (1997):* The psychic life power. Theories in Subjection. Standford: Standford University Press.

[Dan 02] *Danielsen, Oluf, Nielsen, Jannie, Sørensen Birgitte Holm (Ed.) (2002):* Learning and Narrativity in Digital Media. Frederiksberg: Samfundslitteratur Press.

[Del 75] *Deleuze, Gilles (1975):* Woran erkennt man den Strukturalismus. In: Châtelet F. (Ed.). Geschichte der Philosophie, Vol. 8, 110–122. Frankfurt am Main: Suhrkamp.

[Del 04] *Deleuze, Gilles (2004):* Cambridge: Desert Islands and other Texts. Cambridge: MIT Press.

[Fre 00] *Freinet, Célestine (2000):* Pädagogische Werke Bd.2. Paderborn: Schöningh.

[Gae 04] *Gaebe, Wolf (2004):* Urbane Räume: Stuttgart. Ulmer.

[Gai 08] *Gaiser, Birgit (2008). Lehre im Web 2.0 – Didaktisches Flickwerk oder Triumph der Individualität? In e-teaching.org, 1–14. Retrieved March 2013 from: http://www.e-teaching.org/didaktik/kommunikation/08-09-12_Gaiser_Web_2.0.pdf.*

[Hep 09] *Hepp, Rolf Dieter (2009) (Eds):* The Fragilisation of Sociostructural Components. Bremen: Europäischer Hochschulverlag.

[Jäg 98] *Jäger, Mechtild (1998):* Die Philosophie des Konstruktivismus auf dem Hintergrund des Konstruktionsbegriffs. Hildesheim: G. Olms.

[Mas 10] *Mason, Robin, Rennie, Frank (2010). Evolving Technologies. In Rudestam, Kjell Erik, Schoenholtz-Read, Judith (Ed.) (2010):* Handbook of Online Learning, 91–128. Los Angeles: Sage.

[Mea 55] *Mead, George Herbert (1955):* Mind, self, society. Chicago: University of Chicago Press.

[Rei 07] *Reich, Kersten (2007). Interactive Constructivism in Education. In:* Education and Culture 1/2007, 7–26.

[Sie 99] *Siebert, Horst (1998):* Pädagogischer Konstruktivismus. Eine Bilanz der Konstruktivismusdiskussion für die Bildungspraxis. Neuwied: Luchterhand.

[Sch 08] *Schaffert, Sandra, Hilzensauer, Wolf (2008). On the way towards Personal Learning Environments:* Seven crucial aspects. In: eLearning Papers, 9. Retrieved March 2013 from: *http://www.elearningpapers.eu/index.php?page=doc&doc_id=11938&doclng=3*.

[Ter 09] *Terhart, Ewald (2009):* Didaktik. Eine Einführung: Stuttgart: Reclam.

[Zin 08] *Zingel, Stefan, Türker Mustafa Ali (2008):* Formative Interfaces for Scaffolding Self-Regulated Learning in PLEs. In elearningpapers 09. Retrieved July 2012 from: *http://www.elearningeuropa.info/files/media/media15975.pdf*

CONTACT DETAILS

Dr. David Kergel
Carl von Ossietzky Universität
Fakultät I – Institute für Pädagogik
Ammerländer Heerstraße138
26129 Oldenburg
Phone: +49 (0)441798 2840
E-Mail: *kersop@gmx.de*

ThirdSpace: orchestrating collaborative activities in PLEs for formal learning

Yvan Peter, Eloy D. Villasclaras-Fernández, Yannis Dimitriadis

ABSTRACT

ThirdSpace integrates the learner centric Personal Learning Environments (PLE) with the more structured organisation of institutional learning. Collaborative learning best practices are proposed to teachers through the WebCollage authoring tool. The resulting collaborative scripts are modelled using workflow technology and orchestrated automatically. ThirdSpace then publishes and monitors the learning activities in learners' PLEs. This, enables learners to engage in both individual and collaborative activities through their own tools.

Introduction

In this article we propose a platform aiming at the integration of the learner centric and personalised Personal Learning Environments (PLE) with the more structured organisation of formal (institutional) learning. PLEs are built on Web 2.0 services and social software and are inherently user-centred. PLE services are selected, aggregated and managed by the learner, so that the most convenient tools for each person can be used to manage information and relationships on a learning topic. The concept has emerged from the pervasiveness of personal technologies and as a criticism of institutional control represented by closed Learning Management Systems [WIL 07]. PLEs thus represent a shift in terms of control of both the learning environment and the learning objectives [FIE 10]. However, while the learners tend to use their everyday tools as learning support, effectively shaping their learning goals, activities and environment remains difficult and needs support [DAB 12]. For this reason, [HEN 10] advocate that technical support for tool selection and aggregation should be complemented by pedagogical support to achieve the conceptual design and evolution of the PLE. Web 2.0 technologies which form the basis for PLEs are deemed for their support for constructivist pedagogy by facilitating information production and management at an individual or collective level [MCL 10]. The social aspect of Web 2.0 also favours collaborative approaches [DOW 10].

On the other hand, in a formal learning context, the teacher and overall organisation are responsible for the definition of the learning path, resources and environment. Collaborative Learning is one way to organise the learning activities so as to enable interactions that support knowledge construction. Computer Supported Collaborative

Learning proposes collaborative scripts as a way to create the conditions for learning interactions to happen or to structure these interactions into specific activities [KOB 07]. Collaboration design patterns are one approach for script creation specially suited for teachers that may not have extensive expertise in the field of CSCL. Design patterns facilitate the design of these scripts by providing and documenting best practices to support designers [HER 06].

Our belief is that we must preserve the structured approach of formal learning to have the desired learning outcomes while giving more freedom to learners [MCL 10], [DAB 12]. Among the emergent research themes identified during PLE Conference 2012 unkeynotes [CON 12] we are most concerned by the following :

- "The need for structured, guided learning pathways"
- "The balance between loose institutionally controlled systems vs. portable, learner-controlled tools"

We address these issues from the perspective of the learning activities rather than the learning services or resources. Our platform provides support for (a) the design of pedagogically sound collaborative activities by teachers at an institutional level, and (b) the orchestration (i.e. automatic flow control) of the learning activities while learners may still use their own PLE. We believe that, in addition to facilitating the teacher's tasks of orchestration and monitoring of the learners, this will improve learning and motivation of these learners by (i) relying on their chosen tools and personalised environment which they already use for everyday activities (ii) engaging them in collaborative activities which are well supported by web 2.0 and social software.

In the following section, we will present existing approaches toward the integration of institutional/formal learning and personal learning environments. Next, we will show the overall approach we follow, explain the technical architecture and present an illustrating example before conclusion.

Institutional learning and PLEs

Some works already seek to combine the benefits from Web 2.0 and social services with a formal setting. Several LMS now integrate Web 2.0 services such as blogs or wikis. Still, this approach does not respond to the critics about LMS being closed and institutionally oriented systems that do not allow learners to personalise and adapt their learning environment and usually restrict the access to the resources to the duration of the course [DAL 06], [MOT 09].

Other works rather provide the ground for the integration of LMS and PLE services in a common environment. This environment can be as simple as a Web start page like iGoogle or Netvibes. These start pages support the integration of Widgets that are embeddable applications providing a user interface to a remote service. This has been done for instance by [CAS 08] using iGoogle and Widgets based integration of institutional services. Others seek to provide a specific integration environment based on JavaFX to provide a more uniform user interaction [TAR 10]. Marín et al. also rely on a specific Widget aggregator, SymbalooEDU for the integration of institutional and personal services [MAR 12]. SAPO Campus is also an institutional platform that provides services commonly found in PLEs but it seeks to enhance sharing capabilities so as to enable the emergence of learning communities in a safe/institutional context. Enhanced "collaboration, participation, openness and sharing" are a mean to improve the engagement and motivation of the learners [PED 12]. This platform supports openness and sharing including towards people external to the institution. In most of these work the content of the PLE is defined by the institution but the technologies enable the integration of other widgets thus enabling personalisation and appropriation by the learners.

If we consider the management of learning activities in a PLE, we can mention González-Tato et al. which also provide a set of widgets to build an open e-learning platform based on iGoogle [GON 12]. These widgets are dedicated to the management of learning activities from the author, tutor and learner perspectives. [MOD 09] propose an activity oriented mashup based on the Learner Interaction Scripting Language (LISL). LISL relies on {activity – outcome – tool} triplets to define a mashup of widgets to provide a specific and adapted learning environment. Like our use of design patterns, the authors envision that good designs of mashups can be shared based on their language. Again, the definition of the learning environment is driven by the institution or teacher. The activities are supported through a kind of dashboard rather than a plain orchestration.

From design to orchestration within learners' PLEs

Pedagogical scenarios place the focus of attention on the learning activities rather than the resources. They consider the flow of activities, the actors involved as well as the environment in/with which these activities will be done (resources and tools). IMS Learning Design is the prominent standard to describe pedagogical scenarios. It provides a formal representation of the scenarios based on XML that fosters interoperability, enables the sharing of scenario designs and provides the basis for an automatic orchestration of the activities.

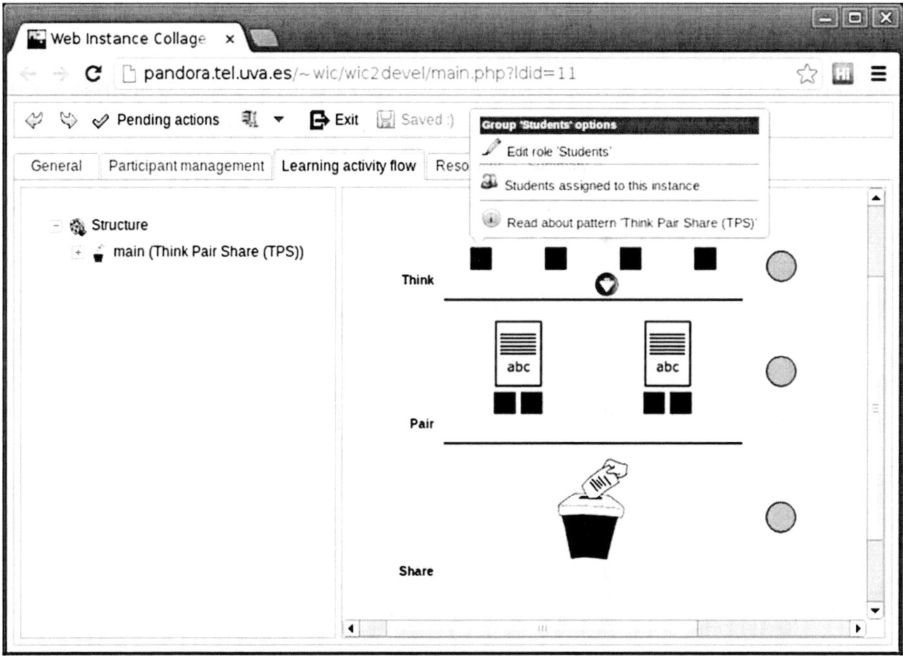

Figure 1: Think Pair Share pattern in WebCollage

Collaborative learning scripts are a kind of pedagogical scenarios where the focus is to foster collaborative learning by a careful design of the activities and/or distribution of roles [KOB 07]. We propose to use Collaborative Learning Flow Patterns (CLFP) to help teachers design collaborative activities. CLFPs capture best practices in terms of collaborative learning activities [HER 06]. Teachers can assemble and adapt known patterns such as Jigsaw or Think Pair Share using the WebCollage authoring tool (Figure 2) which has been evaluated in real-life settings [HER 10]. However, these scripts have been deployed in institutional settings (LMS) leaving no choice of environment to the learners.

Since the pedagogical scenario defines the flow of activity as well as the actors, it is possible to provide a computer supported orchestration that will propose the next available activities to the learners or tutors. Few learning environments embed an IMS LD engine to orchestrate the activities: GRAIL is tightly integrated in the .LRN LMS [DEL 07]; LAMS [DAZ 03] which is an alternative to IMS LD can run standalone but as also been integrated into Moodle. Finally, CopperCore/SLED [MCA 05] is a standalone engine which provides integration APIs but also a standalone support environment that cannot be considered as a full fledge LMS. We have already used workflow technology for the modelling and to provide an orchestration engine for pedagogical scenarios [PET 08]. In general these environments provide the available activities through a dashboard that also enables to mark the activities as completed. They are integrated

in a LMS or provide a limited support environment.

PLEs are appealing because they leverage learners' own tools and social networks providing an open learning environment. We would like to rely on this feature in a formal setting by providing collaborative activities based on CLFPs' best practices in learners' PLEs. The orchestration of these activities (i.e. automatic advancement from one activity to another) in such open environment will lower tutoring needs and provide the following pedagogical advantages:

- Collaborative activities can benefit from the affordance of Web 2.0 and social networks enhancing collective knowledge construction [MCL 07].
- Providing learning activities to the learners directly in their personal services, is a way to scaffold their learning in an open environment and to sustain their motivation [DEL 13].

ThirdSpace combines orchestration of collaboration scripts with self-configured PLEs which implies a distribution of responsibilities. On the one hand, teachers and educational institutions are responsible for creating suitable pedagogical scripts and for managing their deployment on the platform. On the other hand, students are responsible for selecting suitable tools of their choice to accomplish the activities of each course. Based on our previous experience, we use workflow technology for the modelling and orchestration of pedagogical scenarios [PET 08]. We have modeled the CLFPs good practices as workflow processes using Business Process Model and Notation. These processes can then be orchestrated by a workflow engine to manage learners' activities.

The ThirdSpace platform relies on the REST architecture of the Web 2.0 for the integration of personal services with the workflow engine (Figure 2) so as to publish and monitor activities in PLEs.

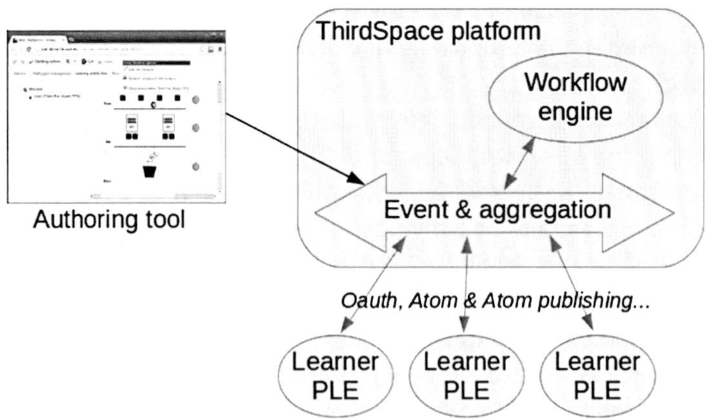

Figure 2: ThirdSpace architecture

Use Case

We will use the Think Pair Share (TPS) pattern as a use case. This pattern organises the activity into three phases to have learners produce a shared view/artefact on a topic or problem. The three phases are :

- *Think* is an individual phase where each learner has to reflect and elaborate on an topic or problem.
- The *Pair* phase let learners confront their productions. This confrontation should help learners build a more thorough understanding of the topic/problem and provide a better solution.
- Finally, the *Share* phase gathers all learners to build a consensus based on previous discussions and productions.

This pattern defines the activities as well as the grouping of the learners during each phase. It could be used in classroom, within the LMS or as proposed in this paper within the learners' PLEs. In the latter case, instead of providing a collaboration tool, the learners are allowed to select their own one. A typical example is the usage of blogs: a learner may select to use her blog as the tool to complete the activities. Using this tool means that the platform must publish the activities on the learners' blogs and let them perform those activities as blog posts or comments.

Considering the teacher's point of view, she will have to select the TPS pattern in Web Collage and customize it to the intended topic and to select the learners and pairing. The deployment of the learning script in ThirdSpace involves exporting the design from Web Collage (activity flow, learners), thus triggering the instantiation of a new process in the workflow engine. From the learners' point of view, they will have to provide information about their personal services and grant access to ThirdSpace so that it can publish information. Then, they will see activities published on their PLE services.

Figures 3 to 5 illustrate the operation of ThirdSpace on the first activity (*Think*) of the TPS pattern deployed by a teacher in ThirdSpace. The instantiation of the process will make the first activity available for the learners associated to that instance. ThirdSpace polls the workflow engine regularly on behalf of the learners. When an activity is available, its description is retrieved and published on the learner's blog (Figure 3).

mercredi 6 juin 2012
Provide a contribution to the following question
Is IMS Learning Design language a good modelling approach for pedagogical scenarios
Publié par Yvan à l'adresse 16:16 0 commentaires

Figure 3: Publication of the activity on the learner's blog

The user can then perform the activity by providing a response to the initial question through a comment (Figure 4). At this stage and with this particular activity, we consider that the activity is done by writing a single comment to the post. We rely on the fact that the blog provides atom feed for posts but also for comments.

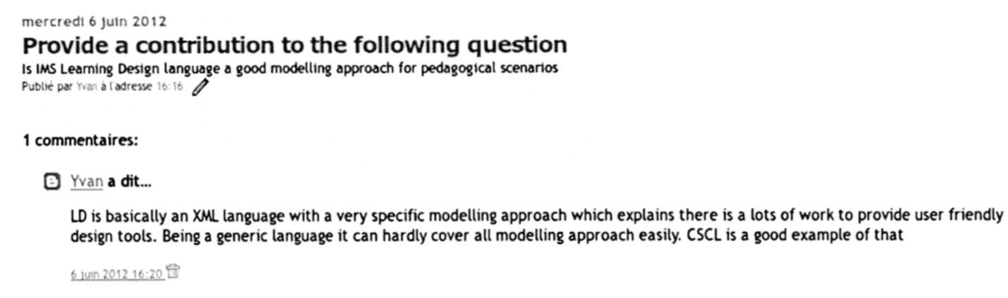

Figure 4: Activity done as a comment to the published activity

By polling the learner's blog comment feed, ThirdSpace is then able to monitor the completion of the activity. In more complex situations where the monitoring of the learners' tools is not enough to detect the completion of the activity we must provide user based declaration either from a tutor or learner to generate the activity completion event.

Upon completion of the activity, ThirdSpace will complete the activity in the workflow engine and post a message on Twitter to support awareness (Figure 5). When the *Think* activity has been done by all learners, the first phase of the pattern will be done and the workflow engine will make the *Pair* activity available.

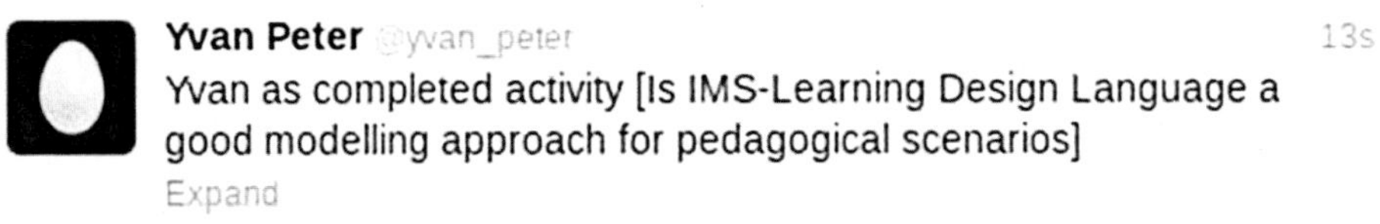

Figure 5: Activity completion posted on Twitter

Conclusions

Our work seeks to enable the structured approach of formal learning in the scope of learners' PLEs. Towards this end, collaborative learning best practices are proposed to teachers through the WebCollage authoring tool. The resulting scripts are modelled and orchestrated automatically by a workflow engine. The ThirdSpace platform then allows the publication and monitoring of the learning activities in learners' PLEs.

Our work does not address the elaboration of the PLE itself. On the institutional side, we provide sound pedagogical design while helping to cope with the tutoring work with the automatic orchestration of activities and awareness features. On the learner side, one can use personal learning services and social networks. Learning activities become available in the chosen services and learners may be aware of other learners progress through social network notification like in the Twitter notification presented in the use case. This provides an awareness of activities. Taking part in collaborative activities proposed in the PLE and being aware of others actions can help learners being conscious of the learning path thus providing a kind of scaffolding for the learning activities. Also proposing activities provides learning objectives that may help sustain learners' motivation [DEL 13].

Integrating formal learning and Personal Learning Environments requires to find the right balance between the necessary structuring of the learning environment (either in terms of resources, services or activities) and a user-centred environment which also encompasses personal activities, relationships and informal learning goals. This balance falls into the middle part of Figure 6 where lies our work and most of the works presented in section 2. They seek to provide an integration environment that lays the ground for extension and personalisation with more personal services and networks.

However, as mentioned among others by [CHA 12] or [DAB 12], learners may not have the digital skills necessary to effectively customize their learning environment to provide a useful learning support and experience. Hence, we will have to take that into account in our work. One direction may be to recommend tools, or provide default tools, that have good affordance for the tasks at hand to help learners organise their environment.

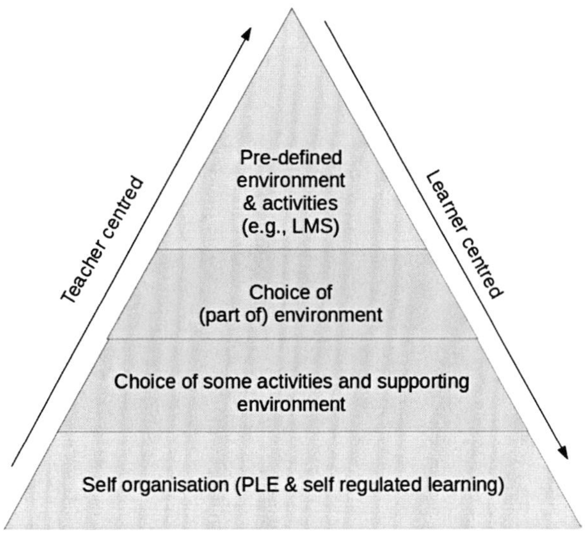

Figure 6: Teacher vs. learner centred

Acknowledgement

This work is partially supported by the STIC-AmSud FUELS project.

REFERENCES

[CAS 08] *Casquero, Oscar; Portillo, Javier; Ovelar, Ramon; Romo, Jesús; Benito, Manuel (2008):* iGoogle and gadgets as a platform for integrating institutional and external services. Mash-Up Personal Learning Environments (MUPPLE'08) workshop at EC-TEL 2008.

[CHA 12] *Chatterjee, Arunangus; Mirza, Mahrukh (2012):* Enhancing Self Regulated Learning Skills for Improved PLE Use: A Problem Based Learning Approach. PLE Conference Proceedings.

[CHA 09] *Chatti, Mohamed Amine (2009):* PLEF: A Conceptual Framework for Mashup Personal Learning Environments. Learning Technology Newsletter 11(3).

[CON 13] *Conole, Gráinne (2012):* The VLE vs. PLE debate, blog post *http://e4innovation.com/?p=590* last accessed June 2013.

[DAA 06] *Daalsgard, Christian (2006):* Social software: E-learning beyond learning management systems. European Journal of Open, Distance and E-Learning, 2006(2), p. 1–12.

[DAB] *Dabbagh, Nada; Kitsantas, Anastasia (2012):* Personal Learning Environments, social media, and self-regulated learning: A natural formula for connecting formal and informal learning. Internet and Higher Education Journal 15(1), 3–8

[DAZ 03] *Daziel, James (2003):* Implementing learning design: The learning activity management system (LAMS). AscilitE, Autralia, 1–10.

[DEL 07] *De-la-Fuente-Valentín, Luis; Pardo, Aberlado; Delgado Kloos, Carlos (2007):* Experiences with GRAIL: Learning Design support in .LRN. TENCompetence Open workshop on current research in IMS Learning Design and lifelong competence development infrastructures.

[DEL 13] *De-la-Fuente-Valentín, Luis; Pardo, Abelardo; Delgado Kloos, Carlos (2013):* Addressing drop-out and sustained effort issues with large practical groups using an automated delivery and assessment system. Computers & Education, 61, 33–42. doi:10.1016/j.compedu.2012.09.004

[DOW 10] *Downes, Stephen (2010):* New Technology Supporting Informal Learning. Journal of Emerging Technologies in Web Intelligence, 2(1):27-33

[FIE 10] *Fiedler, Sebastian; Väljataga, Terje (2010):* Personal learning environments: concept or technology? The PLE Conference 2010.

[GON 12] *González-Tato, Juan; Llamas-Nistal, Martín; Caeiro- Rodríguez, Manuel; Alvarez-Osuna, Javier (2012):* Towards a Collection of Gadgets for an iGoogle e-learning platform. Global Engineering Education Conference (EDUCON)

[HEN 10] *Henri, France; Charlier, Bernadette (2010):* Personal Learning Environment: a Concept, an Application, or a Self-designed Instrument? 9th International Conference on Information Technology Based Higher Education and Training (ITHET), 44–51.

[HER 10] *Hernández-Leo, Davinia; Jorrín-abellán, Iván M., Villasclaras-Fernández, Eloy. D.; Asensio-Pérez, Juan I.; Dimitriadis, Yannis (2010):* A multicase study for the evaluation of a pattern- based visual design process for collaborative learning. Journal of Languages and Computing, 21(6), 313–331.

[HER 06] *Hernández-Leo, Davinia; Villasclaras-Fernández, Eloy D.; Asensio-Pérez, Juan I.; Dimitriadis, Yannis; Jorrín-Abellán, Iván M., Ruiz-Requies, Inés; Rubia-Avi, Bartolomé (2006):* COLLAGE, a collaborative learning design editor based on patterns. Educational Technology & Society, 9(1), 58–71.

[KOB 07] *Kobbe, Lars; Weinberger, Armin; Dillenbourg, Pierre; Harrer, Andreas; Hämäläinen, Raija; Häkkinen, Päivi; Fischer, Frank (2007):* Specifying computer-supported collaboration scripts. International Journal of Computer-Supported Collaborative Learning, 2(2-3), 211–224. doi:10.1007/s11412-007-9014-4

[MAR 12] *Marín Victoria I.; Salinas, Jesús; de Benito, Bárbara (2012):* Using SymbalooEDU as a PLE Organizer in Higher Education. PLE Conference 2012.

[MCA 05] *McAndrew, Patrick; Nadolski, Rob; Little, Alex (2005):* Developing an approach for Learning Design Players. Journal of Interactive Media in Education, (August).

[MCL 07] *McLoughlin, C., & Lee, M. (2007). Social software and participatory learning:* Pedagogical choices with technology affordances in the Web 2.0 era. In ICT: Providing choices for learners and learning. Proceedings ascilite Singapore 2007.

[MCL 10] *McLoughlin, Catherine; Lee, Mark (2010):* Personalised and self regulated learning in the Web 2.0 era: International exemplars of innovative pedagogy using social software. Australasian Journal of Educational, 26(1), 28–43.

[MOD 09] *Modritscher, Felix; Wild, Fridolin (2009):* Sharing Good Practice through Mash-Up Personal Learning Environments. LNCS 5686, International Conference on Web-based Learning (ICWL) – Advances in Web Based Learning, 245–254.

[MOT 09] *Mott, Jon; Wiley, David (2009):* Open for Learning: The CMS and the Open Learning Network. in education, 15(2). *http://ineducation.ca/article/open-learning-cms-and-open-learning-network*, last accessed June 2013.

[PED 12] *Pedro, Luis; Santos, Carlos; Almeida, Sara; Koch-Grünberg, Tim (2012):* Building a Shared Personal Learning Environment with SAPO Campus. Proceedings. Personal Learning Environments Conference, 16 pages.

[PET 08] *Peter, Yvan; Le Pallec, Xavier; Vantroys, Thomas (2008). Pedagogical Scenario Modelling, Deployment, Execution and Evolution. In C. Pahl (Ed.), Architecture Solutions for E-Learning Systems (pp. 283–305). IGI Global.*

[TAR 10] *Taraghi, Benham; Ebner, Martin; Till, Gerald; Mühlburger, Herbert (2010):* Personal Learning Environment – a Conceptual Study. International Journal of Emerging Technologies in Learning (iJET). 5(1), 25–30.

[WIL 07] *Wilson, Scott; Liber, Oleg (2007):* Preparing for disruption: developing institutional capability for decentralized education technologies. World Conference on Educational Multimedia, Hypermedia and Telecommunications (ED-MEDIA), Vancouver, Canada, p. 1386–1395

FIGURES

CONTACT DETAILS

Yvan Peter
Université Lille 1 – LIFL
Bât M3 – Cité Scientifique 59655
Villeneuve d'Ascq, France
E-Mail: *Yvan.Peter@univ-lille1.fr*

Eloy D. Villasclaras-Fernández
The Open University
Institute of Educational Technology
Walton Hall
Milton Keynes – MK7 6AA, UK
E-Mail: *eloy.villasclaras-fernandez@open.ac.uk*

Yannis Dimitriadis
Universidad de Valladolid, GSIC/EMIC
School of Telecommunications Engineering
Paseo de Belén, 15
47011, Valladolid, Spain
E-Mail: *yannis@tel.uva.es*

Technology Enhanced Textbook Provoking active ways of Learning

Wolfgang Neuhaus, Jürgen Kirstein, Volkhard Nordmeier

ABSTRACT

With this contribution we want to present and explain the demonstrators of the »Technology Enhanced Textbook« (TET) that we developed during the last two years and discuss with the active PLE-community whether TET could be a useful component of a personal learning environment. Instead of using the term PLE to refer to the tool itself we prefer to use it to refer to the whole physical and virtual environment which can be influenced and designed by the learner.

Active learning and technological change

As we begin to let visions come true, we start creating new reality. During the process of implementation the new reality reveals to us as a whole of communicating and interacting individuals and the new product arising. In the process of realisation we use knowledge and tools which where handed over to us in varied ways by current or previous generations. These kinds of transmissions happen in personal and informal connections as well as in structured and institutionalized contexts like schools, universities, enterprises, theatres, concert halls, sports, museums, libraries and the Internet. Experiences, newly developed reality and the successively emerging externalised knowledge are passed on to the next generation in many different ways. In his 1916 published book »Democracy and Education« John Dewey referred to this process as "renewal of life by transmission" [Dew 16]. Humans as members of society develop and renew themselves in this manner as well as they influence the social infrastructure connected with them. In the digital age this recurring activity of handing over and renewal leads to a state of permanent innovation, because today production- and development cycles are becoming progressively shorter and more complex. This is what we experience in the food industry, furniture industry, in architecture, medical industry, in the development of our transport networks from aircraft, train to automobile, in the energy sector, in the supply and sewage networks, in media communication networks (television, computer, smartphone, tablets, mp3-player) as well as in the development of software and the Internet. Hereby, the combination of software development and Internet represents a catalyst function across all sectors of society. The handing over of externalised digital knowledge reaches large groups of people in a short time, because today methods of digital copying, networking and distribution are becoming more and

more efficient. From the beginning of mankind to the invention of book culture, as well as from our digital age into the future ahead of us, our capabilities to renew the world are continuously expanding. Over the centuries our inventory of externalised knowledge has been stacked up, cross-linked and continuously developed in sediment-like layers of books, magazines, libraries, cultural assets and digital memories. "Bildung" as scientific term refers to this circular process of transmission and renewal [Neu 12a]. By developing solutions for learning we keep this definition of "Bildung" in mind. The psychological dimensions of learning are characterised by the change of behaviour through experience. Cognitivist, constructivist and behavioural models of learning acknowledge this fundamental view on learning [Lef 86], [Mie 07]. In the teaching-learning research, therefore, action-oriented concepts of learning play an important role [Neu 10].

The basis for the development of specific demonstrators during the TET project is a didactical design (the German term "Didaktisches Design" is different from the traditional term "instructional design" !) that overcomes the confines of traditional instruction-psychologically justified e-learning approaches [Neu 11]. With the design of a textbook of the future we focus on action-oriented educational contexts like "Learning in Context," "project learning", "self-organized learning", "communities of practice", "Problem Based Learning", "Inquiry Based Learning" or "Location-Based Learning".

Currently available mobile media devices, such as smartphones, tablets based on iOS or Android base already allow various forms of proactive interaction with the physical and digital environment beyond the usual communication oriented functions of these devices. You can manipulate experiments, tools, texts, images and other media elements by intuitive touch gestures. Built-in or add-on sensors facilitate measurements, audio and video recordings. You can carry out discussions with other learners and experts or make content available via the Internet. By using GPS, image recognition or augmented reality solutions, location-based phenomena and objects can be identified and individually experienced through interactive experiments and additional multimedia information [Bry 07].

Learning versus e-learning

Before discussing the technological enhancements of the textbook and its potential to provoke active ways of learning, we need to outline the problems that were carried into the educational sciences by the research field of e-learning. In an age of continuous innovation, e-learning seems to be too rigid and inflexible to keep up with the complex dynamics of the globalized development in our society. Numerous studies show that the expectations that many have placed in e-learning were rarely met. Three main characteristics can be found in the literature which could be the reason for the failure of e-learning:

- **The instruction paradigm of the instructional design:** E-learning transferred – since its inception – instruction functions of the teacher to the software (e.g. computer-based training, web-based training). This approach goes back to Robert Gagné who defined principles of instructional design based on his view on the psychology of learning, which stood in opposite to constructivist positions of learning psychology as described in the first section of this article [Gag 73]. Since the constructivist paradigm gained popularity in the psychology of learning, many authors from the field of instructional design made an effort to integrate this constructivist perspective. However, consistent approaches which considered construction as part of instruction were never formulated because: "If learning is primarily determined by the individual and not by the environment and knowledge is understood as individual construction, instruction as a »transfer of knowledge« is strictly impossible" [Blu 98].
- **The idea of controlling learning processes through software:** Until the early 1990s, core of the "Instructional Design" was the management and control of learning processes, e.g. [Mer 88], [Rei 91], even though there were also approaches to integrate context references and constructivist perspectives as seen in Reigeluth. The deficits that resulted from such a perspective in terms of human learning, were explained by Rolf Schulmeister in his book "Grundlagen hypermedialer Lernsysteme". In particular, he criticized the restricted view of Gagné regarding the human memory as a storage system which is a core part of the theory of "Instructional Design": "The validity of the assumption that defined knowledge is stored directly, the so-called "correspondence hypothesis" is rejected by constructivism and [..] been subjected to a detailed critique" [Sch 07: 137]. This dispute between authors of the field of "Instructional Design" and authors relating to the upcoming constructivism was comprehensively documented in [Sch 07].
- **The overvaluation of technology:** Summing up the results of their studies, Gerhard Tulodziecki and Bardo Herzig state that "Overall, the many studies on general media effects (as a comparison between media-based and labour-mediated teaching and learning processes) show that there can not be spoken of a fundamental superiority of learning with electronic media" [Tul 04: 81]. In further articles, Rolf Schulmeister, Gabi Reinman and Michael Kerres came to similar conclusions concerning the meaning of technologies in the context of teaching and learning [Sch 07: 362], [Rei 06: 32], [Ker 07: 3].

Many concepts of e-learning are designed to make learning "easier" for students. However, learning is only effective when the learner actively solves problems and such constructs knowledge. Therefore the "easy" way might not be the most promising one. To address this paradox of traditional e-learning, Joachim Hasebrook asked in a keynote speech in 2009 "Do computers still need humans to learn?" [Has 09]. In educational research it has long been known that there are challenging problems that, once they

are overcome, lead to persistent learning and help to adapt existing mental models to new experiences. Encountering an inexplicable phenomenon, considering competing explanations, implementing goals and actively trying out possible solutions are all important activities related to the learning process but are not adequately considered by many traditional e-learning concepts. Therefore, we recommend to disengage from traditional e-learning. Instead of defining learning from the perspective of the electronic aspects of a learning environment, we believe that it is essential to find ways to encourage communication as well as active involvement with phenomena and learning objects to solve relevant problems. We then have to figure out which role media can play in these kinds of settings. In order to enable individual knowledge construction we need a "mediating" device – a medium – for communication and learning. To make these learning and communication processes transparent we use the German term "mediengestütztes Lernen" (media-supported learning). This term emphasizes that the media devices serve for specific functions especially as tools to communicate and facilitate reflection processes during learning [Neu 11].

Developing the Technology Enhanced Textbook (TET)

Our vision is an interactive textbook – as part of the personal learning environment – which provokes active ways of learning and grows with the learner's experience. The designated user is an active learner who is the author and designer of his/her own personal textbook while going through the learning process. Today's worldwide coverage of interconnected multimedia devices opens new educational perspectives to technologically enhance the traditional textbook. During last two years we had the opportunity to realise and validate our vision in a project fostered by the "Bundesministerium für Bildung und Forschung" (BMBF). The aim of the project is to validate the potential of innovation of our research and to fit our visions to the conditions of the market. Empirical data gained from focus group sessions with our partners of the educational field (schools, universities, educational publishers, museums, radio and television, vocational training) and data from surveys that were answered by experts in the field of learning (teachers, students, lecturers) helped to outline the demonstrators of TET. Instead of trying to promote learning through simply clicking through items on the screen, our focus lies on activities that use both, the physical and virtual environment. To offer students a wide overview, TET uses collaborative, interactive and sensitive media elements to provide opportunities for students to explore their physical environment through experiments, analyses, and measurements. TET also offers experiences for students to control photo-realistic virtual laboratories and "Interactive Screen Experiments" [Kir 07], which will be available on all current mobile devices with Internet access. Between the physical and the virtual world of experiences, learners construct their personal knowledge and become authors of their own personalized textbooks.

The focus groups

We chose to validate our projects using the focus group method. Compared to individual interviews, this method offers the advantage that the targeted solutions emerge out of the concrete experiences of the participants [Göl 05]. The results of the common communication and interaction of the focus group merge directly into the development of the desired product [Boh 03], [Man 60]. The focus group method emerged from research in the United States when it appeared economically reasonable to interview several experts at the same time instead of asking each of them individually [Boh 03], [Gre 98]. In order to generate a group opinion (as a product of collective interactions) discussion groups are compiled and provided with information [Man 60], [Gre 98]. Common applications of the focus group method include the development of new products, generating ideas, capturing user behaviour or the determination of attitudes [Gre 98: 9].

To start producing demonstrators of TET we discussed our ideas with experts of a television company who planned to enhance their educational program (Bayerischer Rundfunk alpha), with experts of museums in Berlin who wanted to give their visitors new ways of exploring their collections (Museum für Naturkunde, Technik-Museum, Spectrum), with experts of textbook publishing houses (DeGruyter, Cornelsen) and with experts in the field of learning (students and teachers of different schools and universities). Three main didactic functions emerged during the focus group discussions with our project partners. These will be the basis for further developments of the demonstrators of TET: (1) to experiment, (2) to communicate and exchange, (3) portfolio functions [Neu 12]:

- **Toolbox function:** Various sensors and technical interfaces are offered to measure, detect, experiment, photograph and record.
- **Communication function:** Learners communicate via chat or video call about their experiences and experiment together online.
- **Portfolio function:** Information can be researched and compiled from browsers, search engines and the cloud based IMPAL-market, the virtual backbone of TET.

Figure 1: Acoustic measuring in the classroom

Learning scenarios

From a constructivist perspective the opportunity to actively carry out scientific experiments with mobile devices holds a special value because here direct action of learners and their initiatives come into focus. Appropriate ways of active learning were discussed with learners and teachers during the focus group talks of the TET project.

- **Measurement and Experimentation:** Current generations of mobile devices provide up to five different internal sensors: microphone, motion sensor, magnetic sensor, camera and GPS receiver. In addition, we developed a wireless interface which is able to process, analyse and visualize the data of external sensors that are usually used in schools and scientific laboratories. In an experiment for determining the speed of sound our students tested a scenario using the sensors of mobile devices In the hallways of our institute building the speed of sound was determined by the microphones of two iPads which were placed at 10 meters distance.

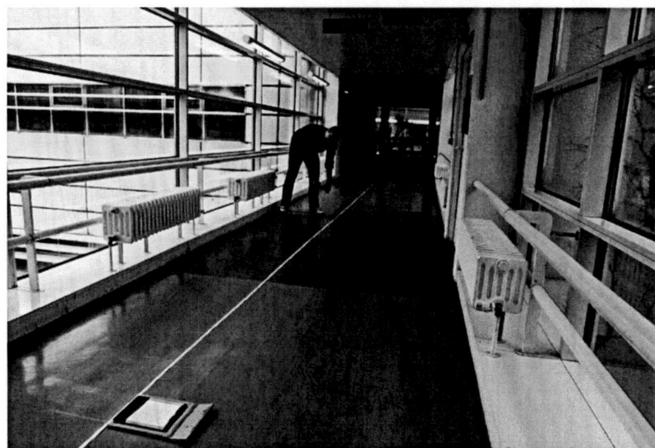

Figure 2: Measuring the speed of sound

With a pair of claves a synchronization sound was generated exactly in the middle of the 5-meter mark. Shortly afterwards, the actual measurement click was generated (spatially behind the iPads). Both clicks were recorded by the two iPads. The high resolution of the used sound editor allowed us to display the exact time interval between the two clicks. From the time difference between the two measuring points, the learner was able to determine the speed of sound (speed = distance / time) rather precisely. Several scenarios to promote active learning are documented on Blog Mediendidaktik (URL below).

- **Virtual Experiments:** Another exciting way to stimulate the learners curiosity is the use of interactive screen experiments (ISE) and interactive laboratories (ISL) as photo-realistic, interactive representations of real experiments and laboratories. They give learners the opportunity to make phenomena immediately tangible by using appropriate virtual experiments. Museum exhibitions, technical equipment and scientific phenomena that users experience in everyday life or appear on television can be discovered, investigated immediately and reflected through ISE and ISL. ISE and ISL can be stored in an individual manner using the portfolio function of TET and can be reused at any time. For TET-users ISE will be made available by the web-based media platform IMPAL [Kir 11].

- **Communication:** In the future, virtual experiments can be operated together, online. TET can provide information on who else is currently working with a specific experiment, or who has already worked with it previously. Users can contact these students via chat to discuss the

Figure 3: Inquiry into the centripetal force

implementation, assessment and evaluation of the experiment. To determine who is available online at a given moment, interfaces to common social Networks like Twitter, Facebook or Google+ will be integrated. Likewise, collaborations between classes from different countries or regions can be realized in the form of joint research projects in which measurements that were made in local environments can be collected and evaluated.

Figure 4: Video-analysis with the tet.folio

- **Portfolio use:** We designed TET as a personalized application on mobile devices which can also be accessed via any Internet-Browser on the web. The portfolio feature of TET allows to store personal externalized knowledge fragments, ISE, ISL, as well as individually collected web content. For this purpose TET offers the possibility to store content in an individually designed structure. Here the focus is put on a clean and intuitive handling, not comparable to the complicated functions of out-dated VLEs. Besides providing each user with the opportunity to individually design content, teachers or publishers are as well able to offer prepared contents that can be included in the individual portfolios of students. The portfolio function of TET allows to track individual knowledge construction with regard to design, as well as research processes by reflecting the personal development steps. All information available online such as "Open Educational Resources" content under Creative Commons License or paid media modules offered by publishers and knowledge brokers can be integrated into the portfolio.

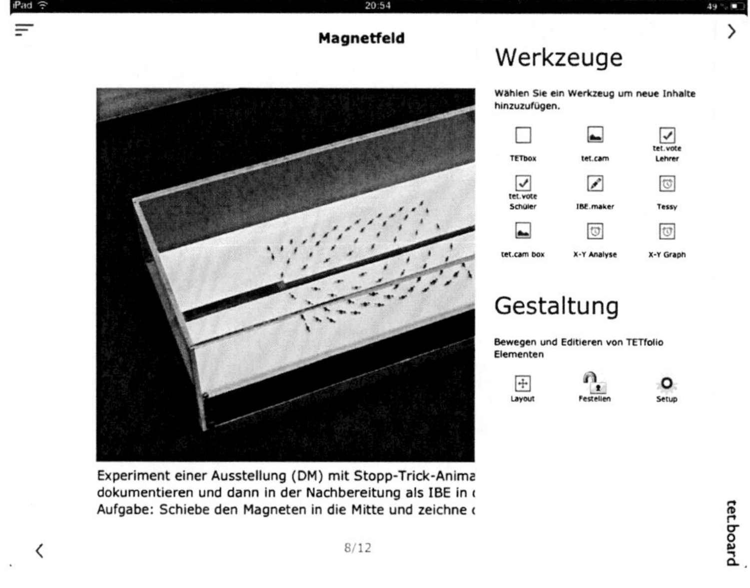

Figure 5: tet.folio page on a computer screen

- To get some impressions of the learning scenarios that we are experimenting with, visit the Blog Mediendidaktik and choose category Lehrszenarien: *http://www.mediendidaktik.org/category/lehrszenarien/*

Figure 6: tet.folio page on a tablet

Existing Demonstrators of the TET

TET as a mobile, interactive textbook supports its future users with didactic-technological extensions of reality, through a high degree of modularity of the content and by a variety of tools for the individual and joint construction of knowledge. TET links proven elements of the textbook with new references to the real life: interactive media modules enable experimentation and exploration in space and in situations that are not available in reality. The following demonstrators of the TET are available for demonstrations:

- **tet.folio:** With the tet.folio learners have access to tools, study materials and the whole Internet. They can bring all of these elements into their own intuitive order, carry out evaluations and make those individually prepared items available to other students and teachers. Active, self-determined forms of learning can be optimally stimulated and supported with the tet.folio. In the tool-area instruments are made available, which are able to record data from external or internal sensors of the mobile device. These records can be evaluated, visualized and processed directly within the tet.folio.
- **IMPAL-Server:** The tet.folio offers access to elements and learning objects of different learning media providers via a cloud-based Internet server (IMPAL) . The user gets access to Open Educational Resources, Creative Commons Licensed media as well as fee-based, high-quality media products of renowned educational media publishers.

- **Interactive Screen Experiments:** Interactive screen experiments (ISE) as photo-realistic, interactive representations of real experiments are no movies and no mathematical simulations. The production of an ISE is based on photo-shootings, during the execution of the experiment, recorded in stop-motion, similar to the production of cartoon animations. Audio and video elements as well as measurement data are inserted to the ISE to enable a realistic perception.
- **ISE-maker:** The ISE-maker allows you to produce Click & Slide animations in an intuitive way. There are no programming skills required. An HTML-based interface allows the user to take photos, to define interactive areas and to animate the resulting ISE. This works on a computer via mouse click, as well as on mobile devices using touch gestures.
- **Tessy:** The "Tessy" sensor interface of the TET enables the user to record values of external sensors wirelessly. It allows you to stream data directly to the digital teaching materials of the tet.folio. The measured values can be streamed in real-time to any place in the classroom. Real experiments can be demonstrated. The measured data of an experiment will simultaneously play the resulting graphics on a Smartboard. Other mobile devices are able to track the live data also, so students using the tet.folio will be able to edit these data streams directly.

These demonstrators help to enrich the personal learning environments of any learner. Aside to these "educationally" demonstrators we developed some more technically driven demonstrators, such as Interactive Screen Laboratories, which offer interactive panorama-views of a real laboratory, the tet.table which offer visitors of a museum ways to interact with real and virtual objects at the same time as well as automation and production systems to realise new media formats for educational television and museums. To get some impressions of the status of the TET-demonstrators and its context visit the tetfolio.de Homepage: *http://tetfolio.de/home/index_engl.shtml* .

Conclusions

The TET project reached a status now where we want to spread the results of our validation process and find partners to go live with the project. Aside to the fact that the developed demonstrators seem to fulfil the needs of the different target groups which were explored, the core results of the validation are: there are three relevant business segments to earn money with our solution: production (service, customization), sale (IMPAL products, multimedia elements and tools) and resale (marketplace, publishing houses). The central idea around the business model at the moment is, to offer the tet. folio free of charge for all systems and to earn money with high quality products around it. In a next step we look for the financing to produce the prototypes of the tet.folio and the IMPAL-server. A beta test phase and activities to build a lively learning community

around it will follow. People and institutions who want to collaborate are always welcome. Up-to-date information about the TET project you can find on our homepage: *http://didaktik.physik.fu-berlin.de/projekte/tet/index_en.html*

REFERENCES

[Blu 98] *Blumstengel, Astrid (1998):* Entwicklung hypermedialer Lernsysteme. Berlin: wvb. Retrieved June 30, 2013, from *http://dsor-fs.upb.de/~blumstengel/main_index_tour.html*

[Boh 03] *Bohnsack, Ralf (2003):* Gruppendiskussionsverfahren und Milieuforschung. In: Barbara Friebertshäuser; Annedore Prengl (Eds.): Handbuch qualitative Forschungsmethoden in der Erziehungswissenschaft, Studienausgabe. Weinheim: Juventa, 492–502.

[Bry 07] *Bryant, Lee (2007):* Emerging trends in social software for education. In S. Crowne (Ed.): Emerging technologies for Learning, Vol. 2, Coventry: Becta.

[Dew 16] *Dewey, John (1916). Democracy and Education. The Macmillan Company Retrieved June 30, 2013, from* *http://www.ilt.columbia.edu/publications/dewey.html*

[Gag 73] *Gagné, Robert Mills (1973):* Die Bedingungen des menschlichen Lernens. Hannover – Berlin – Darmstadt – Dortmund: Hermann Schroedel Verlag.

[Göl 05] *Göll, Edgar; Henseling, Christine; Nolting, Katrin; Gaßner, Robert (2005):* Die Fokusgruppen-Methode: Zielgruppen erkennen und Motive aufdecken. Ein Leitfaden für Umwelt- und Naturschutzorganisationen. Retrieved June 30, 2013, from *http://www.umweltbundesamt.de/umweltbewusstsein/publikationen/Leitfaden-Fokusgruppen.pdf*

[Gre 98] *Greenbaum, Thomas L. (1998):* The Handbook for Focus Group Research. London: Sage.

[Has 09] *Hasebrook, Joachim (2009):* Zukunft des E-Learning: Brauchen Computer zum Lernen noch Menschen? – Foliensatz. Retrieved June 30, 2013, from *http://www.equalification.info/_media/Hasebrook_Zukunft_E-Learning.pdf*

[Ker 07] *Kerres, Michael (2007):* Mediendidaktik. In F. von Gross, & K. – U. Hugger (Eds.), Handbuch Medienpädagogik. Wiesbaden: VS Verlag.

[Kir 07] *Kirstein, Juergen; Nordmeier, Volkhard (2007):* Multimedia representation of experiments in physics. European Journal of Physics, 28 (3).

[Kir 11] *Kirstein, Juergen; Nordmeier, Volkhard (2011):* TET: "Technology Enhanced Textbook"- Ein fachdidaktisches Forschungsprojekt. In: Volkhard Nordmeier; Grötzebauch, Helmuth (Eds.): PhyDid B – Didaktik der Physik – Beiträge zur DPG-Frühjahrstagung 2011. Berlin: Freie Universität Berlin – Ag Nordmeier.

[Lef 86] *Lefrancois, Guy R. (1986):* Psychologie des Lernens. Berlin, Heidelberg, New York, Tokio: Springer.

[Man 60] *Mangold, Werner (1960):* Gegenstand und Methode des Gruppendiskussionsverfahrens. Aus der Arbeit des Instituts für Sozialforschung, Vol. Frankfurter Beiträge zur Soziologie, 9. Frankfurt am Main: Europäische Verlagsanstalt.

[Neu 10] *Neuhaus, Wolfgang; Nordmeier, Volkhard; Kirstein, Jürgen (2010):* IT-gestützte Vermittlungskompetenz – Vernetzung von Lehre und Learning-Community im Learners'Garden Projekt. In: Volkhard Nordmeier; Grötzebauch Helmuth (Eds.), PhyDid B – Didaktik der Physik – Beiträge zur DPG-Frühjahrstagung, 2010. Berlin: Freie Universität Berlin – AG Nordmeier.

[Neu 11] *Neuhaus, Wolfgang, Nordmeier, Volkhard; Kirstein, Jürgen (2011):* Das Lehrbuch der Zukunft – Mediendidaktische Aspekte im Validierungsprojekt »Technology Enhanced Textbook«. In V. Nordmeier; Grötzebauch, Helmuth (Eds.), Phydid B – Didaktik der Physik – Beiträge zur DPG-Frühjahrstagung, 2011. Berlin: Freie Universität Berlin – AG Nordmeier.

[Neu 12-A] *Neuhaus, Wolfgang (2012):* Didaktisches Design und die Transformation von Wissen im digitalen Zeitalter. Berlin: Blog Mediendidaktik. Retrieved June 30, 2013, from *http://mediendidaktik.org/docs/didaktisches-design-neuhaus.pdf*

[Neu 12-B] *Neuhaus, Wolfgang; Kirstein, Jürgen; Nordmeier, Volkhard (2012):* Didaktische Funktionen des Lehrbuchs der Zukunft. In Phydid B – Didaktik der Physik – Beiträge zur DPG-Frühjahrstagung, 2012. Berlin: Freie Universität Berlin – AG Nordmeier.

[Mer 88] *Merrill, M. David (1988):* The Role of Tutorial and Experiential Models in Intelligent Tutoring Systems. Educational Technology, (7), 7–13.

[Mie 07] *Mietzel, Gerd (2007):* Pädagogische Psychologie des Lernens und Lehrens. Göttingen: Hogrefe.

[Rei 91] *Reigeluth, Charles M. (1991):* Reflections on the Implications of Constructivism for Educational Technology. Educational Technology, (9), 34–37.

[Rei 06] *Reinmann, Gabi:* (2006). Ist E-Learning eine pädagogische Innovation? In R. Arnold, & M. Lermen (Eds.), elearning-Didaktik, Vol. 48, Hohengehren: Schneider Verlag.

[Sch 07] *Schulmeister, Rolf (2007):* Grundlagen hypermedialer Lernsysteme. München: Oldenbourg Verlag.

[Tul 04] *Tulodziecki, Gerhard; Herzig, Bardo (2004):* Mediendidaktik: Medien in Lehr- und Lernprozessen. In Handbuch Medienpädagogik, Vol. 2, Stuttgart: Klett-Cotta.

FIGURES

CONTACT DETAILS

Prof. Dr. Volkhard Nordmeier
Freie Universität Berlin
Fachbereich Physik – Didaktik der Physik
Arnimallee 14
14195 Berlin
Phone: +49 (0)30 838 53031
E-Mail: *nordmeier@physik.fu-berlin.de*

The university-wide introduction of an ePortfolio system as transdisciplinary task: Results of an implementation process and perspectives on an optimized process model

Jörg Hafer, Alexander Kiy

ABSTRACT

The introduction of an ePortfolio system at a university represents a complex process. On the one hand, various disciplines, stakeholders and organizational levels are working on different aspects of the overall project and, on the other hand, they have to act together. This article describes the general approach and the first results of the multi-stage introduction and evaluation of an ePortfolio system at the University of Potsdam as part of the project "E-learning in study areas (EliS)". At this point in time we carry out 5 pilot projects with together more than 100 participants based on the software "Mahara". Furthermore, the article attempts to outline general aspects from this procedure for the introduction of ePortfolios at universities. The question is: which success and risk factors can be identified and to what extent can a generic approach to the introduction of such systems be formulated. According to a formative evaluation model, the outcomes from this reflection should serve as criteria for the ongoing implementation process.

Objectives and basic concept of the ePortfolio implementation

Implementing an university-wide ePortfolio

We started an implementation process of a university-wide ePortfolio system, as part of the interdisciplinary project "E-learning in study areas (EliS)[1]" at the University of Potsdam in 2012. This project is based on the assumptions

- that an ePortfolio generates opportunities and options for student-centered approaches to teaching and learning for higher education,
- there is no "one-size-fits-all"-approach for using ePortfolios,
- and that the implementation of an educational software system is a highly interdisciplinary process.

However the ePortfolio is still a fairly open concept. There is no definition how the usage of ePortfolio scenarios will look like exactly. Thomas Häcker [Hae 07] sums up

1 *http://www.elis.uni-potsdam.de/*

30 different terms and concepts of what an ePortfolio is and for what it can be used for. Furthermore, after initial hopes for positive momentum for a "change in learning culture" triggered by ePortfolios, its ambiguity of control and empowerment was recognized and ends up in a fairly different view if and how the use of ePortfolios could support innovations in higher education [Rei 11], [Sch 12], [Mey 11].

Within the eLiS-project we elaborate a specific relation between a "Personal Learning Environment (PLE)" and the "ePortfolio". In our context a PLE is a generic framework for different services and scenarios to support studying and learning. The ePortfolio is a specific "bundle" of functionalities, like content management, content creation and publishing. This portfolio-model is mainly driven by known software-solutions like Mahara, OLAT or PebblePad and the various ePortfolio-taxonomies e.g. as described by Baumgartner & Himpsl [Him 09] or Hornung-Prähauser et al. [Hor 07]. So, in the first step we chose a fairly pragmatic approach to the design the system and took the "first best solution that comes along". This was due to the fact that we won't close the discussion of what an ePortfolio could be in advance. This happens regularly if the project starts with the definition of a fixed set of functionalities and establishes an implicit concept by just a technical decision.

Our ePortfolio project in eLiS does not only aims to carry out explorative scenarios of ePortfolio usage for studying and learning, but has also to prepare the university-wide roll out of an ePortfolio system. In case of the University of Potsdam that means the system has to be prepared for a load about several thousand users (up to max. 10.000 if we take the so called "active user" in the LMS Moodle as a reference value). Also unlike the Learning Management System (LMS) "Moodle", the ePortfolio-system should be prepared for the fact that every user is an author, collector and publisher of content.

The initial application concept: "There is no one-size-fits-all"

For ePortfolios, as well as for other educational technology systems, the intentions and actions of both educational and technical developers, the interests and needs of the users and the technical and organizational limitations create a dynamic context in which the actual educational technology system will be realized. With other words: neither the educational designers nor the developers exactly know how the environment they design will work in practice or if it fulfils the favoured practices of the users. Often functionalities designed "en passant" start over to live their own life and create not intended (but useful) features. For the ePortfolio various authors are in common that we have to deal with a broad concept of what an ePortfolio actually means [Bau 09], [Hae 07].

Therefore, the intention of our implementation approach was offering a set of ePortfolio functionalities represented in the most spreads open-source software "Mahara" plus a set of scenarios of ePortfolio-usages like "tool for reflection", "co-working-site" or "showcase ePortfolios". Additionally we offer consulting and support for instructional design and technical issues. To link the different levels of action and actors, in

order to support a transdisciplinary process that works in the tension between openness and results.

Cope and evaluate the challenges and issues in implementing an educational software system in higher education

For the introduction of educational software systems in higher education a number of process models are in common, which are usually based on a combination of iterative and linear elements. So far, these models say little about the specific situation where several interdisciplinary aspects like organizational processes, information technology and creative and media-didactic aspects come together.

Hornung-Prähauser [Hor 07] described a quite feasible idea of how the introduction of an ePortfolio-system may look like. Figure 1 shows on which stage of the implementation process the matter becomes tricky: At stage 3 ("Adjustment of general framework") the small arrows indicate different tasks, dealing with different actors, professions and different subunits from the university system, but different actors usually follow a different logic of action, for example process modelling of existing applications in software development compared to an open-ended development of media-based learning scenarios in educational conceptualization of teaching.

So, this stage of the project is critical for several reasons:

- Normally there is no interdisciplinary working structure established.
- Mostly the different departments are used to work in their own structure following their own agendas.
- Taking this in account, establishing a stable, effective and sustain project structure remains often difficult or impossible.

This is the reason why implementations a) fail in this stage or b) an actor (often the ICT-Department) take the lead. But this means also that the logic of action of one member is overrepresented.

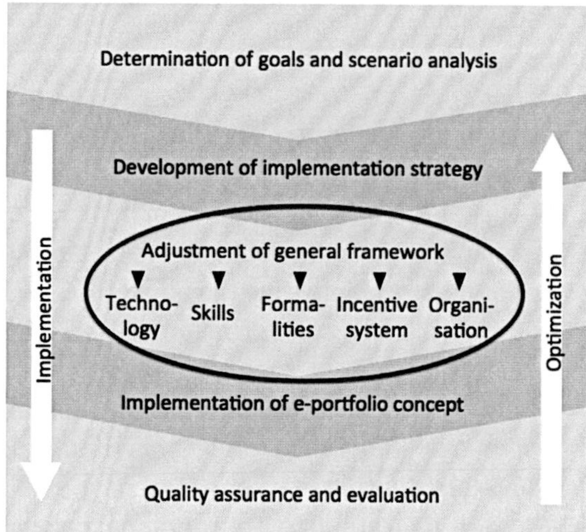

Figure 1: Main fields of operation in ePortfolio implementation [Hor 07: 155] (own translation)

In this context the accompanying evaluation takes an important role to reflect the progress of the project and the alignment according the overall goals. Thus, the project team is challenged to develop an appropriate implementation model focus the fact that the interdisciplinary work is a key factor for a successful project.

Conceptualizing the stages of an introductory period for an ePortfolio system – ADDIE revised

In the instructional/educational project management the ADDIE-scheme is quite common. The phases of analyse, design, development, implementation and evaluation forms the evident periods and working packages of nearly every bigger undertaking. Often the ADDIE-model is annotated that this is not a linear model but should be seen in a more iterative and cyclic way. That means: In real projects the design is often not complete whilst development starts, kind of evaluation take place at every step of the process and the implementation reveals regularly the gaps in the analysis phase.

So, what we did looks more like a new interpretation of A-D-D-I-E:

- Assumptions – instead of making a thorough analysis we took some educated guesses: What would work best in the context of the project to reach our goals?
- Decisions – instead of starting a design process we made decisions: Which software, concepts and patterns support our working concept best?
- Deliver – instead of development we focused to bring selected tools, services and concepts straight into a working environment.

- Involvement – instead of starting an implementation process, we aim to involve key players, target group members and the different actors in university into the introductory phase.
- Evolve – instead of an overall evaluation (which is actual a part of every stage) we aim to develop our concepts, tools and services for a better fit into the overall goals and refine our assumptions.

People, processes, sub-projects, technologies involved in the first implementation phase

We started the implementation project by constitute an "evaluation group" and invited a selected group of persons which are represented the different target groups: faculty lecturers, members of the project team and departments staff which are possible users of the common ePortfolio models (like Career Center, Center for Languages and Key Competencies, Potsdam-Post-Graduate-School, center for evaluation). We offered them the participation in the pilot-project, including supervision and support and gave them an overview of the scenarios of ePortfolio usage. For the first stage in the implementation process we acquired 7 pilot-projects, with together about 100 participants using the ePortfolio software "Mahara" and one group about 25 participants using the Moodle-Extension "Exabis". The specific use of the ePortfolio was not indicated from the project team, but driven from the ideas and needs from the teacher and the participants.

Within the ePortfolio-evaluation-group the participant connected directly to the development team which set up the pilot-server of Mahara, conducting the customization and ensure the operating of the service. Very soon it becomes clear that a lot of questions are communicated directly between the "pilots" and the members of development team bypassing the managers of the evaluation group. Customization of the ePortfolio software Mahara, setup of the necessary software architecture and organizing support were the most important activities in the project management team whilst the first evaluation phase. An important part was to collect information and practical knowledge about how to operate the software and identify the necessary technical and organisational resources for permanent service of a university-wide installation.

During the start-up-phase several small and bigger customizations of the Mahara-Software and technical issues took place. In detail:

- Provisioning of server or virtual machine including "enough" storage for calculated user group
- Installation and configuration of server
- Obtaining an domain for the system
- Getting accesses to central services granted (authentication and storage services)
- Installation of specific software product
- Installation or even compilation of needed software for specific operating platforms (like apache or virus scanners etc.)

- Configuration of software product, connecting to existing services and systems in context of university infrastructure (integration and evaluate integration)
- Obtaining service e-mail alias for support requests and mapping to existing e-mail addresses
- Designing custom views or adopt them to existing website designs, installing specific language packages or customizing text in it
- Fixing little bugs of open source product or report bugs to the community

Furthermore there where several general services which were realized:
- Conceptualizing of user agreement
- Providing initial information for the system (starting page, disclaimer, contact address, help resources, created video tutorials etc.)
- Providing technical insights of project, answering questions of the type "is it possible to achieve..."
- Research for existing plugins to solve problems described and evaluate their functionality
- Creating institutions (groups), enrolling users (external users not listed in university user management yet), granting rights, trouble management (the user xy is not able to log in please check the circumstances)
- Networking with existing projects (information sharing)

Besides of the evaluation group a cooperation derives between the Potsdam Center for Languages and Key Competences (Zessko) and the "EPOS" Mahara Project, developed and operated by the Centre for Foreign Language Learning (Fremdsprachenzentrum der Hochschulen im Land Bremen) in cooperation with the Center for Computing Technologies (Technologie-Zentrum Informatik) of the University of Bremen. The result of this cooperation is the implementation of the EPOS-system within the Zessko in Potsdam beginning at the winter term 2013/2014.

Evaluation and Findings of the first implementation phase

Evaluation is on the one hand an instrument to assess a project from a bird's-eye view. This use of the term is the most common understanding of "evaluation" in the context of education. On the other hand evaluation is a fixed part of an ongoing project work and daily routines. Quality assurance, target vs. actual control, rating the performance of students and reflection of teaching. This use of the term is the most common understanding in software development. In a broader sense "evaluation" is everywhere. To generate an overall picture it will be wise, to consult and assess these different sources of evaluation.

For reporting and evaluating the different working packages and stages of the first implementation phase we differentiate three clusters in which evaluations tasks took place:

1. Evaluation in tasks which are part of the actual project working packages. These evaluations are mainly used to prepare decisions in the course of the project, like selection of software, quality assurance, needs analysis or requirements recording.
2. Evaluation as part of the project management, like generating data for quality assurance, controlling, target performance or achievement analyses.
3. Evaluation as part of the overall project steering activities, like output analysis, overall cost-benefit-evaluation, assessment of the aimed or undesirable effects.

To assess the results and the project status we used the following resources

- An online-survey among the participants of the Mahara-Group with n=33 persons who start the questionnaire and n=20 who has finished it. They represent round 20%.
- An achievement performance analysis of the initial concept document.
- Review of the project documents and resources, like personal notes and memos, mails and the task tracking systems.

Results and findings relate to the actual project working packages

Users experiences with Mahara

In the online-survey we asked for the quality of interaction and the user-satisfaction of the ePortfolio software Mahara. The results were somewhat disillusioning. In open questions the participants wrote about their experiences: “cumbersome, non-intuitive, jerky, confusing, many difficulties, difficult to cope by oneself, not user friendly, difficult to use, high learning curve, bugs, limitations (Editor), complicated functions, hidden functions”. The positive feedback was less and not very enthusiastic: “after training it was just fine, interesting, largely without problems, okay, mainly good to use, with time you find your way quite well”.

Relation of costs and benefits for the user to work into the software

Here the users are divided in two equal parts: The half rate the effort in relation to the benefit too high and vice versa. The half of the persons need more than two hours a week to get used to the software.

Results and findings relate to the project management

In the dimension of project management (goal achievement, input-output performance) the rating of the first implementation phase is characterized from achievements and failures.

Achievements compared to the initial concept

The following topics where planned and realized:

- We have established a group of 6 pilot-users each carrying out a pilot-scenario.
- We have established a test-system and conceptualized a university-wide roll out. The ICT-department of the University is involved and prepared to implement the system as an additional university-wide service.
- We consulted and support the members of the pilot-group and work out a couple of possible scenarios for ePortfolio usage.
- We facilitate that over 100 participants did use the portfolio-software.
- We have learned that the software Mahara – although it's very popular – may not be the best solution. The used functionalities did not cover the possibilities of the software: Blogging, groupwork, filesharing and networking are the main functionalities used. Create and publish advanced personal websites ("Views") did not happen very often. We decided to take a deeper look in alternative technical possibilities to realize these scenarios.

Failures compared to the initial concept

The following topics where planned but we fail to realize them in full:

- We don't reach yet the "normal" lecturers and docents in university; five from six pilot-users belongs to the inner or wider circle of the project group.
- We didn't establish an ePortfolio-expert-group and the planned co-teaching-concept.
- We failed to manage that the users of the software get enough support to work smooth and easy into the software.

Results and findings relate to the overall project steering activities

Assessment of the ePortfolio-concept in general from the participants

We ask the participants how they use ePortfolios. Regardless the poor results of the user experiences with Mahara they rate the possibilities of ePortfolios quite positive: "Content available online, you can see the results of other students, feedback, material immediately accessible to all, greater engagement with the topic, networking, sharing, documentation of work, literacy, common discussions, manage own documents on web page, knowledge exchange, better structured work, fast networking, more structure to information gathering and networking, overview, evaluating the work of other learners".

Failures compared to the initial concept

We ask for which purposes the user think they ePortfolio is most useful. The feedback gives an insight which ideas and concepts the users have from the ePortfolio:

- monitoring and feedback in general (teachers and peers)
- file sharing
- social networking,
- reflection
- manage resources
- organization of work
- creation and release of material

Conclusion from the evaluation

The previous results of the implementation phase at the University of Potsdam indicate that there are on the right way and accomplished the main goals successfully:

- Valuable expert know-how was accumulated for the application of basic technologies and technical integration.
- Lecturers and academic staff are not involved as much as we planned.
- Viable and scalable scenarios of university-wide use of ePortfolios are becoming apparent
- The ePortfolio idea was selectively anchored at the university and at the same time, modified according to the needs of the prospective users
- Important corrections and revisions of the overall concept in particular could be identified by the implementation strategy early on, so that they can be considered as the work continues without jeopardizing the progress of the project

We recognize a rising awareness of the topic in various settings: The Center for Languages and Key Competencies starts a bigger pilot-phase in the winter term, one faculty and the post-graduate school start to think about a post-graduate-network using the ePortfolio and the potential of ePortfolios for orientation to competencies as part of the Bologna-requirements getting more attention.

Perspectives on a generic process and evaluation model

Implementation of ePortfolios as technology system, organizational change and professional development with regard to innovations in teaching and studying is without doubt an interdisciplinary task. For ePortfolios the issue is to establish an "open" concept and to fix at the same time "hard" requirements to prepare the technical service. To align these different perspectives of the actors for the required "adjustment of general framework" the key factor is to involve their practice into a consistent context.

We decided to make use of a process model which is suitable to open concepts of use and at the same time generate the maximum of practical knowledge. This results in the reformulation of the ADDIE-Model (Figure 2)

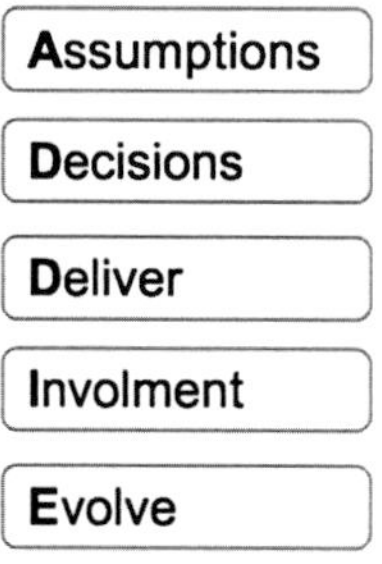

Figure 2: Revised A-D-D-I-E Model

Also an evaluation model was derived from this approach. This model took into consideration that evaluation has different meaning for the different actor groups. The model strives to draw benefits from all perspectives on evaluation on the different project-layers and combine evaluation in the actual project working packages, as part of the project management and as part of the overall project steering activities (Figure 3).

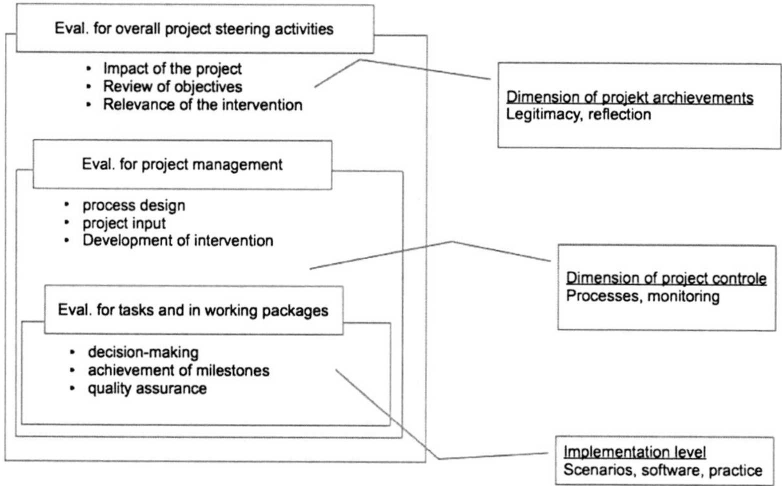

Figure 3: Target levels of evaluation

In the next implementation phase we like to deploy and refine both the process and the evaluation model. Questions which to be answered are, whether the "open" model

of implementation will last sustain if the university-wide roll out should realized and whether the evaluation levels are consistent and practicable to generate useful knowledge in the further course of the project.

REFERENCES

[Bau 09] *Baumgartner, Peter; Himpsl, Klaus; Zauchner, Sabine (2009). Einsatz von E-Portfolios an (österreichischen) Hochschulen:* Zusammenfassung. Teil I des BMWF-Abschlussberichts "E-Portfolio an Hochschulen": GZ 51.700/0064-VII/10/2006. Forschungsbericht, Krems.

[Hae 07] *Häcker, Thomas (2007). Portfolio:* ein Entwicklungsinstrument für selbstbestimmtes Lernen. Eine explorative Studie zur Arbeit mit Portfolios in der Sekundarstufe I, 3, Baltmannsweiler: Schneider Verlag Hohengehren, 2007.

[Hor 07] *Hornung-Prähauser, Veronika; Geser, Guntram; Hilzensauer, Wolf; Schaffert, Sandra (2007). Didaktische, organisatorische und technologische Grundlagen von E-Portfolios und Analyse internationaler Beispiele und Erfahrungen mit E-Portfolio-Implementierungen an Hochschulen. Retrieved from http://edumedia.salzburgresearch.at/images/stories/ePortfolio_studie_srfg_fnma.pdf.*

[Him 09] *Himpsl, Klaus; Baumgartner, Peter (2009). Evaluation of E-Portfolio Software. In:* International Journal of Emerging Technologies in Learning 4 (1), 16–22.

[Him 12] *Himpsl-Gutermann, Klaus (2012). E-Portfolios in der universitären Weiterbildung. Studierende im Spannungsfeld von Reflexivem Lernen und Digital Career Identity. Klagenfurt:* Dissertation.

[Mey 11] *Meyer, Torsten; Mayrberger, Kerstin; Münte-Goussar, Stephan; Schwalbe, Christina (2011) (Eds.):* Kontrolle und Selbstkontrolle. Zur Ambivalenz von E-Portfolios in Bildungsprozessen, 19, Wiesbaden: VS Verlag für Sozialwissenschaften.

[Rei 11] *Reinmann, Gabi; Sippel, Silvia (2011). Königsweg oder Sackgasse? E-Portfolios für das forschende Lernen. In T. Meyer, K. Mayrberger, S. Münte-Goussar, & C. Schwalbe (Eds.), Kontrolle und Selbstkontrolle.Zur Ambivalenz von E-Portfolios in Bildungsprozessen, Wiesbaden:* VS Verl. für Sozialwiss, 185–202.

[Sch 12] *Schulmeister, Rolf (2012). Der Schlüssel zur Medienkompetenz liegt im Begriff der Kontrolle. In:* Zeitschrift für e-Learning, 7 (4), 35–45.

CONTACT

Jörg Hafer
AG eLEARNING
Universität Potsdam
August-Bebel-Straße 89
14482 Potsdam
E-Mail: *joerg.hafer@uni-potsdam.de*

Alexander Kiy
Institut für Informatik
Universität Potsdam
August-Bebel-Straße 89
14482 Potsdam
E-Mail: *alexander.kiy@uni-potsdam.de*

Design as Inquiry: Socially shared PLEs by the example of collaborative note taking. A speed design process.

Heidrun Allert, Sabine Reisas

ABSTRACT

The workshop introduces the pedagogical framework "design as inquiry" which was developed in the context of the multilateral project "Creating Knowledge through Design & Conceptual Innovation" co-funded by the European Union (project website: http://www.knowledge-through-design.uni-kiel.de). The project aims to foster design ability and creative thinking among students and professionals of various disciplines, enabling them to generate innovation and knowledge. Design thereby is understood as an epistemic process that does not only result in new products or services but also provides insights into the situation to be changed. By design we do not refer to a particular profession or discipline, but to a general mode of inquiry that aims to gain insight by means of reflective intervention. This perspective is used as an underlying foundation for the exploration of spaces that encourage active engagement.From this perspective we can assume, that the design of a Personal Learning Environment (PLE) is an ongoing epistemic activity, that is mutually entangled with materiality/ technology and the accompanying social interactions.With the design challenge of this workshop we aim to explore the potentialities of "design as inquiry" for developing spaces that provide collaborative opportunities to co-produce and re-work students' PLEs and encourage them to appropriate spaces for their own needs.

Program

- First, we will introduce you to the pedagogical framework of "design as inquiry" and provide an overview of the design phases. (1/2 hour)
- During a speed design session the participants will experience the whole design circle. To engage a lively discussion the participants will work in small groups. Within this highly interactive phase, we will explore the role of socially shared PLEs by the example of collaborative note taking. (1 1/2 hour)
- After that, we will reflect not only about the process itself, but also about the appropriateness for your own situation, discipline or project and how concepts for developing or facilitating PLEs can benefit from this pedagogical framework. This will also allow us to talk about the role of artifacts, spaces, social factors and the epistemic role of the process. (1/2 hour)

CONTACT DETAILS

Prof. Dr. Heidrun Allert
Christian-Albrechts-Universität zu Kiel
(Kiel University)
Department of Media Education/
Educational Computer Sciences,
Olshausenstraße 75,
24098 Kiel, Germany
Phone: +49 (0)431 880 2956

Sabine Reisas, M.A.
Christian-Albrechts-Universität zu Kiel
(Kiel University)
Department of Media Education/
Educational Computer Sciences,
Olshausenstraße 75,
24098 Kiel, Germany
Phone: +49 (0)431 880 5572
E-Mail: *sreisas@av-studio.uni-kiel.de*

Social badges dynamics in institutional supported platforms

Carlos Santos, Luís Pedro, Sara Almeida, Mónica Aresta

ABSTRACT

In a scenario where the social web promotes the dilution of roles and hierarchies, the attribution of badges as a way to promote integration in educational social platforms is still mostly in the hands of administrators. Aiming to break up this conservative view, this workshop will discuss and work on user-generated badges and peer-support for badges attribution. Throughout a set of activities, participants will be able to create and assign badges to others, following the same set of rules.

Social badges dynamics in institutional supported platforms

SAPO Campus is an educational platform that aims to promote communication and sharing in educational contexts. Despite the institutional approach, where users connect themselves to a well defined and identified institutional space, the dynamics of the platform are almost identical to the ones available in global social networks. Apart from administrative tasks, all users share the same privileges and responsibilities and are able to use the platform as a key part of their Personal Learning Environment.

SAPO Campus Mozilla Open badges support was introduced as a first experience during the PLE Conference 2012 in Aveiro. Since then the team has been working in a deeper integration of Open Badges technology. During the various phases of specification and development the team has been questioning the approach that almost all the social platforms is using for badge integration.

Social web promotes the dilution of roles and hierarchies. But strangely, badges integration in these platforms do not follow this principle. Badges are seen as an exclusive topic in these social dynamics because reputation and recognition of badges could only be achieved if "the gods" are the only ones to create and assign badges to "the common people".

SAPO Campus approach to badges tries to break up with this conservative view related to gamification and badge integration in educational social platforms. Two main concepts are promoted: (A) *user-generated badges* – any user is able to create a group and inside groups the owner is able to create an unlimited number of badges and assign them to group members; (B) *peer-support for badge attribution* – any user is able to express their support for the attribution of a specific badge for a specific user.

During the PLE Conference this approach to badges will already be used by a few thousand users. During this workshop we pretend to explain the rules that are applied in SAPO Campus. Throughout a set of activities the workshop participants will be able to create and assign badges to other participants following the same set of rules. This

experimentation will allow us to question and reflect over the potential impact of this social approach to badges inside educational institutions, namely: motivation, learning and peer-assessment.

Acknowledgements

The authors would like to acknowledge University of Aveiro, SAPO and TMN for the scientific, financial and technical support to the SAPO Campus project and the Labs SAPO/UA R&D activities. This work is part of the Shared Personal Learning Environments (ref: PTDC/CPE-CED/114130/2009) project funded by FEDER funds through the Operational Programme for Competitiveness Factors – COMPETE and National Funds through FCT – Foundation for Science and Technology (Portugal).

CONTACT DETAILS

Carlos Santos
University of Aveiro
Departamento de Comunicação e Arte
Campus Universitário de Santiago 3810-193 Aveiro – Portugal
Phone: +351 (0)234 370389
E-Mail: *carlossantos@ua.pt*

Luís Pedro
University of Aveiro
Departamento de Comunicação e Arte
Campus Universitário de Santiago 3810-193 Aveiro – Portugal
Phone: +351 (0)234 370389
E-Mail: *lpedro@ua.pt*

Sara Almeida
University of Aveiro
Departamento de Comunicação e Arte
Campus Universitário de Santiago 3810-193 Aveiro – Portugal
Phone: +351 (0)234 370389
E-Mail: *saraalmeida340@gmail.com*

Mónica Aresta
University of Aveiro
Departamento de Comunicação e Arte
Campus Universitário de Santiago 3810-193 Aveiro – Portugal
Phone: +351 (0)234 370389
E-Mail: *m.aresta@ua.pt*

PLE Monitor

Ismael Peña, Eva Gil, Raúl Romero, José Mora

ABSTRACT

PLE Monitor proposes a tool to help students and teachers to create, share and effectively use both their own PLEs and their colleagues'. The PLE Monitor maps and aggregates students' PLEs within the LMS, thus enabling participation in the classroom through one's own PLE, creating timelines in terms of topic, platform or individual, the latter is especially designed if the PLE is to be assessed as part of an e-portfolio. Besides their approach as conscious learning strategies, personal learning environments (PLE) can also be described as a set of tools, communities and services that make up educational platforms used by individual students to lead their own learning and pursue their educational goals. What can be seen as a threat to the traditional educational system – based on centralization and standardization – can become an rich learning experience that is able to combine formal and non-formal learning, theory and practice, disciplinary content and professional skills, the academia and the professional environment.

Introduction

To enable the coexistence between institutions and PLEs, the process of creating, monitoring and, if necessary, assessing students' PLEs has to be simple and easy for all the actors involved in order to add barriers to the process of teaching and learning. On the other hand, an ecosystem of PLEs should avoid designs based on the mere inventory of spaces, and be instead integrated in whatever virtual learning system is already in use so that there is no distinction between "inside" vs. "outside", thus blurring the boundaries of the overlapped learning spaces. In this context we will present PLE Monitor: a tool to help teachers and students to create, share and use their PLEs and their colleagues' through a number of features and functionalities aimed at monitor and assess effectively learning processes that occur within these environments

State of play

The PLE Monitor will work in an online course of a Virtual Campus. In this context will find three characters. The first one is a character (named ONcampus) which is a student that, for unspecified reasons, just wants to access the virtual campus to study and that everything that happens on the campus remains unknown for the outer world. The second one is (ON-OFFCampus) that is also a student but he's a accustomed user to social networks, and uses several Web 2.0 tools for learning (call it a Personal Learning Environment), amongst them Twitter, and just does not want to use two nanoblogging tools, one on-campus and another one off-campus, like Twitter. And the last one, a

third character (OFFcampus) is a professional working on eGovernment and, as such, uses Twitter to interact with other people on the field but he doesn't have access to Campus. What you usually would have is two conversations: (1) Inside the campus, a closed conversation that neither benefits from "outside" conversations nor contributes to them; (2) Outside campus, an open but not-permeating-the-campus conversation and that forces some people to attend two conversations on the same field mostly with different people but similar purposes.

Solution

Imagine a nanobloging tool (e.g. StatusNet) installed inside the virtual campus classroom. Everything that happens in there is invisible to the outside world. But everything you tag with #uoc_egov (the "official" hashtag for the course) is published on Twitter. In fact, everything you publish on Twitter with the #uoc_egov hashtag is imported onto the nanobloggin tool installed in the virtual campus, so everyone can see it. Thus allowing people to participate in the closed classroom from outside of the campus. Messages from other people alien to the closed classroom can also be seen insidethe classroom, provided that they add the #uoc_egov hashtag and we have not added a filter to the closed nanoblogging tool that not only filters by hashtag but also by user (in this case, students could participate from their Twitter accounts but the classroom would only be participated by enrolled students).

Benefits

Students can opt to participate only in the classroom and be invisible to off-campus users. Students can opt to participate from outside the classroom and with their own tools. In the limit, they will only participate from their own PLEs and not from the virtual campus. Off-campus students engage in real conversations with "real" professionals and experts in the field. Exposure is likely to be good. Faculty and managers can, if thus desired, use the closed environment to "contain" what is to be monitored or assessed, and without the need to wander around "chasing" spontaneous and ubiquitous contributions from their students.

CONTACT DETAILS

Ismael Peña
Políticas Públicas para el Desarrollo
Estudios de Derecho y Ciencia Política
Universitat Oberta de Catalunya (UOC)
E-mail: ipena@uoc.edu

Eva Gil
Universitat Oberta de Catalunya (UOC)
E-Mail: egilrod@uoc.edu

Raúl Romero
Universitat Oberta de Catalunya (UOC)
E-Mail: rromerogar@uoc.edu

José Mora
Universitat Oberta de Catalunya (UOC)
E-Mail: jmora@uoc.edu